GW01445069

# West Heslerton

# The Anglian Cemetery

# Volume i

**The Landscape Research Centre,**
**Yedingham, North Yorkshire**

**1999**

*Mineral replaced textiles and beads in situ after removal of the runic brooch from Grave 177*

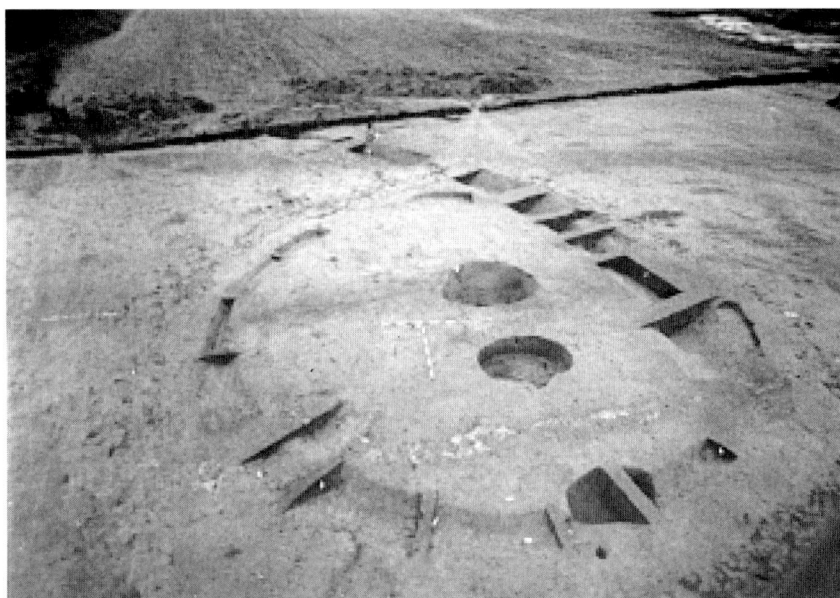

*Excavation in progress on Bronze Age Barrow 2BA264 one of a number of prehistoric monuments which provided the focus for the Anglo-Saxon cemetery.*

# West Heslerton

# The Anglian Cemetery

# Volume i

# The Excavation
# and
# Discussion of the Evidence

by
**Christine Haughton and Dominic Powlesland**

with contributions by
Nigel Blades, Ann Clarke, Margaret Cox, Brian Gilmour, Terry Manby, Penelope
Walton Rogers and Jacqui Watson

1999

*For the volunteers, supervisors, specialists, landowners, enthusiastic colleagues, visitors, sponsors and friends who made this undertaking possible.*

Published by The Landscape Research Centre Ltd.

© The Landscape Research Centre and the individual authors, 1999

Landscape Research Centre
Archaeological Monograph Series
Number 1: Volume 1


ISBN: 0 9537488 0 4

This excavation and its publication has been funded by English Heritage Archaeology Division.

*Designed and typeset by Dominic Powlesland using Aldus PageMaker™ 6.5*

**Printed by Technical Print Services Ltd, Nottingham, England**

# Table of Contents

# List of Figures

# List of Plates

# List of Tables

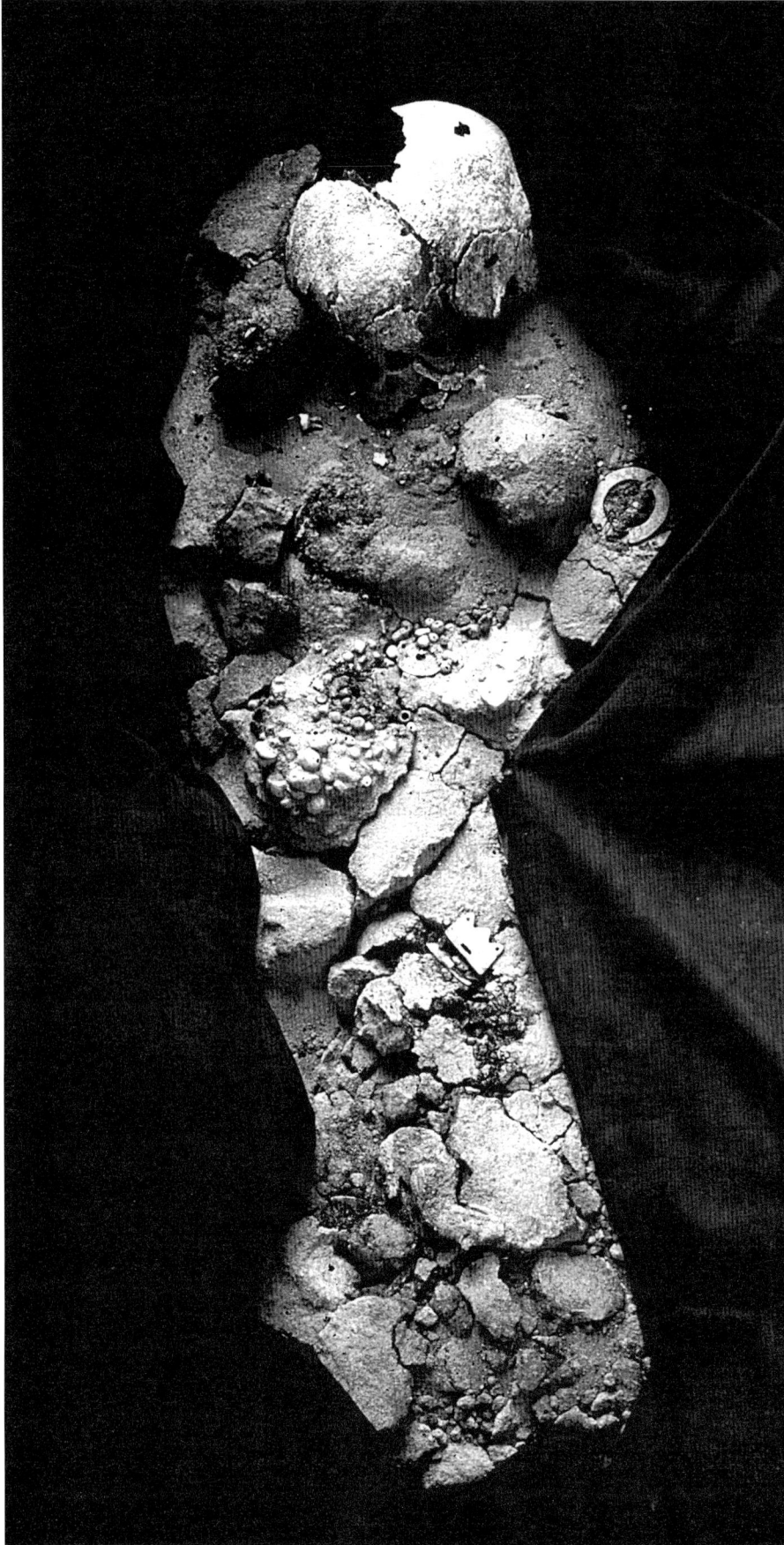

The head and torso of the burial in Grave 86 which was lifted with most of its grave goods in a single soil block (photograph AML)

# Summary

The Early Anglo-Saxon or Anglian cemetery at West Heslerton came to light, like so many sites of this class, as a chance find during mineral extraction operations. The discovery of an Early Anglo-Saxon burial during sand extraction at Cook's Sand Quarry, West Heslerton, North Yorkshire, during the autumn of 1977 led to the instigation of a major programme of rescue excavation. The resulting excavation project was undertaken as part of the national rescue archaeology programme, the funding being provided by English Heritage, formerly the Department of the Environment, through North Yorkshire County Council. The excavations were conducted on a seasonal basis between 1977 and 1987 and involved a large number of volunteers and site assistants without whose efforts, frequently during long days in adverse conditions, none of the results presented here would have been possible.

These rescue excavations, undertaken within the broad research framework of the Heslerton Parish Project, have included the examination of extensive prehistoric and Anglo-Saxon deposits including both an early Anglo-Saxon, or Anglian, cemetery and an associated settlement, the only case in the North of England where the combined elements of settlement and cemetery have been extensively investigated together. This volume brings together the evidence from the cemetery, which spans the period from the Late Neolithic to the medieval periods.

The Anglian cemetery, in use between the late fifth and early seventh centuries, utilised an already established Late Neolithic and Early Bronze Age ritual site as its core and extended over c 8000 square metres of which c 6000 were fully excavated; this included the examination of some 11 prehistoric burials and 201 out of an estimated total of 300 Anglian burials, both inhumations and cremations. The relationship between the Early Anglo-Saxon cemetery and earlier prehistoric ritual and funerary site, also observed at other sites in the region, may reflect a desire to legitimise through what may be described as cultural allusion the emerging 'Anglo-Saxon' society within the context of the prehistoric rather than the Roman past.

The excavation of the cemetery has provided an important new corpus of information, particularly pertaining to textile and costume evidence. There are tantalising indications from the human skeletal material of two distinctive physical types, perhaps representing native and migrant elements in the population. The material culture from the grave assemblages is distinctively 'Anglian' in nature and includes evidence indicating links with Scandinavia in particular.

The excavation, which was undertaken piecemeal over more than a decade, was the setting for the development of a number of innovative techniques in data collection and management, particularly with reference to the application of computers in the field. The methodologies developed during the excavation of the cemetery formed the basis for subsequent work on the associated settlement. The extensive digital archive derived from these two major excavations will be published in full on CD-ROM and incorporated in the report on the settlement.

# Acknowledgements

The success of this excavation owes most to the large number of volunteers, site assistants and supervisors who worked in all weathers, often in the depths of winter, and even through the night under arc-lights when the threat of theft by metal-detectorists was at its greatest. It would be impossible to name them all here: their help and determination is however gratefully acknowledged.

The site was first discovered by Mr Jim Carter, a native of Heslerton, who had worked with the late T C M Brewster at nearby Staple Howe and appreciated the importance of the poorly preserved bones exposed on the windswept edge of Cook's Quarry, West Heslerton. The rapid response of Dr John Dent of the Humberside Archaeological Unit in undertaking a salvage excavation in the winter of 1977-8 prevented the certain loss to quarrying of the first graves to be identified. Once the importance of the site had been identified Mike Griffiths, then County Archaeologist, appealed to Dr John Hurst of the Department of the Environment for rescue funding. Funding was approved and the excavation was supported from 1978 to 1986 by annual grants from the national rescue archaeology budget administered by English Heritage and its predecessor organisations. The subsequent programme of analysis and publication has been funded by English Heritage through the Archaeology Commissions programme. We are indebted to the Inspectorate of Ancient Monuments of English Heritage for their continued support, and in particular to Mr B Startin, Dr R Bewley and Dr G J Wainwright.

This work could not have been undertaken without the necessary permissions and support of the landowners, Messrs. E and R Cook of Cook's Quarry, and the Dawnay Estate, West Heslerton. We are indebted to the many commercial concerns that supported the project by donating equipment and resources, in particular Sharp UK, Commodore UK, Citizen Europe and Sony UK for much of the computing and video equipment used in the project. Many local businesses likewise supported us by providing equipment and services at cost, in particular Massers Camera Shop, Malton.

We are likewise indebted to the many specialists and colleagues whose assistance and advice both during and after the excavation has contributed so much to the results presented here. They include Nigel Blades, Ann Clarke, Margaret Cox, Jean Dawes, Tania Dickinson, Glynis Edwards, Brian Gilmour, Richard MacPhail, Terry Manby, Douglas Moir, Ray Page, Philip Rahtz, Penelope Walton Rogers, Jacqui Watson and Leslie Webster.

We are grateful to Philip Dixon, Chris Scull and Catherine Hills who all read the text and made valuable comments and observations, although any omissions that remain are the responsibility of the two principal authors. Ellen McAdam was kind enough to copy edit the text, ensuring that the final text is both more readable and consistent than it might otherwise have been.

Dominic Powlesland
Christine Haughton
Yedingham, 1992

This preparation of this report was completed in 1992, and has been subjected to only minor revisions since then. It is with considerable regret that, owing to circumstances beyond our control, the final publication of this report has taken so long to come to fruition.

# Introduction

The Early Anglo-Saxon cemetery at West Heslerton is one of a series of cemeteries located on the margins of the Vale of Pickering, which separates the North Yorkshire Moors to the north and the Yorkshire Wolds to the south. Others are known from discoveries at Rillington and Staxton on the southern edge of the Vale and Seamer and Wykeham to the north (Fig 1). The site is one of only four to be extensively examined in the northern Anglian region during the last 20 years, the others being Sewerby and Castledyke, Barton-on-Humber in Humberside (Hirst 1985; Drinkall and Foreman 1998), and Norton in Cleveland (Sherlock and Welch 1992), which collectively provide us with a sample of more than 575 graves excavated using modern techniques in the region as a whole. West Heslerton, like so many other sites of this class, came to light not as a consequence of a planned research programme, but accidentally during mineral extraction. As such the site has provided an important new data set. Much of this evidence was, however, recovered in difficult conditions imposed by the weather, limited resources and the threat of damage from the activities of metal detectorists, a problem exacerbated by the presence of a major trunk road, the A64, crossing the site.

The site is significant for a number of reasons, not least the relatively complete nature of the excavation, which established the limits of the site on all sides. There must still, however, remain some doubt about how much may have been destroyed by quarrying before the start of archaeological work and how many burials remain sealed by the road which bisects the cemetery. Most important of all is the fact that here, for the first time in the north of England, we have been afforded an opportunity to examine both an Anglian cemetery and an associated settlement on a large scale and using modern techniques.

The known distribution of Anglian burials in the northeast of England (Fig 2) owes most to the work of J R Mortimer, who examined more than 30 cemeteries with an Anglian component during the late nineteenth century, and published his results in the superbly illustrated *Forty Years' Researches in British and Saxon Burial Mounds of East Yorkshire,* one of the masterpieces of late nineteenth-century British archaeology (Mortimer 1905). The grave groups recovered by Mortimer and at other more recently excavated sites reveal the rich and distinctive character of Anglian material culture, our perception of which had to a large extent, until the current work on the West Heslerton settlement, been restricted to such information as could be derived from cemeteries alone, and in particular from the grave assemblages such as those excavated by Mortimer, which are preserved in Hull museum.

A feature of the West Heslerton site, which is so frequently paralleled in Mortimer's work that we should perhaps suggest that this is the rule rather than the exception, is the association between Anglian burial and prehistoric ritual sites. We must of course accept that Mortimer generally only investigated barrow cemeteries and that any Anglian burials he discovered were therefore usually thus associated, but we know that had others been reported to him he would have examined them just as he would the upstanding earthworks that were his usual target. This deliberate re-use of prehistoric monuments for burial may signify a desire on the part of the social or political leaders of the emerging Anglo-Saxon society to legitimise the new post-Roman social hierarchy by linking it by association to the earlier prehistoric past. The lack of similarly associated Romano-British burials makes it clear that this marks a break with Romano-British burial tradition, although very little is known about Romano-British rural burial practices in the region in general. The construction of barrows for burial in Early Anglo-Saxon England and the placing of burials within both ring and square ditched enclosures is widely attested, but it is not the norm. It therefore appears that it was the location that was considered important, rather than the practice of burial in barrows.

This excavation was the setting for the introduction of a number of innovative excavation and recording techniques. Particular attention was paid to the recovery of textile and other mineral-replaced organic evidence through the lifting intact of large soil blocks; this allowed many of the grave groups to be excavated in laboratory conditions, guaranteeing the maximum recovery of these fragile materials. Field recording methods underwent a transition during the period in which the site was being excavated, particularly with the increased application of computers and electronic surveying instruments. The graves examined on Site 1 were recorded using conventional paper records, but the bulk of the data was recorded using hand-held computers in the field, with most of the material being individually plotted using an electronic distance meter (EDM). All the graves were photographed vertically; the vertical photographs were printed at scales between 1:2 (for some of the object assemblages) and 1:5, and subsequently digitised within a geographic data management system. During the post-excavation process new context numbers were generated for the features examined between 1977 and 1980 to increase compatibility within the archive; in particular, grave numbers assigned during the 1977–80 seasons were split to generate distinctive grave cut, fill and skeleton records. Subsequently, an all-encompassing sequence of grave numbers has been issued to facilitate cross-referencing and reader comprehension.

The Anglian cemetery was established in the late fifth century within an area defined by an earlier Late Neolithic and Early Bronze age ritual complex comprising a hengiform enclosure, an associated post circle and a series of round barrows. Thirteen burials were associated with the prehistoric monuments, including ten inhumations and three cremations; a single inhumation believed to be prehistoric was discovered in a sample trench some 100m away from the monument complex. The Anglian cemetery was in use for a period of not more than 200 years, spanning the period from the late fifth to early seventh centuries but not covering the full period of the occupation of the associated settlement. The cemetery covered an area of about 8000 sq m of which just under 2000 sq m is currently sealed by the A64. The excavation included the examination of 201 Anglian burials out of an estimated total of *c* 300: 185 inhumations, 15 cremations and a single horse burial. As a percentage of the total the cremations are almost certainly under-represented, since all those identified had been subjected to serious plough damage, in some cases removing everything down to the base of the pottery container. Their distribution is, however, localised and it is unlikely that more than 30 to 40 existed, unless of course they were buried within the ploughsoil itself; in that case, however, despite the poor quality of the ceramics, some evidence should have been observed during the removal of the ploughsoil. As in other cemeteries of this period the burials of young infants are under-represented in the buried population; however, the recovery of a number of infant bones from rubbish deposits in the *Grubenhäuser* in the settlement demonstrates that for infants at least alternative forms of disposal were acceptable.

Contrary to the view recently expressed by Higham (1991 and 1992), the site at West Heslerton does not represent an elite settlement of 'foreigners' in a landscape populated by an invisible native serf population. The evidence from the cemetery indicates the presence of two principal physical groups, the smaller group being best represented in a series of taller, gracile individuals accompanied by weapons. It is unfortunate that the quality of bone

preservation was very poor, since there is insufficient evidence to refine this general observation. It has not yet been possible to subject the remains to DNA analysis that might assist us in the identification of family or genetically distinctive groups. Clearly the examination and comparison of the evidence from the settlement and that from the cemetery will be immensely important for modelling the social structure of the society; this, however, will have to await the full assessment and analysis of the settlement evidence.

# Structure of the report

This report has been prepared in two volumes. This volume, incorporating the synthetic discussion and analysis of the evidence, is presented in four sections: the site, its setting and excavation, the prehistoric activity, the Anglian activity and detailed discussion of the Anglian grave goods by class and type. Volume ii comprises the detailed grave catalogue of the Anglian burials and associated assemblages, bringing together all the evidence from each of the excavated grave deposits on an assemblage basis, including the grave plans, context and object records, and illustrations.

The long duration of the project over many short seasons of excavation coincided with changes in recording methodology and archaeological theory that increasingly emphasised the unique importance of the context as the primary key in recording structures, as opposed to the traditional approach of assigning separate number sequences to different feature classes.

The unique context sequence approach was adopted at West Heslerton from the outset, as it makes data management both much simpler and much more powerful in relation to the analytical potential. Graves were numbered according to the context issued at the time of discovery rather than to a numbered grave sequence. Traditional constructs such as the use of a numbered sequence of 'small finds' were abandoned in favour of a unique numbering sequence for all finds that combined the full context number with a two character object code appended to it. This approach facilitates both the management and analysis of assemblages and maintains the primacy of the context as the unit of record.

# Numbering conventions

The numbered grave sequence used to reference the Anglian graves in this report was applied retrospectively after the first drafts of the report were complete. A context concordance list (Volume ii pp. 371-374) is provided to make it easier for the reader to see at a glance the relationship between the grave numbers and the individual contexts assigned in the field. The excavation of the cemetery took place over a number of years as

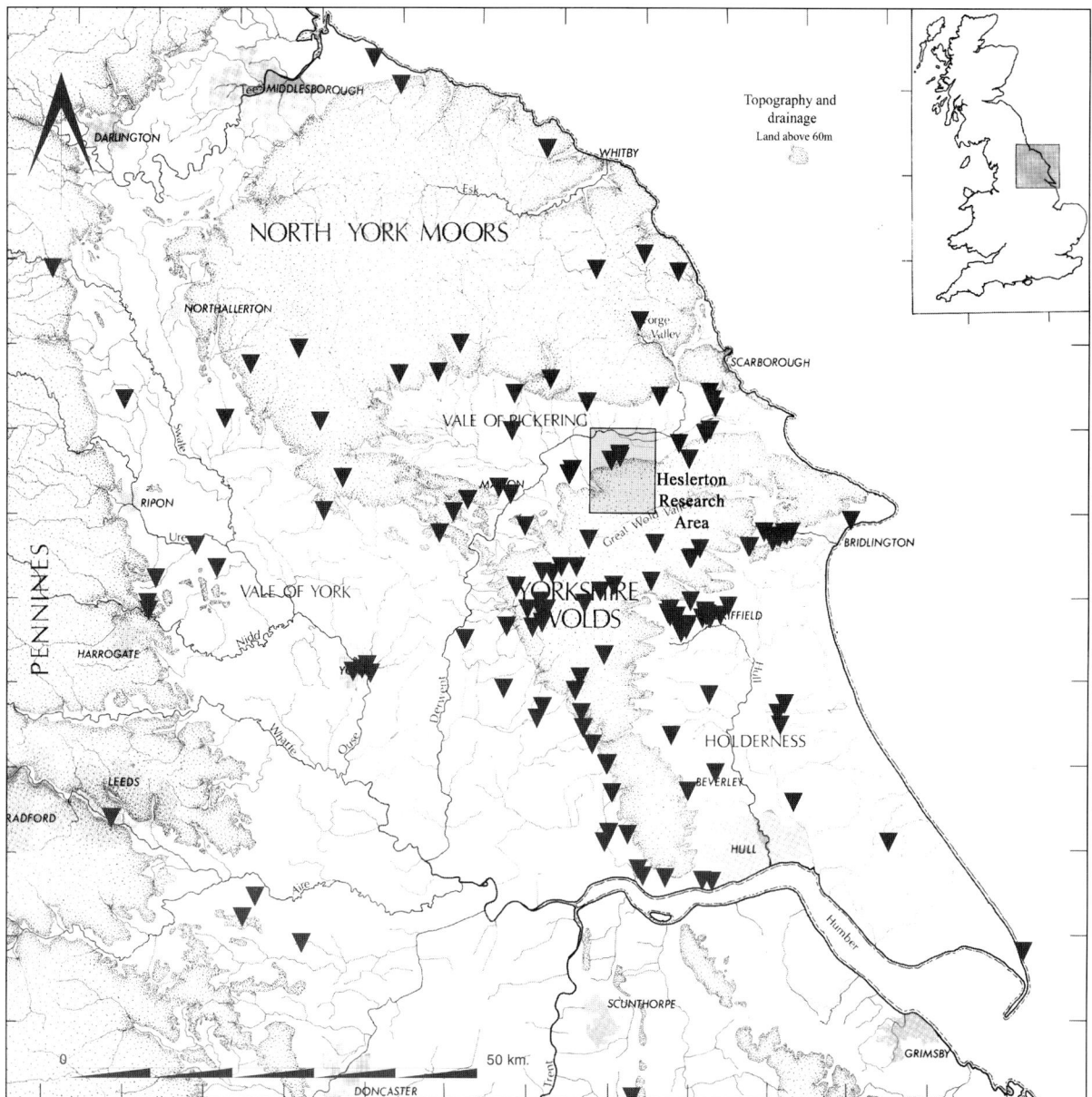

*Figure 1: The distribution of Anglian Cemeteries in Northern and Eastern Yorkshire*

part of a more extensive rescue excavation programme undertaken within a broader research framework, the Heslerton Parish Project, defined to provide a context for the rescue excavations incorporating features from a broad temporal and functional range. A numbering system was defined to cover all potential work in the area, in which individual fields were allotted a three digit site number; excavation areas were defined using a two character code, and contexts within each area were given a five digit number. This approach was adopted as part of a broader initiative to provide a single numbering structure that was directly supported within the Sites and Monuments Record (SMR) for North Yorkshire. Within each context finds were numbered individually using a two character code; thus 002BA00226AA identifies individually an object from Site 2, Area BA, Context 226.

In many cases context numbers were issued sequentially across the excavation, and hence an individual feature may not have a simple sequence of numbers; in order to make it easier both for the reader and for cross-referencing purposes a Grave Number sequence has been applied to the Anglian graves in the cemetery. The original numbers have been retained and a higher level of numbering has been applied to provide a simple sequence of grave numbers. The new numbers are identified by the letter G: thus G3 is the Grave Number assigned to grave cut 01A_00513. Where a specific object is referred to in this volume it is identified firstly by the Grave Number followed by the unique object code issued in the field and also used for the illustrations in Volume ii, as for example, in the case of the sword in Grave 75 which is referred to as G75:2B85AM.

# The site and its setting

## Discovery

The Anglian cemetery at West Heslerton was discovered during September 1977, when quarry worker Jim Carter, who had worked on an occasional basis as an archaeological labourer, observed Anglian burials being eroded out of the quarry surface after the removal of overburden and immediately reported the find to the Humberside Archaeology Unit.

John Dent, then of the Humberside Archaeological Unit, mounted a salvage excavation during the autumn and winter of 1977/78 examining 35 graves in area 1HE (Fig 4). In the spring of 1978 responsibility for the site was transferred to North Yorkshire County Council Archaeology section. Mike Griffiths approached the Inspectorate of Ancient Monuments to raise funds for further examination of the site and appointed Dominic Powlesland project director in the spring of 1978.

This site, like so many others of its type, therefore came to light not as a product of a detailed research programme but as a consequence of casual discovery. The excavations that followed took place within a rescue archaeology framework but have nonetheless produced an important research archive which offers considerable potential for further research.

## Context

West Heslerton is located at the foot of the north-facing scarp slope of the Yorkshire Wolds on the southern margin of the Vale of Pickering, the Anglian cemetery being located just over a kilometre to the east of the present village. The north-facing scarp of the Yorkshire Wolds rises some 300m and is characterised by a steeply sloping face above 100m AOD. At the base of the slope, gently sloping chalk hills are separated by broad shallow dry valleys and extensive hill-wash deposits with numerous spring points emerging at the 55m contour from the junction between the chalk and the Speeton clay beneath. The Anglian settlement at West Heslerton sits astride two of these chalk hillocks, with a spring point at the heart of the settlement. Below this the landscape slopes much more gently towards the centre of the valley to the north, but still features occasional, much lower, chalky knolls

Recent research has demonstrated a much greater density of later prehistoric activity in the Vale of Pickering than had previously been recognised. Air photography, excavation and observations during development work have revealed large numbers of barrows, both individually and in cemeteries, from the Late Neolithic, Bronze and Iron Ages; settlement evidence, particularly for the Late Iron Age and Roman periods, is extensive (North Yorkshire County Council Sites and Monuments Record; Powlesland *et al.* 1986).

By the end of the Iron Age an extensive linear settlement had formed which followed the southern edge of the fenland which then prevailed in the centre of the valley along the 30m contour. The fen edge can be easily identified both by mapping the drainage pattern in the centre of the valley and by examining the cropmark record, which demonstrates the presence of this extensive linear settlement for more than 10 km (Fig 3). Trackways and field systems to the south of the settlement zone indicate that much of the landscape on the lighter soils along the southern edge of the valley was clear and being used for agriculture. Broad trackways leading up onto the Wolds, much of which was enclosed by an extensive network of major late prehistoric boundaries, may indicate that much of the downland landscape of the Wolds was cleared and in use for grazing.

Little is known in detail of the Roman rural economy of the region. However, what we can be certain of is that in the post-Roman period, as in every other part of lowland Britain, the Roman settlements were generally deserted in favour of new sites. The work still in progress on the Anglian settlement at West Heslerton is providing much needed new evidence of this period of transition. The reasons behind what appears to be a fundamental change in the settlement structure of lowland Britain remain far from clear. Some have argued that this change in settlement represents a determined effort on the part of invading continental Angles, Saxons and Jutes to impose their will upon the landscape. One is tempted, however, to suggest that here we are seeing a response to an essentially economic and environmental change rather than an overtly political one. Evidence recovered in sample

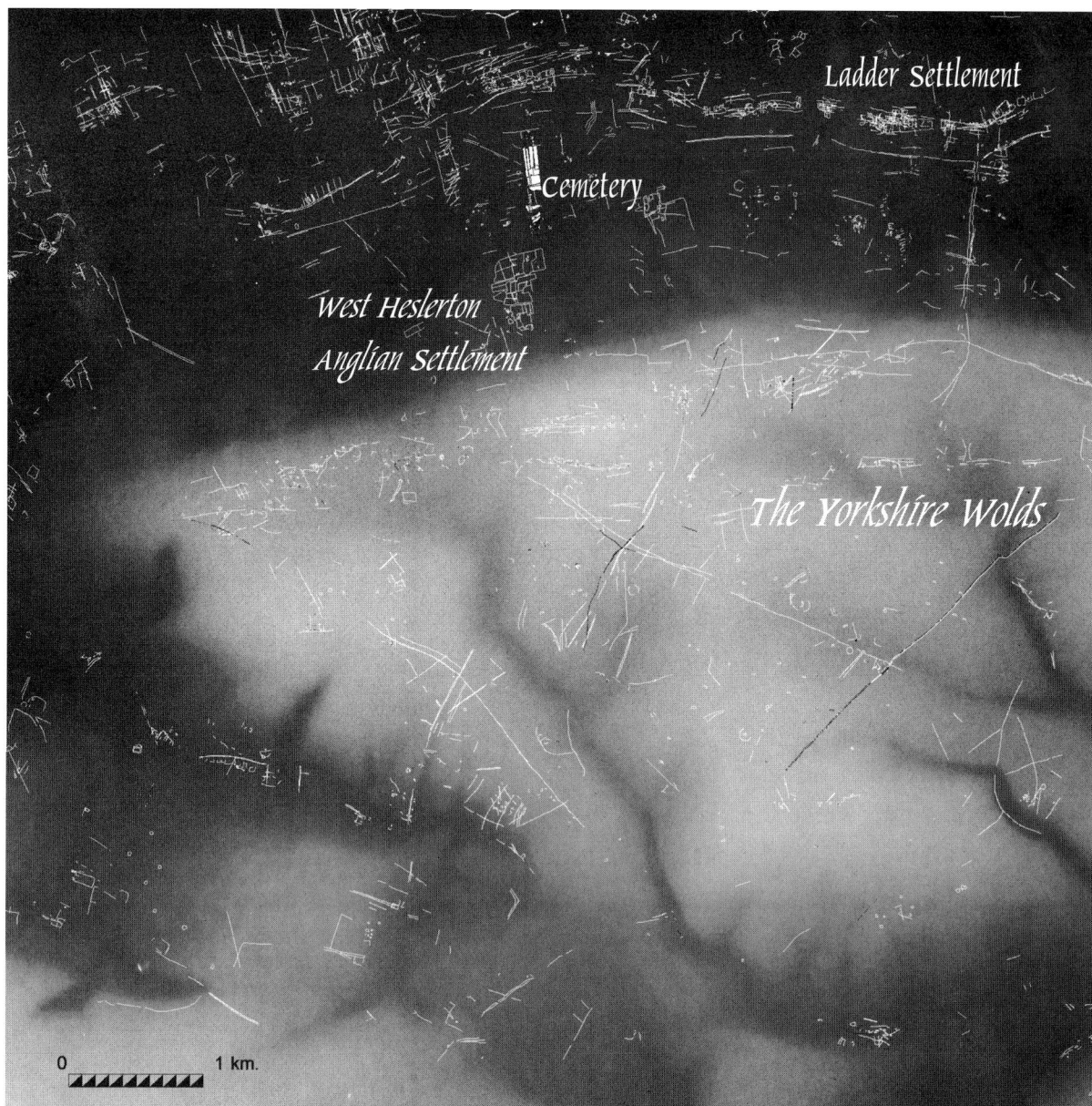

*Figure 2: The location of the Anglian settlement and cemetery at West Heslerton*

excavations of the linear settlement at Sherburn 5km to the east of West Heslerton demonstrates that during the late Roman period ground-water problems increased dramatically, supporting the generally accepted view of environmental deterioration during the late Roman period. It appears that conditions in the fen edge settlement were far from ideal for settlement throughout the latter part of the fourth and into the fifth century, and one is forced to ask why the settlement was not deserted sooner. It is possible that the shift in settlement came about as a consequence of the breakdown of the Roman system of land tenure, allowing land that was not previously available for settlement to be freed, and thus providing the impetus for a change in the overall settlement structure.

Evidence from Wykeham, Seamer Crossgates and Sherburn in the Vale of Pickering demonstrates that during the fifth century a distinctly Anglian component emerges in these settlements in the form of Anglian ce-

ramics and the ubiquitous *Grubenhäuser*; these sites do not, however, go on to develop through the early Anglian into the Middle Saxon period (Moore 1965, Pye 1976, 1983). This evidence has hardly been studied and much needs to be done to clarify the dating of the Anglian material and the sequence which led to the establishment of the Anglian settlements like that at West Heslerton.

By the end of the fifth century the Vale of Pickering supported a substantial population, as demonstrated by the presence of Anglian cemeteries at Staxton, Rillington, and West Heslerton and by emerging evidence of settlements on the southern and northern margins of the valley. The distinctive Anglian material culture identifiable in the grave goods from the cemeteries demonstrates the continental links in the population, not the percentage of Scandinavians as opposed to Britons occupying the countryside. Nor can we draw upon place-name evidence to suggest that the frequency of Anglo-

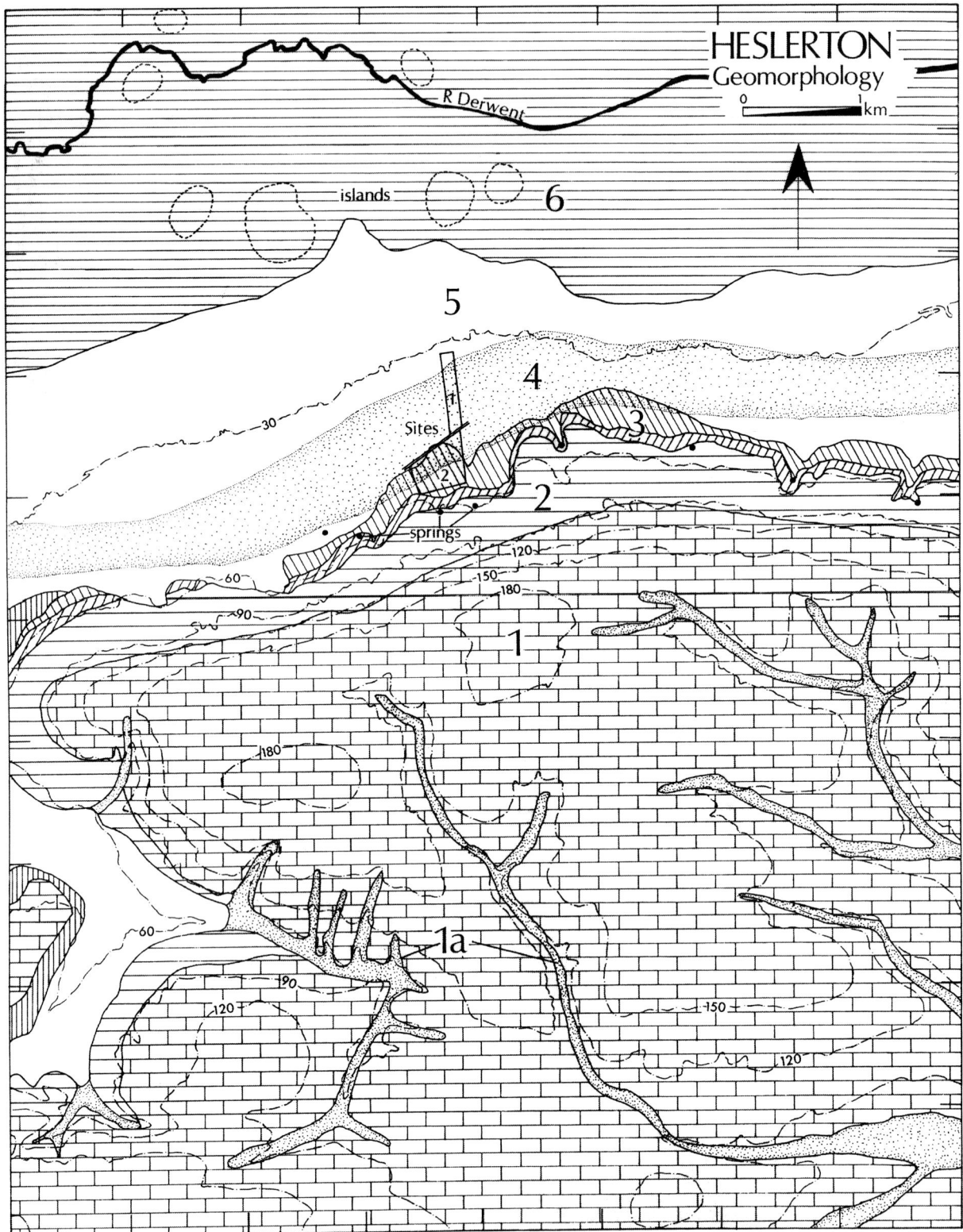

Key:            Heslerton: Geomorphological zones
Zone 1:         The Wold Top, chalk downland
Zone 2:         The Wold Scarp, chalk with eroded chalk knolls
Zone 3:         The Speeton clays with outcrops of chalk and Old Red Chalk
Zone 4:         The blown sand, aeolian sand overlying slight chalk knolls and post-glacial sands and gravels
Zone 5:         Post-glacial sands and gravels
Zone 6:         The wet Vale, fenland in antiquity, bisected by many relict stream channels once filled with peats
                which are rapidly drying out

*Figure 3: Heslerton geomorphology and landscape zones*

Saxon place-names is such as to demonstrate that the level of migration was correspondingly large. The place-names cannot be identified for the first time until much later in the Saxon period, at a time when the early Anglo-Saxon settlements themselves are being deserted in favour of new Middle Saxon sites which emerge as the named villages. Whether we view the development of Early Anglo-Saxon England as a consequence of large-scale invasion and domination, something not adequately supported in the archaeological record, or as the emergence of a small new social and political elite whose material culture was willingly assimilated by the native population, one thing is clear: by the beginning of the sixth century the population in Eastern Yorkshire, later to become Deira, had adopted Anglian dress and burial practices.

# Geology

The geology and soils along the southern edge of the Vale of Pickering show considerable uniformity, with heavier soils at the foot of the Wolds where Speeton clays are to be found in between the chalky outcrops (Fig 3). Sands and gravels derived from glacial outwash form the dominant soils along the southern edge of the valley, and have provided the parent material for the substantial aeolian sand deposits which are a feature of this part of the valley between the 35m and 45m contour. They extend up to 1km to the north of the foot of the Wolds, where gravels become more numerous. The cemetery is situated at the northern limit of the distribution of a series of slight chalk knolls, at a break in the slope which then descends gradually towards the centre of the valley to the north at the junction between geomorphological zones 3 and 4. The eroded chalk outcrop that effectively defines the southern edge of the cemetery formed a shallow arc running across the southern edge of the cemetery, the ground falling away on all sides. To the south, hill-wash and windblown deposits seal the natural sands and gravels, which extend to the next major chalk outcrop 200m to the south. The base sands and gravels, covering most of the area occupied by the Anglian cemetery, are composed of a soft sand and gravel comprising chalk and a very poor flinty chert derived from erosion of the chalk face of the Wolds by glacial outwash.

The very free-draining nature of the sands and gravels provided a poor environment for bone survival, although the soils are now markedly alkaline; this may be a consequence of chalk enrichment occurring once the Wolds were brought under extensive open agriculture. The upper metre of the natural sands is characterised by the presence of numerous very thin solution lines where fine particles have concentrated in undulating bands. These frequently pass right through the archaeological features, making the excavation and identification of body stain features, which survived well in the more sandy areas of the sites, particularly difficult. The localised soil conditions and geology of the cemetery meant that it was highly susceptible to both natural erosion and deposition, as well as to damage resulting from agricultural practices both in the medieval period and more recently.

# Location of the cemetery

The prehistoric and Anglian cemetery at West Heslerton was established just to the north of a slightly elevated natural chalk knoll situated between 40m and 45m AOD between two stream channels, the source of which lay at the base of the Wolds some 450m to the south. One of the streams, the Ass Beck, which forms the parish boundary between East and West Heslerton and ran due north 75m to the east of the cemetery, still survives today. The other, which defined the western limit of the cemetery, emerged from its source at the heart of the contemporary Anglian settlement some 450m to the south-west, but was redirected along a man-made channel during the later medieval period. The focal point of the cemetery appeared to lie in the centre of an area defined on the west by the stream and to the south and east by a series of prehistoric monuments: a Neolithic hengiform enclosure, which effectively encloses most of the chalk knoll, an adjacent post circle and later round barrows to the north-east and the north, which occupied the remaining high part of the knoll. Around the knoll the subsoil comprised the post-glacial sands and gravels whose extraction led to the discovery of the site in 1977. The choice of location for the Anglian cemetery, combining both the presence of the earlier ritual sites and the relatively light soils around the chalky knoll, is closely paralleled at other sites such as Rillington 5km to the west, where the Anglian cemetery forms the final phase in a large cemetery that includes at least one long barrow, many round barrows and a large group of Iron Age square barrows.

The distribution of the Anglian burials indicates that the northern part of the enclosure ditch (2BA38) and barrow (2BA130) were probably visible at the time that the cemetery was in use (Fig 6). Two further barrows, one in the centre of the enclosure (2BA174) and a second partially sealing the ditch on the western side (2BA264), produced no indication of any secondary activity and their mounds, which were in any case probably small, may have been obscured by aeolian sand. A prehistoric boundary, defined initially by a pit alignment (2BA603) and later by a series of gullies, perhaps indicating the presence of a hedge, may have constrained the development of the northern half of the cemetery (Site 1) but appears not to have done so over the southern half (Site 2). To the north of the cemetery the ground slopes gently down towards a Late Iron Age and Roman period linear settlement a kilometre to the north, following the edge of the fenland environment which once extended over much of the area at the centre of the Vale of Pickering.

Following the Anglo-Saxon period the cemetery was lost beneath rig and furrow fields and later bisected by a road, now the A64.

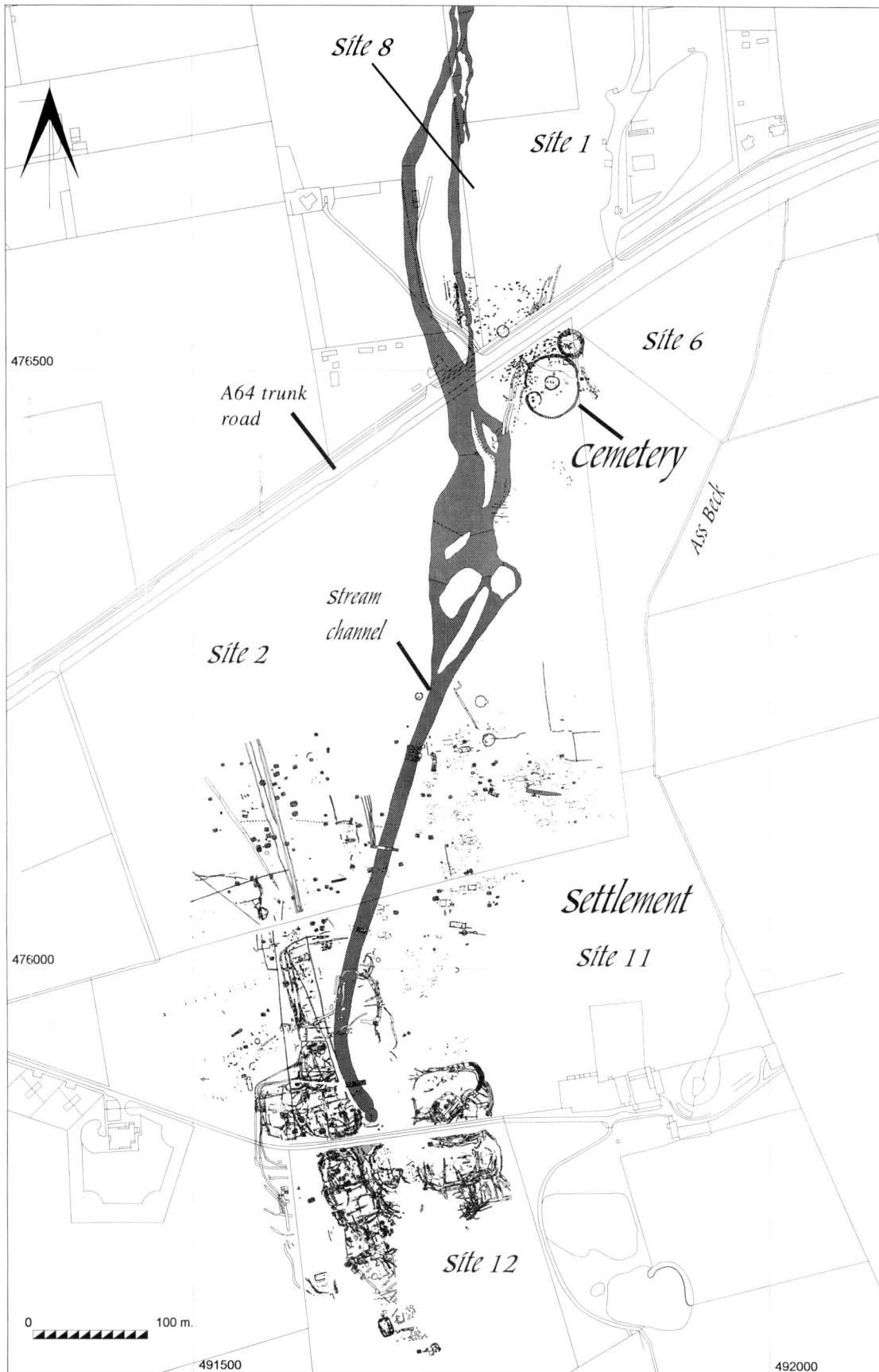

*Figure 4: West Heslerton: plan showing the relationship between the Anglian settlement and cemetery*

*Plate 1: aerial view looking across the excavation towards the north-east*

*Plate 2: aerial photograph taken from a helium balloon over the centre of area 2BA during the backfilling*

The topography of the cemetery is not instantly apparent to the casual viewer because of the presence of the A64, which was cut into the aeolian deposits that covered some parts of the cemetery and built up against the hedged field boundaries which cross the site. Evidence from a salvage excavation ahead of the introduction of a new water main indicates that further burials are likely to remain preserved beneath the road. Despite the damage caused by the building of the A64 and the loss of the area to the north in the quarry it remains clear that the cemetery occupied a slightly elevated position determined by the location of the prehistoric monument complex at its core. The combination of plough damage, road construction, quarrying and the variable build-up of blown sands adjacent to the field boundaries make it impossible to reconstruct the ancient land profile with any certainty. To the east the ground falls away fairly rapidly towards an active stream, the Ass Beck, whilst to the south the ground falls away gradually before rising again towards the settlement.

# The Excavation

## The excavation sequence

The West Heslerton Anglian cemetery was excavated piecemeal over a number of years following the discovery of the cemetery in 1977. The site extended over four principal excavation sites defined by current field boundaries with sub-areas on two of the sites: Heslerton Parish Project Sites 1A, 1B, 1C, 1HE, 2A, 2B, 2BA, 2BB, 6AA and 8AA (Fig 5). The cemetery contained both cremations and inhumations; the cremations had, however, suffered particularly badly from plough damage and although parts of 15 cremations were examined we can assume that a number of others had been entirely destroyed by ploughing.

The excavation programme between 1978 and 1985 was determined largely by quarrying activity to the north of the cemetery, where features of the Late Neolithic and Early Bronze Age, Late Bronze and Early Iron Age, and Roman periods were examined, although a number of graves were examined in areas 1A (17 Graves) and 1B (11 graves) during 1979 and 1980. Further graves discovered as part of a sampling operation to identify the southern limits of the cemetery in areas 2B (11 graves) and 2C in and 2F (4 graves) in 1982. It was decided during the excavation at Cook's Quarry, Site 1, that the prehistoric and Roman evidence should be published separately, since further examination of the cemetery was likely to take place, and thus this material was published in 1986 (Powlesland *et al* 1986).

During 1985 excavation of the cemetery was resumed with the examination of Site 8AA; work continued in 1986 and 1987 on Sites 2BA, 2BB and 6AA. A total of 185 Anglian inhumations and 15 Anglian cremations were examined, in addition to a number of Late Neolithic and Early Bronze Age burials discussed below. Although the limits of the cemetery were established on all sides it was not possible to examine the cemetery in total; a substantial portion remains preserved beneath the A64 modern trunk road which bisects the cemetery. It is estimated that up to a hundred graves may remain sealed by the road and adjacent paths and hedges, giving an overall cemetery population in the region of three hundred individuals. A single Anglian burial in area 1C (1C464), a hundred

metres to the north of the main excavated area, was probably an outlier; the area between the main cemetery area and this individual grave had already been lost to quarrying by the time the cemetery was discovered. It is unlikely that this area contained a high density of burials as the eventual discoverer of the site, Jim Carter, walked over the area on a daily basis and observed nothing.

## The excavation areas

### Site 1: Areas A, B and HE

Topsoil removal had already taken place prior to the discovery of the site in area 1HE and over much of areas 1A and 1B (Fig 5). The subsoil in these areas was sand; in contrast to areas excavated further to the north blown sand deposits were less extensive in this part of the site. Towards the eastern end of area 1A, beyond the limits of the cemetery and adjacent to the hedged southern boundary, blown sand deposits had protected features from modern plough damage and concealed a gently domed sub-surface profile, indicating that the cemetery had been established upon a slightly elevated knoll. It was impossible to establish the shape of the old land surface with any precision since for the most part the area had been stripped before the start of the excavation and the area immediately to the south had been partially truncated when the A64 Trunk Road was established. Although the dense deposits of soft sand in these area made excavation relatively easy the definition of the graves, which had been backfilled with the same material with little additional topsoil, was very poor. It was necessary to lower the whole of the ground surface over most of the area to ensure that no graves were missed.

Area 1HE (1549 sq m) was examined during the winter in salvage conditions. It had been thought that the limits of the cemetery had been reached in the investigation of area 1HE; however, the discovery of further graves in Areas 1A (635 sq m) and 1B (738 sq m) during 1978 showed that this was not the case. The constant threat from metal detecting meant that the graves in these areas had to be excavated very rapidly, with work often continuing through the night under arc-lights. It was not possible to fully investigate the whole area during 1978 and

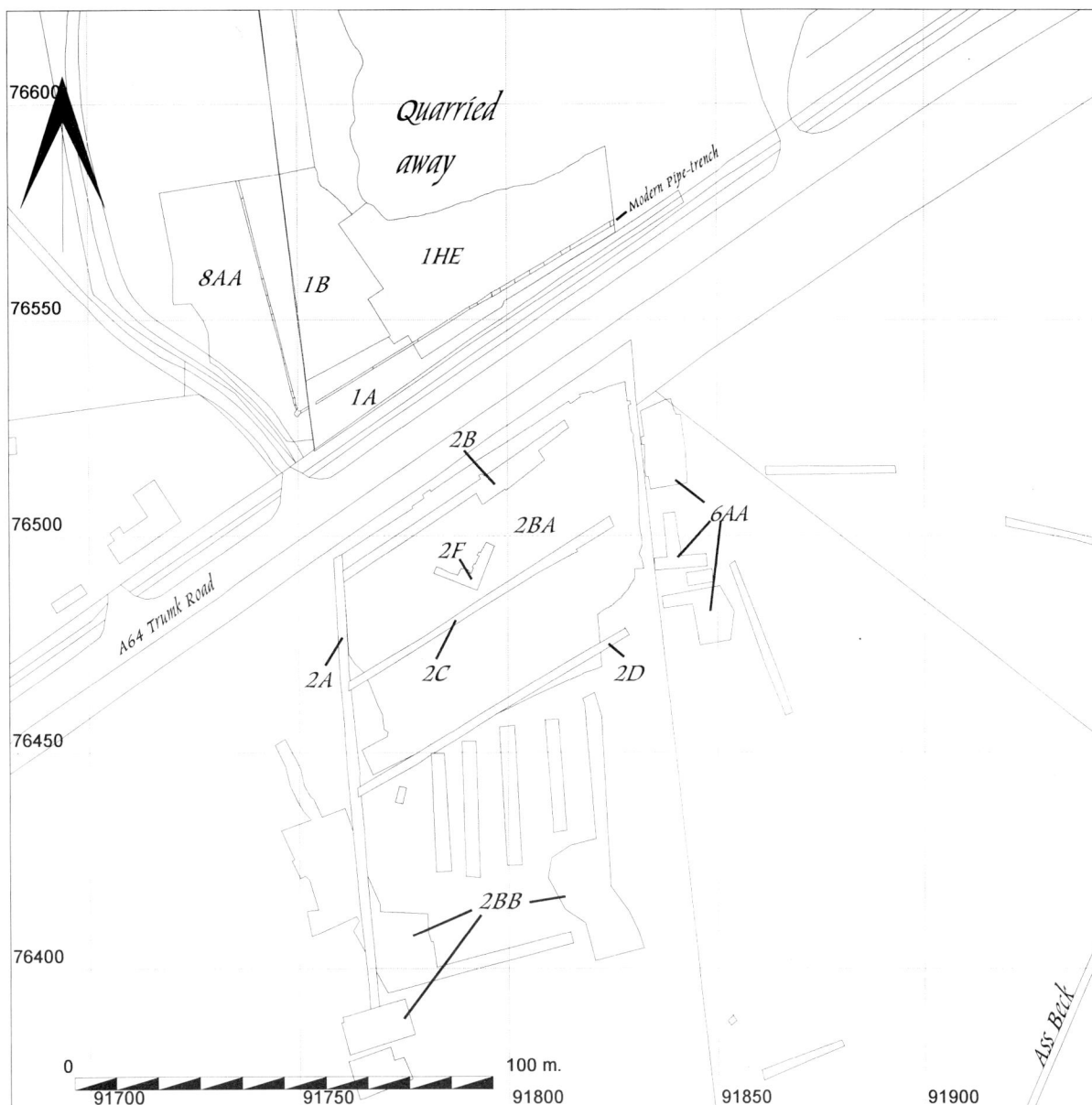

*Figure 5: Plan showing the excavation areas*

part of area 1B, which remained sealed beneath a spoil-heap, was finally examined in 1979. A problem characteristic of the natural sands on Site 1 was the incorporation of thin *c*2mm clay varves or pans which occur as horizontal bands in the natural but also run through the features. These varves made excavation particularly difficult as the survival of skeletal material in these areas was poor and these relatively dense deposits frequently obscured the fragmentary skeletal material and associated staining.

## Site 2: Areas 2A, 2B, 2C, 2D, 2E and 2F

During 1982 a sampling strategy was devised to assess Site 2 and to determine whether the cemetery extended to the south of the A64 Trunk Road which bounded Site 1 (Fig 5). It was proposed to open a grid of 2m trenches spaced at 20m intervals; in the event three trenches were opened by machine. 2B, 2C and 2D ran parallel to the field boundary and a fourth, 2A, ran north–south connecting with the other trenches at the western end. Following the discovery of the relict stream channel in 2A a fifth trench, 2E, was opened by machine to check the course of the stream channel. A sixth trench, 2F, was opened by hand in the centre of the area between 2B and 2C, where evidence of modern plough damage was immediately apparent. As on Site 1 the adjacent field boundaries, forming the northern and eastern boundaries of the area, had restricted plough damage in these areas and encouraged the deposition of blown sand, affording those graves that lay adjacent to the field boundaries a higher degree of protection than was normally the case.

## Site 8: Area 8AA

During the spring of 1985, following the completion of the excavation report concerning the pre-Anglian activity on Site 1, attention was turned again towards the cemetery with the examination of Site 8 immediately to the West of Site 1, within the areas proposed for further mineral extraction (Fig 5). An area of 1344 sq m was stripped by Hy-Mac under archaeological supervision, delimited by the eastern edge of the relict stream channel which marked the western limit of the Anglian cemetery. This area, excavated with a small team, contained seven Anglian burials running up to but not beyond a minor stream channel with a series of late prehistoric boundary features following the eastern bank of the main channel further to the west. The sand which formed the subsoil over areas 1A and 1B was bounded to the west by the stream channel where it gave way to mixed deposits of sand and chalk/chert gravels. Although this area had suffered some plough damage this had only recently cut into the archaeological deposits. Adjacent to two of the graves patches of denser sand were thought at the time to indicate the presence of spoil heaps derived when the graves were originally cut; they were impossible to further define as they disappeared upon cleaning. The presence of this material was taken to indicate that in this area at least, plough damage had been minimal and that the stripped surface must have been very close to the old land surface.

## Site 2: Areas 2BA and 2BB

Following the completion of excavation on Site 8, area excavation was begun on Site 2, initially in area 2BA where over 3800 sq m was stripped and then extended to cover over 1900 sq m in area 2BB (Fig 5). The trial trenches opened in 1982 gave a false impression of the extent and complexity of the archaeology in this area and thus excavation continued for longer than had been intended, continuing throughout 1985 and the first half of 1986. This area had clearly contained the focus of the Anglian cemetery and incorporated areas where plough damage had reached a critical point, and others where preservation had been assured by the build-up of blown sands against the hedge boundaries. Whereas the natural geology in the rest of the cemetery comprised sand with some involutions bringing chalk and chert gravel to the surface, the natural in areas 2BA and 2BB included a solid chalk knoll which had been incorporated in the construction of a hengiform enclosure. This had been missed in the earlier trial trenches; trench 2C had run straight though the western entrance to the monument. The interior of the hengiform enclosure appears, initially at least, to have been reserved for cremation burial; a number of graves cut into the filled in ditch of the enclosure benefited from the more chalky environment which had reduced the level of post-depositional decay of the skeletal material. The natural subsoil over nearly half of the enclosed area comprised frost-shattered chalk gravels lying above solid chalk bedrock into which the enclosure ditch had been cut on the northern and eastern sides; the remainder of the area was covered with sand. The natural sand deposits in areas 2BA and 2BB were more granular and less cohesive than in the areas examined to the north and tended to dry out very quickly, at which point they became very difficult to work. The sides of the grave cuts became very unstable and liable

both to collapse and erosion from the wind. In the sandy areas, as on Site 1 to the north, the grave cuts were so difficult to see clearly that it was necessary to take down the whole surface to be sure that no burials had been missed.

## Site 6: Area 6AA

The last part of the area to be examined, in 1987, lay adjacent and to the east of Site 2BA on Site 6, where the ground fell away from the hedge boundary towards an active stream, the Ass Beck, which had once defined the boundary between the now merged parishes of East and West Heslerton (Figs 4,5). Three small areas amounting to less than 500 sq m were opened against the boundary with Site 2 to confirm the presence and limits of the prehistoric monuments extending into the area from Site 2 and to determine whether the Anglian cemetery extended beyond these monuments; these appeared to define the eastern edge of the cemetery. Soil conditions here were effectively the same as in area 2BA, divided between pure granular sand and fractured chalk bedrock with solution holes. A single unaccompanied but almost certainly Anglian burial was identified cut into an earlier prehistoric barrow. To the south of the barrow and 19.5m to the south-east of the eastern entrance of the hengiform enclosure a cremation beneath an inverted Food Vessel appeared to be an isolated flat-grave. Four 2m wide machine trenches were opened to the east and south of the area, on the slope running towards the stream, but no further archaeological features were identified.

| | Inhumations | Cremations | LNeo/EBA |
|---|---|---|---|
| 1A | 18 | | |
| 1B | 9+1 Horse | | |
| 1C | 1 | | |
| 1HE | 35 | | 1 |
| 2B | 11 | | |
| 2BA | 98 | 13 | 6+2cr |
| 2BB | 1 | | |
| 2F | 4 | | |
| 2C | | 1 | 1 |
| 8AA | 7 | | |
| 6AA | 1 | 1 | 1 |
| **TOTAL** | **186** | **15** | **11** |

*Table 1: grave counts by excavation area*

# Condition of the graves

The subsoils over most of the area covered by the cemetery were dominated by free-draining sands and gravels and, despite the fact that the soils are now quite alkaline, the level of bone preservation was generally poor. Much of the cemetery had suffered serious plough damage and, coupled with the fact that most of the topsoil had been removed on Site 1 before the start of the excavations, this made any attempt to reconstruct the original depths of the graves impossible. Where the graves had been cut into sand the sandy grave fills were frequently almost indistinguishable from the natural sand subsoil and could

*Figure 6: Plan of the excavated areas showing the course of the stream channel and all excavated features*

only be successfully isolated by lowering the natural surface across the site as a whole.

Plough damage was particularly severe on Site 1 and in part of Site 2, Area 2BA, where an Anglian bronze-bound wooden bucket (2F2AA ) was retrieved from the base of the ploughsoil after having been partially cut away by modern ploughing (Plate 3). In one part of the cemetery, the north-east corner of Site 2, aeolian sands had built up against the current field boundaries in such a way that we can be confident that the upper fills of the graves had not been seriously truncated. In the north-eastern part of 2BA large fragments of Anglian pottery, recovered from the deposits sealing the graves, may be derived from vessels used as grave markers; their survival indicated a lack of post-depositional damage in this area.

Post-depositional damage to the graves and their contents was not, however, confined to plough damage. The soft soils were heavily burrowed, disturbing grave goods, particularly the bead necklaces, and in areas close to the modern field boundaries tree roots had caused further disturbance. A number of graves had been partially cut away by a modern sewerage pipe running though Sites 1 and 8, and others were disturbed by medieval rig and furrow on Site 2 (Fig 6) or later Anglian graves, although the frequency with which graves intercut was very low, demonstrating that the graves must have remained visible during the life of the cemetery whether deliberately marked or not. The close proximity of a main road meant that the site was under constant threat from metal detector users; one grave was disturbed and a substantially complete Anglian pot was removed from the site one night. A second effect of the road was that traffic vibrations could dislodge complex assemblages from the drying sand during excavation and lifting.

*Plate 3: recent plough damage showing as dark plough marks during initial cleaning*

# Excavation and recording procedures

## Summary

Excavation of the West Heslerton cemetery continued intermittently over a decade, a period during which, as already noted, archaeological recording systems and excavation methodologies went through a number of fundamental changes, particularly as a consequence of the introduction of computers for on-site recording. By 1978 pro-forma recording sheets had been introduced into most excavation recording systems to ensure a consistent standard of record. During the life of the excavation the pro-forma sheets introduced at the start of the excavation were first replaced with a more comprehensive series of recording forms designed to maintain compatibility across all excavations in the county and then superseded by a heavily computerised record, utilising hand-held computers in the field for recording all contexts and objects. In 1984 the Electronic Distance Meter (EDM) was introduced as standard recording equipment and all subsequent finds were individually recorded with their 3-D location. Records generated in the early seasons have been re-formatted to ensure compatibility within the excavation archive.

The need to excavate and remove grave assemblages quickly and therefore minimise the risk of theft from the site meant that photography, both still photographs and, during the final season, video, were used extensively to supplement field drawings. The introduction of Computer Aided Design software (CAD) in 1984 provided a mechanism by which detailed plans could be compiled using a variety of source materials at different scales. The detailed plans in the catalogue have been compiled using a combination of field sketches and vertical photographs, all the grave plans being digitised from originals at scales from 1:2 to 1:10. As the excavation progressed it became clear that the high incidence of mineral-replaced or preserved organic materials deserved particular attention and thus much thought was given to determining methods of lifting objects individually or as groups in soil blocks so that the maximum return of data could be secured through micro-excavation in the laboratory.

## Excavation methods

With the exception of the trial trenches, cut when isolating the presence of the cemetery on Site 2, Areas 2A–2F, all excavation was carried out using open area techniques. Most of the topsoil on Site 1 was stripped before the start of excavation as part of preparation for quarrying operations; elsewhere a Hy-Mac with a straight-edged 3m blade was used to remove the ploughsoil under archaeological supervision. The soft sands which characterise much of the site were ideal for shovel-scraping and, after machining, all areas were shovel-scraped to expose the archaeological features. Following some unsuccessful attempts to excavate graves in areas 1A and 1B maintaining a half section, all graves were excavated in plan. As already noted, when the limits of an individual grave could not be satisfactorily identified, the natural surface around the grave was lowered until either the grave outline became clear or the burial was exposed. This approach had the added benefit that once the grave group was exposed work could continue unhindered by the limits of the grave pit and without risk of the soft sides of the feature collapsing and destroying hours of careful cleaning work. Before the introduction of the EDM finds occurring in the upper fills were plotted using a planning frame and levelled before removal; once the EDM was introduced all finds were given a unique 'tag number', the 'tag' locations then being recorded by the EDM.

*Plate 4: Christine Haughton and John Hanson excavating one of the weapon burials on Site 8AA. Excavation of each grave had to be rapidly undertaken to reduce the risk of theft of material*

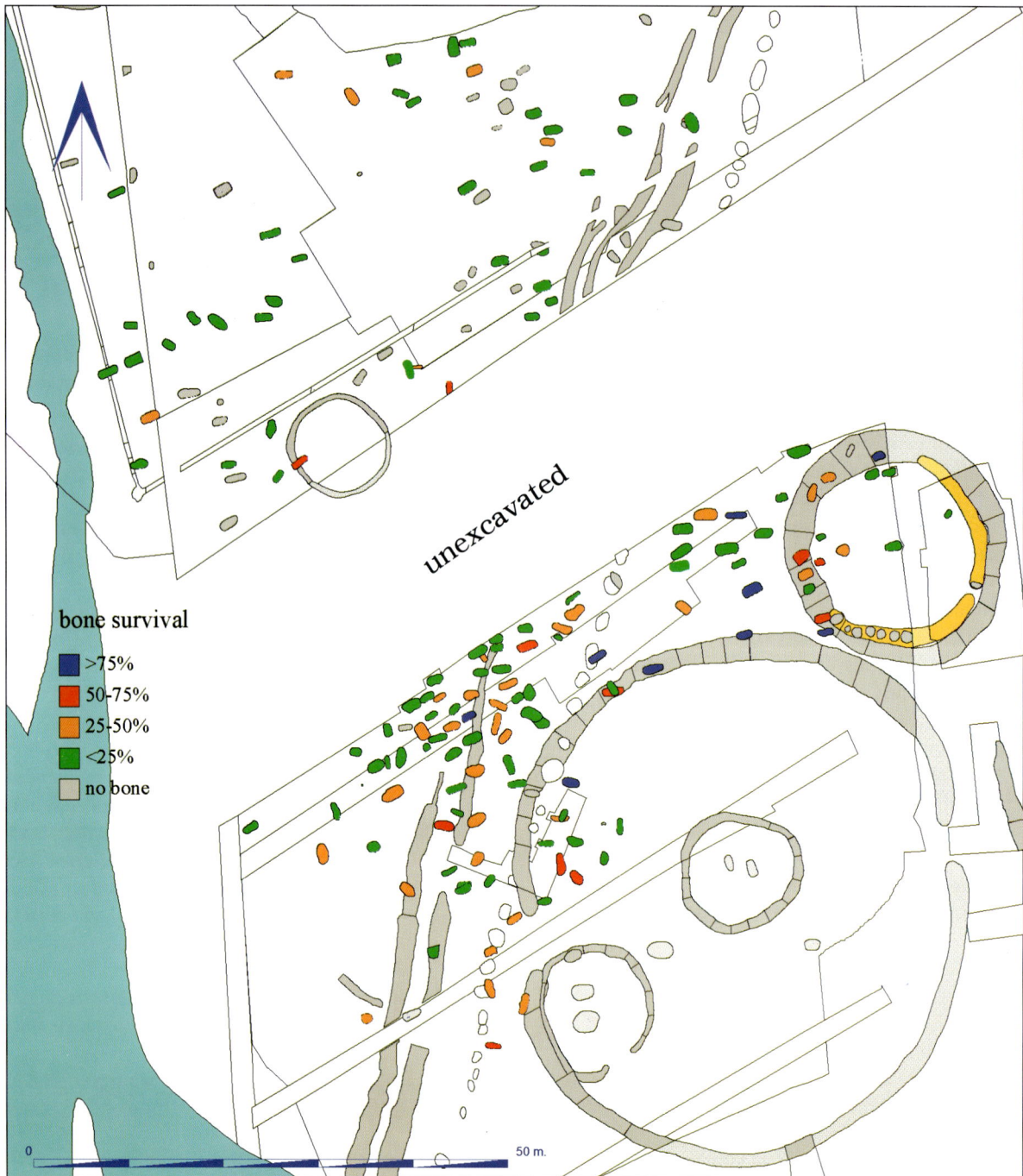

*Figure 7: plan showing the variation in bone preservation across the cemetery*

Very few finds were recovered from the upper fills of the graves. Among those that did occur, most were beads that had become displaced as a result of animal burrowing. It had been hoped that the careful examination of the upper grave fills might produce evidence of funeral meals and other evidence associated with the burial ritual, but this was not the case (Powlesland 1980).

# Condition of the skeletal remains

The frequent location of Early Anglo-Saxon cemeteries on light, well-drained sandy soils introduces a bias into the skeletal record of the period at a national rather than a purely local level. In the Vale of Pickering, for instance, all the known Anglian cemeteries are located on well-drained sandy soils in which good bone preservation would be the exception rather than the rule. The condition of the Anglian skeletal material was generally poor, with half of the graves containing either no skeletal material at all (16%) or only fragments of bone or tooth enamel (34%) (Fig 7). Only in those few cases in area 2BA where the graves had been cut into chalk was there reasonable preservation of skeletal material. In a number of graves, concentrated in areas 1A, 1B and 1HE, all that remained of the skeletons was the enamel from the tooth crowns. Even in some of the better preserved skeletons the bone was frequently badly eroded and tended to fall apart once exposed. Although the skeletal material survived badly, the sandy soils had provided a good envi-

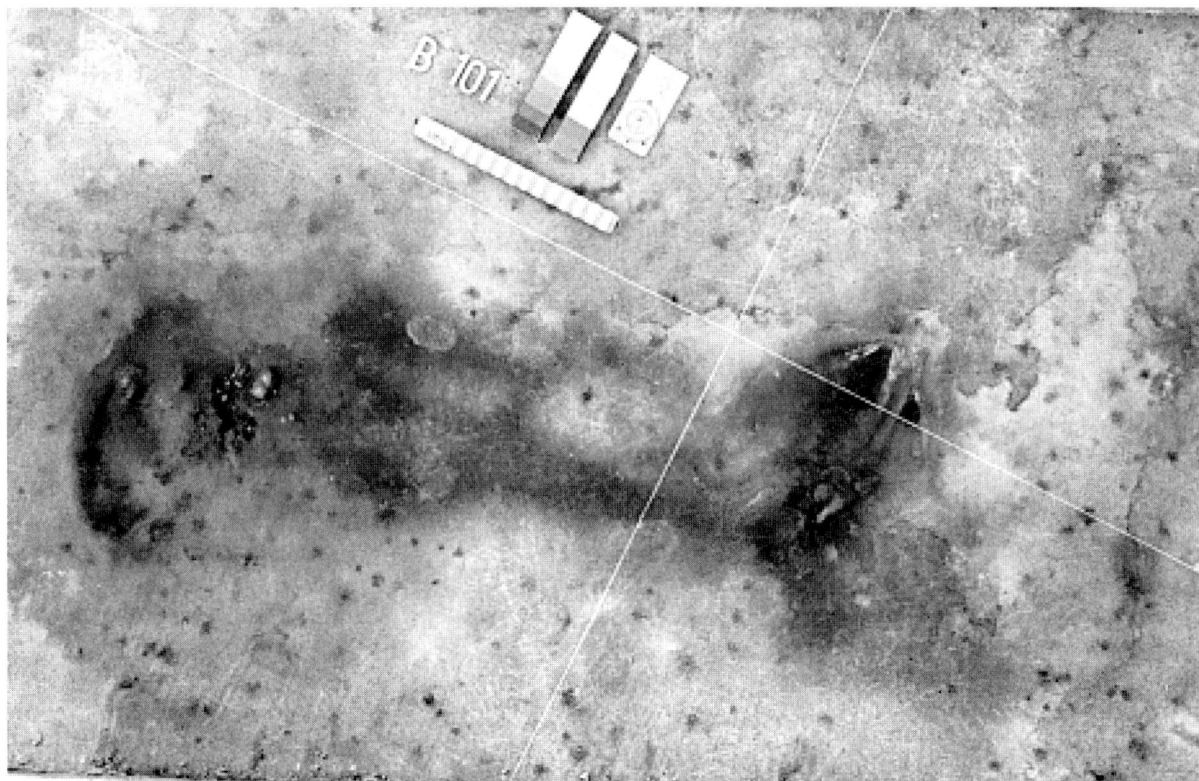

*Plate 5: body stain in Grave 27 (1B101) during excavation*

ronment for the formation of body stains or shadows in the sand. There seemed to be no way of predicting the presence of body stain features, which often could be identified not so much by changes in colour as by a change in texture, body stain features having a characteristic density and 'stickiness', and frequently incorporating very thin slivers of bone in an almost crystalline compact matrix. Chemical tests were undertaken to determine the variation of phosphate concentrations in the graves with a view to enhancing the resolution of the body stain features, but no appreciable difference in the levels of phosphate, even in the visible body stain features, could be identified; this approach was therefore abandoned.

Direct association with decaying metalwork, particularly those items made of copper alloy, had contributed towards the preservation of some bone, the copper salts released during the corrosion process reducing nematode activity. This has had an effect upon the statistics of bone condition measured against sex, particularly with reference to the fragmentary survival of female skeletal material. The assumption that adult skeletal material should survive better than that of children is questioned by Margaret Cox (pers comm) and is not supported by the evidence recovered.

The distribution of bone survival, although to a small extent demonstrating the presence of an increasingly alkaline environment in area 2BA, cannot easily be explained. The factors which contribute towards bone survival are numerous and we have at present little indication of the relative effects of burial in coffins or of clothing worn by the deceased. There is a slight correlation between increasing grave depth and bone survival; however, even here we are hampered by the fact that we cannot accurately estimate the original grave depth and, while this may be a consequence of reduced oxygen levels at greater depths, it may simply be a consequence of increased alkalinity, since the level of chalk inclusions in the sand areas increased with depth.

# The examination of the body stains

The treatment of each burial was determined by the condition and survival of the skeletal remains and the complexity and preservation of any accompanying grave assemblage. Following the discovery of the first body stain features in Area 1A during 1979 considerable effort was devoted to the excavation of body stains in relief; although this was a worthwhile exercise it proved both very slow and, more importantly, highly susceptible to excavator moulding. The intense animal burrowing activity that the site had been subjected to and the relatively poor quality of the body stain features meant that the temptation to sculpt the body stain into a recognisable form was too great; moreover, the end product was frequently unintelligible. A more satisfactory solution was to examine the body stains in plan, gradually removing centimetre-thick spits and re-photographing the changing form of the stain; where some bone survived in association with extensive staining a composite method of exposure of the bone and removal of the stain in spits was employed. The variability of bone preservation and survival of body stain features did not have any exclusive geographical distribution except that, where graves were cut into chalk or large quantities of chalk gravel were introduced into the grave backfill, bone preservation was much better. Recognisable body stain features were generally confined to graves in Area 1A with occasional examples in Areas 2B, 2BA and 8AA.

# Recovery of the soil blocks

Many of the graves at West Heslerton contained fragile assemblages, frequently incorporating mineral-preserved or -replaced organics. During the period of the excavation a number of different methods were used to attempt to recover this material in soil blocks in as intact a condition as possible. It was felt that this was one area where the site offered a large body of new data quite different from that generally recovered from earlier excavations in the region. It was believed that by recovering the grave goods in their own soil there was less likelihood of rapid decay of the fragile organic materials and that the potential for the recovery of organic materials, whether surviving or mineral-replaced, would be increased. This proved to be the case, particularly for material in contact with copper alloy and iron objects. The first attempts in area 1B were made by isolating the required material in a pedestal that was then wrapped in cling film and plaster bandage. Once the plaster had set the block was marked with the grave details, a north point and a location before the pedestal was cut away. Once the block had been cut away it was inverted and some of the sand removed from the base, which was then sealed by pouring plaster into the void. The resultant blocks were highly stable and not susceptible to movement or distortion; some conservators, however, felt that the use of plaster made opening the blocks difficult and so, apart from a single plaster-encased block from area 2BA, subsequent blocks were encased in polyurethane foam or within plastic boxes of varying sizes.

The use of the more hazardous foam produced blocks that were lighter but tended to be less rigid. As more blocks were lifted the techniques were refined, so that by the end of the excavation methods had been developed that would enable us to lift very large blocks. The most difficult aspect of the polyurethane foam method was finding a way to contain the foam around the block without purpose-building a timber casing for each block as required. The natural sand at West Heslerton was for the most part highly cohesive when damp and so it was decided that rather than build cases to go around each block the sand could itself be used to contain the foam. This meant that a narrow trench 0.10-0.15m wide had to be cut around each block; using a plasterer's leaf or spoon, tunnels were then dug beneath the block at the base of the trench into which the foam would flow when poured. The method proved for the most part highly effective, and a large number of groups were lifted intact in this way. It was of course important to ensure that the base of the block was well below the level of the grave goods, but not so far down as to make the block too heavy or too difficult to tunnel beneath. Once the foam around and beneath the block had partially set, cling film or tinfoil could be placed over the top of the block, which was then sealed beneath further foam, leaving projecting tabs to indicate the top of the block. Once labelled, one or two three-dimensional co-ordinates were marked on the foam surface and then the block was removed and inverted, sometimes to have the base strengthened by the addition of more foam.

Plate 7: recording a 3D location on a soil block before lifting

Plate 6: preparing a soil block for lifting in the field

The blocks, once removed, were then taken to the Ancient Monuments Laboratory of English Heritage where they could be dismantled following the preparation of X-radiographs giving detailed information on the materials within them. It is most unlikely that some of the more exceptional detail on the organic material from the graves could have been retrieved without this removal technique. In particular the large quantity of textile information recovered at West Heslerton owes much to this method of recovery. The principal problem arising from this approach is the time involved in dismantling the soil blocks; in the case of West Heslerton the material remained in the laboratory until the spring of 1992, nearly six years after the completion of the excavation. If this approach is adopted again a local processing facility should be established to ensure rapid examination of the blocks. The soil conditions were ideal for this approach and in similar circumstances there is a good argument for lifting entire graves for excavation off-site in the laboratory, where a far more detailed record can be made than is possible in the field.

Plate 9: using the EDM, an electronic distance measuring device attached to a theodolite

# Recording procedures

The excavation of the cemetery took place over a ten-year period, between 1977 and 1986, a period in which there was widespread discussion between those actively engaged in excavation regarding both excavation methodologies and documentation procedures. This debate may be seen as a product both of the vastly increased level of excavation undertaken within the framework of 'rescue archaeology' and the emergent emphasis within the academic institutions upon theoretical archaeology. For the community of diggers much of this discussion took place in local pubs after long days in the field rather than in the classroom. There was a general concern with the philosophies behind different recording strategies and, with the more widespread availability of personal computers, an evolving view of archaeology as an increasingly 'scientific discipline'. Much of this discussion revolved around the key issue of objectivity, something reflected in Britain by the development of pro-forma recording sheets and associated procedures during the late 1970s and early 80s. At Heslerton the scale of the excavations, which by 1986 covered more than 15 acres of which the cemetery represented about a third, and the multi-period and multi-function nature of the evidence, provided the necessary environment for the development of a unified recording strategy. Old constructs such as 'small finds', 'bulk finds' and feature numbers were discarded in favour of a unified context number system with all finds being individually recorded using a standard record structure and contexts handled in a similar fashion. Some aspects of the record were dropped simply on practical grounds, in particular the production of full

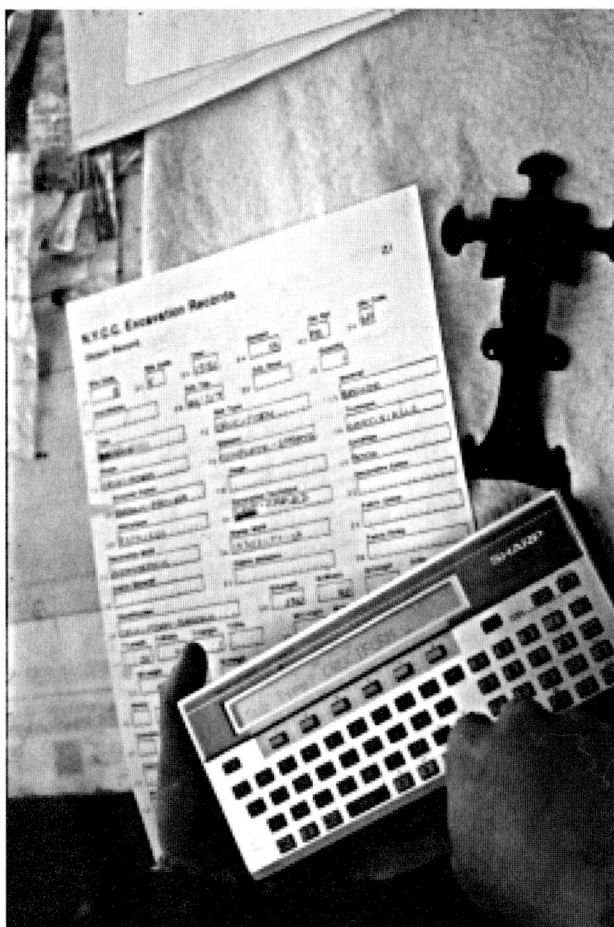

Plate 8: recording systems in transition. Transferring data from pro-forma recording sheets into a hand-held computer

colour field drawings and stone-by-stone draw-ings of the natural. The use of a standardised context sequence employing a key identifier that combined a site number, area code, con-text number and in the case of the objects an additional two character object code radically improved data management potential.

By 1981, working closely with Mike Griffiths, then County Archaeologist, and his team, a computerised recording system had been de-veloped which fed directly into the County Sites and Monuments Record. Pro-forma sheets were completed in the field and then transcribed into the mainframe computer-based database using a remote terminal; the system offered immense long-term archive and research potential. There were problems arising from line failures and the remote loca-tion of the database at County Hall, 50 miles from the excavation HQ; more importantly, the data was often not logged until after the excavation season was over, pre-cluding any opportunity for checking the data while work was in progress.

During 1984 a local solution was developed, which em-ployed hand-held computers in the field, programmed in BASIC and generating small format printouts which were pasted into traditional site notebooks; data collected us-ing the Sharp hand-held computers was downloaded on a daily basis to a personal computer at the excavation HQ and copies passed on to the SMR. At the same time we became aware of the potential of the Electronic Dis-tance Meter (EDM), the forerunner of the surveyors 'Total Station', that made it possible to rapidly record individual object locations to within one centimetre in three dimen-sions. The application of hand-held computers and the EDM meant that we could rapidly record in a standard-ised fashion, incorporating accurate spatial locations throughout the record establishing a system of record that was to remain largely unchanged during the later exca-vation of the associated settlement. Following the devel-opment of the hand-held data logging system, effort was concentrated on the graphical data with all plans being digitised using a Computer Aided Design (CAD) pack-age. Whilst the digital plans produced in this way of-fered great versatility it was, at that time, impossible to link these with the conventional data held in a series of simple flat file databases. This position was resolved through the development of a fully integrated Geographic Data Management System, G-Sys, developed at week-ends and in the evenings over a number of years. This software tool remains at the core of the Heslerton record-ing system, providing interactive plotting and manage-ment of database, plan and image data.

The database structures developed for data collection on

*Plate 10: John Hanson, excavation supervisor recording a grave using a hand-held computer*

site employed a hierarchical structure with a field struc-ture designed to facilitate analysis and extraction in par-ticular. In order to maximise the benefit from the small hand-held data collectors, which only had 8k of data stor-age, most fields initially employed numeric codes; these were automatically translated to text once the data was printed or displayed on the PC. Only limited space was available for free text; however, the field structure was such that most of the descriptive, spatial and preliminary interpretive data were held in a series of required fields, reducing the need for extensive descriptive free text which is poorly adapted for analytical purposes. Rather than use an elaborate relational database model, a simple struc-ture was adopted which comprised a series of flat files, supported by look-up tables for code translation, and in-corporating the Context, Object and Graphical records, all of which were related by the combined field of Site, Area and Context number termed the Key_ID. Digitised line drawings were in turn linked to the rest of the data-set using the same Key_ID which is embedded in each drawn object when imported into G-Sys.

Following initial experiments in which the graves were excavated using running cross-sections this approach was abandoned in favour of excavation in plan, the locations of individual objects being recorded in 3D using the EDM. With much of the fieldwork taking place during the winter the drawing of conventional field drawings of the grave plans was abandoned in favour of vertical pho-tographs incorporating known and marked reference points which were then printed at scales between 1:2 and 1:5 and used as the basis for the production of the digital plans used in the accompanying Grave Catalogue.

# Prehistoric activity

## Summary

Although the best known aspect of this site is its use as an Anglian cemetery, this was only the last phase of its intermittent use for ritual purposes. The discovery of an important sequence of prehistoric landscape features which provided the focus of the later activity is no less important and, indeed, the apparent relationship between the Anglian re-use and the earlier ritual site is of considerable regional significance.

The earliest activity at the site is indicated by a Mesolithic lithic assemblage which adds to that already discussed from Site 1 to the north (Powlesland et al 1986). The stream channel that was ultimately to define the western boundary of the cemetery formed the focus of Late Mesolithic activity on Site 1, a picture repeated here with concentrations of Mesolithic material increasing towards the banks of the now relict channel. Sample trenches across the channel revealed a complex stratigraphic sequence dominated by redeposited materials and multiple channels that could not be interpreted without much more extensive excavation than was possible within the objectives and resources available. The level of erosion and deposition, combined with the difficulty of identifying well dated and uncontaminated deposits, was such that work was restricted to identifying the line of the main stream channel and the investigation of two late Prehistoric pit alignments. One of these extended into the stream channel area from the cemetery to the north-east the other ran along the opposite stream bank to the west (Fig 6).

The excavations and associated research at West Heslerton over the last 15 years have revealed that the rich late prehistoric sequence long identified on the Yorkshire Wolds extends into the Vale of Pickering. There was very extensive activity both along the southern edge of the valley and on slightly elevated platforms or islands in the fenland environment that existed at the centre of the valley during the later prehistoric period. The excavations in the cemetery and to the north on Site 1 have produced evidence of both ritual and domestic landscapes during the Late Neolithic and Early Bronze Age, including major monuments of the type more commonly associated with the Wessex Downs or the Yorkshire Wolds.

These features contribute to an emerging picture of the Vale of Pickering in which the landscape was at least as heavily used as that of the Yorkshire Wolds immediately to the south. The view of minimal activity in the Vale during the later Neolithic and Bronze Age offered by Pierpoint and based on the distribution of artefacts must now clearly be discarded (Pierpoint 1980). Furthermore, excavation on the heavier soils in the area of the Anglian settlement 450m to the south indicated that the level and nature of the prehistoric activity in this area was quite different from that found on the lighter sandy soils in the area of the cemetery and to the north. In addition to the Late Neolithic post alignments and Late Neolithic and Early Bronze Age barrows identified on Site 1, a hengiform enclosure, a post circle, three barrows and a number of flat graves form part of what is clearly an extensive Late Neolithic and early Bronze Age ritual landscape. A number of pits of a more domestic nature, containing Peterborough and Grooved Wares in a sample area (2BB) some 45m to the south of the hengiform enclosure, form an important addition to the more disparate Peterborough style pit groups isolated on Site 1 to the north. This perhaps indicates a focus of domestic activity in the area between the heavier soils at the foot of the Wolds to the south and the more sandy soils which extend from the cemetery site to the north. There was no evidence of activity during the Middle Bronze Age.

By the Late Bronze Age the structure of the landscape had been clearly defined by the construction of a series of major pit alignment boundaries, later succeeded by complex linear earthworks. Known locally as the 'Wold Entrenchments', these boundary earthworks frequently survive on the Wolds and are often retained in the current parish boundaries (Mortimer 1905). During this period the focus of activity appears to have been divided between relatively high-status elevated palisaded enclosures such as Staple Howe (Knapton) and Devil's Hill (West Heslerton), situated on knolls part-way down the north-facing scarp of the Wolds, and open and unenclosed settlement areas adjacent to the principal boundaries in the Vale (Brewster 1963, Powlesland et al 1986). A pit alignment boundary passing through the cemetery may belong to this period, suggesting that at least some indication of the earlier importance of the site remained visible at this time. By the Late Iron Age and during much of the Roman period settlement activity is concentrated along the fen edge a kilometre to the north of the cemetery. There is little indication of activity in the cemetery area other than the fact that the pit alignment boundary running through the later cemetery area continues to function as a minor boundary, the pit alignment being replaced by a series of simple shallow ditches, possibly defining a pathway. The distribution of the Anglian burials provides some confirmation that at least some signs of the prehistoric use of the site remained visible, with groups of inhumations cut into the ditches of both the hengiform enclosure and the final ditched phase of the adjacent post circle.

# The Mesolithic

The small lithic assemblage demonstrating activity in the Mesolithic is discussed by Clarke below. The distribution of the material follows the same general trend as that from Site 1 to the north, with the quantity of material increasing along the eastern margin of the stream channel that ran along the western margin of area 2BA and was partly exposed in sample areas in 2BB (Fig 6). The stream channel, fed by springs at the foot of the Wolds nearly 500 metres to the south, was redirected further south along a man-made channel during the medieval period and subsequently filled with alluvium and blown sands. Without much more extensive excavation in areas some distance from the banks of the stream it is difficult to assess the relative importance of the stream area in the Mesolithic and later prehistoric periods. It is quite possible that the banks of the stream channel merely provided an easy line of communication between the open fenland environment in the centre of the Vale to the north and the heavier and probably more extensively wooded areas at the foot of the Wolds to the south. It is most unlikely that the stream was large enough to support an edible fish population, although it may have provided a suitable hunting environment for wildfowl and smaller animals. The Mesolithic assemblage, which includes more than 50 microliths, was mostly derived from two generalised contexts, 2BA500 and 2BA518, generated as part of the cleaning exercise to expose the grave cuts. In no case could cut features of the Mesolithic be inferred from the lithic evidence, which might best be viewed as an indicator of generalised activity following the banks of the stream.

# The Late Neolithic and Early Bronze Age

The excavation of the cemetery has added considerably to the corpus of Late Neolithic and Early Bronze Age material already recovered, and confirms and supports the picture of widespread use of this part of the landscape during the Late Neolithic and Early Bronze Age already observed at Site 1 (Powlesland et al 1986).

Pit pairs containing ceramic assemblages of Fengate/Peterborough type in association with carbonised hazelnut shells, possibly representing storage pits, were a feature of Site 1 to the north and were also found in the cemetery. A small hengiform enclosure, measuring c50m in diameter with opposed entrances to the west and east, may be related to a possible occupation area some 65m to the south which included a number of pits and possible postholes containing Peterborough and Grooved Ware ceramics. Immediately to the north-east of the hengiform enclosure a series of massive post settings arranged in a horse-shoe shape closely resembles monuments at Dorchester, Oxon, although the association with cremation burial argued for the Dorchester examples is not supported by the evidence here (Atkinson et al 1951, 51–9). This feature was ultimately replaced by a large ring ditch, probably a barrow, the ditch cutting into the postholes of the earlier monument. The enclosed area was badly damaged by ploughing and the cutting of a medieval or later field boundary. The hengiform enclosure ultimately formed the setting for the construction of two small ditched round barrows and a number of flat graves. One of the barrows was located centrally, the ring ditch of the second being cut into the ?partially filled ditch of the earlier enclosure. Although the Beaker/Food Vessel date of the barrow cemetery is broadly the same as that of the barrow cemetery excavated on Site 1, 200m to the north, the monuments and burial rites are quite different in character, the barrows being much smaller and effectively single phase monuments. To the north-west of the enclosure in Area 8AA a series of shallow gullies running north to south adjacent and to the east of the stream channel, which formed the western boundary of the Anglian cemetery, contained material possibly indicating a Late Neolithic or Early Bronze Age date, but their function remains unclear.

# Fengate-Peterborough pit groups

Shallow, often elongated, pits frequently in pairs and containing assemblages incorporating Peterborough and Fengate type ceramics in association with carbonised hazelnut shells, are a feature of the Late Neolithic landscape at West Heslerton and on the Wolds as well as elsewhere in Britain. At West Heslerton the soil conditions on Site 1 and in the area of the cemetery precluded the survival of animal bone in these assemblages. Further examples incorporating animal bone have, however, subsequently been discovered during the excavation of the Anglian settlement to the south, where such pits are less densely distributed. These features are distinctive not only on account of the assemblages they contain but also by reason of the very dark, almost black soil fills, perhaps indicating that they originally contained a high volume of organic matter.

The apparently random distribution of the pits and their lack of obvious association with other classes of feature raises questions about their function. They are not associated with structural remains except perhaps in area 2BB where a group of smaller pits contained Grooved Ware in addition to those containing Peterborough and Fengate style ceramics. Apart from their remarkable ceramic assemblages, in which only parts of a number of different vessels are represented, and the fact that they often occur in pairs, the single distinguishing feature of these pits is the ubiquitous presence of carbonised hazelnut shells. One is tempted to suggest that these pits served originally as storage pits for hazelnuts, which were broken into as and when required and then deliberately backfilled with domestic rubbish and food waste. There is nothing topographically distinctive in their distribution and if they served this purpose then one might suggest that their location was related to the existence of standing hazel trees. At Heslerton the presence of hazel trees during the Anglo-Saxon period at least is implied by the Anglo-Saxon place-name, meaning 'the hamlet in the clearing amongst the hazel' . Even if this were the case, however, the mixed and fragmentary nature of the ceramic assemblages implies that the rubbish, if that is what this material is, derives from more than a single visit or, alternatively, that it represents a deliberately selected group of material. Perhaps they contain only residual material from a more extensive surface midden deposit which has subsequently been removed by ploughing and

other destructive agencies. The large number of small and abraded sherds found in less securely stratified deposits than the pits may give some support to this view. The context of these features is perhaps easier to explain within the monumental landscape in which they occur, although whether they are a product of some sort of ritual associated with the construction of the monuments or of a more domestic and nomadic behaviour cannot be determined. Their relative proximity to monumental features such as the hengiform enclosure or the barrows may indicate a direct association with the monuments. In the absence of large excavated areas without significant monumental constructions we cannot be sure that these pits are not part of a much more widespread distribution quite unrelated to the monuments. In the area of the Anglian settlement both Late Neolithic monumental structures and these distinctive pits are rare; however, the settlement is in a different ecological and morphological zone to that of the cemetery, which appears to have been less heavily used in the Late Neolithic. If we are to interpret the pits within a ritual context then we need to determine whether the remarkable assemblages they contain represent deliberate and selective deposition. Clearly the subject deserves more detailed investigation than is possible here, and whatever the function of these pits it is unlikely that a single explanation fits all.

The ceramics from these Late Neolithic deposits are discussed in detail by Manby below. The presence of a broad range of types, forms and decorative motifs is of considerable interest, but until compared with well dated and definitely domestic assemblages will continue to present an enigmatic interpretive problem.

*Plate 11: excavation of the Late Neolithic pits in progress in area 2BB*

# Monumental features

Area 2BA was dominated by two large Late Neolithic monumental features (Fig 8), a hengiform enclosure *c*60m x 55m with opposed entrances to the west and to the east, and an adjacent post circle. The latter was superseded by the construction of a ring-ditch measuring *c*23m in diameter, which cut away parts of the earlier massive post pits.

There is also the evidence for Late Neolithic post-alignments, perhaps forming part of an avenue on Site 1 to the north, and another hengiform enclosure recently identified in a magnetometer survey at East Heslerton less than 1500m to the east and situated in a directly comparable position. Taken as a group, these features indicate that the Vale of Pickering contains similar monument complexes to those found elsewhere at, for instance, Dorchester-on-Thames (Whittle *et al* 1992). Their discovery demonstrates that valley areas such as the Vale of Pickering were at least as important a feature of the Late Neolithic landscape as the upland areas such as the Yorkshire Wolds, where features of this period have remained more visible. The presence of aeolian sands, colluvial and alluvial build-up and the lack of rocky parent material incorporated in the construction of earthen monuments have contributed to the lack of visibility of prehistoric monument complexes in areas such as the Vale of Pickering. Only with detailed air and ground-based remote sensing or large-scale open-area excavations such as at West Heslerton are we able to get any idea of the density of these features in this environment. Even then, the difficulties raised by the presence of masking deposits make the identification of landscape complexes much more fragmentary and difficult than on the gravel terraces of the Thames or in the Millfield basin. After 15 years of intensive air-photographic survey, a substantial amount of excavation, and geophysical and airborne multi-spectral surveys, the later prehistoric ritual landscape of the Vale of Pickering is only now starting to emerge. It is most unlikely that this area is in any way unique, and the level of work here indicates the investment of time and energy required to assess realistically the potential of these seemingly flat and barren landscapes.

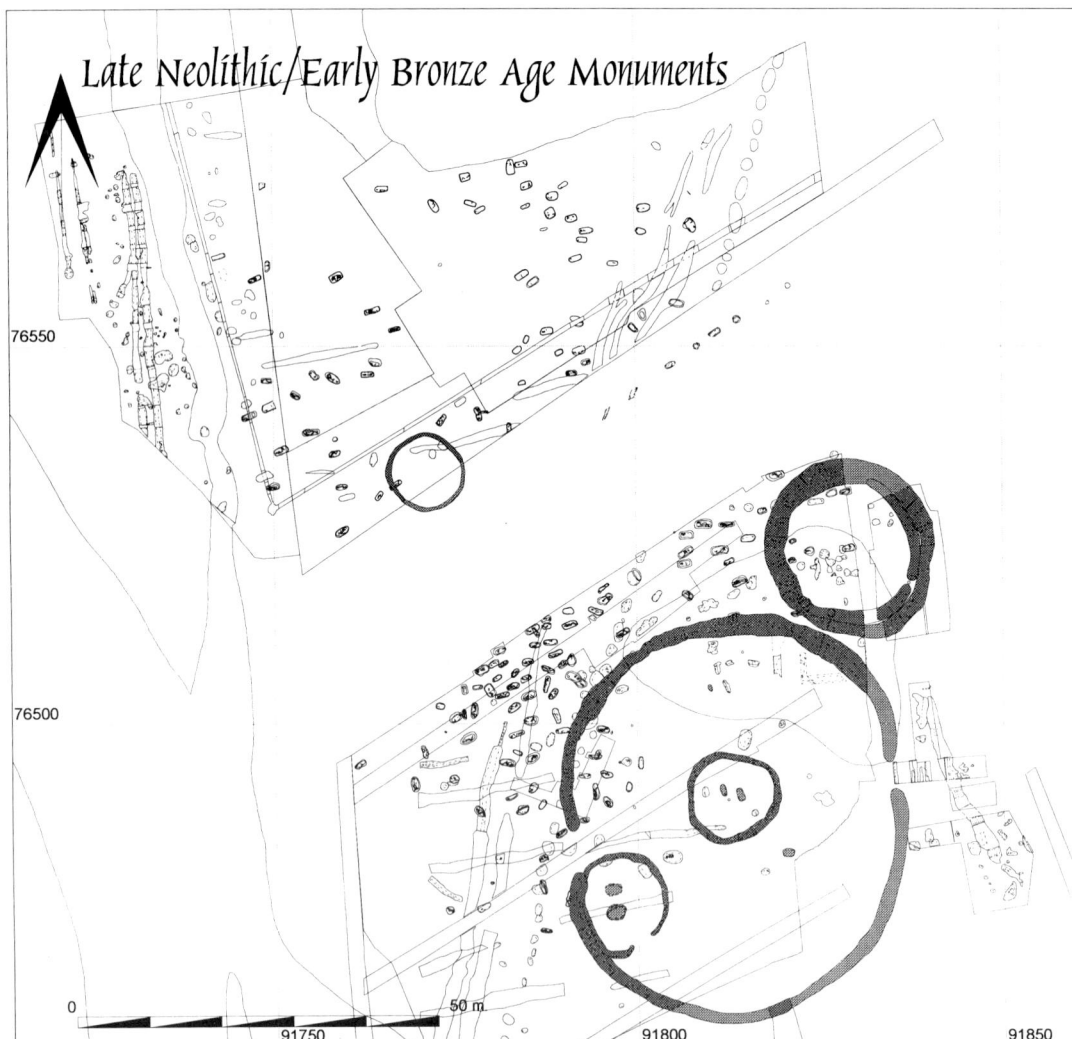

*Figure 8: Monumental features of the Late Neolithic and Early Bronze Age (shaded)*

# The timber circle

A timber circle (2BA1354), of which only a semi-circular arc measuring *c*18.5m in diameter could be securely identified, was located in the north-east corner of area 2BA, extending into Site 6AA to the east (Fig 9). This monument showed three principal phases of construction: firstly as a post circle, which appears to have been replaced by the construction, slightly off-centre, of a palisade which itself appears to have been partially cut away by the construction of a ditch. Although there was no directly surviving stratigraphic relationship with the adjacent hengiform enclosure, the substantial ditch of the final phase appears to have been open at the same time as the enclosure ditch, suggesting that this structure was the earliest of the Late Neolithic/Early Bronze Age monuments on the site. No independent dating evidence was recovered. The field drawings of the sections through the construction trench and post holes of the circle, the later palisade and ditch and the hengiform show tip-lines of substantial chalk rubble which could be used to argue that the barrow ditch was in part filled from spoil derived

from the cutting of the enclosure ditch; this interpetation is, however, far from secure (Fig 10).

The timber circle, if indeed it was ever a full circle, was constructed using up to 60 massive timber uprights set in a deep and vertically sided construction trench. The extent to which the posts of the timber circle formed a complete circle could not be identified; the later palisade and ditch may have cut away all evidence on the north and north-western sections of the circle. It was felt during the excavation that had the circle been complete some evidence should have survived on the north and north-western parts of the circle. It was not possible to investigate the north-eastern portion of this monument and it is possible that the later ditch, which appears in plan to be off-centre relative to the identified section of the post-circle, entirely removed all traces on the northern side. It was clear from a detailed examination of the recorded evidence that where this feature was cut into sand no sectional evidence relating to the post circle or later pali-

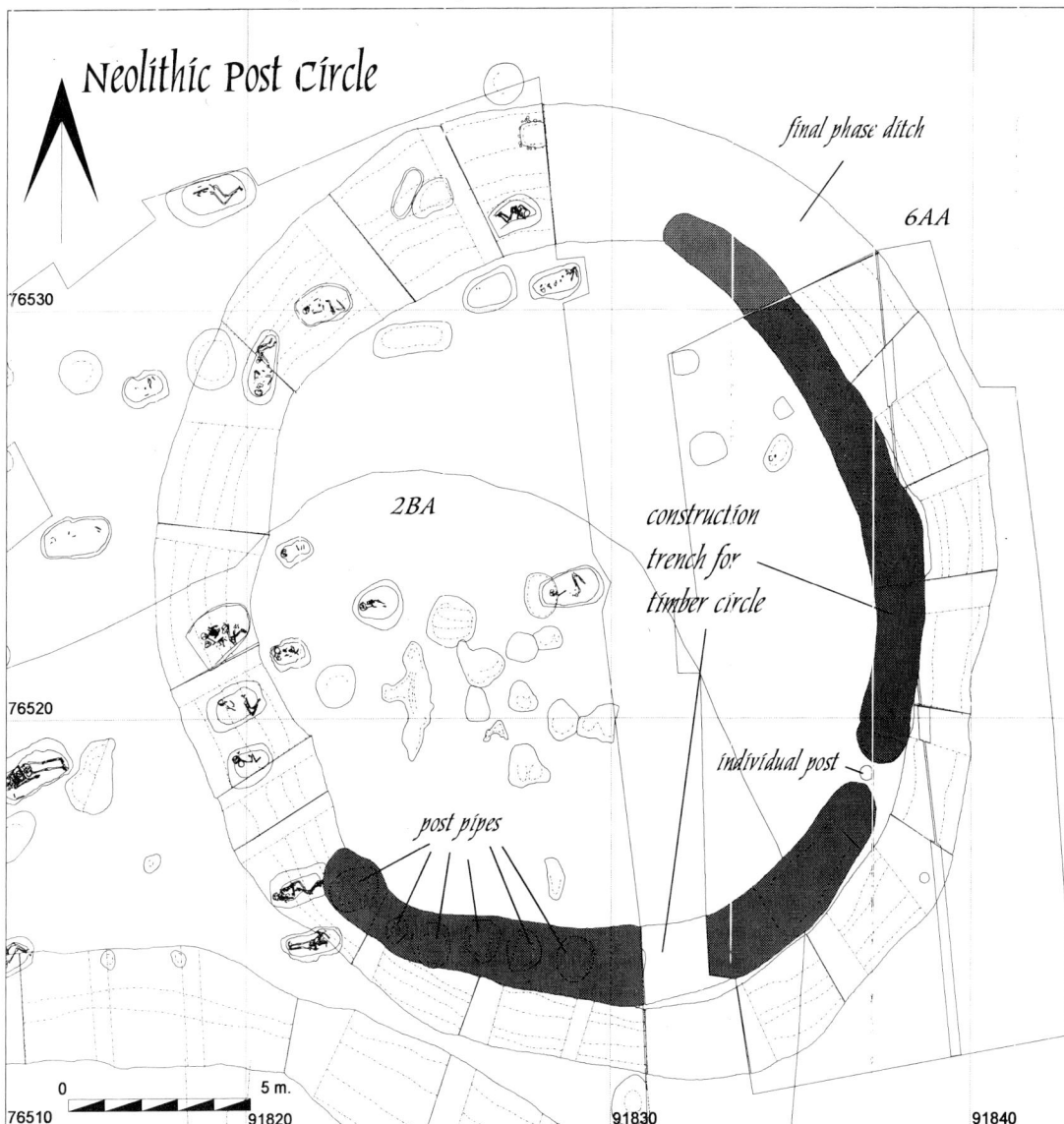

*Figure 9: plan showing the Late Neolithic timber circle and later ditch*

sade survived, a situation not dissimilar to that occurring in the adjacent hengiform enclosure. The alternative is that the arrangement was more penannular or horse-shoe shaped. On the southern side a series of well defined post-pipes were identified, indicating that the posts were massive timbers up to 1.1m in diameter and set into a construction trench measuring up to 1.7m in width and over a metre deep. The posts had been set into two construction trenches forming two segments of a semi-circular arc with a gap of 70cm between the two construction trenches on the south-eastern side; a single, much smaller

post *c*30cm in diameter occupied a central position in the gap and aligned with the inside edge of the larger post-pipes. This structure has much in common with those examined by Atkinson at Dorchester-on-Thames and recently reassessed by Whittle *et al* (Atkinson 1951, Atkinson *et al* 1951, Whittle *et al* 1992).

In area 2BA the individual post-pipes could be clearly identified, indicating an arc open towards the north-west (Fig 9, Plates 12, 13, 14). Seven individual post-pipes could be seen clearly enough to allow excavation. In area

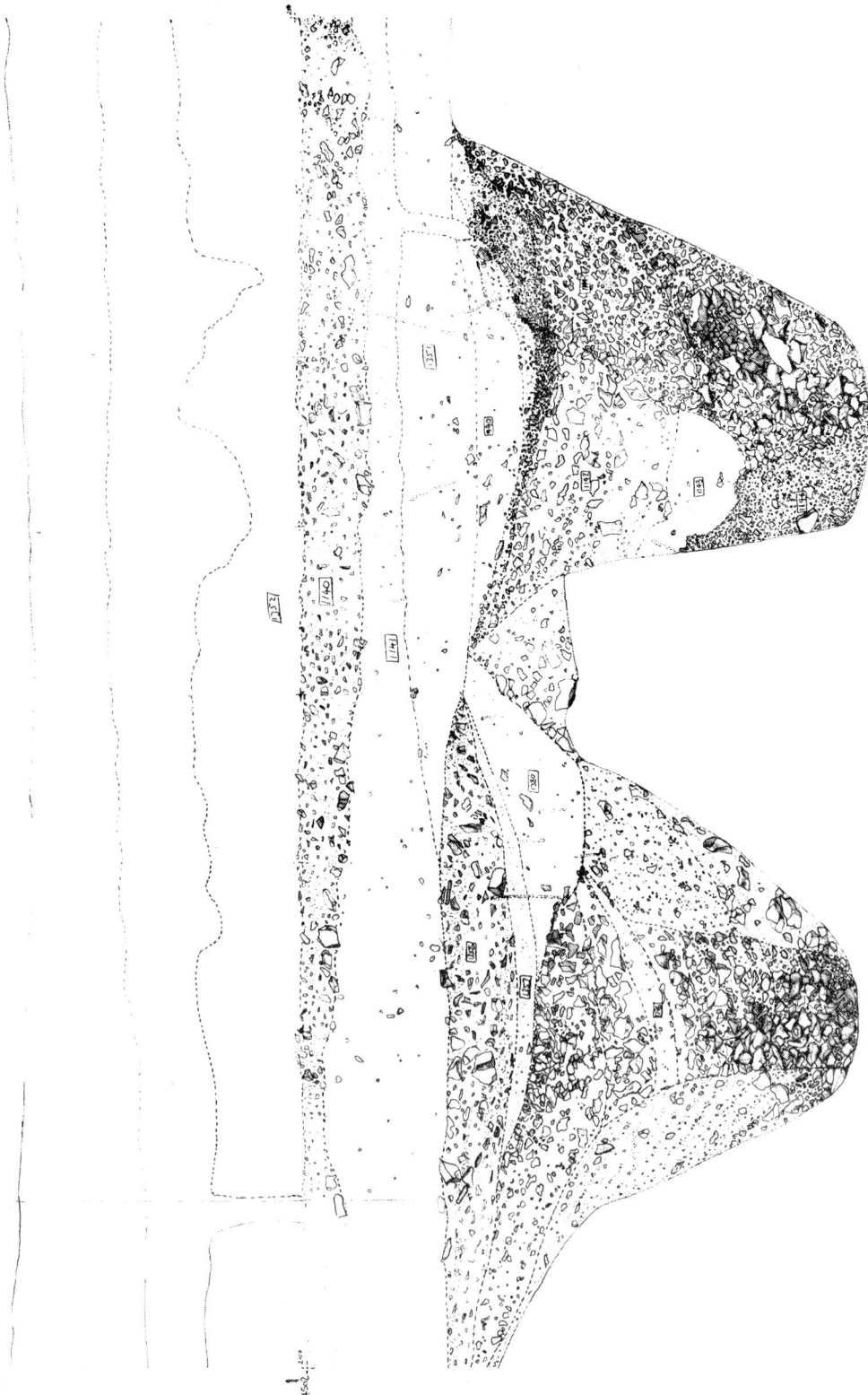

*Figure 10: Field drawing showing the section through the post-trench and later ditch (scale 1:20)*

6AA to the east, the chalk bedrock gave way to sand and the individual post-pipes could not be clearly identified. The natural sand from the construction trench and used to backfill around the posts as packing would have quickly collapsed once any *in situ* posts decayed, leaving little chance for the post-pipes to remain visible. There is considerable temptation to interpret the individual small post in the gap between the two construction trenches, in 6AA, as some sort of marker or sighting post (Fig 9). The survival of the post-pipes and lack of distortion of the upper edges of these features suggests that the posts rotted *in situ* before the construction of the palisade. No charcoal nor any directly associated cultural debris which could be used for primary dating evidence was recovered. A series of shallow features within the area enclosed by the posts may be contemporary but again lack finds; a few scraps of cremated bone were recovered from one of these features but the quantity was minimal and, given the pres-ence of a number of Anglian cremations nearby, could well post-date this structure. The stratigraphic context and the parallels elsewhere do, however, indicate a Late Neolithic or Early Bronze Age date for this feature.

In the second phase a new construction trench of similar size was constructed enclosing the earlier circle on the southern side; individual post-settings were not identified and it would appear that much of the evidence of this second phase of timbering was removed when the feature was recut as a ditch. A careful examination of the section drawings indicates that this palisade trench contained slightly smaller timbers, up to *c*7m in diameter, set on the inside of the trench. The trench had been backfilled with chalk rubble packing (Plates 13, 14).

Ultimately the post circle and palisade were superseded by the cutting of a substantial ditch (Barrow 2BA130),

*Plate 12: the post-circle and later palisade and ditch during excvation from the SW*

*Plate 13: oblique view of a section through the construction trench for the post-circle and later palisade slot.*

*Plate 14: west facing section through the post-circle construction trench and later palisade slot*

which cut away the outside edge of the first phase post-trench and much of the second phase palisade slot (Fig 11). It was unclear during excavation whether the cutaway of the outer edge of the post-trench occurred as the ditch was dug or as a consequence of later erosion (Fig 10). The ditch is described in the record as a 'Barrow Ditch'; however, no prehistoric burials were recovered from within the area enclosed by the ditch.

## Barrow 2BA130

The largest of this group of probable barrows, 2BA130 was defined by a steep-sided ditch which cut away parts of the post-circle 2BA1354 which it replaced (Fig 11). The material derived from the ditch would have created a considerable mound. It is likely that this monument was still visible during the Anglian period as it effectively marks the eastern limit of the cemetery. That the ditch remained visible in the fifth century is indicated by the number of Anglian graves that had been cut into its softer fills in preference to the harder bedrock adjacent. The interpretation as a barrow is problematic as no identified

prehistoric burials were discovered within the enclosed area. One feature, a shallow slot containing a few very small fragments of cremated but unidentifiable bone may indicate that this was a late Neolithic burial structure. It is possible that this cremated bone may relate to an Anglian cremation in which case the slot-like cut that contained the material would be an unusual feature. All the definite graves identified within the enclosed area were of Early Anglo-Saxon date.

## The hengiform enclosure

Many small hengiform enclosures have been identified in the air-photographic record from the north of England (Harding and Lee 1987). The example excavated at West Heslerton (2BA38), comprised two roughly semicircular ditches forming a flattened circular enclosure measuring c45m from east to west and c53m from north to south (Fig 12). The monument, which showed two principal phases, had opposed entrances to the east and west. The western entrance, c5m wide, was flanked by the slightly in-turned terminals of the enclosure ditches; it was not

*Figure 11: Plan of the post-circle and later palisade and barrow 2BA130*

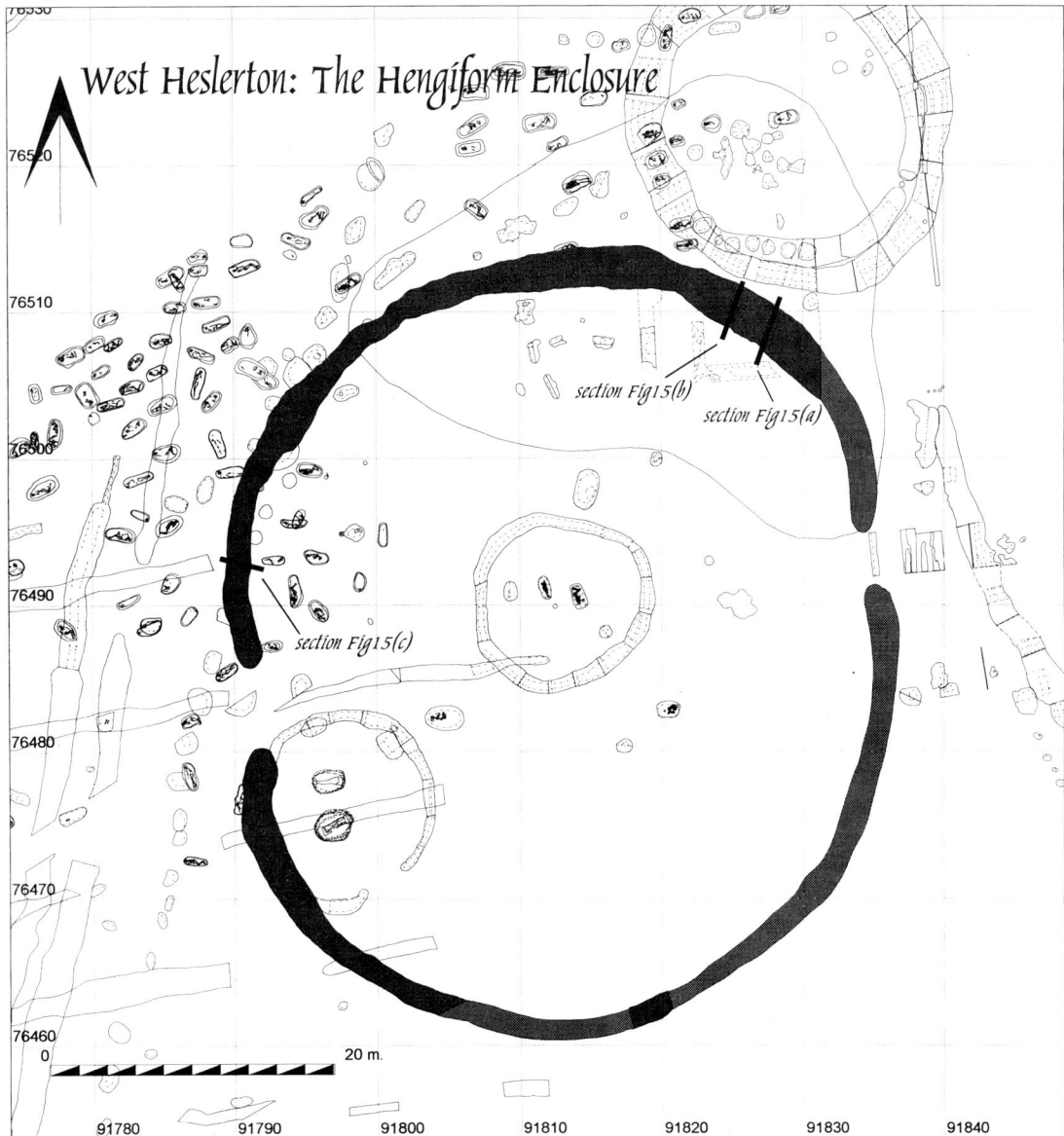

Figure 12: plan of the hengiform enclosure 2BA38 and related features

Plate 15: a full section across the construction trenches of the post-circle, hengiform and succeeding palisaded enclosures at the point where both structures are at their closest

*Plate 16: site 2BA following excavation the northern arc of the hengiform enclosure*

possible to excavate the eastern entrance fully. A similar but larger feature measuring *c*75m by *c*67m has since been identified from the air in an almost identical topographic position at East Heslerton only 1500m to the west (Fig 13).

The enclosure ditch incorporated, within its northern half, a slightly raised platform of chalk which had been badly truncated by plough damage. In the second phase a palisade trench was cut into the partially filled in ditch. No certainly contemporary internal features could be identified; although a pit containing a large Fengate

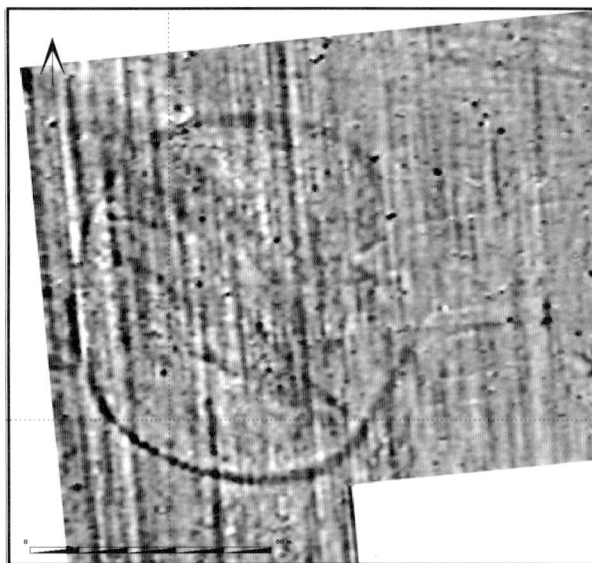

*Figure 13: geophysical survey of a hengiform enclosure at East Heslerton (Scale 1:1500)*

ceramic assemblage was excavated, its association remains unclear. Two barrows and a number of flat graves were later constructed within the enclosure. One of the barrow ditches (2BA264) was flattened to the west where it also cut into the infilled enclosure ditch (Figs 12, 17).

The enclosure ditch varied in form, with a relatively shallow profile on the western and southern sides where it had been cut into sand. In the north-eastern quadrant the scale of the ditch increased to over 3m in breadth and up to 1.5m in depth compared to a breadth of 2.2m and depth of 0.45m on the southern side (Figs 13, 15) . The eastern side, which was partially sealed by the current field boundary, had suffered less plough damage; however, plough marks in the interior suggested that even here some damage had occurred before the establishment of the present field boundary, the date of which is unknown. Its description as a 'hengiform' enclosure owes most to the morphology and general context of the feature; plough damage had removed all trace of any associated bank. The location and flattening of the western side of Barrow M264 (see below), which cut into the fill of the enclosure ditch, may indicate that this feature was constructed to respect an upcast bank on the exterior of the enclosure or, alternatively, that it respected the palisade constructed in the second phase.

The interpretation of the devopment sequence of this monument was problematic as the appearance and fills of the ditch where it had been cut into bedrock (Figs 14 (a), (b)) were in marked contrast to those where it had been cut into sand (Fig 14 (c)).

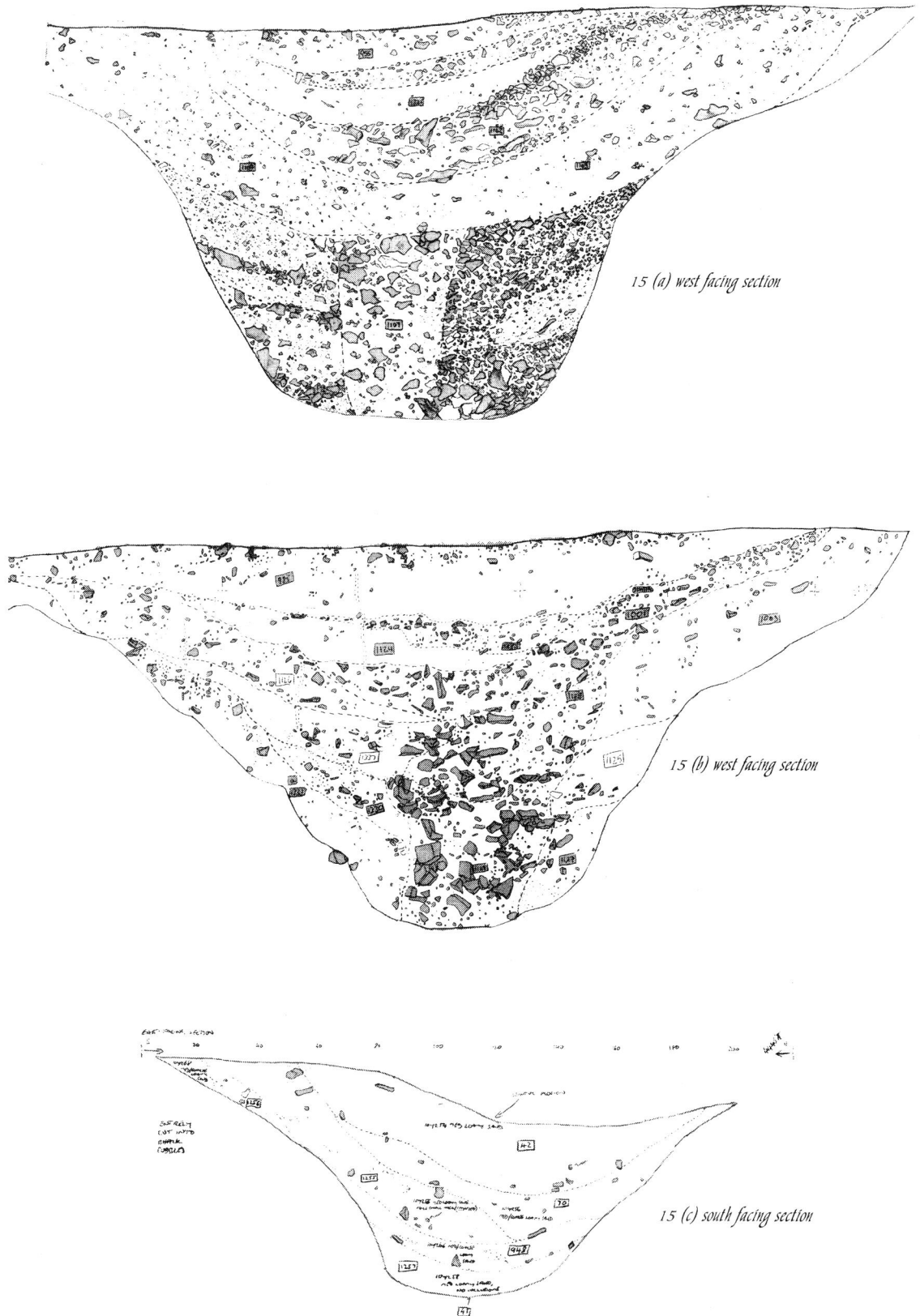

*15 (a) west facing section*

*15 (b) west facing section*

*15 (c) south facing section*

*Figure 14: West Hesleton: hengiform enclosure. Field drawings of the ditch sections, the lower example showing the difference where the enclosure was cut into sand rather than chalk bedrock (Scales 1:20)*

Excavation was initially concentrated on the northern part of the monument; the trial trenches cut to test the extent of the cemetery had missed this monument entirely, one trench (2C) passing straight through the western entrance. It was some weeks before the extent of the feature became clear. Where the ditch had been cut into chalk gravel and bedrock a distinct central cut with an almost vertical face on the inside edge was interpreted as a palisade slot (Figs 14 (a), (b)).

The palisade slot was present and clearly visible, both in plan and section, following most of the northern arc of the monument. Where the feature was cut into sand no such central slot could be identified (Fig 14(c)). In contrast to the timber circle, individual post-pipes could not be recognised, indicating that the palisade was deliberately dismantled. This interpretation is given support by the evidence recorded in section, revealing that the outer face of the palisade slot lacked the vertical and well defined inner face. It seems most likely that any timbering was deliberately removed by pushing the timbers out from the inside of the enclosure, giving rise to the irregular profile of the slot on the outer face.

On the northern side the enclosure ditch had a flattened V-shaped profile with a U-shaped base. The palisade slot had been cut into the partially filled ditch; there was some indication that a later cleaning of the ditch had truncated the filled-in slot. It was quite clear in a number of sections that the deposits on either side of the slot had been cut through rather than being formed from packing material. The slot, where best defined, had a breadth of up to 0.4m with the lower 0.6m surviving in the base of the 1.3m deep ditch. On the southern side, the lack of clear evidence for the palisade trench could indicate that the palisade was only partial; this seems unlikely. A more likely interpretation is that the coarse natural sands in this part of the site rapidly eroded and any evidence of the later phase was lost.

The was no conclusive dating evidence either from the ditch, which cut away the edge of a pit containing Peterborough ware at a high level (this may have resulted from a late recut), or from the palisade slot. The final phase of the monument must have pre-dated the barrow (2BA264), which contained a Food Vessel burial. Ceramics were rare and abraded and lithic debris could not certainly be associated with the feature. In the base of the slot on the northern side a pair of roe deer antlers and a fragment of a very much larger antler appeared to represent a deliberate deposit. The upper fills of the enclosure, which appeared to derive from natural accumulation, incorporated material ranging in date from the Neolithic to early Mediaeval periods. A context for the enclosure may be found in what appears to be an occupation area outside the enclosure c65m to the south in area 2BB.

*Plate 17: the southern half of the post-circle and barrow and north-east segment of the hengiform enclosure seen during excavation. The close relationship between the two monuments and lack of intersection indicates that one was constructed respecting the other, but the sequence remains unclear*

# Possible occupation area

A number of sample areas were opened up by machine to the south of the hengiform enclosure in order to locate the southern extent of the enclosure ditch and to test the potential for the recovery of evidence of associated or other prehistoric activity in the area. The southern side of the enclosure ditch was identified, cut into sand, some five metres beyond the limit of excavation. A 3.5m wide trench was extended 32m to the south where a small area covering just under 350 sq m was opened following the discovery of a sealed land surface incorporating prehistoric ceramics and cut by pits containing small fragments of cremated bone, charcoal and carbonised hazelnut shells (Fig 15). The poorly preserved and leached buried soil was sealed by nearly a metre of blown sand and hill-wash. A scatter of abraded Early Iron Age sherds on the old ground surface indicated that the main build-

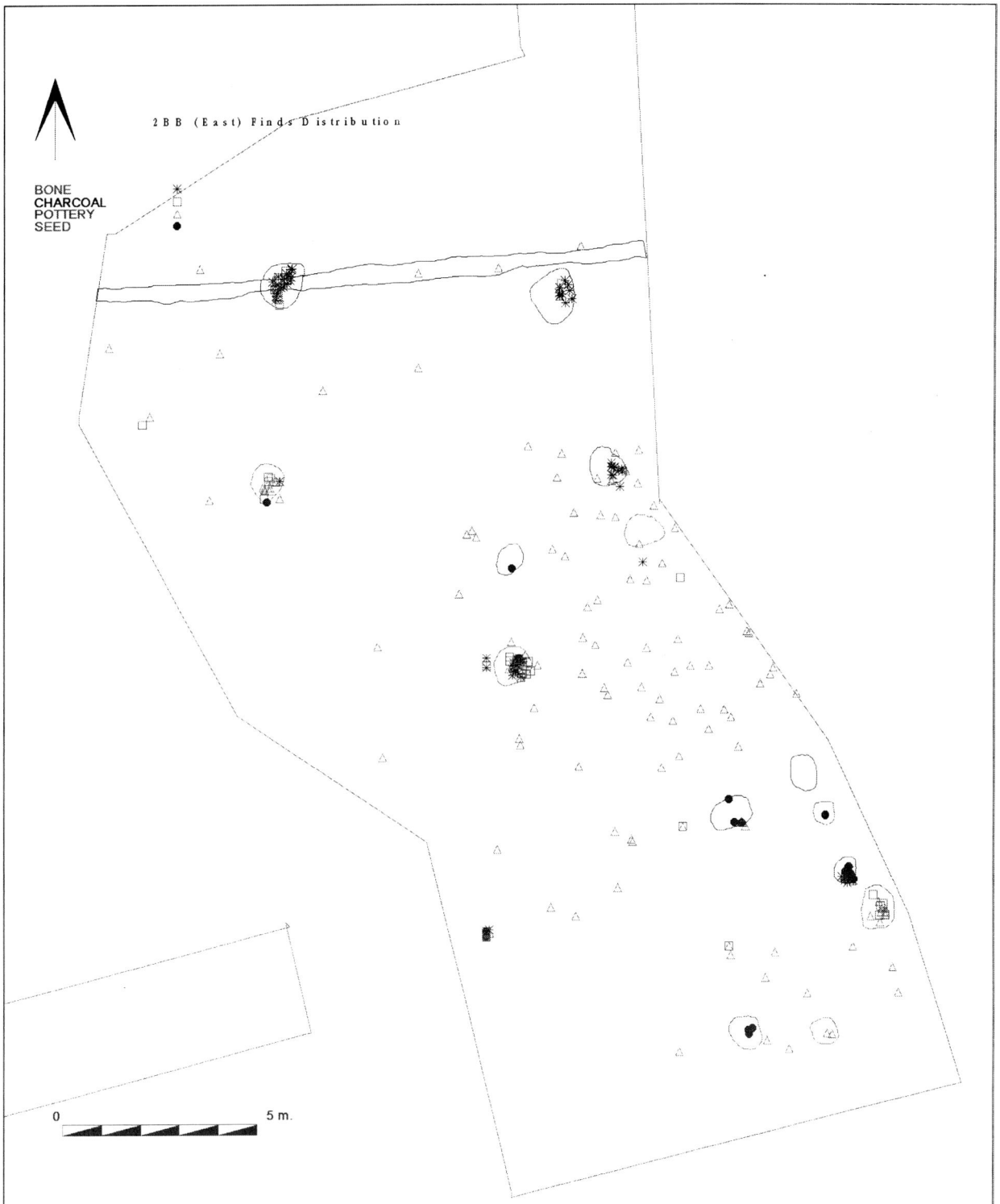

*Figure 15: plan of part of area 2BB showing the distribution of Late Neolithic pits or postholes*

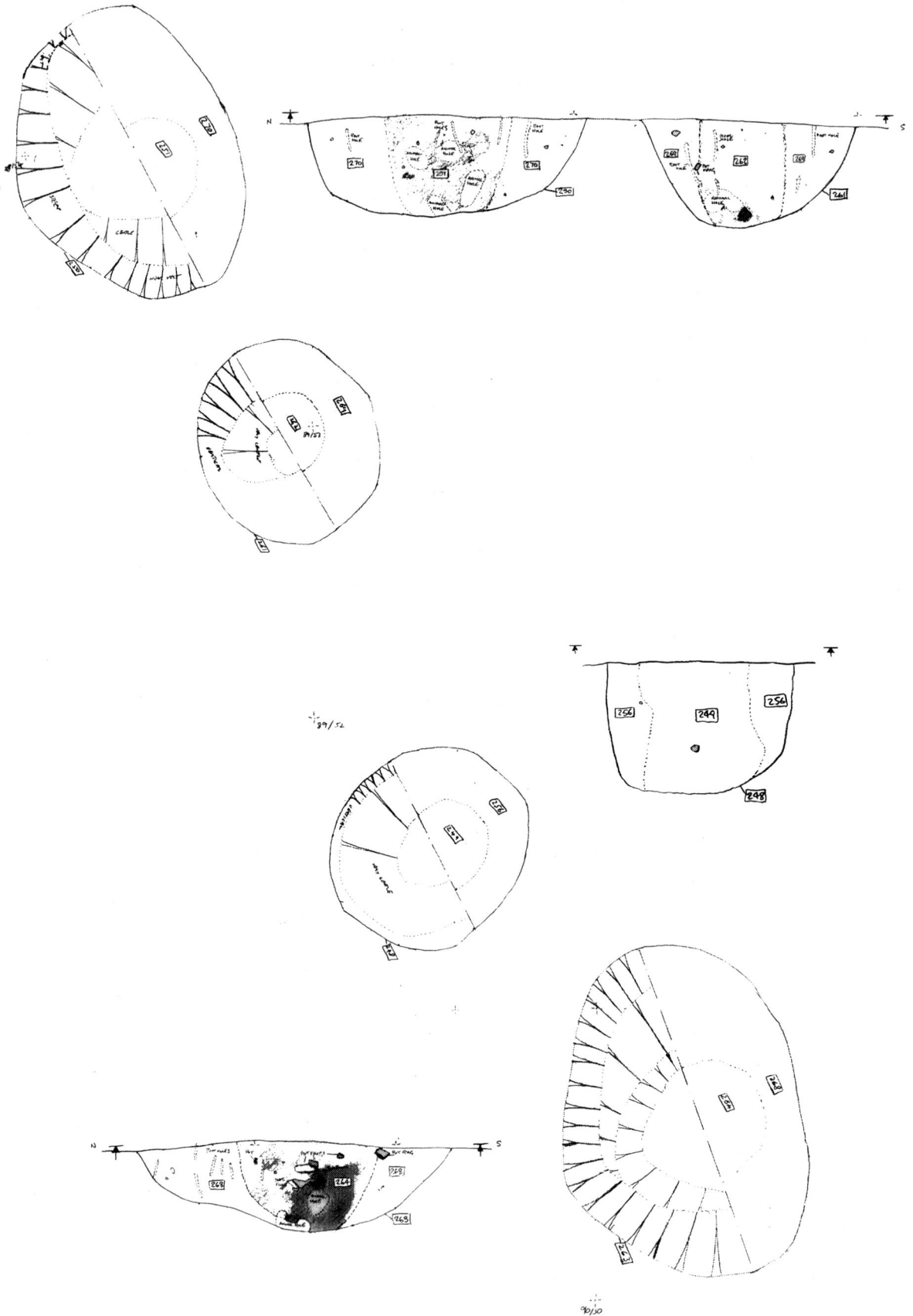

Figure 16: field drawings, plans and sections of four of the Late Neolithic pits / ? postholes examined in area 2BB (Scale 1:20)

up of aeolian and colluvial deposits post-dates this period and probably was a consequence of woodland clearance and agricultural activity towards the foot of the Wolds during the Roman period. Cut into or associated with the buried soil a series of 14 small pits were identified and excavated. The depth at which the features were buried meant that they were not threatened by plough damage and thus the area examined was not extended. The evidence recovered clearly identified the potential for recovery of important deposits possibly domestic in character, within the immediate vacinity.

The pits examined were all roughly circular or ovate in plan ranging from 0.7m to 1.3m across with depths ranging from 0.2 to 0.45m. Five of the pits contained significant quantities of calcined or cremated bone and charcoal; the fragments were however very small and it was impossible to determine whether they were human or animal in origin. These features were initially interpreted as cremations; however, the quantities of cremated bone were minimal. The presence of carbonised hazelnut-shells in three of the five pits containing cremated bone fragments indicates that this material is more likely to have been derived from domestic rather than funerary activity. Of the remaining pits, four contained only carbonised hazelnut shells and one no material culture evidence at all. The sand filling of many of these features was uniform and very dark indeed, and leaching out of the organic component made it exceptionally difficult to identify any real edges to these features. It was, for instance, difficult to determine whether many of the features had had vertical sides even when box-sectioned. Although some appeared to have been simple pits, others seemed to be postholes, with poorly preserved post-pipes visible in section. One of the pits, situated to the west of the main group, contained much of a Grooved-Ware vessel of Durrington Walls style (Fig 43, 2BB239AI, AF, AE)

A line of four pits next to the eastern limit of excavation may represent part of a wall line (Fig 16); however, no intelligible structural pattern could be determined within the limited area exposed. Two of these pits incorporated substantial groups of Peterborough ware. The presence of Peterborough, Grooved Ware and Grimston style ceramics associated with these features indicates that if the evidence sampled here does relate to domestic activity it is most likely to have been associated with either the construction or use of the monument complex. Its location c50m away from the complex itself may therefore have some significance. Excavation in this area, which was sealed by blown sand, was hampered by the difficulty of identifying the boundary between the sealing deposits of hill-wash and the almost identical material into which the features had been cut. Potential clearly remains to clarify the tantalising evidence recovered in this part of the site, particularly towards the south and east, where deep deposits of hill-wash and blown sand are likely to preserve further evidence of activity. To the north of this area, between this pit complex and the hengiform enclosure, the natural sub-surface rises to a point where medieval and modern ploughing had truncated it. This was identified in a series of trenches running from north to south to the south of the enclosure and containing only evidence of recent plough damage and rig and furrow. It is not at all clear whether the apparent absence of activity between this group of pits and the enclosure represents a deliberate buffer zone or a product of subsequent damage. Whether the evidence recovered from this small sample area derives from activity associated with the construction, or subsequent use of this monument complex, the relatively high density of activity indicates that the landscape associated with the complex is very extensive.

# The Early Bronze Age Barrows

The monument sequence established during the Neolithic was added to in the Early Bronze Age when the post-circle was replaced by a ring ditch and a minimum of three round barrows defined by circular ditches were constructed. Four flat-graves including three inhumations and a cremation were also identified within or just outside the hengiform enclosure.

This small group of graves is important as it includes Beaker, Food Vessel and Food Vessel Urn burials in what seems to be a contrasting burial rite to that in the barrows

excavated c200m to the north on Site 1(Powlesland et al 1986). The three barrows examined on Site 1 were relatively large (between 20 and 30 metres in diameter), had partially preserved mounds, substantial ditches and long sequence of burials. In contrast, the barrows examined in the area of the later Anglian cemetery were smaller, had no surviving mounds, were defined by very shallow ring-ditches and contained no more than two grave pits. The ring ditch 2BA130 and was interpreted as a barrow had different attributes to both barrow series.

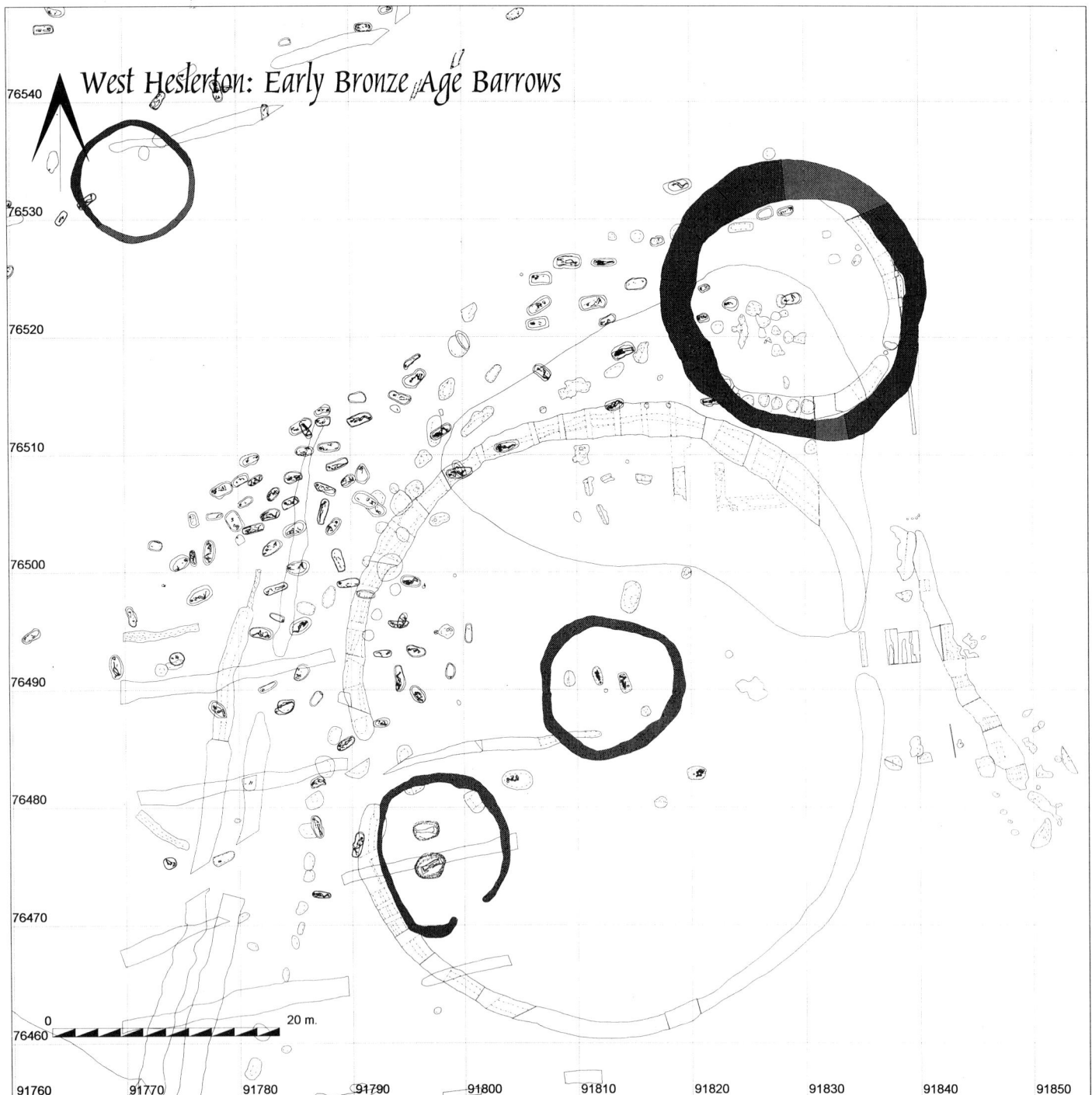

*Figure 17: distribution of Early Bronze Age barrows*

# Possible Barrow in area 1HE

The discovery of a Beaker accompanied by a flint knife, cut away by what appears to be two successive Anglian burials in area 1HE (G43, G49 Vol ii, 76), (Fig 19). indicates that a barrow had probably exisited in this location. This interpretation is given added support by the alignment and gaps of a pair of probably Roman gullies that flank a path or define a boundary. These extend to the north-east and south-west but are splayed and interrupted as if respecting a barrow mound at this location. There was no evidence of any encircling ditch.

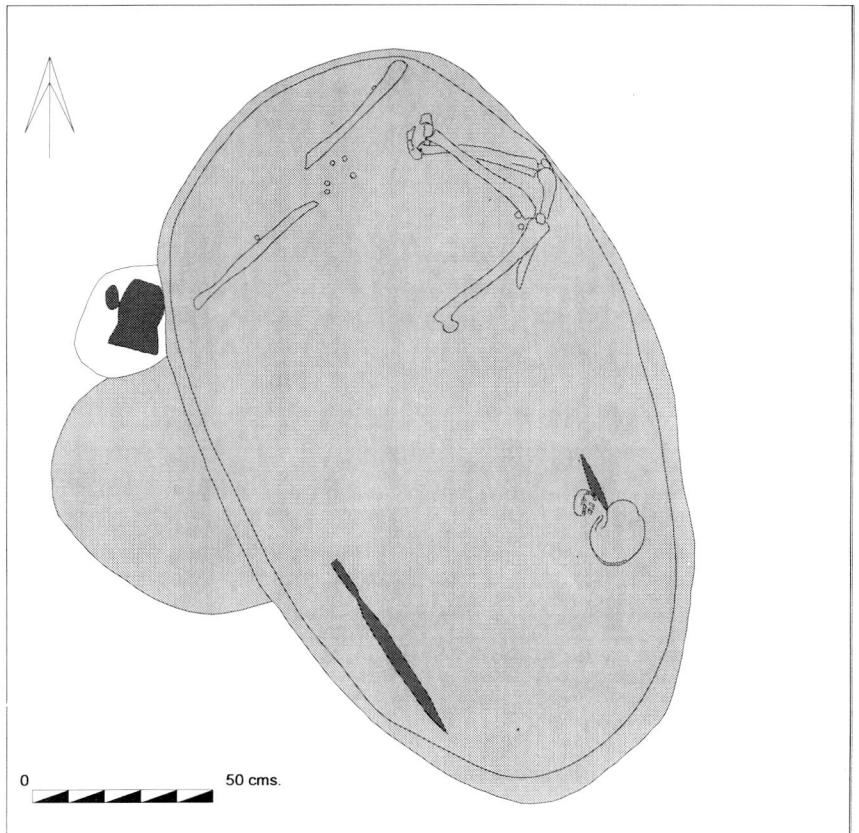

Figure 18: plan of Grave 1HE318, cut by the later graves G43 and G49

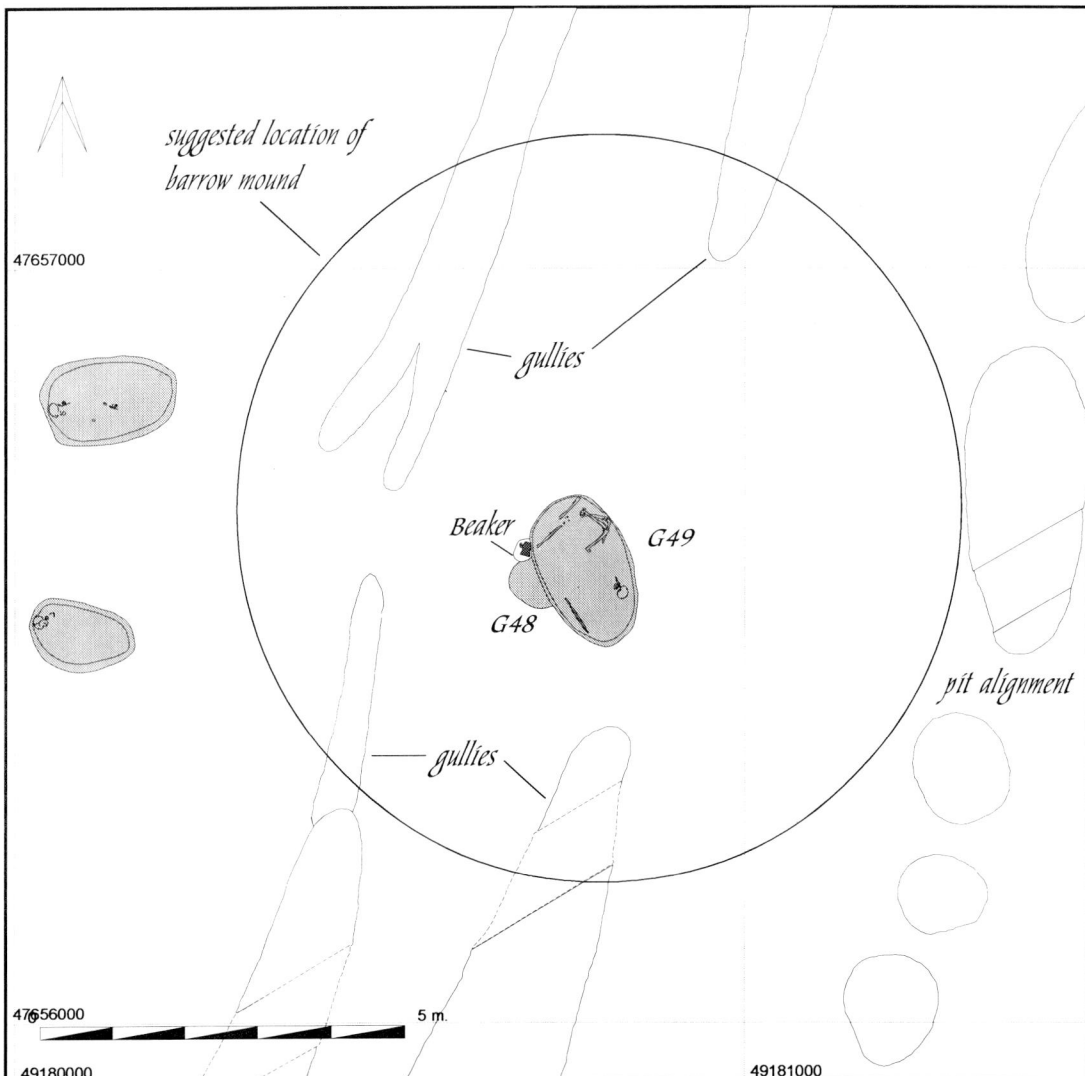

Figure 19: showing the divergance and absence of the later gullies to the north and south of the mostly cut away Beaker burial

# Grave 1HE318

| Cut: | 1HE318 | Length: | 0.55 |
|---|---|---|---|
| Fill: | 1HE218 | Breadth: | 0.30 |
| Beaker Group 1HE18 | | Depth: | 0.11 |
| Grid ref. | 80700/56627 | | |

## Summary:

Beaker and accompanying plano-convex flint knife in a small pit partially cut away by graves G48 and G49. The Beaker, which had been partially cut away during the removal of the overburden, lay on its side with the flint knife beneath. Despite detailed cleaning of the surrounding area no other evidence for a grave was identified. This association is most unlikely to have occurred outside a funerary context.

## Flint knife:

**18EA** Large grey flint single edge retouched knife, 80mm long and 42mm broad, with a milky white cortex on one face.

**Beaker:** 1HE18DW **(see below)**

# Barrow 1A521

A second probable barrow was identified *c*50m to the south-west of grave 1HE318. A partially exposed ring-ditch in area 1A, which extended beyond the limit of excavation to the south, probably relates to a barrow. The ditch, half of which was within the excavation area with a maximum breadth of 0.85m and depth of 0.35m, indicates a monument 10m in diameter. The excavated section was not a true arc: rather it incorporated three curved sections with sharper curves where they joined. It is just possible that this may be a distorted square barrow, in which case it would be an isolated example. This monument had been truncated by ploughing, being partially cut away by a fragment of rig and furrow and by more recent agriculture. An unaccompanied prone burial was found in a grave cut through the ring ditch (G6,Vol ii, 9). The grave may be prehistoric; however, without independent dating evidence it has been discussed in the context of the Anglian cemetery.

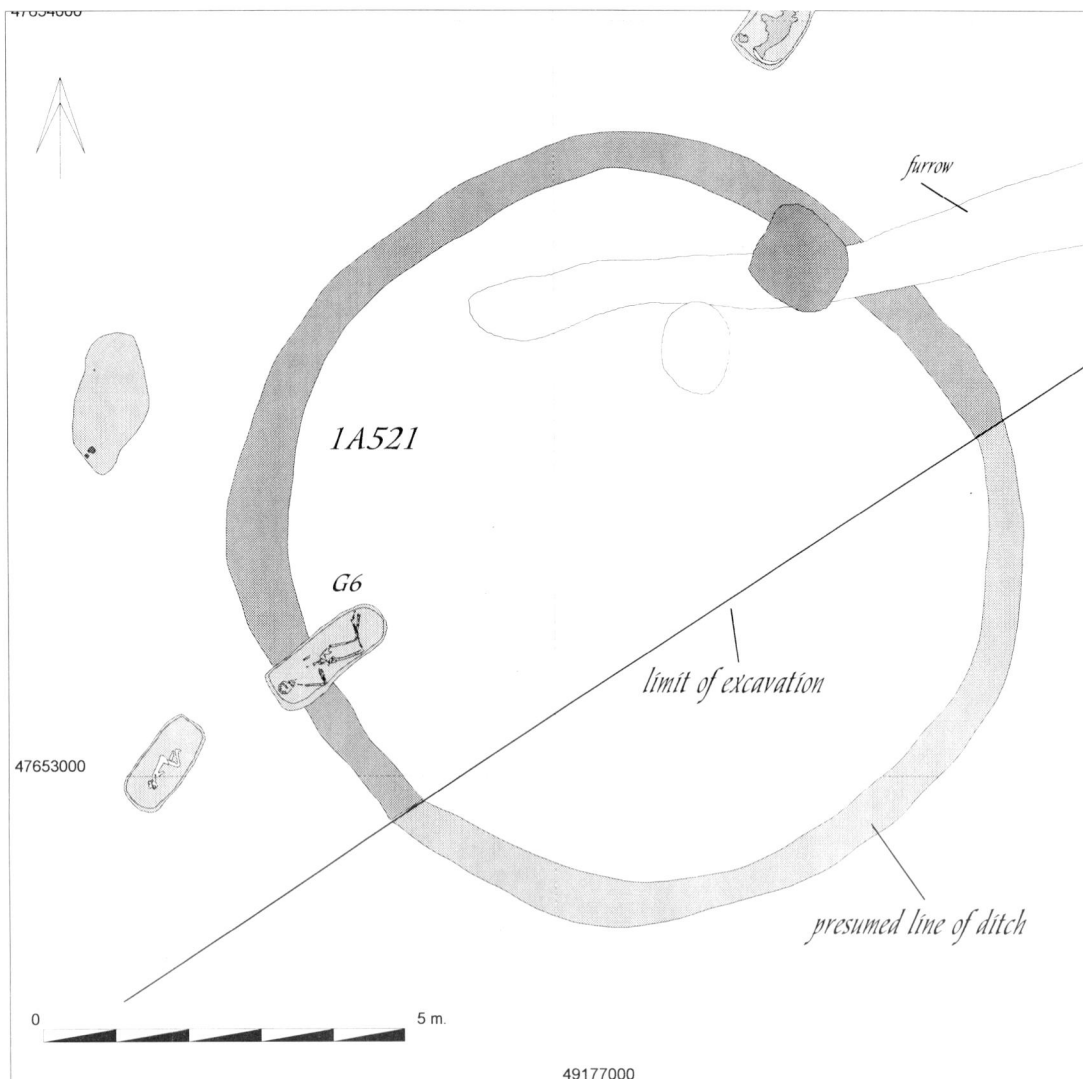

*Figure 20: plan showing the ring-ditch of Barrow 1A521 and later features*

# Barrow 2BA174

Barrow 2BA174, situated at the centre of the enclosure, was defined by a shallow U-shaped gully no more then 0.55m deep, enclosing an area of *c*88 sq m and measuring 13.3 x 12.5m to the outside of the gully (Fig 21). The gully appears to have been dug in short straight segments, the result being somewhat irregular. At the centre of the enclosed areas two large grave pits, both aligned north–south, were cut to a considerable depth. Both graves were over a metre deep, the eastern grave 2BA219 being over 1.5m deep. In both cases the primary deposit was an inhumation accompanied by a Food Vessel and in both cases a secondary burial, a cremation, had later been inserted into the grave. Both of the graves associated with this monument were thus defined by massive grave pits, both showed a similar sequence of re-use and both

contained an inhumation, probably in a tree-trunk coffin, although evidence from this could only be seen in 2BA219. The backfilling of this grave included 59 clearly visible different deposits, and although most comprised varying mixes of sand and gravel derived no doubt from spoil generated by cutting the grave, loamy deposits within the series suggest that the feature may have lain open for a considerable time before final backfilling was completed. The second of the two cuts showed no clear evidence of this sequence although in both cases a cremation was later inserted into the top of the grave. Both the cremations 2BA230 and 2BA243 appeared by the distribution of material to have been contained within some sort of bag or container.

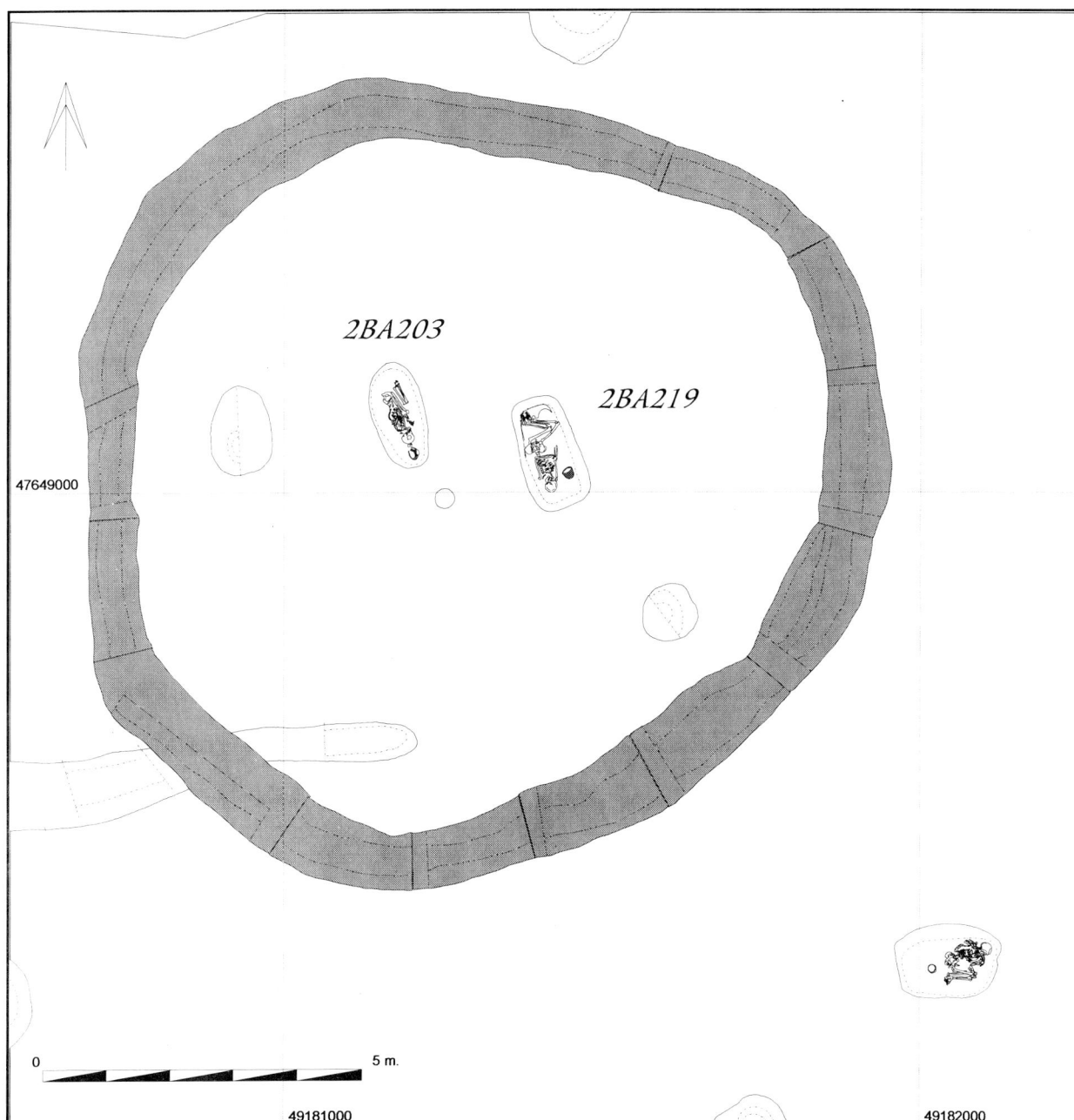

*Figure 21: plan of Barrow 2BA174 showing the location and orientation of the two graves 2BA203 and 2BA219*

*Plate 18: work in progress during the excvation of Barrow 2BA219*

# Grave 2BA219

| Cut: | 2BA219 | Length: | 2.77 |
|---|---|---|---|
| | | Breadth: | 1.10 |
| Skeletons: 2BA241, 2BA241A | | Depth: | 1.45 |

Cut into by cremation pit 2BA230

| Grid ref. | 81275/48906 | Level: | 43.28 |
|---|---|---|---|
| Age: | Adult 25-35, Juvenile | | |
| Sex: | Male,      Unknown | | |

## Summary:

This grave was distinguished not only on account of its size but also by the large number (59) of distinct fills it contained (Fig 22). Many of these represent tip-lines in the backfilling of the grave but even then, loamy deposits within them may indicate that backfilling did not all take place at a single time. At the base of the grave pit a crouched skeleton accompanied by a Food Vessel lay on its right side with the head to the south and facing east (Fig 23, Plate 19). The body had been placed in a tree-trunk coffin, evidence of which survived as staining in the base of the grave. Beneath the coffin a fine silty sand had accumulated. When the grave had almost completely filled, a cremation contained in some sort of bag and incorporating a burnt barbed and tanged arrowhead had been placed in a deep secondary cut towards the southern end of the grave where it was accompanied by a Food Vessel. Examination of the human remains indicates that

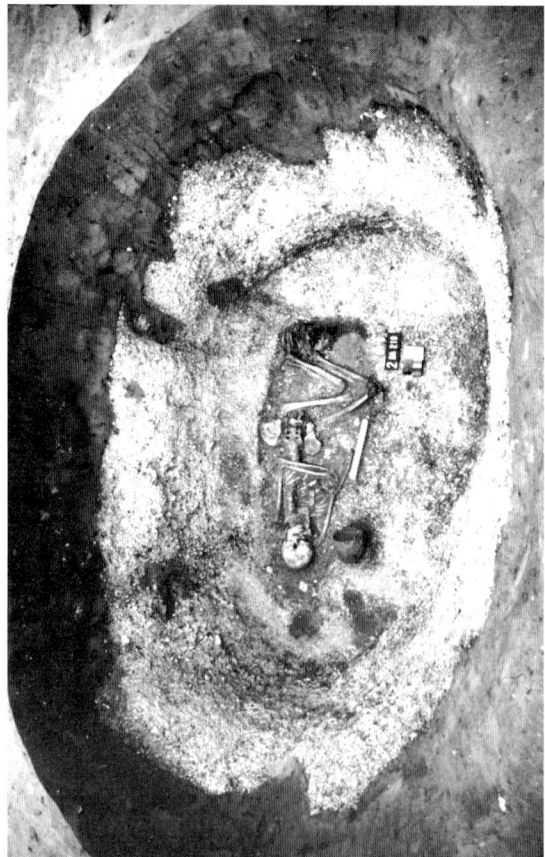

*Plate 19: Grave 2BA219 prior to the removal of the skeleton(s) and accompanying Food Vessel*

*Figure 22: field drawing of the section through grave 2BA219 and showing the cut for cremation 2BA230 with associated Food Vessel (Scale 1:20)*

*Plate 20: vertical photograph of the burial and accessory vessel in grave 2BA219*

the grave had in fact contained two burials, that of an adult male accompanied by a juvenile.

## Skeleton:

Most of the bones of inhumation 2BA241 represented an adult male and the accompanying juvenile bones were renumbered 2BA241A.

The adult, aged 25-35 on the basis of attrition, had mild discitis affecting the bodies of lumbar vertebrae 3 and 4. The skeleton exhibits extosis; the lateral edge of the attachment of deltoid to the left clavicle has ossified, with the entire insertion site raised above the normal bone contour; this is indicative of trauma. It must be considered that the skeletal evidence for trauma will only reflect either injury directly involving the bone, where soft tissue infection involves the bone, or where soft tissue injury results in calcification of the damaged tissue. This skeleton also exhibits ankylosis. The costal cartilage of the right first rib has ossified, fusing it to the manubrium. This individual, whose attritional age is 25 to 35, appears to be a 'bone former' despite his apparently young age. As noted above the attachment of deltoid to the left clavicle has ossified, as has the thyroid cartilage. There is an enthesophyte on the tip of the odontoid peg.

## Flint blade:

**2BA241AR:** Shallow retouch down one side of a large blade. ?Knife. ML 75mm; MW 24mm; MT 7mm

## Food Vessel: 2BA241AT **(see below)**

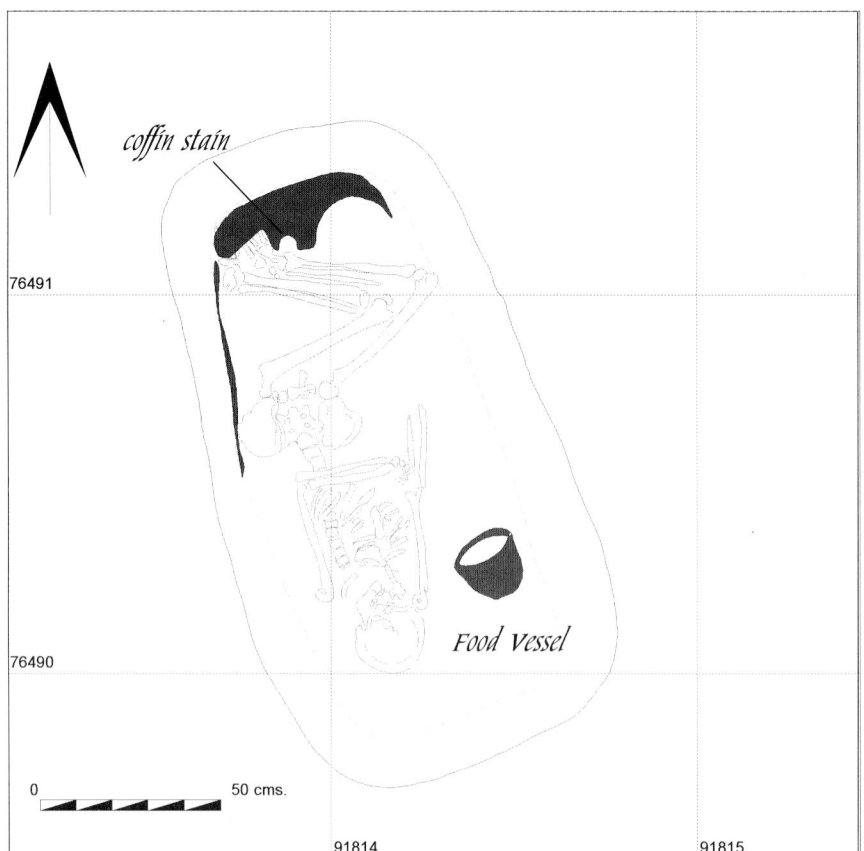

*Figure 23: plan of Grave 2BA213*

# Cremation 2BA230

| | | | |
|---|---|---|---|
| Cut: | 2BA230 | Length: | 0.85 |
| Fill: | 2BA231 | Breadth: | 0.60 |
| Cremation: | 2BA227 | Depth: | 0.14 |
| Cuts into Grave | 2BA219 | | |
| Grid ref. | 81419/49051 | Level: | 44.10 |
| Age: | Unknown | | |
| Sex: | Unknown | | |

## Summary:

Secondary cremations had been inserted into both the inhumations in Barrow 2BA174; in this case the cremation was accompanied by a Food Vessel lying on its side (Plate 21). The cremation itself appeared to have been buried in some sort of bag, the shape of which was preserved in the form of the deposit (Plate 22). The cremation was accompanied by a Type 1A (iii) Food Vessel and contained a burnt barbed and tanged arrowhead.

## Skeleton:

A few fragments of cremated bone, white in colour.

## Food Vessel: 2BA227AI: (see below)

# Grave  2BA203

| | | | |
|---|---|---|---|
| Cut: | 2BA203 | Length: | 2.27 |
| Fills: 2BA204, 234, 262, 263, 282 | | Breadth: | 1.51 |
| Skeleton: | 2BA283 | Depth: | 1.00 |
| Grid ref. | 81177/49116 | Level: | 43.52 |
| Cut into by Cremation Pit 2BA243 | | | |
| Age: | Adult | | |
| Sex: | Female | | |

The second of the two graves in this barrow was far less complex. At the base of the grave the crouched and possible bound inhumation was once again buried on its right side with the head to the south and facing east (Fig 24). Just to the south of the skull a Food Vessel, tipped over from an upright position, was placed accompanied by two rather poor quality flint flakes situated as if they had been in a small bag or pouch. There was no evidence of a tree-trunk coffin in this case; however, a lens of charcoal and organically enriched soil beneath the body may indicate a less substantial timber coffin. A large cremation pit, 2BA243, had been cut into the grave at the southern end and, as in the example above, the cremated bone was tightly packed and appeared to have been originally contained within a bag.

## Skeleton:

This adult female skeleton has moderate osteophytic lipping affecting the vertebrae from thorax to sacrum and slight but widespread degenerative changes to the extra-spinal joints. Schmorl's nodes on thoracic vertebrae 9 and 12 could indicate considerable physical stress during adolescence and early adulthood.  Schmorl's nodes

Plate 21: cremation pit 2BA230 during excavation; the Food Vessel can be seen in the section

Plate 22: bag–shaped deposit of cremated bone 2BA227

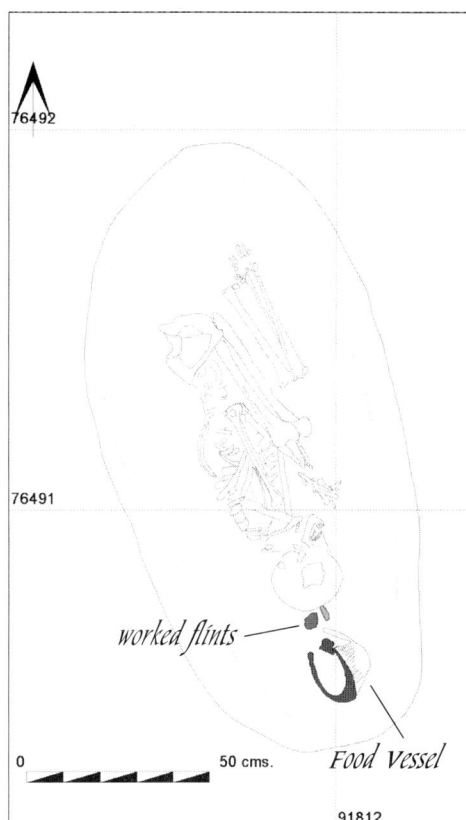

Figure 24: plan of grave 2BA203

234

262

263

283

204

DARKER SAND WITH MORE CHARCOAL WITHIN

204

204

263

283

SKULL

343

FLINT

POT

*Food Vessl*

262

343

CREMATION

245

*cremation*

244

243

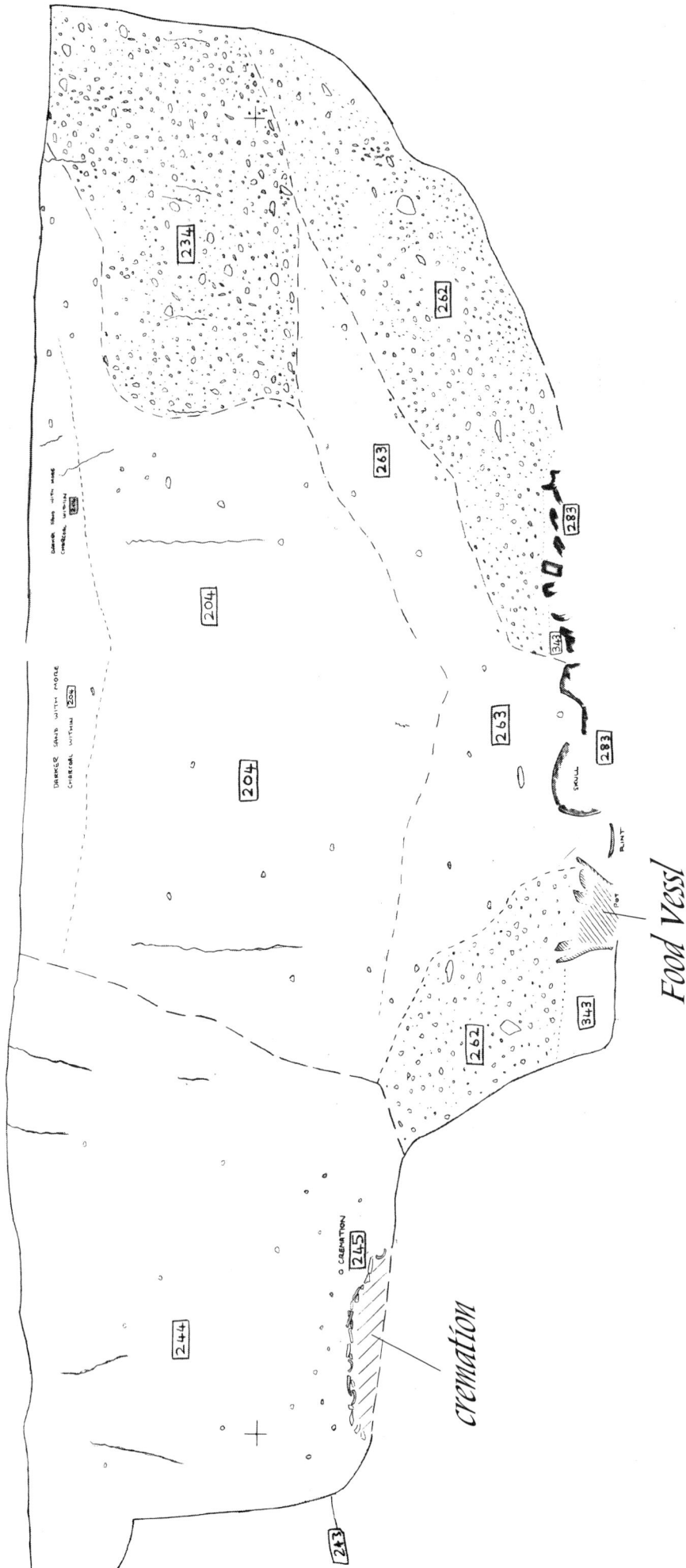

*Figure 25: field drawing of the section through Grave 2BA203 showing the cut for cremation 2BA243*

can progress to spondylosis deformans (Kelly 1982), crescent shaped lesions on the anterior portion of the discal bodies, the epiphyseal rings of the centrum being completely destroyed.

**Food Vessel: 2BA283AP: (see below)**

# Cremation 2BA243

| Cut: | 2BA243 | Length: | 1.12 |
|---|---|---|---|
| Fills: | 2BA244 | Breadth: | 1.11 |
| Cremation: | 2BA245 | Depth: | 0.66 |
| Grid ref. | 81258/48984 | Level: | 43.97 |

Cut into Grave 2BA203

A deeply cut cremation pit filled with a homogeneous sandy fill with very few inclusions had been dug into the filled in grave 2BA203. At the base of the pit a mass of cremated bone fragments lay as if they had been contained in a bag.

*Plate 23: excavation of Grave 2BA203 in progress, Cremation 2BA243 can be seen in the foreground*

**Skeleton:**

A mass of fragments of cremated bone white in colour, unaged and unsexed.

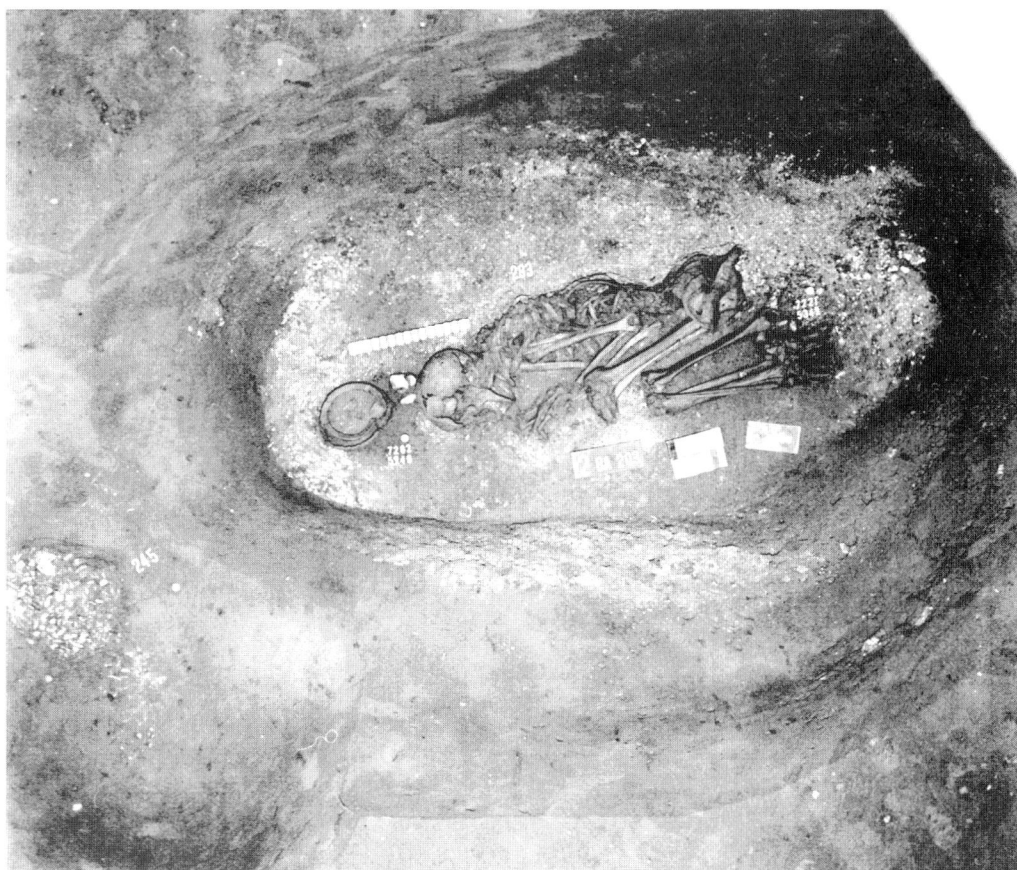

*Plate 24: Grave 2BA203, fully excavated prior to removal of the skeleton and associated Food Vessel*

# Barrow 2BA264

7.5m to the south-west of 2BA174 a second small barrow (2BA264) was likewise defined by an irregular penannular gully (Fig 26, Plate 25). It is likely that originally the ditch had entirely enclosed the burial area, since this area had clearly been subject to both plough damage and wind erosion. The gully, enclosing an area of 100 sq m and measuring 11.85m x 12.83m, was very shallow with an average depth of no more than 0.25m. The most significant aspect of this feature was its relationship to the hengiform enclosure 2BA38. The ditch or gully, which was in no place greater than 0.40m deep, was clearly flattened on its western side where it cut into the upper fill of the enclosure ditch. It is possible that the very obvious flattening of the ring ditch on the western sides reflects some then upstanding component of the hengiform enclosure; perhaps the barrow was constructed

butting up against the second phase palisade. No sectional details survived in the sandy ditch fill to confirm or disprove this interpretation. On the eastern side the gully contained a high concentration of worked flints, perhaps derived from a disturbed flint scatter incorporated in the mound matrix. Extensive aeolian activity coupled with the light sandy soils meant that although lithic material was common its stratigraphic integrity was doubtful; much of the flint recovered from the area was exposed as the natural sand eroded in windy weather.

This monument contained two grave cuts, both aligned roughly east–west, where the aggressive sandy environment had almost completely destroyed all skeletal evidence, leaving only the body stains. In both cases the graves appeared to have contained burials within tree-trunk coffins.

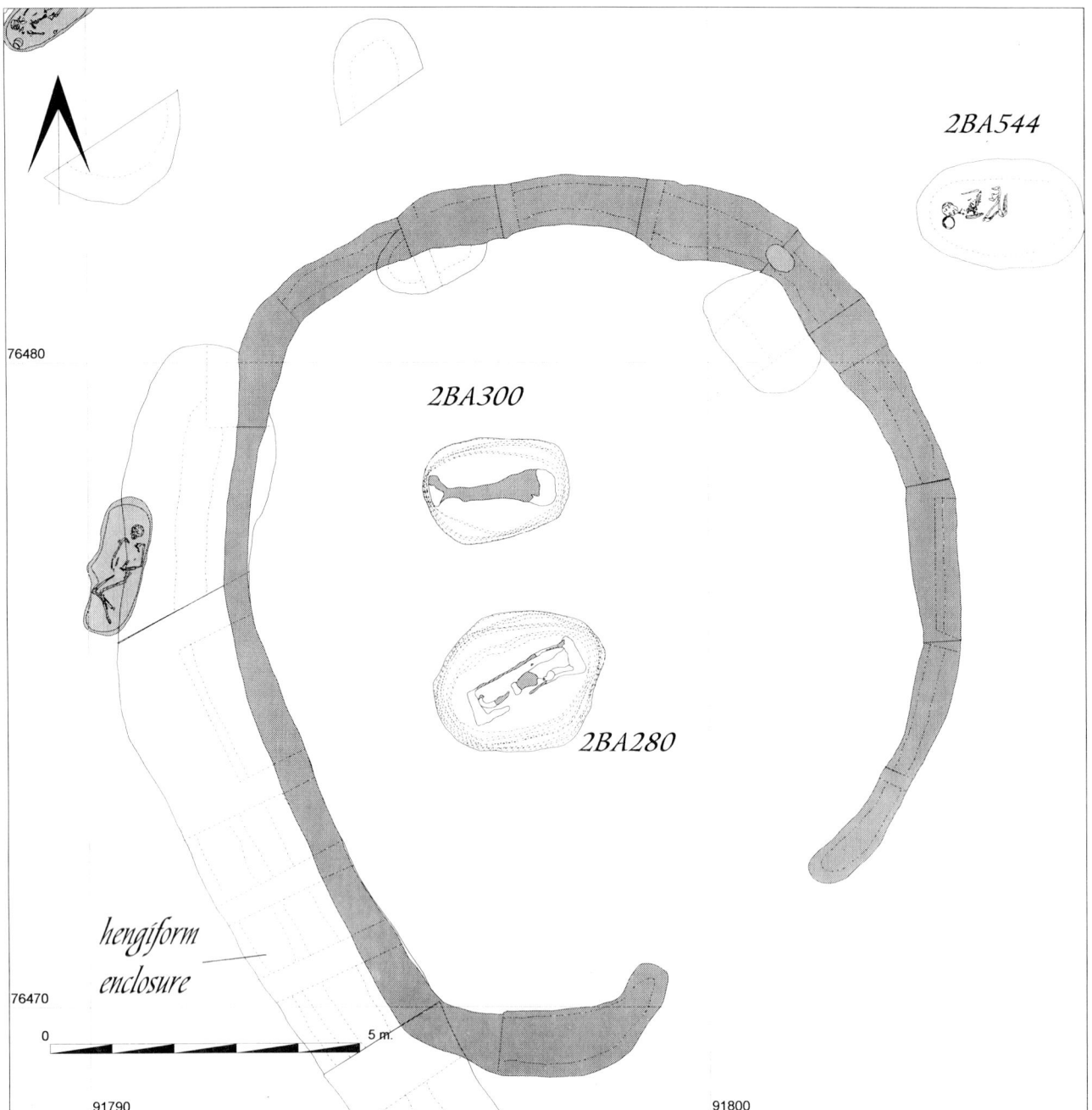

*Figure 26: plan of Barrow 2BA264 situated cutting the western side of the hengiform enclosure*

*Plate 25: Barrow 2BA264 after excavation. The ditch of the hengiform enclosure, partially cut away by the barrow ditch, can be seen in the background*

# Grave 2BA280

| Cut: | 2BA203 | Length: | 2.25 |
|------|--------|---------|------|
| Fills: | 2BA281,306 | Breadth: | 1.47 |
| Skeleton: | stain and teeth only | Depth: | 0.60 |
| Grid ref. | 5698/4006 | Level: | 44.10 |
| Age: | Unknown | | |
| Sex: | Unknown | | |

**Summary:**

This, the smaller of the two graves in the barrow, lay in the northern half of the ring ditch (Fig 27, Plate 26). The grave was filled with uniform re-deposited natural sand with staining in the base indicating both the presence of a wooden coffin and the body position with the head to the west (indicated by some fragments of tooth enamel). The planform and profile of the stain indicated that the coffin had probably been a hollowed out tree-trunk. There were no associated finds.

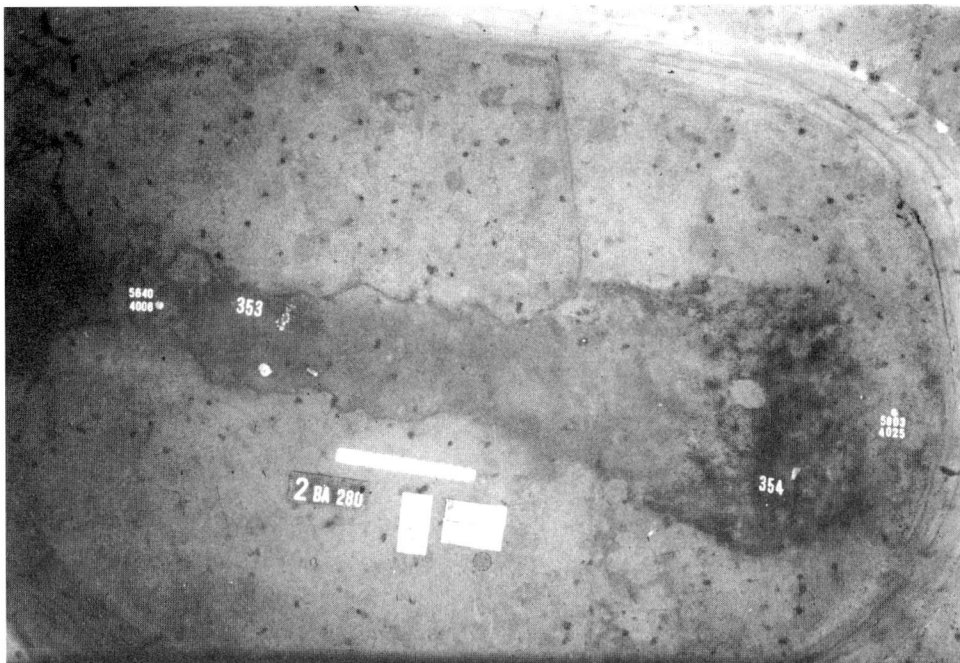

*Plate 26: vertical photograph showing the stain of a tree-trunk coffin in grave 2BA280*

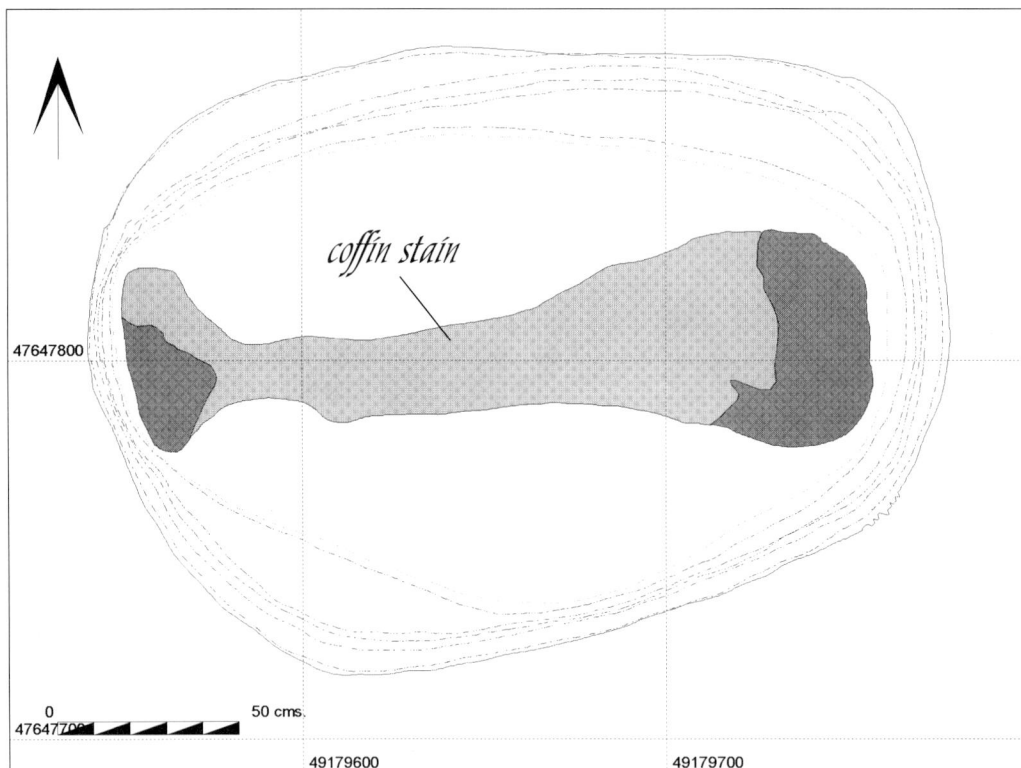

*Figure 27: plan of grave 2BA280 and staininng of tree-trunk coffin*

# Grave 2BA300

| | | | |
|---|---|---|---|
| Cut: | 2BA300 | Length: | 2.85 |
| Fills: | 2BA301, 307, | Breadth: | 2.20 |
| | 355, 428, 429 | Depth: | 1.01 |
| Skeleton: | stain only | | |
| Grid ref. | 79650/47800 | Level: | 44.10 |
| Age: | Unknown | | |
| Sex: | Unknown | | |

This large grave pit, aligned east-west and situated just to the south of the centre of the ring ditch, contained an outstandingly well preserved stain or 'ghost' of a tree-trunk coffin (Fig 28, Plates 27, 28). The grave was filled with uniform re-deposited natural sand. The profile of the coffin survived to a depth of 0.25m in the sandy soils into which the grave had been cut. The coffin stain which measured 2.2 by 0.6m survived as a compact, stained and clay–enriched deposit. As in grave 2BA280, bone survival was exceptionally poor, with none recoverable. The position of the head at the eastern end of the coffin could be clearly distinguished and recorded but in this case not even the tooth enamel had survived. A single flint blade midway along the northern side of the coffin may have been a grave good, but there were no other associated finds.

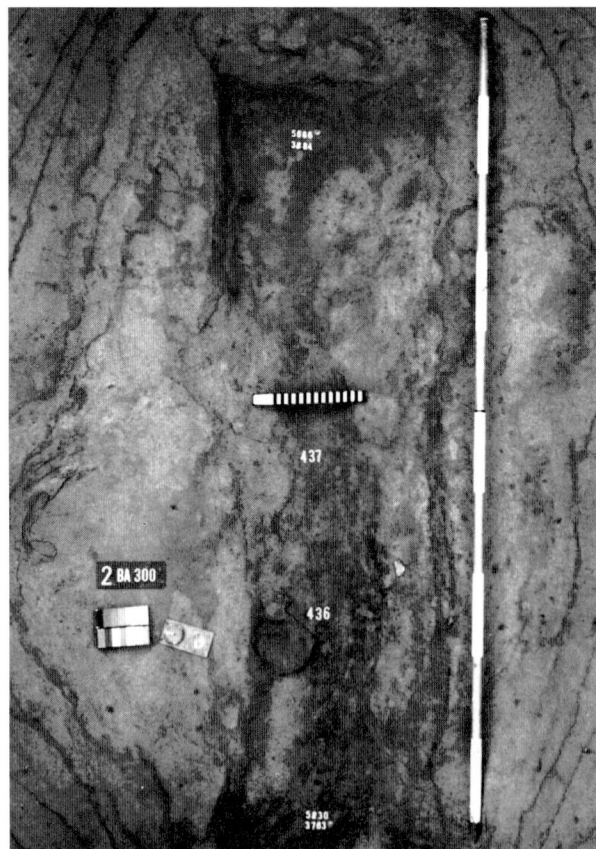

*Plate 27: vertical photograph of coffin-stain and stain from the skull area in grave 2BA300*

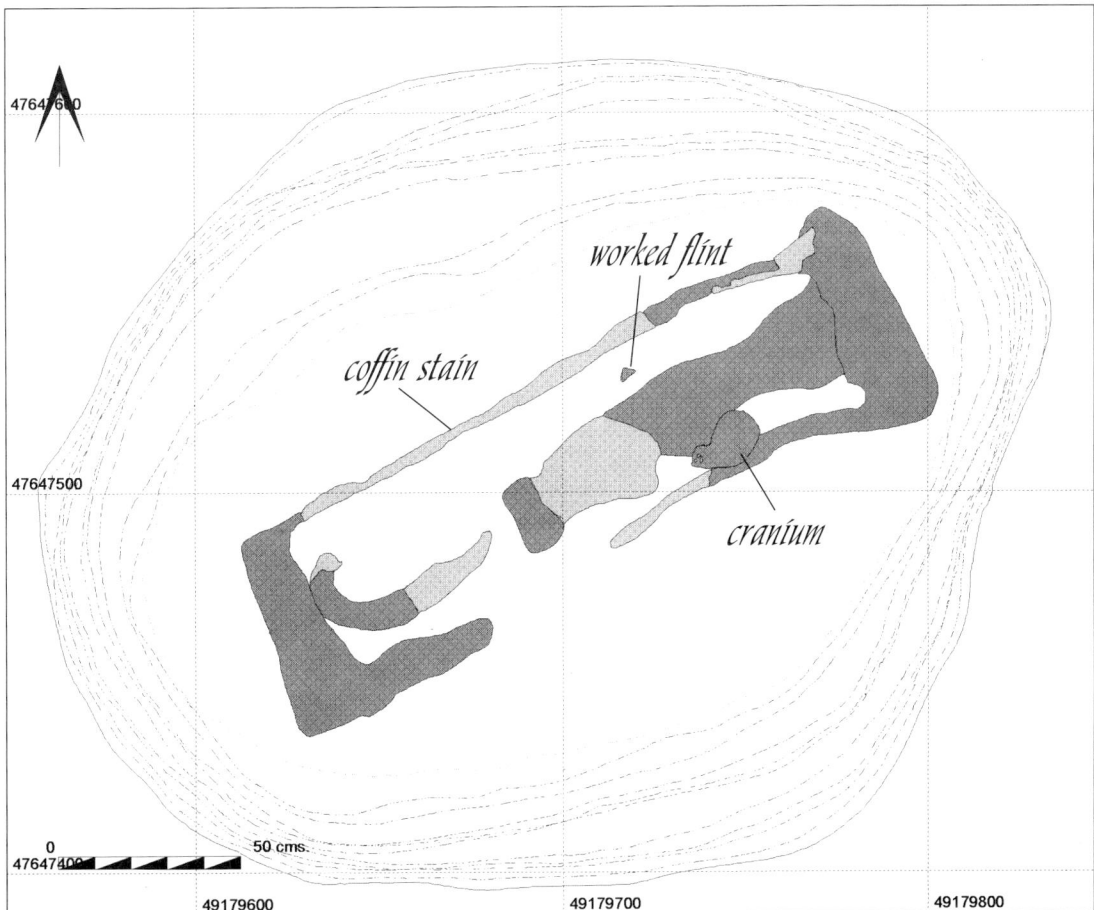

Figure 28: plan of grave 2BA300 and staininng of tree-trunk coffin

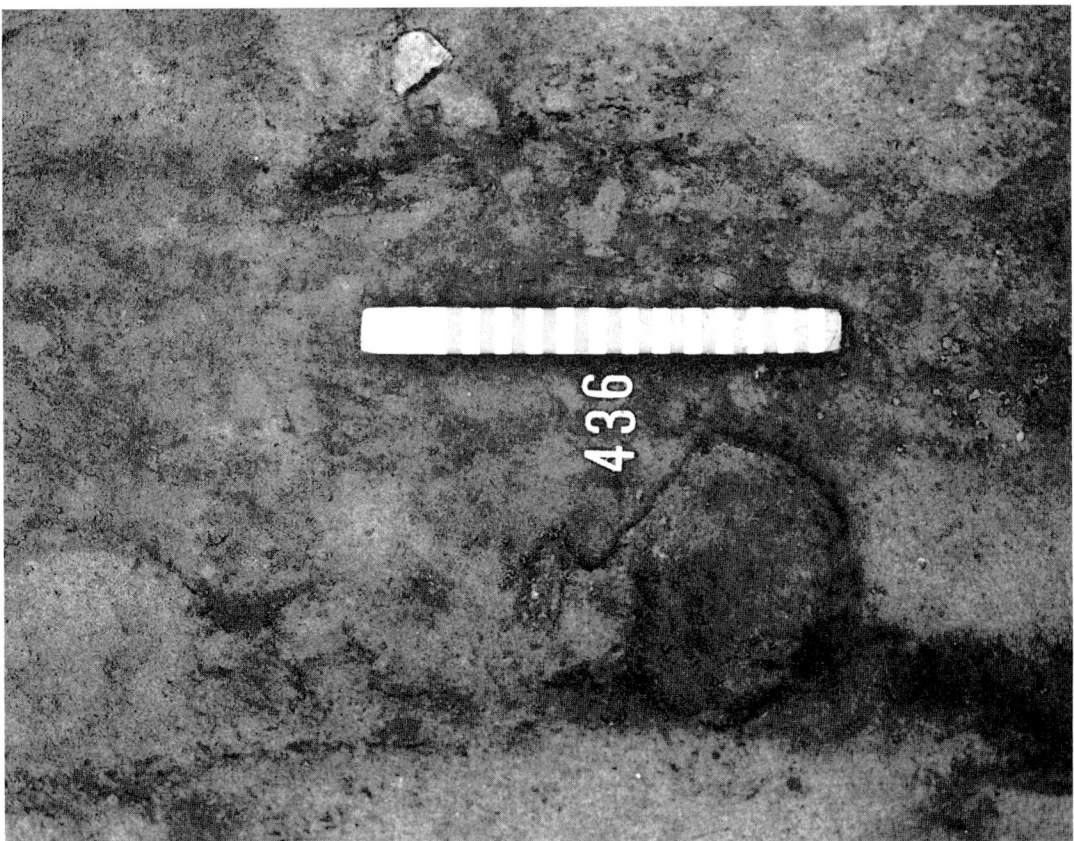

Plate 28: detail photograph of the staining from the skull, with flint blade to the top of the photograph. Grave 2BA300

# Four flat graves

In addition to the graves associated with potential barrows, three flat graves containing inhumations accompanied by Beaker or Food Vessel accessory vessels and a cremation beneath a Food Vessel Urn complete the evidence for Early Bronze Age burial in the area. In one and possibly two of the flat graves the presence of a tree-trunk coffin was indicated. Although the presence of both Beakers and Food Vessels in this area indicates that this small cemetery of the Early Bronze Age is broadly comparable in date to the barrow cemetery excavated on Site 1 only 200m to the north, the burial mode and monument construction are quite different. A fourth, undated flat grave (2BB116) situated over 150m to the south of the cemetery is likely to be of prehistoric date.

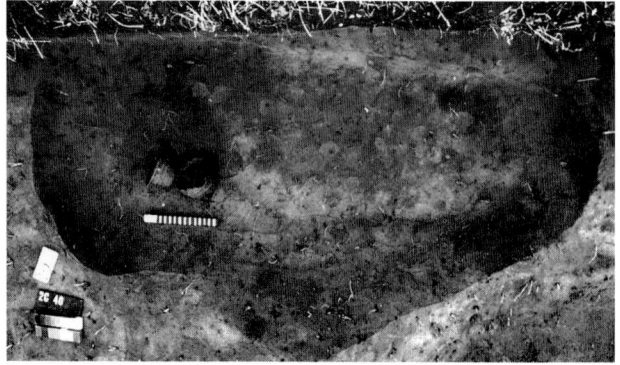

*Plate 29: grave 2C40 during excavation*

# Grave 2C40

| Cut: | 2C40 | Length: | 2.20 |
| Fills: | 2C41,2C42 | Breadth: | 0.90 |
| Skeleton: tooth caps only | | Depth: | 0.45 |
| Grid ref. | 77853/47571 | Level: | 44.24 |
| Age: | Unknown | | |
| Sex: | Unknown | | |

Situated ten metres to the west of the western entrance of the hengiform enclosure, this grave was discovered in a trial trench excavated as part of a campaign to identify the southern limits of the cemetery before the area excavation of area 2BA. The grave aligned roughly east-west, had contained a body, probably lying on the left side, facing north with the head to the west. The grave, which was cut into sand, was very shallow, perhaps reflecting the suspected high levels of erosion and plough damage in the sandier parts of the site. The aggressive burial en-

vironment had contibuted to the total decay of the body; the only evidence of the body consisted of fragments of tooth caps and two small areas of staining, one around the tooth caps and the second along the northern side of the grave. The burial had been accompanied by two small Yorkshire Vase Food Vessels, tipped over behind where the skull would have been, and a plano-convex flint knife and copper awl lying togther as if they had been in a pouch or small bag just beneath or in front of the skull.

*Plate 30: detail photograph showing the two Food Vessels in 2C40 in situ*

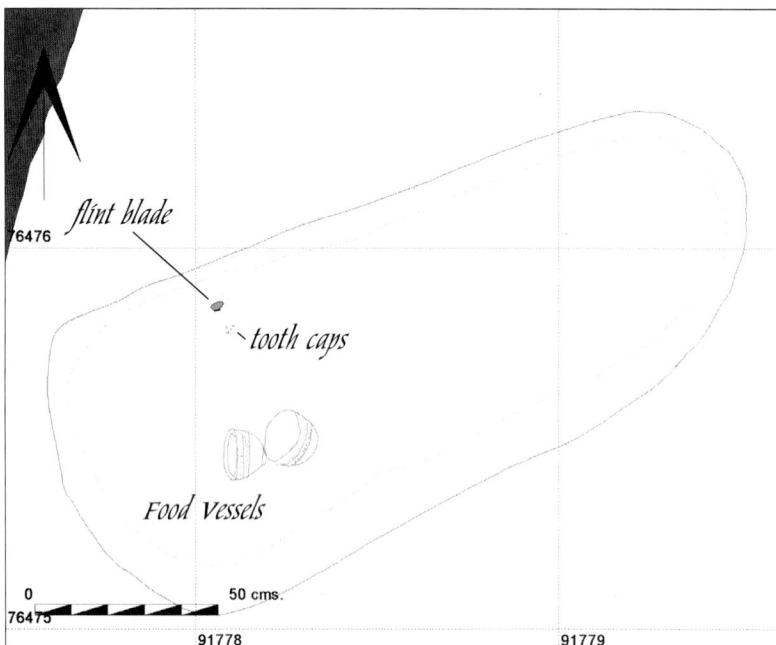

*Figure 29: plan of grave 2C40*

# Grave 2BA217

| | | | |
|---|---|---|---|
| Cut: | 2BA217 | Length: | 1.85 |
| Fills: | 2BA218, 239, 235, 237 | Breadth: | 1.70 |
| Skeleton: | 2BA229 | Depth: | 0 .69 |
| Grid ref. | 82063/48297 | Level: | 44.06 |
| Age: | Adult | | |
| Sex: | Male | | |

This grave, 4.5m to the south-east of the ditch of barrow 2BA274, was cut into hillwash, sand and tightly packed chalk gravel. It contained the fairly well preserved skeleton of an adult male in a tightly crouched position on the left side with the head to the east and facing south. At the feet a Beaker had been placed in an upright position (Fig 30). A V-perforated jet button was situated at the waist; there were no other grave goods. A thin lens of dense organic staining was noted, both in section and in plan at the eastern end of the grave; it appeared to be both beneath and around the body. This material was quite distinctive and looked as if it had served as some sort of organic wrapping in which the body had been buried. It appeared during excavation to have a coherent structure and was thought to have been derived from the decay of

some sort of basketry; however, the material was unrecoverable and it could eaqually have derived from either an animal pelt or a heavy textile. It appears that this individual died from a severe blow to the chin.

## Skeleton:

Congenital pathologies are those which represent conditions present at birth. The only congenital defect apparent in the material from this cemetery is in the skeleton from this grave, 2BA229, an adult male. This individual has unusually narrow left and right auditory meatus. The auditory ossicles are not present but may have been lost post-mortem. There is no evidence of infection or of tori auditivi. Allowing for soft tissue, it is likely that his hearing would have been severely impaired. As a result he

*Plate 31: vertical photograph of the fully excavated grave 2BA217 prior to lifting of the skeleton and grave goods*

may have had a speech impediment, speech is very dependent upon hearing.

Skeleton 2BA229 also showed evidence of two fractures. The left ulna of this individual has a healed closed fracture approximately mid-haft; no infection was contracted during healing. The radius has not survived. Midshaft lower arm fractures are know as Parry fractures and are considered to be the result of parrying a blow to the head or the body with the arm. The right mandibular condyle has a compression fracture that is consistent with an upward blow striking beneath the right side of the mandible. On the posterior aspect of the mandibular condyle, which survives in good condition, the cortex is fractured revealing the diploe. There is no evidence of healing but the nature of the lesions and condition of the bone clearly suggest that these are not post-mortem in origin. The posterior zone of the mandibular fossa is unusually angulated and the projecting angle fits into another fracture line at the border of the joint surface; again the diploe is exposed and there is no sign of healing, suggesting that this fracture occurred shortly before or at the time of death. It is impossible to determine if this trauma resulted from an awkward fall or from a deliberate blow, although

the latter explanation seems more plausible. If this is correct, when considered in conjunction with the healed Parry fracture, it seems that this male was subject to physical assault on at least two separate occasions. If this man was physically abused, his fractures considered in conjunction with his hearing and almost certain speech defects suggest that his communication disabilities caused him social problems.

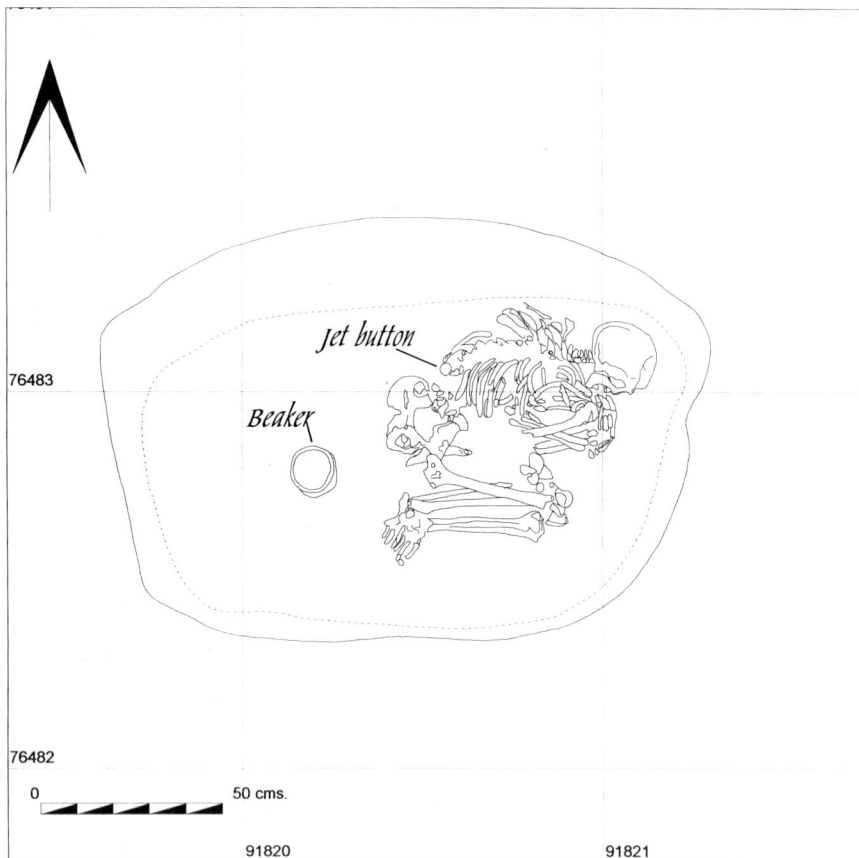

*Figure 30: plan of Grave 2BA217 showing the crouched burial in the eastern half of the grave pit and the still standing Beaker vessel in the centre*

# Grave 2BA544

| | | | |
|---|---|---|---|
| Cut: | 2BA544 | Length: | 2.68 |
| Fills: | 2BA545, 573, 588, 589 | Breadth: | 1.72 |
| Skeleton: | 2BA589 | Depth: | 0.91 |
| Grid ref. | 80481/48230 | Level: | 43.80 |
| Age: | Unknown | | |
| Sex: | Unknown | | |

This large and deep grave cut was situated between the two barrows within the hengiform enclosure. It had contained a tree-trunk coffin with a poorly preserved skeleton. The coffin, which had left a clear stain, in the sand into which the grave had been cut, measured 1.82m x 0.67m with a depth of 0.24m. The burial lay in a supine position, the forearms drawn across the chest, but with the right leg tightly contracted and drawn up to the elbow, and the left leg tightly contracted across the right. The head was to the west and facing south. A Yorkshire Vase Food Vessel had been placed within the coffin just in front of the skull (Fig. 31).

*Plate 32: photograph showing the Food Vessel against the skull in 2BA544*

*Plate 33: vertical photograph of grave 2BA544 before removal of the skeleton and Food Vessel*

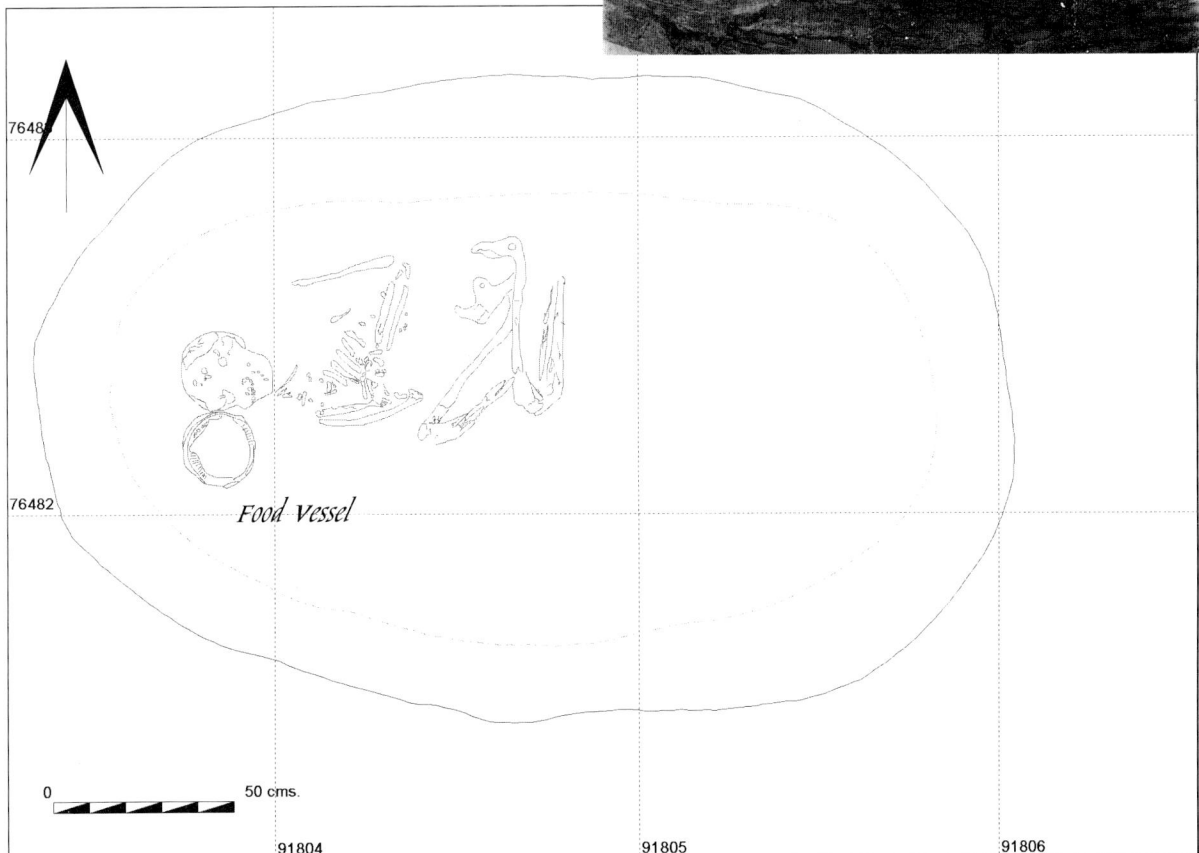

Food Vessel

*Figure 31: plan of Grave 2BA544 showing the burial and Food Vessel*

# Grave 2BB115

| Cut: | 2BB115 | Length: | 1.17 |
|------|--------|---------|------|
| | | Breadth: | 0 .81 |
| Skeleton: | 2BB116 | Depth: | 0.32 |
| Grid ref. | 77545/37386 | Level: | 45.25 |
| Age: | Adult (25-35) | | |
| Sex: | Unknown | | |

Over 150m to the south of the centre of the cemetery an isolated burial was discovered in a grave cut into the eastern bank of the stream channel (Fig 32). The burial, in a crouched position on the right side with the head to the north, was unaccompanied and cannot be dated on either stratigraphic or independent grounds. It seems more likely that it is prehistoric than Anglo-Saxon, given its relatively remote position and the lack of any grave goods. Its discovery in the section of a trial trench designed to sample the stream channel gives no guarantee that it was indeed isolated, as excavation in this area was not pursued further.

### Skeleton:

Very fragmentary remains of an adult skeleton. The cranium set in soil was recovered in a soil-block but proved too fragmentary and fell to pieces when the block was dismantled. There is no sexing information; the three surviving molars have attrition falling in the 25-35 age bracket. The lamboid suture is fusing ectocranially and has fused endocranially.

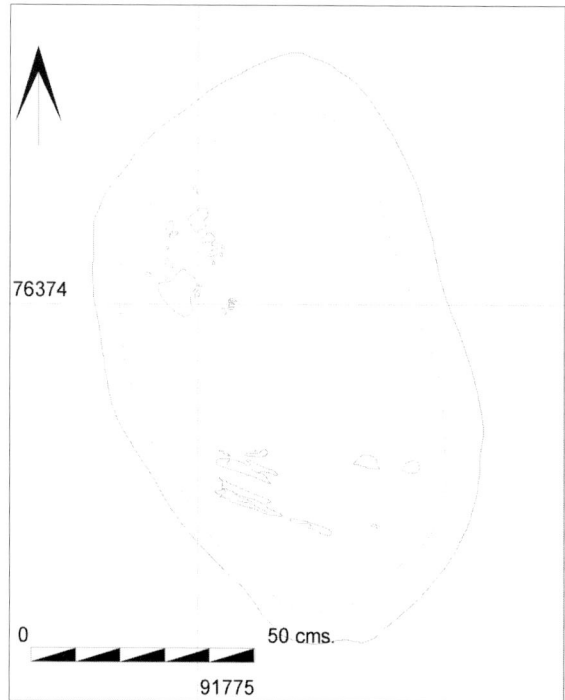

*Figure 32: plan of the undated grave 2BB115*

# Food Vessel Urn Cremation 6AA4

| Cut: | 6AA4 | Length: | 0.36 |
|------|------|---------|------|
| Cremation: | 6AA3 | Breadth: | 0.34 |
| | | Depth: | 0.20 |
| Grid ref. | 85039/48984 | Level: | 44.55 |
| Age: | Child | | |
| Sex: | Unknown | | |

A series of small trenches were opened in the field immediately to the east of area 2BA with a view to gaining further insight into the construction and sequence of the post-circle and to attempt to identify any eastern entrance to the hengiform enclosure. This burial, located some 13m to the east of the hengiform enclosure, where a small pit with vertical sides was identified, comprised a cremation of a young child of indeterminate sex lying beneath an inverted Food Vessel Urn (Plates 34, 35).

*Plate 34: photograph showing the inverted Food Vessel Urn in 6AA4 prior to its removal*

*Plate 35: photograph showing the cremation in 6AA4 after removal of the Food Vessel that covered it*

# Later Prehistoric and Roman activity

Pit alignments are a feature of the later prehistoric landscape of Eastern Yorkshire and a number of other parts of Britain. Examples already excavated on Heslerton, Site 1, include a major boundary established by the Late Bronze Age at the latest and comprising regularly spaced pits as large as 2m square and over 1.5m deep, and a much smaller affair forming what appeared to be a Roman period field boundary, comprising small elongated pits measuring up to 2m in length but no more than 1.5m wide and 0.75m deep (Powlesland *et al* 1986, 129,162).

A pit alignment bisected the Anglian cemetery, respecting the hengiform enclosure and running up to the eastern bank of the stream channel to the south of the cemetery (Fig 33, Plates 36,37). A second alignment followed the line of the stream channel on the opposite bank. Futher segments of the same system were examined in the settlement excavation, over 250m further to the south. In common with boundary features in general, these pit alignments produced little in the way of secure dating evidence. The presence of a few unabraded sherds of Iron Age pottery in the upper fills of these pits indicates an Iron Age date but the quantities of material were very small. The pits in both alignments are very similar in both form and scale to the examples dated to the Roman period, on the basis of association with a Roman trackway on Site 1; in neither case is the dating evidence very secure. Regardless of whether the date of these features is Iron Age or Roman it is likely that they were planting pits for hedges. In contast to the Late Bronze Age alignments which produced large quantites of spoil that formed banks on either side of the pit alignment, as can be seen from upstanding examples identified on the Wolds and the North York Moors, the pits in these alignments were too small to serve as quarry pits for major embanked features. There is no evidence that they served as any form of post pits, and the nature of the filling indicates that they were deliberately backfilled with topsoil, as would be the case if they were planting pits.

Following the establishment of the pit-alignment / hedged boundary, a trackway or path was established to the west of the boundary defined on both sides by shallow ditches or gullies. The date of construction is once again unknown; however, the recovery of a Roman coin in one of the segments examined in John Dent's excavation in area 1HE indicates that the ditches remained open during the Roman period.

*Plate 36: the pit alignment on the western side of the relict stream channel before excavation, looking south*

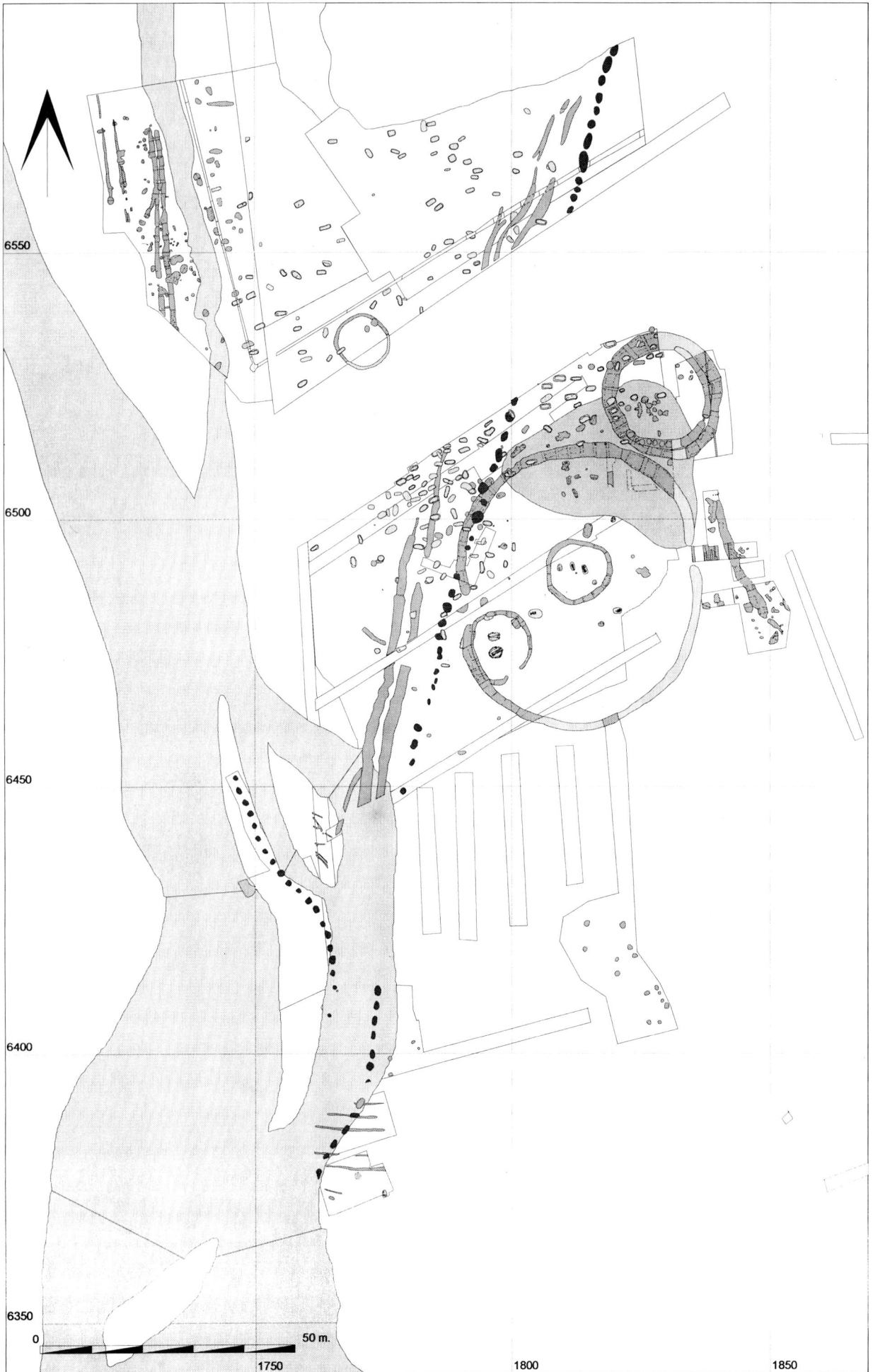

*Figure 33: plan showing the relationship of the later prehistoric pit alignments to the stream channel and earlier monumental features*

*Plate 37: photograph looking south across one of the excavated segments of the later prehistoric pit alignments*

# A relict stream channel

Sample trenches were cut across the stream channel which forms the western boundary of the cemetery. The stream appears from work undertaken on the settlement, to have been redirected down a man-made channel further to the west, during the eleventh century or later.

The many channels up to 2m deep contained deposits with large quantities of animal bone, much of which was both water-worn and partially mineralised. Much of this material may have derived from the Anglian settlement to the south, but both the lithic assemblage and some of the faunal material indicated that these deposits incorpo-

rated material derived from Mesolithic and later prehistoric activity. Clearly the stream channel is of considerable importance in the prehistoric and later landscapes. It served as the western boundary of the Anglian cemetery but its detailed examination was beyond the scope of this excavation. Excavation in the area of the Anglian settlement to the south indicated that the stream had been a focus of prehistoric activity and that it played a major role in the Anglian settlement, perhaps supporting a water mill. A series of shallow gullies following the eastern bank of the stream on site 8AA are likely to have been of prehistoric origin but they are not securely dated.

# The flints

by Ann Clarke

The flint assemblage comprises over 2000 pieces and is detailed by type and area in Table 2. No detailed analysis has been attempted to determine the specific characteristics or distribution of the flakes, blades and debris which comprise the bulk of the assemblage. Instead, this report concentrates on the type and location of the retouched pieces. The 107 retouched pieces include a wide variety of tool types spanning the Mesolithic period through to the Bronze Age (Table 3).

## Mesolithic

Microliths are a common tool from the site and include backed blades, points and scalene triangles; many of the pieces were too fragmented to determine the specific type. They occur mainly in area 2BA, particularly from 2BA500 and BA518 and in Neolithic ditch fills, but are also present from areas 2BB and 8AA, mainly cleaning spits. Other probable Mesolithic tools include an awl from 2BA500 and a series of blades and flakes with specific abrupt retouch along the edges. These retouched blades are much broader than those on which the microliths are produced and they exhibit abrupt retouch or blunting down one side, with occasional notching, or are obliquely retouched on an end. Sometimes it can be seen that this retouch was carried out by chipping the edge of the flint while resting it on an anvil; this is known as enclume work and is generally considered a Mesolithic element. A series of flakes exhibit abrupt retouch around the edge of the piece, which often forms an irregular notched outline.

The blades are most commonly found in BA while the abruptly retouched flakes occur mainly in BB, specifically the stream deposits. There are also a few from 6AA and there is one from 8AA. The scrapers are less well defined in terms of chronology and are dealt with later.

## Neolithic/Bronze Age

One complete leaf point and one fragment from a probable leaf point are present. The former is from a cleaning layer over the barrow in 2BA while the latter is from ditch BA649. Two chisel arrowheads are also present, one from BA666 and the other from 8AA1. Green (1980) notes that chisel arrowheads have a high density in the Yorkshire Wolds and span the period 2500–1500 BC. They are often associated with Grooved Ware, although some are found with early Beaker types, and they are most commonly found in domestic rather than burial contexts.

Three barbed-and-tanged points are present; two are of the Sutton type (Green 1980) from 2BA609 cleaning over

a barrow and 2BB242. One fine burnt Conygar Hill point was recovered from a Bronze Age cremation. Green (1980) notes that the Conygar Hill type points are most frequently associated with cremation burials in Food Vessel graves and are also associated with Collared Urns in the timespan 1650–1200 BC.

Five serrated blades are present, one of which is also tanged. One is from a grave fill 2BA545, also associated with a number of flakes and blades. The rest are from barrow deposits of BA and cleaning layers in 2BB and 8AA.

A probable plano-convex knife was associated with a skeleton 2BA589. This is made on a blade and has been retouched unifacially around the edges but still retains an uncharacteristic hump in profile. One other retouched piece was associated with coffin 2BA437 and this is a primary flake with fine, shallow retouch on two edges.

Two retouched blades were recovered from Anglian graves: one has been retouched bifacially down one side while the other is a larger blade with unilateral shallow retouch.

Scrapers, or those retouched pieces with a steeply formed edge, have been dealt with separately. As a tool they are relatively difficult to define chronologically, particularly when they are from mixed contexts. Four possible thumbnail or horseshoe scrapers are present, one from a Bronze Age ditch, one from an Anglian context and the others from the stream and cleaning layer in 8AA. Other scrapers of a probable Bronze Age date are defined solely by their regular shape, and to some extent their size, and the presence of a faceted platform. These are particularly associated with the Bronze Age ditches and barrows and with cleaning layers in BB. One scraper with a faceted platform comes from an Anglian grave 2BA74. The remaining scrapers may be of any age but there are several associated with the stream deposits of 2BB which may, through association with other material, be regarded as Mesolithic.

Finally a note must be made of a cache of ten flint nodules and fragments from 2BA430. Three are complete nodules and the rest are fragments from the splitting of such nodules. They are similar in character, tabular in form and of a mottled grey flint, and they have a restricted size range of 90–115mm in length. None of these pieces shows any particular form of working and any flakes which may have been detached from the parent nodule are likely to be the result of incidental flaking while the nodule was being split rather than produced as a result of core working.

| Type\Area | 2BA | 2BB | 6AA | 8AA | TOTAL |
|---|---|---|---|---|---|
| Flakes | 870 | 162 | 45 | 141 | 1218 |
| Blades | 352 | 80 | 14 | 87 | 533 |
| Cores | 64 | 21 | 9 | 27 | 121 |
| Chunks | 61 | 30 | 2 | 13 | 106 |
| Retouched | 58 | 31 | 5 | 13 | 107 |
| Total | 1405 | 324 | 75 | 281 | 2085 |

*Table 2: flint types by area*

# Retouched Flints

Abbreviations: ML Maximum length; MW Maximum width; MT Maximum thickness; Th Thickness

## Arrowheads

**2BA227 AB:** Barbed-and-tanged point. Very fine piece with squared barbs and tang. Base of arrowhead slightly convex in plan. Conygar Hill type (Green 1980, 117). ML 39mm; MW 29mm; Th 4mm.

**2BA609 AC:** Barbed-and-tanged point, fragment missing. ML 17mm; MW 17mm; Th 3mm.

**2BA649 AE:** Fragment from probable leaf-shaped arrowhead. Straight-sided with very fine invasive retouch on both faces. Not measured.

**2BA666 CC:** Chisel arrowhead. Bifacially worked down one side and unifacially worked down opposite side. Abrupt retouch along broad 'chisel' end. ML 35mm; MW 25mm; Th 4mm.

**2BA945 BG:** Leaf-shaped point. Invasive retouch bifacially from edges. ML 45mm; MW 20mm; Th 3mm.

**2BB242 AD:** Barbed-and-tanged point. ML 23mm; MW 23mm; Th 3mm.

**8AA1 AP:** Chisel arrowhead. Abrupt opposing bilateral retouch with shallow retouch on 'chisel' end. ML 26mm; MW 29mm; Th 3mm.

## Microliths

**2BA136 AB:** Scalene triangle. ML 12mm; MW 5mm.
**2BA309 AM:** Bilateral backed fragment ?Point.
**2BA309 AU:** Partially backed bladelet. ML 31mm; MW 6mm.
**2BA309 BD:** Backed fragment. 4mm wide.
**2BA500 BN:** Backed fragment. 5mm wide.
**2BA500 CF:** Backed fragment. 4mm wide.
**2BA500 ED:** Backed fragment. 5mm wide.
**2BA518 0X:** Backed fragment. 5mm wide.
**2BA518 1F:** Backed fragment. 7mm wide.
**2BA518 GG:** Point. ML 22mm; MW 3mm.
**2BA518 NS:** Bilateral backed fragment ?Point. 5mm wide.
**2BA518 NZ:** Backed fragment. 5mm wide.
**2BA518 TH:** Backed fragment. 5mm wide.
**2BA518 TR:** Backed blade. ML 17mm; MW 4mm.
**2BA518 XL:** Scalene triangle. ML 12mm; MW 4mm.
**2BA597 AC:** Backed fragment. 3mm wide.
**2BA598 AW:** Point. ML 12mm; MW 3mm.
**2BB68 DL:** Backed blade. ML 20mm; MW 5mm.
**2BB197 AD:** Fine point. ML 24mm; MW 3mm.
**2BB226 AS:** Backed fragment. 7mm wide.
**2BA226 AW:** Backed fragment. 5mm wide.
**8AA1 FW:** Scalene triangle. ML 18mm; MW 5mm.
**8AA155 AA:** Point fragment. 3mm wide.

| Type\Area | 2BA | 2BB | 8AA | 6AA | TOTAL |
|---|---|---|---|---|---|
| Barbed-and-tanged point | 2 | 1 | | | 3 |
| Leaf point | 2 | | | | 2 |
| Chisel arrowhead | 1 | | 1 | | 2 |
| Microliths | 17 | 4 | 2 | | 23 |
| Serrated blades | 3 | 2 | | | 5 |
| Tanged blade | 1 | | | | 1 |
| ?Plano-convex knife | 1 | | | | 1 |
| Scrapers | 17 | 14 | 3 | 1 | 35 |
| Awl | 1 | | | | 1 |
| Obliquely retouched blades | 3 | 2 | | | 5 |
| Large backed blades | 5 | 2 | | | 7 |
| Edge retouched | 6 | 9 (8) | 3 (1) | 4 (3) | 22 (12) |
| Total | 58 | 31 | 13 | 5 | 107 |

*Table 3: retouched flint by type and area*
*Numbers in brackets refer to those edge retouched flints with abrupt retouch.*

## Scrapers

**2BA2 DH:** End scraper. Blade. ML 28mm; MW 19mm; MT 6mm.

**G87 AC:** Horseshoe type scraper. Flake. ML 26mm; MW 30mm; MT 9mm.

**2BA74 AQ:** End and side scraper. Flake/ blade. Faceted platform. ML 32mm; MW 21mm; MT 7mm.

**2BA108 AL:** End scraper. Flake. ML 26mm; MW 33mm; MT 6mm.

**2BA173 AG:** End scraper. Thick primary flake. ML 42mm; MW 36mm; MT 12mm.

**2BA173 AU:** End and side scraper. Large blade. ML 70mm; MW 28mm; MT 12mm.

**2BA176 AA:** End scraper. Flake/ blade. ML 35mm; MW 32mm; MT 6mm.

**2BA279 AB:** Horseshoe type. Flake/ blade. Faceted platform. ML 25mm; MW 23mm; MT 8mm.

**2BA353 AA:** Side scraper. Flake. Fragment.

**2BA486 AM:** End scraper. Flake/ blade. Faceted platform. ML 33mm; MW 25mm; MT 8mm.

**2BA507 AA:** Fragment of probable scraper made on a flake.

**2BA518 VA:** End scraper. Stubby flake/ blade. ML 22mm; MW 23mm; MT 12mm.

**2BA573 AO:** Scraper edge down both sides. Flake/ blade. Fragment.

**2BA743 AF:** End scraper. Flake. Fragment.

**2BA783 AC:** End scraper. Flake/ blade. ML 23mm; MW 23mm; MT 11mm.

**2BA783 AH:** End scraper. Flake/ blade. Utilised on all other edges. Faceted platform. ML 60mm; MW 35mm; MT 8mm.

**2BA993 AE:** Side scraper. Thick secondary flake. ML 41mm; MW 32mm; MT 13mm.

**2BA1066 AB:** End scraper. Primary flake. Very nice. ML 37mm; MW 40mm; MT 10mm.

**2BB22 AB:** Scraper edge down both sides. Flake. ML 33mm; MW 27mm; MT 5mm.

**2BB63 AC:** Concave scraper edge on side. Stubby blade. Fragment.

**2BB67 AX:** Side scraper. Blade. Fragment.

**2BB68 AB:** End and sides scraper. Blade. Faceted platform. ML 37mm; MW 26mm; MT 8mm. **2BB68 AS:** End scraper. Primary blade. Utilised down one side forming notch. ML 45mm; MW 22mm; MT 6mm.

**2BB94 AA:** End scraper. Flake/ blade. Utilised down one edge. Faceted platform. ML 47mm; MW 30mm; MT 7mm.

**2BB122 BS:** Thumbnail scraper. Flake/ blade. ML 24mm; MW 22mm; MT 6mm.

**2BB125 AB:** End and side scraper. Flake. ML 30mm; MW 21mm; MT 5mm.

**2BB132 AM:** End and side scraper. Flake. ML 25mm; MW 19mm; MT 5mm.

**2BB136 AA:** End scraper. Flake. ML 30mm; MW 25mm; MT 8mm.

**2BB226 AH:** Thumbnail type. Flake/ blade. ML 20mm; MW 20mm; MT 5mm.

**2BB254 AA:** End scraper. Flake/ blade. Utilised on other edges. Faceted platform. ML 51mm; MW 36mm; MT 6mm.

**2BA254 AN:** End scraper. Blade. Utilised down sides forming notches. ML 43mm; MW 25mm; MT 9mm.

**2BB340 AC:** Concave scraper edge on side. Secondary flake. ML 34mm; MW 32mm; MT 13mm.

**6AA86 (23105):** End scraper. Chunky flake. ML 52mm; MW 32mm; MT 16mm.

**8AA115 BE:** Horseshoe type. Flake. ML 17mm; MW 25mm; MT 7mm.

**8AA278 AB:** End scraper. Blade. Utilised on one side. ML 45mm; MW 26mm; MT 6mm.

**8AA323 AA:** End scraper. Flake/ blade. ML 26mm; MW 19mm; MT 7mm.

## Retouched blades

**2BA225 AB:** Obliquely blunted. Enclume. Possible edge damage. ML 53mm; MW 15mm; MT 5mm. **2BA303 AA:** Blunted down one side. Enclume. ML 35mm; MW 8mm; MT 4mm.

**2BA500 EN:** Retouched on end to isolate a point. Probable awl. ML 32mm; MW 21mm; MT 4mm.

**2BA500 IF:** Blunted down one side. Edge damage. Fragment. MW 11mm.

**2BA518 YL:** Blunted down side. Enclume. ML 33mm; MW 9mm; MT 4mm.

**2BA591 AN:** Oblique retouch. ML 44mm; MW 25mm; MT 6mm.

**2BA626 AC:** Partial concave end worked. ML 25mm; MW 15mm; MT 2mm.

**2BA636 AA:** Abrupt retouch on end and side. ML 33mm; MW 16mm; MT 5mm.

**2BA1072 AC:** Obliquely blunted. ML 44mm; MW 15mm; MT 5mm.

**2BB39 AM:** Obliquely blunted. ML 36mm; MW 14mm; MT 5mm.

**2BB68 CL:** ?Obliquely blunted. ML 32mm; MW 13mm; MT 3mm.

**6AA2 (19058):** Abrupt retouch to form concave edge/ notch. ML 28mm; MW 10mm; MT 3mm.

**8AA115 AY:** Partial blunting of one side. ML 36mm; MW 9mm; MT 3mm.

**8AA140 AM:** Blunting down one side. ML 40mm; MW 10mm; MT 4mm.

## Miscellaneous edge retouched

**G198 AB:** Miscellaneous bifacial retouch down one side of a blade. ML 32mm; MW 17mm; MT 10mm.

**2BA50 AM:** Fragment with steep retouch.

**2BA241 AR:** Shallow retouch down one side of a large blade. ?Knife. ML 75mm; MW 24mm; MT 7mm.

**2BA437 AD:** Fine shallow retouch down one edge and part of another. Primary flake. ML 38mm; MW 39mm; MT 7mm.

**2BA518 NB:** Fragment with denticulate outline.

**2BB61 AA:** Abrupt retouch on sides and end of flake fragment.

**2BB68 AG:** Abrupt retouch on ends of flake. ML 17mm; MW 26mm; MT 5mm.

**2BB107 AC:** Abrupt retouch on side of blade forming concave edge. ML 32mm; MW 16mm; MT 3mm.

**2BB119 AH:** Abrupt retouch round edges of flake forming concave edges. ML 19mm; MW 16mm; MT 3mm.

**2BB133 AB:** Abrupt retouch on end of flake. ML 19mm; MW 27mm; MT 6mm.

**2BB247 AA:** Abrupt retouch on side of blade forming concave edge. ML 26mm; MW 20mm; MT 7mm.

**2BB283 AC:** Nibbling retouch on end and sides of blade. ML 39mm; MW 22mm; MT 9mm.

**2BB317 AA:** Abrupt retouch on ends and sides of flake forming concave edges. ML 22mm; MW 16mm; MT 4mm.

**2BB317 AD:** Abrupt retouch on end and side of secondary flake. ML 25mm; MW 31mm; MT 9mm.

**6AA2 (20160):** Abrupt retouch on part of a blade/ flake. ML 29mm; MW 14mm; MT 5mm.

**6AA2 (21008):** Abrupt retouch on side of flake fragment.

**6AA75 (18092):** Abrupt retouch around flake edge. ML 24mm; MW 31mm; MT 8mm.

**8AA1 GI:** Abrupt retouch around most of flake edge. ML 31mm; MW 24mm; MT 5mm.

**8AA140 AA:** Shallow retouch on end of flake. ML 17mm; MW 28mm; MT 3mm.

**8AA221 CR:** Shallow flaking down one side of primary flake. ML 44mm; MW 27mm; MT 9mm.

## Miscellaneous

**2BA545 AX:** Blade, serrated down one side. ML 68mm; MW 24mm; MT 11mm.

**2BA589 AL:** ?plano-convex knife. Blade retouched from the edges although quite humped in profile. ML 65mm; MW 25mm; MT 9mm.

**2BA993 AY:** Fragment with cortex. Possibly serrated down one side.

**2BA1070 BK:** Blade, serrated down both sides. ML 41mm; MW 15mm; MT 5mm.

**2BB226 AO:** Tanged blade. Long, pointed blade with possible serrations down one side and utilised on opposite edge. ML 65mm; MW 26mm; MT 18mm.

**8AA1 BD:** Fine blade serrated down both sides. ML 65mm; MW 18mm; MT 5mm.

**8AA1 GJ:** Blade, serrated down one side. ML 48mm; MW 14mm; MT 7mm.

# The prehistoric pottery

by Terry Manby

## Catalogue of accessory vessels

**1HE18DW**: Beaker Clarke N3      Lanting and van der Waals Step 5 **(Fig 34)**
Height: 180 mm; Rim diameter: 120 mm; Base diameter: 75 mm

Complete profile, large piece cut away from one side of the vessel. Short funnel neck, ovoid body above simple foot, slightly hollow base. Hard smooth reddish orange exterior, orange brown interior, dark grey core; crushed dolerite temper >8mm long. Decorated with coarse comb impressions (4 teeth to 10 mm), bands of short vertical between horizontal lines. Plain band between neck and body decoration that is topped by a fringe of diagonal lines. Illustrated and discussed in Powlesland *et al* 1986, Fig 44.

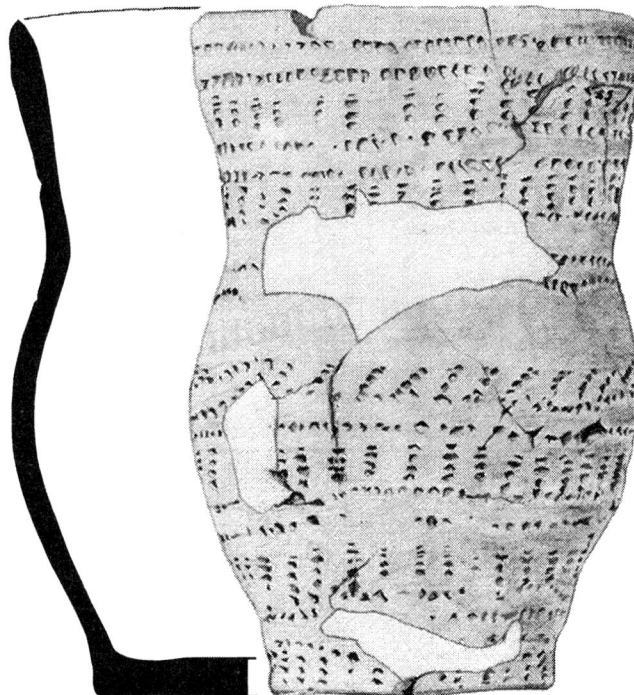

**1HE18DW   1:2**

*Figure 34: Beaker 1HE18DW*

**2BA229AQ 1:2**

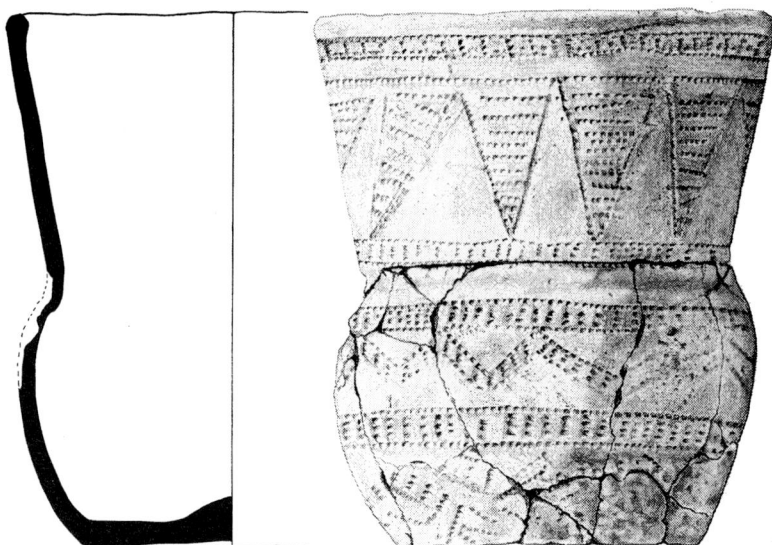

*Figure 35:Beaker 2BA228BQ*

**2BA229AQ**: Beaker       Clarke S1 (W)
Lanting and van der Waals Step 5 **(Fig 35)**
Height: 143 mm; Rim diameter: 125 mm; Base diameter: 80 mm.

Complete vessel; marked shoulder high on the body, funnel neck with rounded, slightly expanded rim. Concave base with internal boss. Hard compact orange-buff fabric with orange patches; light grey core. Surface pitted from the solution of the temper, especially internally towards the bottom. Small chalk and calcite tempering. Decorated with large square comb impressions (5 teeth to 10 mm). Bands of short vertical lines between single horizontal lines divide the metopes; infilled pendant triangles on the neck and on the body; two filled bar-chevrons with diagonal hatched triangles around the base.

**2BA227AI**: Food Vessel   Type 1a (iii) **(Fig 36)**
Height: 96 mm; Rim diameter: 120 mm; Base diameter: 62 mm.

Slack profile, internal bevel to weak rim, wide shallow shoulder groove spanned by five low lugs, equally spaced (unperforated). Compact smooth buff surfaces, orange toned, grey core. Grog and stone tempering - white flint, chalk and ironstone. All-over decoration of short vertical incised strokes in rows; also on the rim bevel arranged radially until varying to the diagonal.

**2BA241AT**: Food Vessel   Type 4 **(Fig 37)**
Height: 125 mm; Rim diameter: 145 mm; Base diameter: 80 mm.

Internal rim bevel, globular body on plain base. Compact orange-buff fabric, light grey tones, dark grey core. Scattered temper of large angular fragments 10 mm long – flint, chalk and ironstone fragments. All-over decoration of thick cord impressions, closely spaced overlapping rows of horizontal and diagonal lines, distinct in places bur overlapping and obscured over most of the exterior. The rim bevel has rows of short diagonal impressions.

**2BA227AI 1:2**

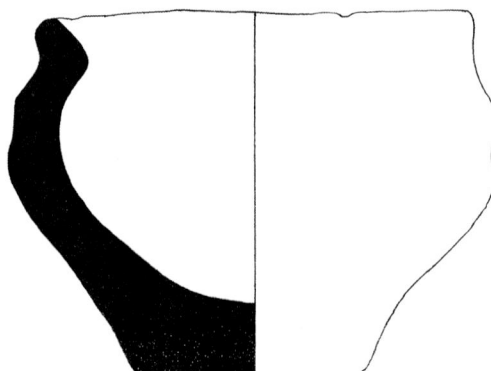

*Figure 36:Food Vessel 2BA227AI*

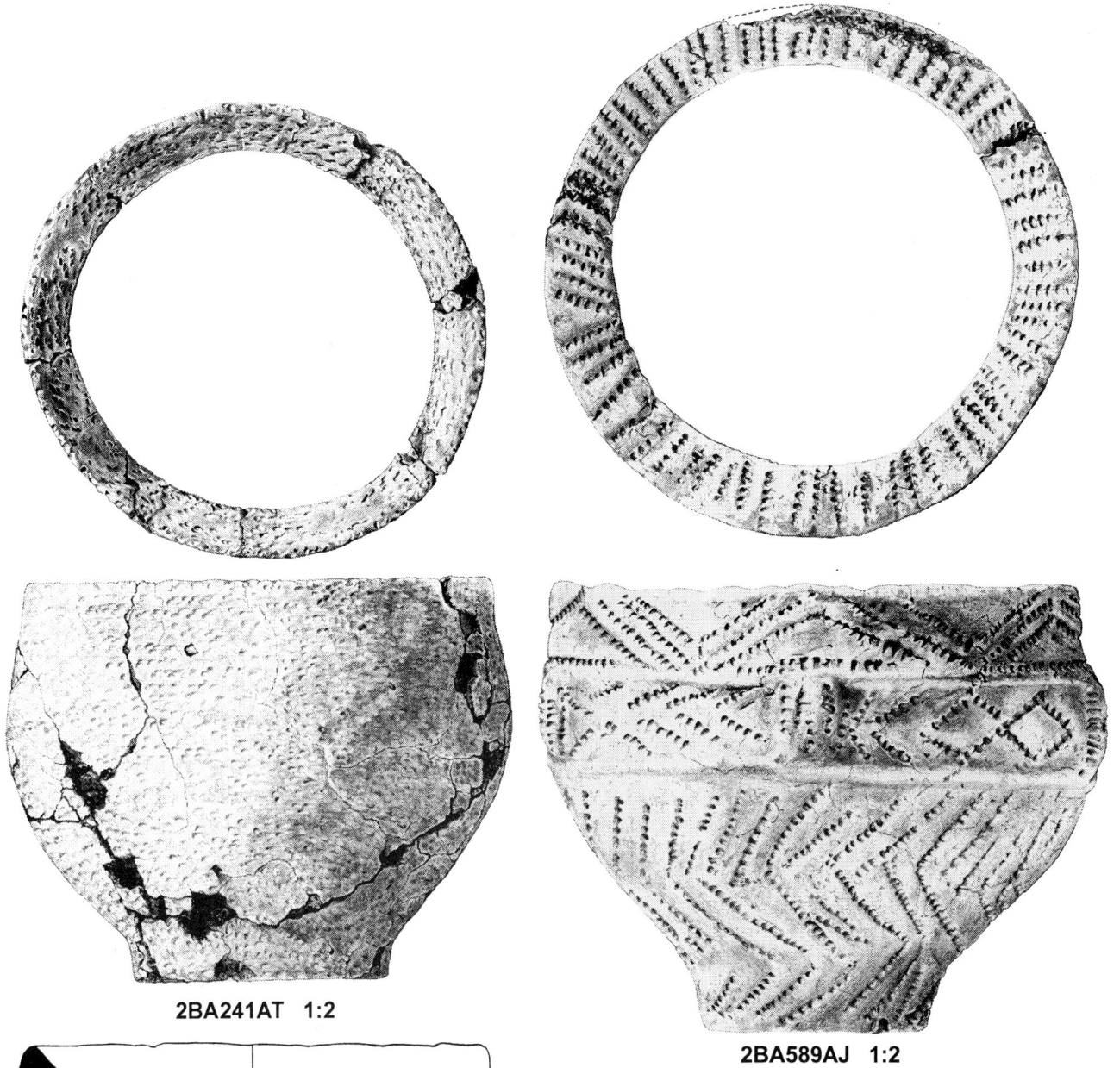

**2BA241AT 1:2**

**2BA589AJ 1:2**

*Figure 37:Food Vessel 2BA241AT*

*Figure 38:Food Vessel 2BA589AJ*

**2BA589AJ**: Food Vessel    Type 1a (iii) **(Fig. 38)**
Height: 138 mm; Rim diameter: 168 mm; Base diameter: 73 mm.

Broad internal rim bevel, shallow neck, broad shallow grooved spanned by five strip lugs, equally spaced and unperforated. Hollow base. Orange fabric, dark grey core; profuse temper erupting through the surfaces; pieces of dolerite >8mm long and some flint >10 mm long. All-over decoration made by thick whipped cord (5 turns per cm) impressions. Widely spaced herringbone pattern over the exterior. Radial lines on the rim bevel.

**2BA283AP**: Food Vessel    Type 3 (ii) **(Fig. 39)**
Height: 118 mm; Rim diameter: 150 mm; Base diameter: 80 mm.

Internal rim bevel, shallow neck profile down to rounded shoulder, simple base. Compact orange-brown fabric, grey core, light brown interior. Fine quartz sand temper. All-over decoration of closely spaced herringbone pattern in horizontal rows, impressed with a finely whipped cord (c15 turns per cm).

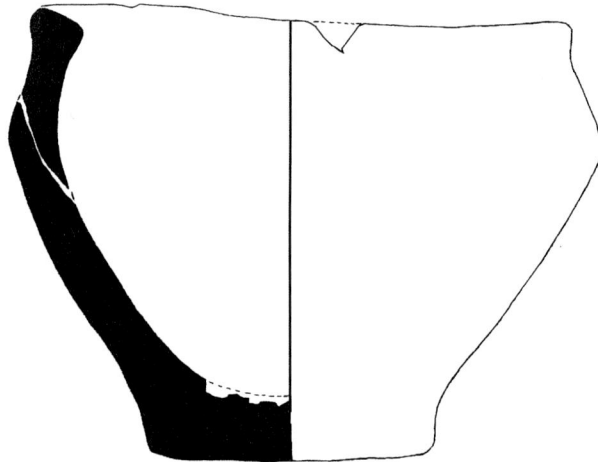

**2BA283AP   1:2**

**6AA3AA**: Food Vessel    Type 2 (iii) **(Fig. 40)**
Height: 203 mm; Rim diameter: 195 mm; Base diameter: 95 mm.

Weak internal rim bevel, soft profile with rounded ribs, shallow neck and shoulder groove, moulded foot, slightly concave base. Orange-buff fabric with some greyish toning, grey interior. Decorated with casual rows of short maggot impressions each made up of three or four turns of a thick twisted cord. Decoration over the rim bevel and down the exterior, dying out halfway down the body.

*Figure 39:Food Vessel 2BA283AP*

| Step | Beaker Class | Number | Reference (Powlesland *et al* 1986) | Association |
|------|------|------|------|------|
| 1/2 | A O C | 2BA 1002A B-A C | | Scattered Sherds |
| 3 | E-N/N R | 1S777A A | 1986, fig 42 | Grave |
| 4 | N 3 | 1HE18D W | 1986, fig 44 | Grave |
| 5 | S 1 (W) | 2BA 229A Q | this vol. Fig 35 | Grave |
| 4 | N/N R | 1R302A C | 1986, fig 32 | Grave |
| 6 | S 2 (E) | 1M 345A A | 1986, fig 27 | Grave |
| 7 | S 4 | 1L20A A –BB | 1986, fig 19 | Grave |

**Table 4:** *the Beaker series by class*

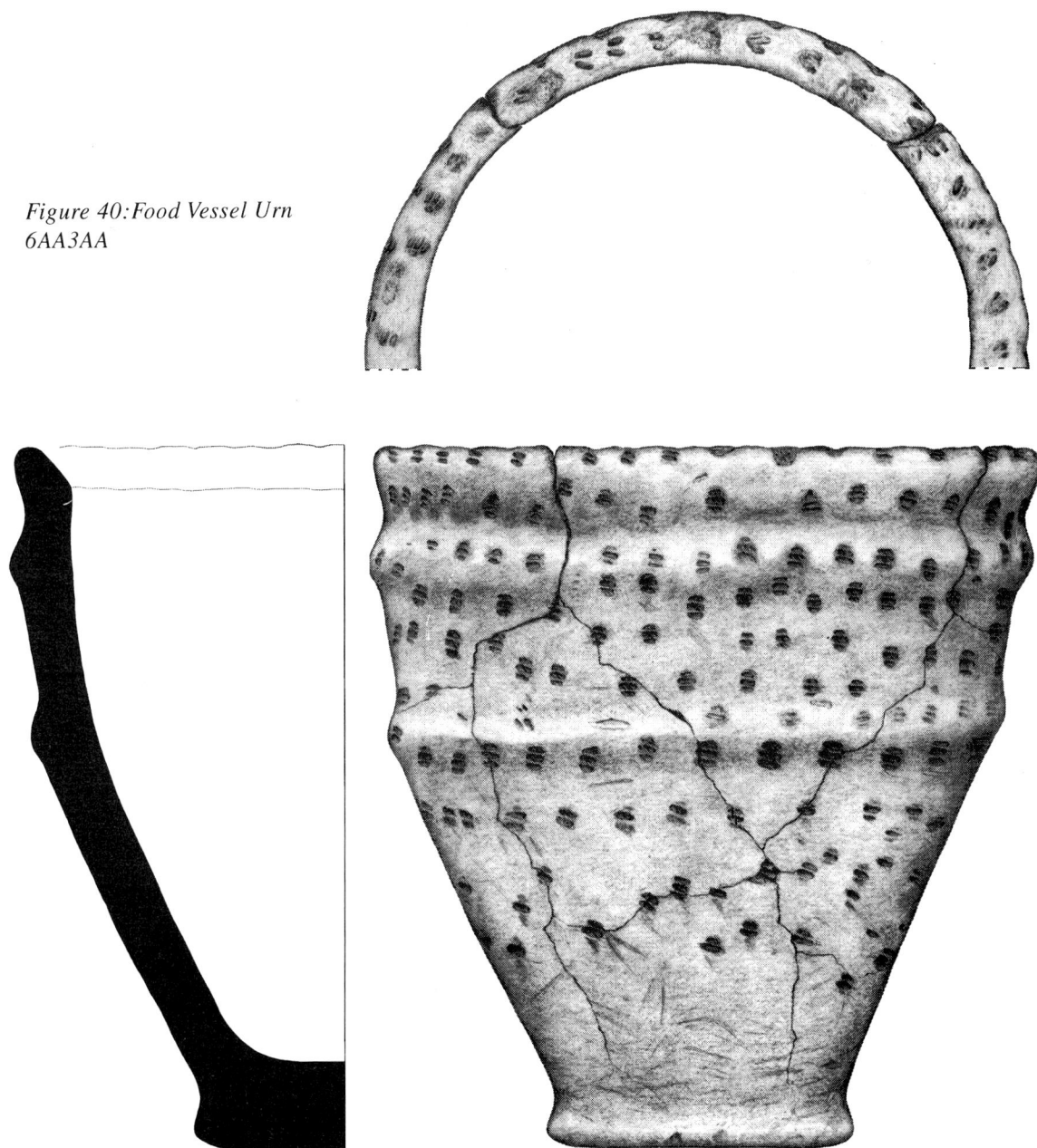

*Figure 40:Food Vessel Urn 6AA3AA*

**6AA3AA 1:2**

# Commentary on the accessory vessels

## Beakers

The Beaker finds from the sandy zone along the foot of the northern Wold escarpment were the subject of the report on the Site 1 excavations (Powlesland *et al* 1986). However, one Beaker, 1HE18DW, illustrated in that report (*ibid*, 113, fig 44), was not described or included in the discussion. This Beaker, of Clarke's N3 class, along with the most recent finds, serves to consolidate the range of vessel types at Heslerton (Table 4). They now represent the full span of regional Beaker development

(Lanting and van der Waals 1972, 39–40), apart from the earliest Step 1/2. Alternatively, only the Middle and Late Beaker styles of Case's Beaker classification are present here in burial associations (Case 1977), the Late style appearing at the end of the third millennium BC with the advent of Step 5 Beakers.

In terms of fabric, profile, decorative technique and motifs, the Heslerton Beakers have parallels within the eastern Yorkshire region, especially those of the Northern and Southern British Beaker Groups (Clarke 1970, 153–245). The chronological range of Middle and Late style Beakers by stratigraphy and associations extends across the transition from the Late Neolithic into the mature Early Bronze Age. In regional terms Step 3 and 4 Beakers are well placed in Late Neolithic 2, *c* 2750–2000BC (Manby 1988, 62–4), equating nationally with Burgess's

Mount Pleasant Phase (Burgess 1980, 37–78). Continuing development during the Early Bronze Age had Beakers of Step 5 and 6 as a major element of the Fargo Phase, c 2000–1800BC (Burgess 1986, 350–1). Regionally, the Earlier Bronze Age phasing requires further refinement utilising the later twentieth-century excavation evidence relative to the Food Vessel series that are the dominant contemporary ceramic type in eastern Yorkshire barrow associations.

# Food Vessels

The national and regional background of Early Bronze Age Food Vessel types was reviewed in the previous Heslerton excavation report (Powlesland *et al* 1986, 120–3). Eastern Yorkshire provides the greatest concentration of Food Vessels in the British Isles, almost exclusively in burial associations. Like the previously reported Heslerton vessels, the present finds are a significant addition to the regional corpus of Food Vessels, and each displays aspects of shape and decoration that are characteristic of the regional series (Pierpoint 1980, 63–123).

Previous studies at a regional level have recognised that linkages can be established between shapes, fabric and particular decorative characteristics that can be sufficiently alike to suggest they are the work of individual potters. Such comparisons are possible for pottery variously deposited in adjacent graves and/or neighbouring barrows, from localities up to 10km apart, and even more distant (*ibid*, 119–29). Such linkages are significant for their implied chronological and geographical connections. However, the materials used as temper in the potting clay, flint, chalk, sand and crushed dolerite, support an entirely local manufacture of all the present group of Heslerton Early Bronze Age pottery.

**2BA227AI: (Fig 36)** A well modelled vessel of Type 1a(iii) with five low lugs in the shoulder groove. Single motif decoration of short vertical strokes in horizontal rows all over the exterior and the rim bevel. Among Type 1a Food Vessels the great majority have four equally spaced lugs in the shoulder groove, but up to 16 equally spaced lugs can occur among the multi-lugged variants that occur in eastern Yorkshire, Lincolnshire, Northumberland and the Peak District. Of these, the five-lugged variant is the most common in eastern Yorkshire, known from 14 sites on the Wolds and North York Moors; the two from West Heslerton are a local concentration comparable with the three examples from Riggs Barrows 36 and 41 (Mortimer 1905, 173, 181; figs 434, 436, 456).

**2BA241AT: (Fig 37)** A finely modelled globular vessel of Type 4. Notable for the intensive decoration of unusual character applied to the exterior and the bevel. Globular forms of Food Vessel are an uncommon type that is scarce in eastern Yorkshire; there are comparable simple bevelled rimmed vessels from the Wold area. A pot from

Goodmanham 111 has all-over herringbone decoration by whipped cord (Kinnes and Longworth 1985, 86). Versions with additional features and elaborate all-over cord decoration are a small pot with boss lugs from Acklam 205 (Mortimer 1905, 87, fig 201) and the North Newbold bowl with perforated lugs and a cruciform foot (Manby 1969, 281, fig 3.5). From central Yorkshire, Ainderby Quern Howe had a plain-bodied globular Food Vessel accompanying one of the primary cremations (Waterman 1951, fig 7.1).

Some globular Food Vessels have deep heavy rims, like that from Sherburn, a barrow on the Wold 6km southeast of West Heslerton, which has all-over decoration by a coarse horizontal cord (Kinnes and Longworth 1985, 35). More distant finds are elaborately decorated vessels from sites along the coast of Northumberland (Gibson 1978, Nos 70, 72, 73 and 77). South of the Humber at Crosby Warren, the cord decoration is confined to the upper third of the vessel (May 1976, 83, fig 46.2). Some globular forms are present amongst the Food Vessels of the Peak District (Manby 1957, 9); they are also proportionately more numerous among the widely dispersed Welsh Food Vessel series (Savory 1957, 205–7) where they are grouped as 'Irish-influenced'.

**2BA589AJ: (Fig 38)** This is a large vessel of Type 1a and is notable for the five equally spaced lugs of ribbon-like character and the use of comb for all-over herringbone decoration. Comb imprinting like the running vertical bar-chevron on the neck was only rarely employed in the eastern Yorkshire Food Vessel group. This is an S-Beaker derived motif that is also present on the Type 2 Food Vessel from Heslerton Barrow L (Powlesland *et al* 1986, 123, fig 18), where comb imprinting is combined with false-relief impression. In general shape, fabric, the use of comb imprinting and motifs, these two vessels show particular close affinities. The bar-chevron motif was used on the S1-Beaker 2BA229AQ, and on Beakers of Steps 5 and 6 (Lanting and van der Waals 1972, fig 3), and its adaptation to Food Vessels is a useful indicator of contemporary dating.

**2BA283AP: (Fig 39)** A well modelled vessel of Type 3 with a shallow neck, all-over decoration in well executed whipped cord impressions including horizontal herringbone pattern. Its characteristics are typical of the Yorkshire Food Vessel series; in profile, and the use of whipped cord and herringbone motifs, it is immediately comparable with a Food Vessel from nearby Barrow 1L (Powlesland *et al* 1986, 83 and 123; fig 19).

**6AA3AA: (Fig 40)** This vessel is notable both for its inversion over a cremation and for being the largest of the Food Vessels of the Heslerton barrow cemetery. When measured in terms of height/rim diameter, an analysis of eastern Yorkshire Type 2 Food Vessels, or the tripartite form, shows the size grouping concentrated between 100/110mm to 180/180mm. A rim diameter greater than the height is characteristic of the Yorkshire Food Vessel series. Vessels in excess of 180/180mm fall within the lower end of the size range of the Food Vessel Urns series (Cowie 1978, 20–4, fig 2) characterised by height in excess of rim diameter. However, within the regional series there are grounds for seeing vessels of the c200/200mm cluster as intermediate between accessory Food Vessels and Enlarged Food Vessel Urns; the majority of the latter are also of the Type 2 profile.

The Heslerton vessel can be linked in profile to vessels serving an accessory function with inhumation burials from two nearby barrows on the Wolds. The first, which also has cord maggot decoration above the shoulder, is from Sherburn Barrow 13 (Greenwell 1877, 154; Kinnes and Longworth 1985, 35, Burial 3). It has incised decoration on the body; this in turn serves as a link with a vessel even closer in profile to the Heslerton vessel from Ganton Barrow 17 (Greenwell & Rolleston 1877, 157; Kinnes and Longworth 1985). Both of these vessels are slightly smaller than the Heslerton vessel, and fall at the very top of the main Food Vessel size range. The above barrows belonged to the Potter Brompton Wold barrow group (centring on SE976/754) at 5.6km east of the Heslerton site. All three are so alike in their features and distribution as to be the productions of the same potter.

The other vessels of the 200/200mm size cluster were also used in accessory function with inhumations on the Wolds at Kilham and at Sharp Howe, Folkton (Kinnes and Longworth 1985, 111, Burials 11 and 12, Burial 2). The associations of the fourth vessel from Warter are unknown (Cowie 1978, 102). However, the fifth is a multi-ridged type (Type 2a) that accompanied a cremation at Ampleforth (unpublished, Yorkshire Museum), on the Hambleton Hills of the North Yorkshire Moors. Across eastern Yorkshire Food Vessels have an accessory role both with inhumation graves and with the minority rite cremation burials (Manby 1980, 316). The inversion of vessels over cremation deposits is the usual role for Enlarged Food Vessel Urns and Early Series Collared Urns in eastern Yorkshire. The employment of Food Vessels in this role in Wold barrows is rare but occurred at Garton Slack Sites 7 and 8 (Brewster 1980, 219, 249, 276). Inversion of the Food Vessel over a cremation occurred at the North York Moor sites of Brotton Warsett (Hornsby and Stanton 1917, 236) and Hinderwell Beacon (Hornsby and Laverick 1920, 446) both on the Cleveland coast, and at Ampleforth, Pye Rigg Barrow 4 (unpublished excavations by G F Wilmott) on the Hambleton Hills. The Brotton and Hinderwell vessels would allow for their being late in the period of Food Vessel usage. It is thus likely that they belong to a period when the older inhumation practice was being replaced in the region by the cremation rite with its associated Collared Urn. The change from serving as an accompanying vessel to the function of covering the burial de-

posit represents a major realignment of the cultural purpose of Food Vessels, a change that is further reflected in the increasing size of vessels and continued by the change in height/width ratio of the Enlarged Food Vessel Urns.

# Catalogue of other prehistoric ceramics

## GENERAL ASPECTS

The pottery is generally small, suffering solution of the tempering agents by deep surface weathering. Only a limited number of sherds can be joined; the only group of large sherds where extensive reconstruction was possible is a series of Fengate style bowls and cups. The ceramic traditions present are:

**Peterborough Ware:** The majority of sherds are of vessels in the Peterborough Ware styles. These divide as small sherds of Mortlake and early Rudston style bowls widely distributed across the site; in contrast, the Fengate style assemblage comes from a limited number of contexts.

**Grooved Ware:** Two vessels represented by sherds belonging to bucket-shaped vessels of the Durrington Walls style.

**Beaker:** Represented only by two sherds of AOC Beaker.

**Later Bronze Age:** The second commonest group of sherds are of Late Bronze Age type, some with finger-tip decoration. The sherds are generally small in size and weathered; only rarely does any calcite or chalk tempering survive undissolved.

## Site 2BA

**2BA2AE:** Late Bronze Age (LBA) rim, pinched-up lip, internal bevel. Very hard, buff exterior, grey interior, profuse flint temper >5mm. Wall thickness 7mm. **(Fig 43)**

**2BA2AJ:** Large LBA body sherd, same as 2BA2AE above, with finger-tip wiping.

**2BA2CL:** Weathered LBA sherd. Buff exterior, grey interior, pitted, ?calcite/chalk. Wall thickness 11mm.

**2BA2DS:** Weathered LBA sherd. Brown, dark toned interior, pitted to an open texture, calcite/chalk >9mm.

**2BA5AC:** Sherd. Buff, reddish core and interior, sand and erratic temper (dolerite) pebble.

**2BA24AK:** Weathered sherd. Laminated, dark grey, brown exterior, scattered flint >6mm. Interior scaled off.

**2BA24AN:** Weathered flake. Reddish exterior, dark grey core, interior flaked off, laminated, sand temper. Stick or bone end imprints.

**2BA40AE:** Rim, Peterborough Ware; simple externally bevelled lip. Dark grey, orange coated surfaces. Transverse fingernail imprints on the lip. Wall thickness 8mm.

**2BA42AN:** Small weathered sherd, rolled and pitted.

**2BA50AX:** Weathered fragment, ?LBA. Brown exterior, dark grey interior, pitted; ? organic temper.

**2BA50BJ:** Shoulder or base angle; LBA. Compact buff exterior, dark grey interior, sand temper. Wall thickness 8mm.

# Peterborough

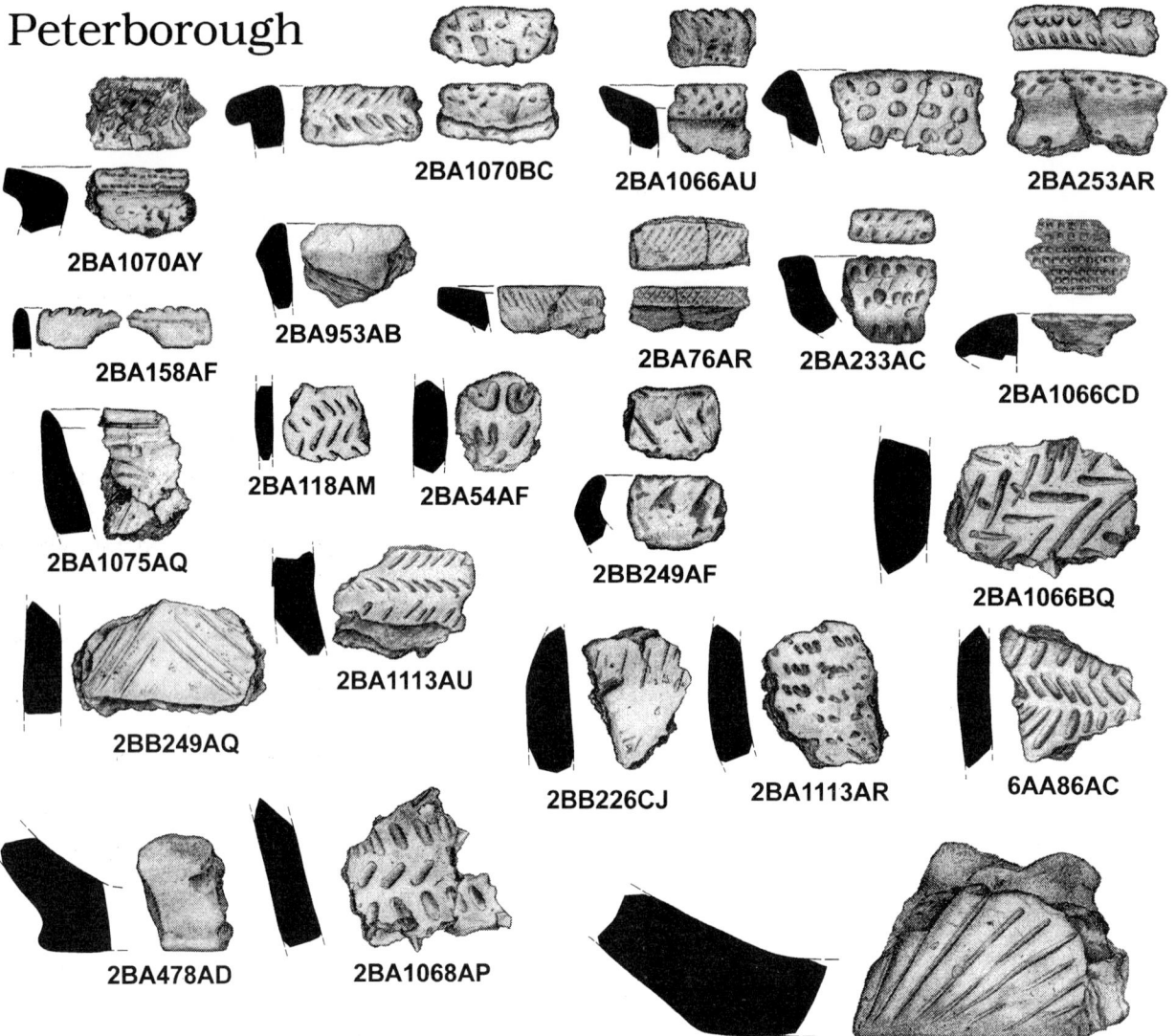

2BA1070BC  2BA1066AU  2BA253AR
2BA1070AY
2BA953AB
2BA158AF  2BA76AR  2BA233AC
2BA1066CD
2BA118AM  2BA54AF
2BA1075AQ  2BB249AF
2BA1066BQ
2BA1113AU
2BB249AQ  2BB226CJ  2BA1113AR  6AA86AC
2BA478AD  2BA1068AP
2BA1072AH

# Rudston

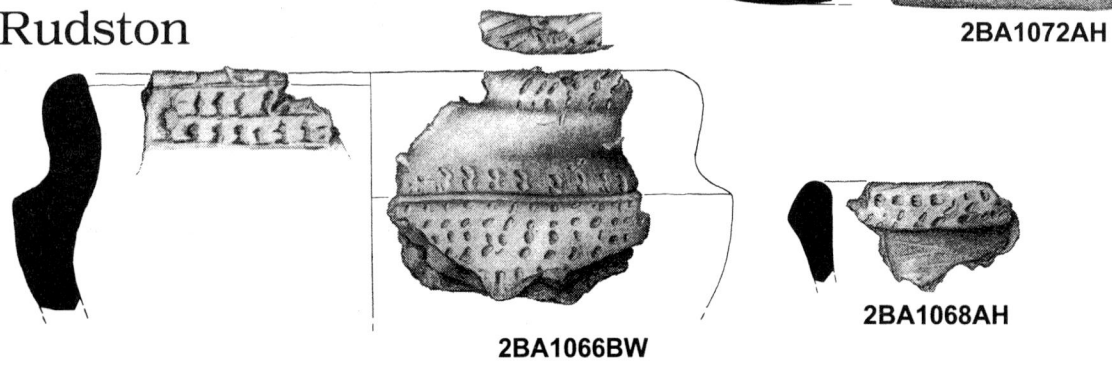

2BA1066BW  2BA1068AH

# Mortlake

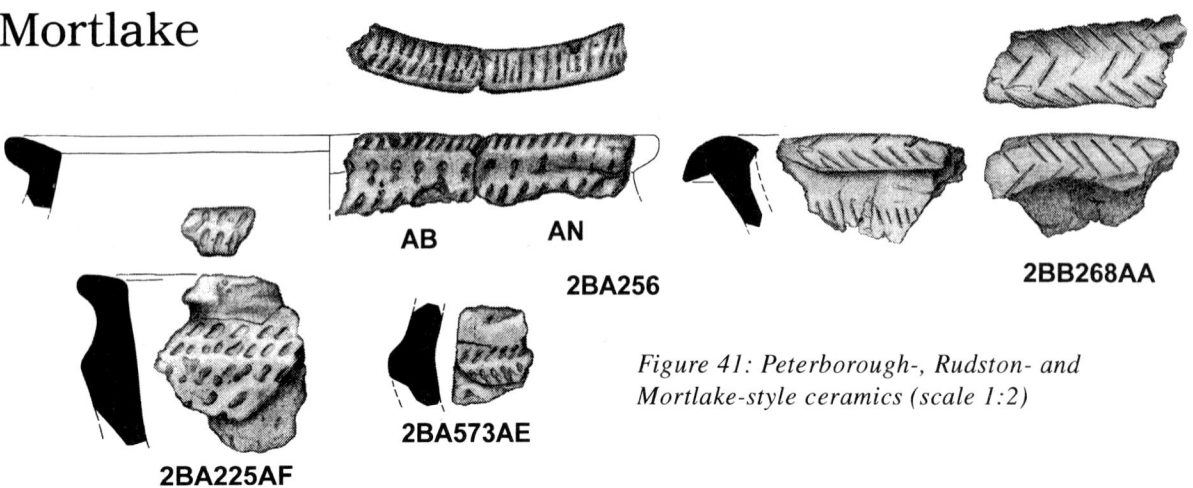

AB  AN
2BA256  2BB268AA

2BA573AE

2BA225AF

*Figure 41: Peterborough-, Rudston- and Mortlake-style ceramics (scale 1:2)*

**2BA50CH**: Weathered sherd. Orange surfaces, dark grey core, some erratic temper >7mm.

**2BA50CI**: Small LBA sherds. Buff exterior, grey interior, grog and sand temper. Wall thickness 11mm.

**2BA50CJ**: Small weathered LBA sherd. Surfaces flaked off, dark grey core, pitted, calcite/chalk temper dissolved.

**2BA50CK**: Crumb.

**2BA50CS**: Weathered sherd. Orange-buff exterior, dark grey interior, tempered with sand and small dolerite pebbles.

**2BA54AF**: Weathered sherd. Buff with reddish-toned surfaces, brown core, soapy feel. Much fine sand temper with black particles. Impressed decoration of uncertain character. Wall thickness 9mm. **(Fig 41)**

**2BA54AG**: Weathered LBA sherd. Brown exterior, grey interior, deeply pitted, erratic temper >3mm. Wall thickness 12mm.

**2BA54AI**: LBA sherd. Buff exterior, brown interior, grey core, some calcite temper. Wall thickness 7mm.

**2BA54AJ**: Large LBA sherd. Orange exterior, brown interior, grey core, pitted, ? calcite/chalk and sand. Vertical finger-tip stroking on the exterior, wiping marks on the interior. Wall thickness 8mm.

**2BA60AI**: Weathered flake.

**2BA60AJ**: Sherd, same fabric as 2BA60AQ. Wall thickness 10mm.

**2BA60AK**: Sherd and three crumbs. Same fabric as 2BA60AS and 2BA452AG, AK, AM, AW and AX. **(Fig 42) Joins AX**.

**2BA60AL**: Small weathered sherd, same fabric as 2BA452AW.

**2BA60AM**: Segment of a roughly modelled wide-mouthed cup, convex base with angle. Coarse laminated orange fabric tempered with flint, chalk and quartz sand. Plain, 45mm+ high, 50mm rim diameter, 38mm base diameter. **(Fig 42)**

**2BA60AO (i)**: Three sherds, compact orange-buff, scattered flint >9mm and pitting left by solution of calcite/chalk and sand. Wall thickness 22mm. Same fabric as 2BA452AW.

**2BA60AO (ii)**: Sherd, orange-buff, grey core. Pitted by solution of large temper, chalk, flint >9mm and sand. Wall thickness 12mm. Same fabric as 2BA452AW.

**2BA60AP**: Rimsherd of a large Fengate style bowl. Deep collared rim with internal bevel. Hard orange fabric with flint temper >6mm. Incised alternating diagonal hatching on the collar and a finger-tip scooped pit below the lower edge of the collar. Wall thickness 10mm. **(Fig 42)**

**2BA60AQ (i)**: Two joining rim sherds of a large Fengate style bowl. Deep collared rim with internal bevel, well modelled. Hard heavy orange laminated fabric, scattered flint temper >6mm. Incised alternating diagonal hatching on the collar, stick-end imprints on the bevel, finger-tip scooped pits below the lower edge of the collar. Same vessel as 2BA60AJ and 2BA945BH.

**2BA60AQ (ii)**: Body sherd in the same fabric as 2BA452AW. Wall thickness 10mm. Also crumbs in other fabrics. **(Fig 42)**

**2BA60AQ (iii)**: small rim fragment, inturned lip. Hard compact grey. Fingernail imprinting as a pair of horizontal lines on the rim. Top and inside of lip notched.

**2BA60AR**: Rim and body sherd of Fengate style bowl. Collared rim with internal bevel. Hard compact buff, dark tones and dark core. Flint and sand temper. Diagonal rows of stick-end imprinting on the collar with groups of diagonal incised lines. Same vessel as 2BA60 AQ and AX. **(Fig 42)**

**2BA60AS**: Rim of a Fengate style bowl. Collared rim with internal bevel. Orange fabric, dark grey core, flint and sand temper. Incised decoration. Same vessel as 2BA60AK, AL and 2BA452AK, AW, AX, AY. **(Fig 42)**

**2BA60AT**: Sherd. Heavy compact orange-buff. Dark grey core, scattered angular flint temper >10mm and sand. Wall thickness 12mm.

**2BA60AU**: Sherd, same fabric as 2BA452AX.

**2BA60AV**: Sherd. Orange-buff exterior, grey interior. Large angular flint >15mm and grog temper. Wall thickness 13mm.

**2BA60AW**: Rim of small bowl, Peterborough Ware. External lip. Laminated brown, dark grey interior, rough fissured exterior, scattered flint temper, sand and erratics. Fingernail imprints inside and in places outside the rim.

**2BA60AX**: Rim and body sherd of a Fengate style bowl. Collared rim with internal bevel. Hard, compact, buff, darker tones and grey core, laminated. Erupting temper, flint >8mm, chalk and fine sand, some coarse quartz pebbles. Diagonal fingernail impressions on the lip. Horizontal wipe marks over the interior. Wall thickness 7–8mm. Same vessel as 2BA60AQ and AR. **(Fig 42)**

**2BA60AY**: Rim sherd, Fengate style. Rim folded down to form a deep collar with internal bevel. Compact orange fabric with scattered chalk and flint temper >10mm. Groups of alternating diagonal cord lines on the collar. Wall thickness 10mm.

**2BA63AK**: Base angle; LBA, slight foot. Hard, brittle, orange exterior, brown interior, scattered flint >4mm and sand. Wall thickness 8mm.

**2BA63AS**: Small sherd, Peterborough Ware. Orange-buff exterior, grey interior, laminated, tempered with sand and some flint. Possible impressed decoration. Wall thickness 12mm.

**2BA64AM**: LBA base, acute angle, 120 mm diameter. Brown exterior, grey interior, pitted, some dissolved temper, calcite and sand. Grass impressions on the underside.

**2BA71AA**: Small sherd, Peterborough Ware. Hard dark grey, much angular flint temper >5mm. Closely spaced herringbone pattern of whipped cord impressions.

**2BA76AR**: Rim, Peterborough Ware. Everted rim with internal bevel. Laminated, orange-buff surfaces, grey core. Some flint temper. Fine cord line impressions in diagonal rows on the exterior and as herringbone on the bevel. **(Fig 41)**

**2BA93AK**: LBA sherd. Orange exterior grey-brown interior, some pitting, ?calcite temper. Wall thickness 8mm.

**2BA93AL**: Weathered sherds; Peterborough Ware. Soapy orange, grey core, sparse temper, ?grog and fine sand. Articular bone end impressions. Wall thickness 12mm.

**2BA99AC**: Weathered LBA sherd. Orange-buff, grey core, pitted ?calcite temper.

**2BA99AB**: Small LBA sherd. Brown exterior, grey interior, pitted, ?calcite/chalk and sand. Wall thickness 7mm.

**2BA105AA**: Small weathered LBA sherds. Orange-buff exterior, dark grey interior. Pitted, ?calcite/chalk tempering. Wall thickness 6–7mm.

**2BA105AM**: Crumb.

**2BA105AN**: LBA sherd. Hard, compact, reddish exterior, brown interior, pitted, ?calcite/chalk and sand. Wall thickness 8mm.

**2BA105AY**: Small weathered sherd. Orange, pitted, ?calcite/chalk and sand.

**2BA109AB**: LBA sherd. Brown exterior, grey interior, pitted, calcite/chalk. Wall thickness 10mm.

**2BA109AD**: LBA sherd, same fabric as 2BA2AE and AJ, but orange to buff surface. Wall thickness 8mm.

**2BA109AE**: Weathered crumb, pitted.

**2BA109AF**: Weathered LBA sherd. Brown surfaces, grey core, deeply pitted, ?organic and flint temper. Wall thickness 10mm.

**2BA109AH**: LBA sherd, same fabric as 2BA156AZ.

**2BA109AI**: Grooved Ware sherd. Brown surfaces, grey core, deeply pitted by solution of temper, ?organic. Light-weight fabric. Incised decoration of a pair of vertical lines with open triangles each side. Wall thickness 10mm. Same vessel as 2BA158AA. **(Fig 43)**

**2BA109AK**: Small LBA sherd, simple base angle. Buff exterior, dark grey interior, pitted, ?calcite/chalk.

**2BA109AL**: Crumb; dark grey.

**2BA109AM**: LBA sherd. Orange to brown exterior, dark grey interior, pitted, calcite. Wall thickness 7mm.

**2BA109AN**: Fragment of LBA, flat-based. Brown-buff exterior, dark grey body, pitted, ?calcite. Wall thickness 16mm.

**2BA116AH**: Weathered and rolled LBA sherd. Grey fabric, much pitted.

**2BA118AM**: Exterior flake, Peterborough Ware. Compact orange-buff. Rows of short incised herringbone pattern. **(Fig 41)**

**2BA118AQ**: Large LBA sherd. Orange-buff, reddish interior, pitted, ?calcite/chalk and some flint temper. Wall thickness 10mm.

**2BA119AA**: Crumb.

**2BA119AB**: Crumb.

**2BA119AC**: Crumb.

**2BA123AB**: Small weathered sherd. Brown exterior, dark grey interior, Pitted.

**2BA136AA**: Small sherd. Brown, orange interior, sand tempered. Fine incised herringbone decoration.

**2BA156AC**: Weathered LBA sherd, light grey, orange exterior, some pitting, ?calcite/chalk and sand. Wall thickness 9mm.

**2BA156AE**: Weathered LBA sherd.

**2BA156AG**: Small weathered LBA sherd. Brown exterior, dark brown interior, pitted, ?calcite/chalk and sand. Wall thickness 7mm.

**2BA156AH**: LBA sherd, same fabric as 2BA156AI, AJ and AW.

**2BA156AI**: LBA sherd, same fabric as 2BA156AH,AJ and AW.

**2BA156AJ**: LBA sherd. Same fabric as 2BA156AH, AI and AW.

# Fengate

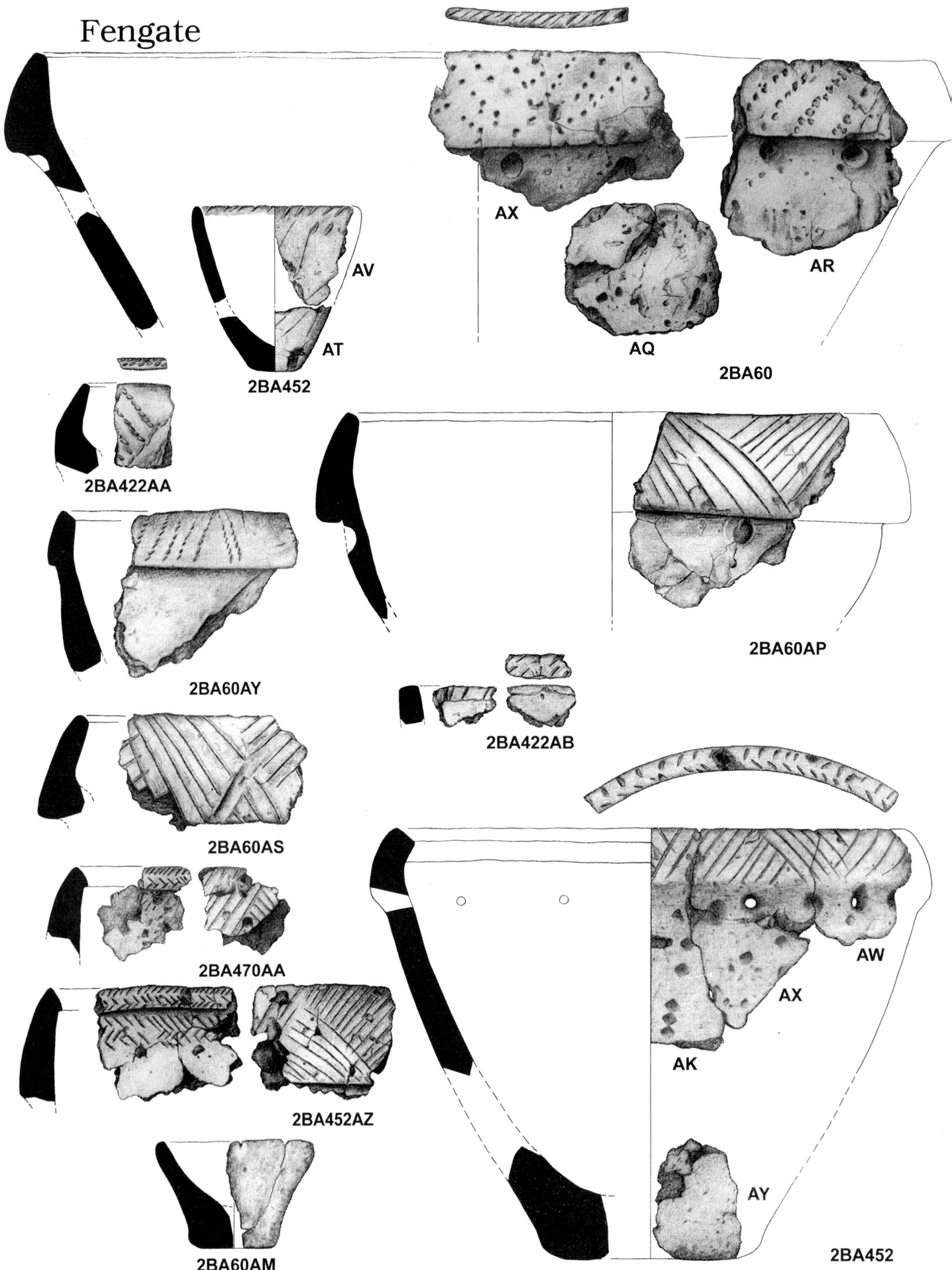

AV

AT

**2BA452**

AX

AQ

AR

**2BA60**

**2BA422AA**

**2BA60AY**

**2BA60AP**

**2BA422AB**

**2BA60AS**

**2BA470AA**

**2BA452AZ**

**2BA60AM**

AW

AX

AK

AY

**2BA452**

*Figure 42: Fengate-style ceramics (scale 1:2)*

**2BA156AL:** Weathered sherd. Brown surfaces, grey core, deeply pitted, ?calcite/chalk and sand temper. Incised lattice decoration. Wall thickness 10mm.**(Fig 43)**

**2BA156AM:** Sherd, same fabric as 2BA156AL. **(Fig 43)**

**2BA156AN:** Weathered LBA sherd. Dark grey, pitted, ?calcite/chalk and coarse quartzite temper.

**2BA156AT:** Angle of a convex base, Peterborough Ware. Orange-buff exterior, dark grey core and interior. Pitted, ?organic temper and sand with a flint pebble >7mm.

**2BA156AV:** Same fabric as 2BA156AZ.

**2BA156AW:** LBA sherd, same fabric as 2BA156AH–AJ.

**2BA156AZ:** LBA sherd. Orange-buff exterior, dark grey interior, pitted, ?calcite/chalk, grog and some erratic temper. Wall thickness 7mm. Same as 2BA156AV.

**2BA158AA:** Grooved Ware sherd. Brown surfaces, dark grey core. Pitted by solution of organic temper. Incised vertical lines and diagonal lines, possible infill of dots by a sharp point. Wall thickness 11mm. Same vessel as 2BA109AI.

**2BA158AF:** Rim, Peterborough Ware. Everted lip with internal bevel. Dark grey, brown surfaces, some pitting. Plain except for notching on the lip made by a point.**(Fig 41)**

**2BA158AH:** Sherd. Buff exterior, smooth grey interior, laminated. Wall thickness 11mm. Fabric like 2BA998AD and 2BA1070BO.

**2BA158AJ:** Small flake. Orange-buff exterior, grey core, sand temper.

**2BA165AG:** LBA sherd.

**2BA165AH:** LBA sherd, orange-brown, pitted, ?calcite/chalk with flint and quartz. Wall thickness 7mm.

**2BA165AJ:** LBA rim, lip rolled outwards. Orange-buff exterior, grey interior, pitted, calcite/chalk, flint and sand. Fingernail notching across lip. Wall thickness 7mm.

**2BA170AC:** Two LBA crumbs.

**2BA170AD:** Four LBA crumbs.

**2BA170AE:** LBA crumb.

**2BA204AB:** LBA rim, thick-walled, internal bevel. Brown, pitted, ?calcite/chalk. Wall thickness 11mm.

**2BA204AH:** Weathered LBA sherd. Orange-buff exterior, grey interior, pitted, ?calcite. Wall thickness 7mm. Same fabric as 2BA204AI.

**2BA204AI:** LBA sherd, same fabric as 2BA204AJ.

**2BA204AJ:** Sherd, same fabric as 2BA452AX.

**2BA214AA:** Sherd. Light-weight, buff exterior, orange interior, light grey core. Pitted, grog temper. Wall thickness 7mm.

**2BA225AD:** LBA sherd. Compact brown, greyish interior, some pitting, ?calcite. Horizontal wiping in the surfaces, finger-tip printing in a row on the exterior. Wall thickness 8mm.

**2BA225AF:** Rim and shoulder fragment, Mortlake style. Small bowl with internally bevelled rim, concave neck. Laminated orange; cord decoration on the bevel, rim, shoulder and body in a herringbone pattern. Possibly the same vessel as 2BA573AE.**(Fig 41)**

**2BA233AC:** Rim, Peterborough Ware, expanded with external bevel. Laminated, brown exterior, sand temper. Two row of diagonal cord maggot imprints, inside rim are rows of crescentic imprints.**(Fig 41)**

**2BA253AR:** Rim of Peterborough Ware and crumbs. Out-turned overhanging rim. Brown, grey core, laminated. Pitting caused by the solution of temper, ?calcite and grog. Plain neck, lines on the rim, rounded impressions inside. Wall thickness 8mm.**(Fig 41)**

**2BA255AF:** Two crumbs.

**2BA255AG:** Crumb.

**2BA255AH:** Eight crumbs. Brown surfaces, grey core.

**2BA255AI:** Small sherd Peterborough Ware. Laminated, brown surfaces, grey core, flint >6mm and sand temper. Wall thickness 10mm.

**2BA255AJ:** Weathered sherd. Brown, buff surfaces, grey core, pitted, ?calcite/chalk and sand temper.

**2BA255AP:** Sherd. Buff-orange exterior, grey interior, grog and sand temper. Wall thickness 15mm.

**2BA256AB:** Rim, Mortlake style, everted with internal bevel. Brown, darker tones, pitted in places, fine sand temper. Stick-end impressions on the neck, lip and bevel. Wall thickness 7–8mm. Same vessel as 2BA256AN. **(Fig 41)**

**2BA256AM:** Small weathered sherd, Peterborough Ware. Dark brown.

**2BA256AN:** Rim sherd, everted lip with internal bevel. Brown, darker toned interior, pitted. Same vessel as 2BA256AB.**(Fig 41)**

**2BA305AH:** Weathered rim, Peterborough Ware, overhanging rim. Compact brown, fine sand temper. Rows of stick-end imprints on the interior.

**2BA305AI (i):** LBA sherd. Reddish brown exterior, reddish core, grey interior, sand temper. Wall thickness 13mm.

**2BA305AI (ii):** Sherd, Peterborough Ware. Orange-grey exterior, grey interior, grog temper. Wall thickness 16mm.

**2BA338AA:** Sherd. Heavy brown fabric, lighter surfaces, grey core, laminated, sand temper. Wall thickness 11mm.

**2BA338AD:** Sherd, Peterborough Ware. Compact, gritty, orange-buff exterior, laminated. Much angular flint temper >18mm. Plain. Wall thickness 12mm.

**2BA338AF:** Weathered LBA base angle. Hard, compact grey, pitted, ?calcite/chalk temper and sand. Wall thickness 8mm.

**2BA361AG:** Weathered sherd. Orange exterior, grey interior, coarse erupting temper, quartzite fragments and sand. Wall thickness 7mm.

**2BA373AE:** LBA base angle. Hard buff, interior scaled off, sand tempering.**(Fig 43)**

**2BA373AL:** LBA sherd. Brown exterior, grey core and interior, pitted, ?organic temper with some quartzite. Wall thickness 9mm.

**2BA382AB:** Sherd. Hard orange-brown exterior, dark grey interior, sand temper. Two rows of short vertical imprints. Wall thickness 9mm.

**2BA422AA:** Rim, Fengate style, collared rim with simple lip. Hard laminated brown with darker tones. Sand tempered. Cord lines on the exterior in alternate groups of diagonal lines leaving a reserved triangle between. **(Fig 42)**

**2BA422AB:** Rim, Fengate style. Dark brown, grey core, laminated and gritty. Sand temper. Fingernail imprinting on the lip and inside.**(Fig 42)**

**2BA423AA:** Small sherd, Peterborough Ware. Dark grey, buff-orange exterior, laminated, interior scaled off.

**2BA452AA:** Three crumbs, dark brown.

**2BA452AE:** Sherd, Peterborough Ware. Fabric like 2BA478AP but with some large pieces of angular flint >12mm. Wall thickness 10mm.

**2BA452AF:** Crumb.

**2BA452AG:** Small sherd. Hard brown, interior scaled off. Sand temper with black particles.

**2BA452AH:** Small sherds and crumbs. Orange, dark grey core.

**2BA452AJ (i):** Base angle, Peterborough Ware. Rounded edge to steeply rising body profile. Tempered with scattered flint >15mm and sand.

**2BA452AJ (ii):** Compact orange with lozenge-shaped imprinting, scattered flint temper. Wall thickness 12mm. Joins 2BA452AM.

**2BA452AK:** Rim of a Fengate bowl, badly weathered. Joins 2BA452AG and AX. **(Fig 42)**

**2BA452AM:** Three rim and body sherds of the Fengate style bowl. Same Vessel as 2BA452AG, AK, AQ,AW, AX, AY. The body has scattered lozenge-shaped imprints. Joins 2BA452AJ(ii).

**2BA452AO:** LBA sherd, interior flaked off. Hard compact brown, calcite >6mm.

**2BA452AQ:** Small sherd. Brown, dark grey core, sand temper.

**2BA452AR:** Small sherd, Peterborough Ware. Dark brown, laminated, fine sand temper. Fine incised diagonal lines. Possibly same vessel as 2BA470AA.

**2BA452AT:** Base of a small Fengate style vase. Narrow base 20-25mm across. Roughly modelled, grey, brownish surfaces, laminated. Scattered flint >8mm. Fine incised criss-cross lines on the exterior. Same fabric as rim 2BA452AV. **(Fig 42)**

**2BA452AU:** Sherd, Peterborough Ware. Hard dark grey, orange-toned exterior. Flint and sand temper. Wall thickness 8mm.

**2BA452AV:** Two sherds of Peterborough Ware. Upper part of a small open bowl or cup. Simple rim, hard dark brown, buff-toned interior, scattered flint temper >5mm and fine sand. Below the lip a row of fingernail impressions, fine diagonal lines below. Wall thickness 7–8mm. Possible the rim of 2BA452AT. **(Fig 42)**

**2BA452AW:** Rim that joins 2BA452AX showing a pair of perforations below the collar at 50mm centres with pits between.

**2BA452AX:** Upper part of a Fengate style bowl. Rim diameter 180mm, collared with an internal bevel, a perforation bored through after firing below the lower edge of the collar. Orange, dark grey core, tempered with flint and chalk >8mm, fine sand including a white quartzite pebble. Incised decoration, alternate diagonal line hatching on the collar and herringbone on the bevel. Small lozenge-like imprints on the neck area which is badly eroded on this sherd. Wall thickness 8mm. Same vessel as 2BA60AL, AO (i), AS, AU, BK; 2BA204AJ; 2BA452AJ, AK, AM, AW, AY; 2BA478AQ and 2BA518DY. **(Fig 42)**

# Grooved Ware

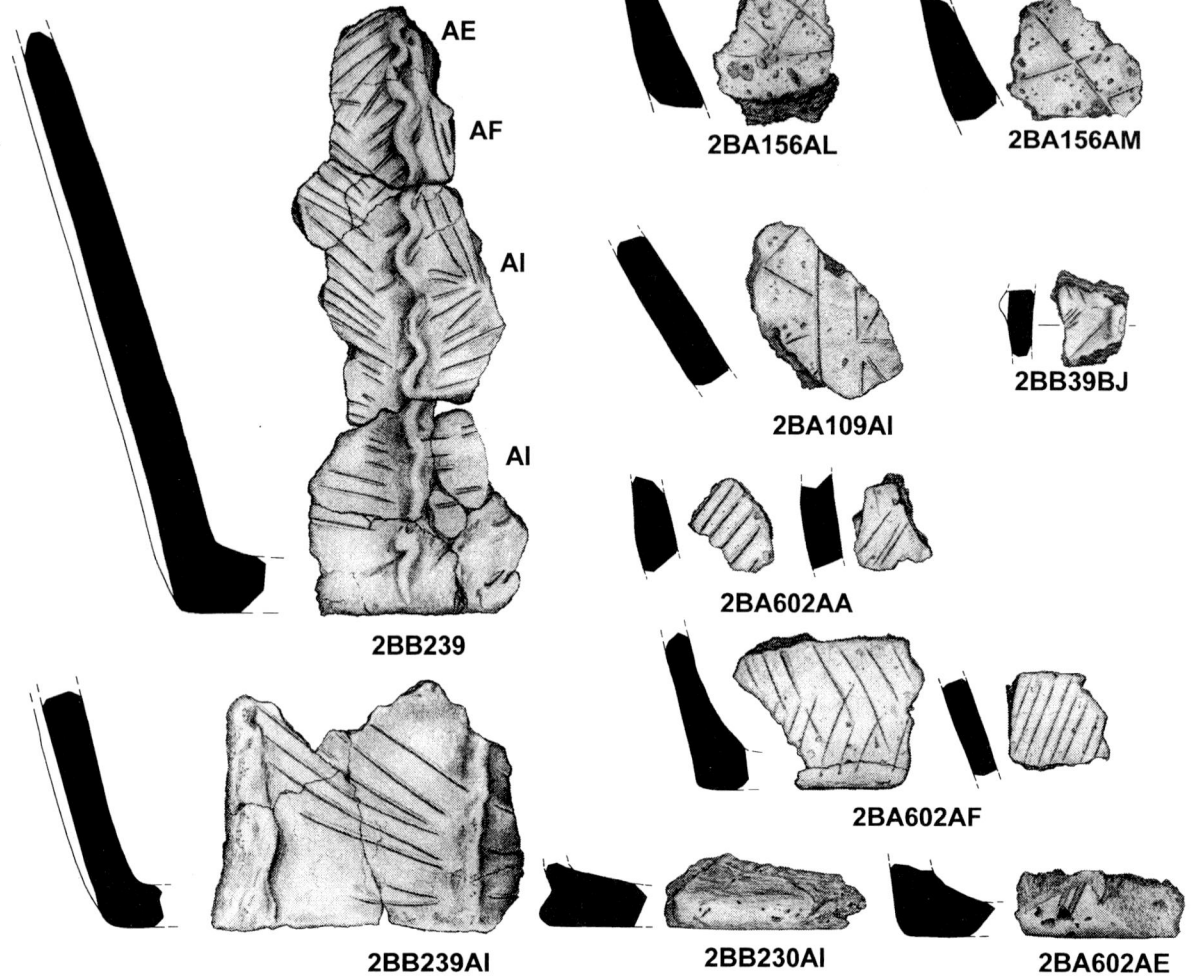

## Beaker

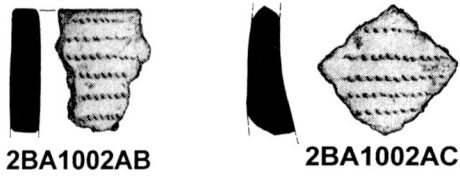

# Late Bronze Age

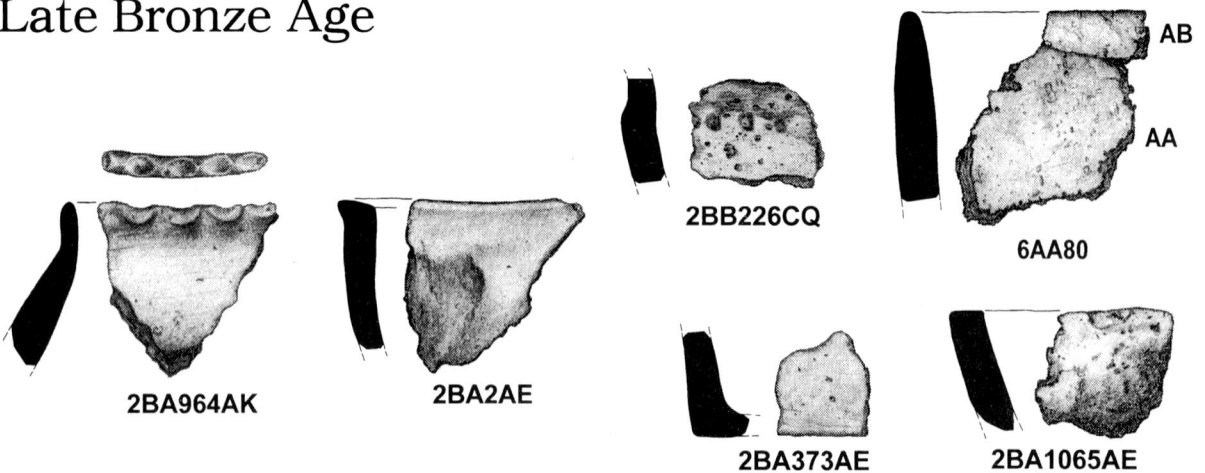

*Figure 43: Grooved Ware, Beaker and later prehistoric ceramics (scale 1:2)*

**2BA452AY**: Base angle of same vessel as 2BA452AX. **(Fig 42)**

**2BA452AZ**: Rim, Fengate style bowl. Deep collared rim with internal bevel. Fine buff exterior, dark grey core and interior, laminated. Voids, ?calcite and sand temper. Finely incised herringbone pattern on the bevel and interior, hatched alternating triangles on the exterior. Same vessel as 2BA470AA and 2BA1066AG. **(Fig 42)**

**2BA457AC**: Large LBA sherd. Very hard orange-buff, profuse flint temper >7mm and sand. Wall thickness 7mm.

**2BA457AL**: ?Rim sherd, Peterborough Ware. Hard orange-buff interior, grey core, laminated. Flint and sand temper. Incised diagonal lines on the interior.

**2BA470AA**: Rim of Fengate style bowl, inturned with internal bevel, probably a collared rim. Buff exterior, dark grey core, voids left by solution of temper, calcite and sand. Finely incised herringbone pattern on the bevel and interior, hatched alternating diagonal lines on the exterior. Same vessel as 2BA452AZ and 2BA1066AG. **(Fig 42)**

**2BA478AA**: Weathered LBA sherd, lower body to base angle of a small pot. Orange surfaces, brown core, pitted, ?calcite/chalk and some flint. Wall thickness 8mm. Also two weathered and rolled small sherds.

**2BA478AD**: Base of a large Peterborough Ware bowl with protruding foot to a convex base. Laminated hard orange-buff surfaces, dark grey core. Scattered angular flint temper >10mm and sand and coarse quartz temper. **(Fig 41)**

**2BA478AE (i)**: Weathered sherd, Peterborough Ware. Laminated dark grey, reddish exterior. Some flint >8mm and sand temper.

**2BA478AE (ii)**: Small sherd. Compact, orange surfaces, grey interior, some flint temper. Wall thickness 9mm.

**2BA478AG**: Crumb. Brown.

**2BA478AI**: Sherd, same as 2BA60AT.

**2BA478AJ**: Small LBA sherd. Brown.

**2BA478AK**: Small weathered sherd. Laminated, dark grey.

**2BA478AL**: Sherd. Heavy pinkish-buff exterior, buff interior, grey core. Smoothing marks on the interior, large erratic temper (dolerite) >6mm. Wall thickness 13mm.

**2BA478AM**: Exterior flake. Orange surface, grey inside. Short vertical strokes.

**2BA478AO**: Two body sherds of Peterborough Ware. Hard orange-buff, laminated. Large flint temper >12mm and sand. Two short elliptical impressions. Wall thickness 11mm. Fabric like 2BA452AJ (i).

**2BA478AP**: Sherd, Peterborough Ware. Hard, heavy, laminated, reddish exterior, brown interior, dark grey core, smoothing on the interior. Some flint and sand temper. Wall thickness 10mm.

**2BA478AQ**: Sherd. Same fabric as 2BA452AX.

**2BA500NW**: Weathered sherd, brown pitted fabric.

**2BA518AS**: Base angle, Grooved Ware, slight foot. Hard orange-buff exterior, dark grey interior, laminated, sand temper.

**2BA518DY**: Sherd, same fabric as 2BA452AX.

**2BA518GO**: LBA sherd. Reddish brown exterior, dark grey interior, much sand and some coarse quartz temper. Wall thickness 12-15mm.

**2BA518OL**: Small sherd, Neolithic. Laminated dark brown, profuse flint temper >5mm and sand. Wall thickness 10mm.

**2BA518OM**: Small LBA sherd. Reddish surfaces, grey core, pitted, ?calcite/chalk and quartz sand. Wall thickness 6mm.

**2BA535AJ**: Sherd. Dark grey, hard. Much angular flint temper >8mm. Laminated. Wall thickness 11mm.

**2BA573AE**: Weathered shoulder sherd, Peterborough Ware. Laminated orange, sparse flint temper >5mm. Diagonal cord impression in the shoulder angle forming a herringbone. Possibly the same vessel as 2BA225AF. **(Fig 41)**

**2BA590AD**: Small sherd, Peterborough Ware. Dark grey, flint temper.

**2BA602AA**: Weathered body sherds, Grooved Ware. Orange-brown surfaces, dark grey core. Tempered with profuse fine sand and coarse quartz sand. Decorated with shallow lines. Wall thickness 10mm. **(Fig 43)**

**2BA602AE**: Base angle Grooved Ware. Same as 2BA602AA and AF. **(Fig 43)**

**2BA602AF**: Base angle and sherd, Grooved Ware. Orange exterior, dark grey interior. Grog and sand temper. Decorated on the body with shallow strokes forming a close herringbone pattern. Carbon layer over the interior. Joins 2BA602AA. **(Fig 43)**

**2BA652BH**: Weathered LBA sherd. Hard buff, scattered flint temper >3mm. Wall thickness 12mm.

**2BA652BI**: Sherd, brown gritty, flint and sand temper. Wall thickness 7mm.

**2BA822AA**: Weathered LBA sherd. Dark grey, traces of buff exterior, pitted, ?calcite. Wall thickness 8mm.

**2BA836AB**: Weathered sherd, Peterborough Ware. Hard dark brown, sand temper. Imprinted with the articular end of a small bone.

**2BA945BF**: LBA/EIA sherd. Heavy, laminated, orange surfaces, grey core, pitted, ?calcite and sand. Grass marks on interior. Wall thickness 12mm.

**2BA945BH**: Base angle of a Fengate style vessel, same fabric as 2BA60AJ.

**2BA953AB**: Rim, Peterborough Ware. Deep external sloping rim. Laminated, dark grey, sparse flint and quartz temper. **(Fig 43)**

**2BA957AB**: Weathered sherd, Peterborough Ware. Heavy, laminated orange to buff exterior, grey interior. Profuse crushed dolerite temper >7mm and sand. Faint worn traces of an incised horizontal herringbone pattern on the exterior. Wall thickness 12mm.

**2BA964AJ**: Sherd. Brown exterior, dark grey core, evidence of ring building, pitted, ?calcite/chalk and sand.

**2BA964AK**: LBA rim. Hard compact brown, grey core, pitted, ?calcite and sand temper. Finger tip 'pie-crusting' on the lip. Wall thickness 11mm. **(Fig 43)**

**2BA993AF**: Body fragment of a large vessel, Peterborough Ware. Orange-buff exterior, grey interior. Flint temper >15mm, sand and small pebbles including ironstone. Wall thickness 22mm.

**2BA993AQ**: Weathered sherd, Peterborough Ware. Laminated brown, orange core, flint temper >6mm. Row of diagonal coarse cord imprints.

**2BA993BF**: Sherd. Heavy laminated brown exterior, dark grey interior, scattered flint >8mm. Faint incised diagonal lines. Wall thickness 11mm.

**2BA993BH**: Body sherd, Peterborough Ware. Hard, orange-buff surfaces, grey core. Flint temper >7mm and sand. Evidence of ring building. A pair of fingernail impressions. Wall thickness 13mm.

**2BA993 BK**: Sherd, Peterborough Ware. Hard orange-buff exterior, grey core. Scattered flint >6mm, chalk, quartzite and sand.

**2BA998AD**: Sherd, Peterborough Ware. Orange-buff exterior, grey interior. Temper dissolved, organic. Rows of indistinct imprints made by a broken-ended tool. Wall thickness 9mm.

**2BA998AE**: Sherd, Peterborough Ware. Laminated brown surfaces, dark grey core. Scattered pitting from dissolved calcite/chalk. Possible line decoration. Wall thickness 10mm.

**2BA998AF**: Flake. Orange, smooth exterior, incised herringbone, same as 2BA118AM.

**2BA1002AB**: Rim, AOC Beaker, flat lip. Compact orange-brown, sand temper. Fine horizontal cord line impressions, 7 turns per 10mm. Wall thickness 8mm. Same vessel as 2BA1002AC. **(Fig 43)**

**2BA1002AC**: Sherd, body of an AOC Beaker. Same as 2BA1002AB. **(Fig 43)**

**2BA1065AB**: Weathered LBA sherd. Buff exterior, brown interior, deeply pitted, some calcite or chalk temper remaining. Wall thickness 15mm.

**2BA1065AE**: Weathered LBA rim, simple with internal bevel. Brown surfaces, grey core, pitted, calcite temper >2mm. Wall thickness 10mm. **(Fig 43)**

**2BA1065AM**: LBA sherd. Brown exterior, grey interior, pitted, partly dissolved calcite >5mm. Wall thickness 12mm.

**2BA1066AO**: Weathered LBA sherd. Orange exterior, dark brown interior, pitted, ?calcite/chalk and coarse quartz sand. Wall thickness 12mm.

**2BA1066AG**: Rim fragment, Fengate style, same as 2BA452AZ.

**2BA1066AK**: Sherd, Peterborough Ware. Buff, dark grey interior, laminated. Pitted by solution of temper, calcite/chalk. Wall thickness 15mm.

**2BA1066AU**: Weathered Peterborough Ware rim, thick everted lip with internal bevel. Laminated dark grey, thin brownish surface in places. Flint temper >5mm. Short ?cord line impressions on the rim and bevel. Wall thickness 8mm. **(Fig 41)**

**2BA1066BC**: Weathered LBA sherd. Compact orange-buff exterior, dark grey core, pitted, ?calcite/chalk and sand. Wall thickness 12mm.

**2BA1066BI**: Weathered sherd, Peterborough Ware, possibly a shoulder. Dark grey, grey core, laminated. Deeply pitted by solution of temper, calcite/chalk, also quartz sand. A diagonal row of incised lines on the neck, two horizontal converging lines on the interior. Wall thickness 10mm.

**2BA1066BQ:** Sherd, Peterborough Ware. Reddish-buff exterior, grey interior, laminated. Flint temper >10mm, fine sand and dolerite fragments. Incised herringbone decoration. Wall thickness 13mm. **(Fig 41)**

**2BA1066BW:** Rim and shoulder of a Rudston style bowl. Rounded rim and sharp shoulder profile. Hard dark grey with brown interior, laminated. Profuse flint temper >5mm and coarse sand. Incised diagonal lines over the lip, continuing inside alternating with rows of bird bone impressions. Wall thickness 15mm. Horizontal wiping on the interior. Same vessel as 2BA1068AH. **(Fig 41)**

**2BA1066CD:** Small rim, Peterborough Ware, internal bevel. Laminated dark grey, brown surface. Voids left by solution of temper. Horizontal lines on the bevel made with a ?comb. **(Fig 41)**

**2BA1068AH:** Rim, Rudston style bowl, flat lip with external rim bevel. Laminated dark grey with thin buff surface. Scattered temper of flint and sand. Incised diagonal lines on lip, false cord impression inside and out. Same vessel as 2BA1066BW. **(Fig 41)**

**2BA1068AP:** Sherd, Peterborough Ware. Hard compact, buff exterior with reddish to grey tones, grey interior, scattered flint >10mm and sand. Short cord impressions in herringbone rows. Wall thickness 10mm. **(Fig 41)**

**2BA1068AQ:** Crumb.

**2BA1068AR:** Crumb.

**2BA1068AS:** Sherd, Peterborough Ware. Oxidised buff to leave only a thin interior grey layer. Flint temper >7mm, dolerite, sand and quartz. Wall thickness 18mm. Similar to 2BA1068CD.

**2BA1068AV:** Crumb. Orange, flint temper.

**2BA1068AX:** Two small crumbs. Flaky, dark brown.

**2BA1068AY:** Sherd, Peterborough Ware. Reddish orange exterior, grey interior. Profuse flint >5mm, some dolerite fragments >15mm and sand. Wall thickness 14mm.

**2BA1068BA:** Two sherds and crumbs, Peterborough Ware. Hard compact orange to reddish brown exterior, grey interior, laminated. Scattered large flint temper and sand. Wall thickness 12 mm.

**2BA1068BB:** Sherd, Peterborough Ware. Buff exterior, dark grey interior, laminated. Flint temper >3mm and sand. Wall thickness 3mm.

**2BA1070AF:** LBA sherd. Compact, grey-buff exterior, dark grey interior, some pitting, ?calcite/chalk. Wall thickness 7mm.

**2BA1070AG:** Weathered sherd, Peterborough Ware. Hard orange exterior with reddish tones, dark grey interior. Scattered flint temper >9mm. Rows of short coarse cord impressions.

**2BA1070AJ:** Flake, Peterborough Ware. Dark grey laminated, small crushed flint temper. Traces of incised herringbone decoration.

**2BA1070AK:** Weathered shoulder fragment, Peterborough Ware. Orange-toned exterior, grey interior, laminated, voids left by solution of temper. Diagonal incised lines on the shoulder ledge. Wall thickness 10–14mm.

**2BA1070AL:** Small weathered sherd, same fabric as 2BA1070AR and AU.

**2BA1070AM:** Weathered sherd, Peterborough Ware. Reddish surfaces, light grey core, pitted. Wall thickness 10–15mm.

**2BA1070 AN:** Compact grey, dark grey core, some pitting. Stab and drag impressions in a herringbone pattern. Wall thickness 7mm.

**2BA1070AQ:** Sherd, Peterborough Ware. Hard compact, dark grey exterior surface over a reddish layer, light grey core, orange interior, flint >5mm, grog and sand temper. Closely spaced diagonal cord maggot. Wall thickness 10mm.

**2BA1070AR:** Sherd. Light grey laminated, same fabric as 2BA1070AL.

**2BA1070AT:** Sherd, Peterborough Ware. Brown exterior, dark grey interior, laminated. Pitted by solution of temper, calcite/chalk, and flint >3mm. Short cord lines in diagonal rows. Wall thickness 10mm.

**2BA1070AU:** Sherd, Peterborough Ware. Laminated, light grey. Scattered coarse quartz temper. Wall thickness 8mm. Same fabric as 2BA1070AL and AR.

**2BA1070AY:** Weathered rim, Peterborough Ware. Everted rim with broad internal bevel. Hard dark grey with some buff surface remaining. Much flint temper >7mm, sand and coarse quartz. Diagonal cord lines on the bevel, horizontal on the lip. **(Fig 41)**

**2BA1070AZ:** Weathered Peterborough Ware rim of a small diameter bowl. Hammer-head rim, concave neck. Hard orange exterior, buff interior, dark grey core, flint temper >6mm and sand. Plain exterior, diagonal cord maggot on the interior.

**2BA1070BC:** Rim, Peterborough Ware, broad and overhanging. Or-

ange exterior, brown interior, grey core. Incised herringbone on the rim, imprinting inside, ?cord knot. **(Fig 41)**

**2BA1070BD:** Rim, same vessel as 2BA1075AQ and 2BA1070BM.

**2BA1070BM:** Rim, same vessel as 2BA1075AQ and 2BA1070BD.

**2BA1070BN:** Sherd, Peterborough Ware. Orange-buff, grey core, grog and sand temper. Wall thickness 13mm.

**2BA1070BO:** Sherd, Peterborough Ware. Orange-buff exterior, grey interior. Temper, dissolved organic and sand. Traces of cord decoration, short diagonal lines. Wall thickness 12mm. Similar fabric to 2BA998AD.

**2BA1072AG:** Weathered body sherd, Peterborough Ware. Laminated buff exterior, pitted by solution of temper, grog inclusions. Rows of short vertical cord lines in rows. Wall thickness 10mm.

**2BA1072AH:** Base angle, Peterborough Ware. Thick heavy reddish-toned buff surfaces, grey core, laminated. Profuse angular flint temper >5mm and coarse sand. Incised diagonal lines. Wall thickness 6mm. **(Fig 41)**

**2BA1075AA (i):** Peterborough Ware. Compact orange-buff exterior, grey interior. Scattered flint temper >6mm and sand. Maggot impressions, a horizontal line flanked by rows of diagonals. Wall thickness 11mm.

**2BA1075AA (ii):** Peterborough Ware. Soapy light brown, grey core. Tempered with flint >5mm and sand. Coarse cord line, a horizontal with diagonals above and below. Wall thickness 10mm.

**2BA1075AA (iii):** Peterborough Ware. Dark brown, grey interior, light weight, pitted. Plain. Wall thickness 7mm.

**2BA1075AH:** Rim. Same vessel as 2BA1075AQ and 2BA1070BD.

**2BA1075AL:** Weathered LBA sherd. Brown, orange beneath surface, crushed quartzite temper. Wall thickness 7mm.

**2BA1075AQ:** Rim, Peterborough Ware, internal bevel. Grey fabric, buff interior, pitted, ?calcite/chalk >3mm and sand temper. Same as 2BA1070BM and 2BA1075AH, BD.

**2BA1075AR:** Small flake, light grey. Incised diagonal lines 15mm apart.

**2BA1084AD:** Small sherd, Peterborough Ware. Orange-red, crushed flint temper >5mm.

**2BA1086AA:** Small Neolithic rim sherd. Hard coarse dark grey, buff patches on surface, laminated. Flint and sand temper.

**2BA1113AE:** Sherds and crumb, Peterborough Ware. Orange-reddish exterior, dark grey interior, voids, ?calcite and sand. Wall thickness 10mm.

**2BA1113AR:** Body sherd, Peterborough Ware. Compact buff, grey core, tempered with >5mm flint and fine sand. Short cord impressions in rows. Wall thickness 8mm. **(Fig 41)**

**2BA1113AU:** Body sherd, Peterborough Ware. Laminated dark grey, lighter toned inside. Tempered with grog and fine sand. Incised herringbone decoration. Wall thickness 8mm. **(Fig 41)**

**2BA1113 AZ:** Sherd, Peterborough Ware, exterior scaled. Laminated buff-brown. Tempered with flint and igneous rock fragments >6mm. Wall thickness 6mm. Carbon layer on the interior.

**2BA1113BA:** Small Neolithic sherd. Laminated dark brown, profuse flint temper >5mm and sand. Wall thickness 10mm.

**2BA1156AY:** Sherd, Peterborough Ware. Orange-buff exterior, grey interior, laminated. Profuse small flint temper, >6mm, and sand. Wall thickness 10mm.

## Site 2BB

**2BB39BJ:** Small weathered sherd, Grooved Ware. Laminated dark grey, buff-toned surfaces. An applied moulded rib, herringbone decoration incised with a sharp point. Wall thickness 7mm. **(Fig 43)**

**2BB42AV:** ?LBA flat base. Deeply weathered and fissured by solution of temper. Thickness 12mm.

**2BB44AB:** Rim, slight internal bevel. Grey, buff surfaces, pitted by solution of temper, ?calcite, a shale pebble inclusion. Wall thickness 6mm.

**2BB46AH:** Crumb, pitted dark grey.

**2BB68BV:** Weathered sherd. Buff, pitted by solution of temper. Wall thickness 8mm.

**2BB94AM:** LBA sherd. Compact orange-buff surface, dark grey core. Surface pitted by solution of temper, ?calcite; also flint and fine sand. Wall thickness 4–7mm.

**2BB132CE:** LBA sherd. Orange surfaces, dark grey core, much temper dissolved, organic, also sand. Wall thickness 9mm.

2BB184AA: LBA base angle or shoulder fragment. Orange-buff to buff surfaces, grey core. Pitted due to solution of temper, ?calcite or chalk. Wall thickness 11mm.

2BB226AI: Base angle with splayed foot, LBA. Orange-buff, brown-grey interior. Pitted by solution of tempering, ?calcite/chalk with fine sand.

2BB226BH: LBA ?rim. Slightly outsplayed and thickened. Compact orange surfaces, dark grey core, scattered tempering, sand and flint.

2BB226CF: Sherd. Orange-brown, grey core. Pitted by the solution of tempering, ?calcite/chalk with fine sand. Wall thickness 8mm.

2BB226CG: Sherd, Grimston type fabric. Compact dark grey-brown surface over orange-brown core. Scattered temper >3mm, flint, iron-stained chalk pebbles and fine sand. Wall thickness 5mm.

2BB226CH: Neolithic sherd. Laminated, orange-buff, grey core, large flint tempering >12mm. Wall thickness 14mm.

2BB226CI: LBA sherd. Buff exterior, dark grey interior. Pitted by the solution of temper, ?calcite/chalk, with much fine sand. Wall thickness 10mm.

2BB226CJ: Shoulder, Peterborough Ware. Hard, heavy grey, harsh surface. Angular flint temper >6mm and coarse sand. Incised diagonal lines above the shallow shoulder angle. Wall thickness 6-12mm. (Fig 41)

2BB226CL: LBA sherd. Brown, dark grey core, pitted, fine sand temper. Wall thickness 9mm.

2BB226CM: LBA sherd. Compact orange, grey core, pitted. Wall thickness 7mm.

2BB226CN: Weathered sherd. Dark grey, flint temper >6mm with sand.

2BB226CO: LBA sherd, slight shoulder. Dark brown exterior, grey interior, pitted, with fine sand.

2BB226CP: ?LBA crumb. Buff exterior, dark grey interior, sand tempering. Incised horizontal line with a diverging diagonal.

2BB226CQ: Shoulder fragment with finger tip printing; LBA. A carbonised layer over the interior. Brown, lighter toned exterior. Pitted by solution of temper, ?calcite/chalk, with much fine sand. Wall thickness 8mm. (Fig 43)

2BB226CR: ?Rim with simple lip, weathered. Orange-buff, grey core, interior scaled off, pitted by solution of organic tempering, with sand.

2BB226CS: Weathered sherd. Buff exterior, brown interior, grey core, small pitting caused by solution of temper. Wall thickness 8mm.

2BB226CV: Weathered sherd. Buff exterior, grey core, scaled interior, pitted by solution of temper, ?calcite/chalk with flint.

2BB226CW: Crumb.

2BB226CX: Sherd. Compact, brown exterior, orange interior, grey core, pitted by solution of tempering, ?calcite, with flint and sand. Wall thickness 8mm.

2BB230AI: Base angle Grooved Ware. Orange exterior, grey interior. Pitted by solution of ?calcite temper. (Fig 43)

2BB230AK: Sherd, weathered and very pitted, externally eroded. Orange-buff surfaces, dark grey core, pitted by solution of temper, ?calcite. Wall thickness 8mm.

2BB232AE: Sherd. Orange-buff, grey core. Pitted by solution of tempering, ?calcite/chalk with flint and sand. Wall thickness 10mm.

2BB239AD: Grooved Ware, same as 2BB239AE.

2BB239AE: Base of a Durrington Walls style Grooved Ware jar. Orange exterior, dark grey interior, brownish core. Pendant strips down to base angle, wavy outline by finger tip moulding, spaced at 56–60mm intervals. The intervening spaces are infilled with diagonal lines incised with a sharp point. Same vessel as 2BB239AI. (Fig 43)

2BB239AF: Grooved Ware, joins 2BB239AE. (Fig 43)

2BB239AH: Grooved Ware, moulded strip and incised decoration,. Same as 2BA239AE.

2BB239AI: Lower body and base angle of a Durrington style Grooved Ware vase. Base diameter 185 mm. Joins 2BB239AD,AE, AF and AH. (Fig 43)

2BB241AC: Small sherd, deeply weathered. Hard brown, greyish surface harsh to the touch, pitted, ?calcite and sand. Wall thickness 8mm.

2BB245AK: Flat base fragment; Bronze Age, rolled and weathered. Orange-buff, grey core.

2BB249AF: Rim, Peterborough Ware, exterior scaled. Rounded top with internal lip rolled over. Hard brown-orange, grey interior. Tempered with scattered large flint >6mm and sand. Incised herringbone decoration on top of the rim and interior. (Fig 41)

2BB249AG: Sherd, possibly the same as 2BB254AF. Light buff, sand

and flint temper. Decorated with casual fingernail impressions. Wall thickness 7mm.

2BB249AH: Crumbs, Peterborough Ware, same as 2BA249AO.

2BB249AO: Sherd of a thick-walled pot, Peterborough Ware. Orange-buff, profuse large angular flint temper >10mm, also chalk, sand and a quartz pebble. Wall thickness 15mm.

2BB249AP: Sherd, Peterborough Ware, same as 2BB249AO.

2BB249AQ: Sherd, Peterborough Ware. Orange exterior, grey interior, large flint temper >7mm, also sand. Incised herringbone decoration. Wall thickness 10mm. (Fig 41)

2BB249BF: Crumb.

2BB249BL: Peterborough Ware, same as 2BB249AO.

2BB249BN: Sherd, Peterborough Ware, same as 2BA249AO.

2BB254AF: Rim, Peterborough Ware, weathered. S-profile with rounded lip. Light buff fabric, grog temper. Coarse incised line decoration. Wall thickness 8mm.

2BB254AH: LBA sherd. Hard dark brown, lighter interior, some pitting, ?calcite, flint and sand temper. Wall thickness 9mm.

2BB254AI: LBA sherd, interior scaled off. Buff, grey core, organic and sand temper.

2BB254AM: Crumb.

2BB254BC: Small shoulder fragment. Dark grey hard fabric, soapy feel, some pitting, ?calcite and sand. Wall thickness 8mm.

2BB254BD: LBA sherd. Orange-buff, dark grey core. Scattered pitting caused by solution of temper, ?calcite and much fine sand. Wall thickness 10mm.

2BB268AA: Mortlake style rim, everted with rim bevel. Grey-brown fabric with flint >3mm and sand temper. Incised herringbone on lip and bevel. (Fig 41)

2BB275AA: Sherd. Interior scaled off. Buff, laminated.

## Site 6AA

6AA2AA: Rim, outbent and thickened, Early Bronze Age. Compact grey, brown exterior, surface pitting caused by solution of temper, ?calcite and fine sand. Decorated with diagonal lines below the lip made by a sharp point. Wall thickness 13mm.

6AA80AA: Sherd, disintegrating external surface. Orange exterior, dark grey interior, scattered chalk and calcite temper >7mm. Wall thickness 10–12mm. (Fig 43)

6AA80AB: Rim sherd, barrel-shaped ?jar. Rounded lip. Dark grey, laminated structure, surface cavities caused by solution of temper, profuse calcite >8mm. Wall thickness 12mm. (Fig 43)

6AA82AA: Sherd. Brown exterior, grey interior and core, pitting caused by solution of temper, calcite, quartz sand and grog. Wall thickness 8mm.

6AA86AA: Sherd, Early Bronze Age. Buff exterior, dark brown interior, profuse large stone temper, dolerite >8mm, and fine sand. A cord maggot impression.

6AA86AB: Weathered sherd, ?Neolithic, Grimston type fabric. Compact laminated brown, scattered temper, flint >6mm and fine sand. Wall thickness 7mm.

6AA86AC: Sherd, same as 6AA86AA. Compact, orange-buff exterior, dark grey interior, profuse large stone temper, dolerite >5mm and fine sand. Closely spaced herringbone pattern of cord maggot impressions. Wall thickness 10mm. (Fig 41)

6AA86AD: Sherd, Early Bronze Age. Orange exterior, dark grey core, interior scaled off. Stone and quartzite temper. Wall thickness 14mm.

6AA96AA: Sherd, Late Neolithic. Orange, dark grey core, harsh surface, scattered temper, white flint, fine sand and coarse quartz sand. Wall thickness 12mm.

6AA97AA: Sherd. Heavy fabric, orange exterior, dark grey interior, tempered with dolerite fragments and grog. Wall thickness 15mm.

6AA97AB: Small weathered sherd. Grey, buff exterior, grog temper. Wall thickness 14mm.

6AA100AA: Sherd, ?Neolithic, Grimston style fabric. Compact orange brown exterior, grey interior, laminated structure, scattered temper, white flint >5mm, fine sand and coarse quartz sand, and a shale pebble >6mm. Wall thickness 12mm.

6AA112AA: Sherd. Brown exterior, dark grey interior, surface pitting caused by the solution of temper, calcite. Wall thickness 10mm.

6AA113AA: Weathered rim sherd, squared lip. Light to dark brown, grey toned, light grey core. Pitting caused by the solution of temper, calcite. Wall thickness 12mm.

6AA141AA: Abraded sherd with large flint temper.

# The Anglian cemetery

## The development and layout of the Anglian cemetery

Although the excavations covered only about 75% of the total area occupied by Anglian graves, the unexcavated area forms a transect across the site (Fig 44). The similarities between the graves and their contents both to the north and south of the area sealed by the A64 road indicate that the sample of data recovered is representative of the cemetery as a whole. There is considerable variation in grave density across the site; even allowing for the total loss of some graves due to plough damage, a number of grave clusters can be identified as well as apparent linear arrangements of graves. Burial modes and grave assemblages vary considerably, as do the scale and form of the grave pits themselves. Although it is not possible to provide precise dating for material from this period, individual graves can be assigned to one or more overlapping phases.

## Limits of the cemetery

One of the more important aspects of the excavation was that the limits of the cemetery were established on all sides, allowing us to see the site in the broader context. It is perhaps surprising that there appears to have been no attempt to define the limits or contain the cemetery within an enclosed area. The cemetery was overlooked by the associated settlement situated on more elevated ground between 500 and 800 metres to the south. The evidence indicates that at the time it was in use the prehistoric monuments that provided the focus for the later graves must have remained visible features in the landscape. The lack of any physical enclosing feature may indicate either that there was little pressure for agricultural land and thus the cemetery could spread in an unconstrained fashion without affecting productive ground or, alternatively, that it was deliberately left open within an area of grazing which, if well managed, could have assisted in the maintenance of the cemetery and prevent it from becoming overgrown. We have no environmental evidence which would allow us to assess the state of the land in the immediate vicinity of the cemetery, whatever its use. The sandy land is of the poorest

quality available locally, and may have become exhausted during the preceding periods. Even with modern fertilisers the sandy soils cannot be relied upon to produce good crops. Whether or not the poor quality of the land contributed to the choice of location, it is likely that the presence of the prehistoric monuments was a more important factor.

The fact that there were so few intercutting graves, a feature which the site has in common with most Early Anglo-Saxon inhumation cemeteries, indicates either that the graves were well marked, of which there is little evidence, or that the cemetery was carefully maintained. Without careful maintenance, perhaps supported by knowledge of its layout passed down by oral tradition, it seems likely that far more graves would have intercut. It is possible that the limits and even some areas within the cemetery itself were marked by trees and hedges, which have left no evidence. The intervisibility of the cemetery and the settlement may have been an important factor in the spatial relationship between the two; if this is the case then it presupposes that the ground between the two was open and not covered with trees which would have obscured the view between these two complexes. To the north of the cemetery the land falls away slightly more steeply for about 400 metres and, had it been established in this area, it would have been much less visible from the settlement.

If site 2BA not been excavated then the interpretation of the development of the cemetery would have been fundamentally different, since in the areas examined to the north of the A64 it appeared that the cemetery had been bounded on the eastern side by a boundary following a pit alignment of probable Iron Age date (Fig 44). Excavation to the south of the road demonstrated that this was not the case. However, there was a reduction in grave density to either side of the pit alignment boundary, indicating that some upstanding feature or hedgeline may have remained. The frequent proximity of Early Anglo-Saxon cemeteries to parish boundaries has been discussed

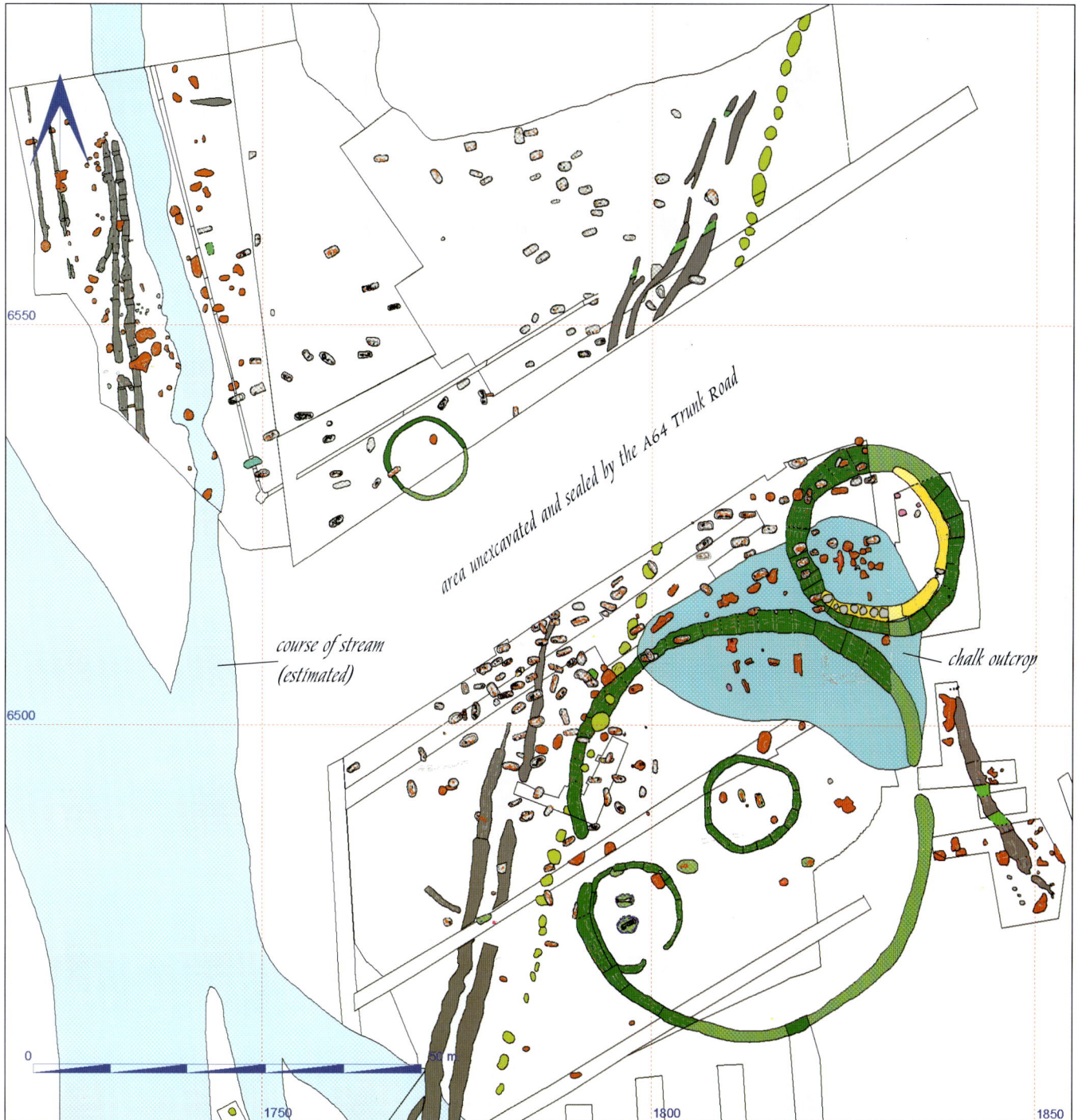

*Figure 44: plan showing the distribution of the Anglian graves in relation to earlier features and the stream channel*

by Arnold (1982), and it is interesting to note that the present boundary between East and West Heslerton lies only 75m to the east of the cemetery. At one point it was thought possible that the pit alignment boundary, which is subsequently replaced by a series of shallow gullies perhaps indicating the presence of a hedge, could have provided the line for an earlier parish boundary, with two contemporary cemeteries, one on either side, serving different communities. The evidence from the settlement and the fact that the parish boundary follows a natural watercourse argue against this. During the period that the cemetery was in use it appears that the settlement covered over 15ha and supported a considerable

population, certainly sufficient to generate a cemetery of this size.

Although no Anglian boundary features have been identified, the cemetery was bounded only a few metres to the west by a watercourse up to 2m deep. To the south and east it appears to be substantially contained by the presence of a number of barrows and the Late Neolithic hengiform enclosure, with the ground falling away to the next watercourse in the east. We can be less certain about the area to the north since this was mostly quarried away before the beginning of the excavation, and although one burial, G30, lies in isolation over 120m to the north, we believe this to be an outlier. Although most of the area between this burial and the cemetery had been quarried prior to the start of project, a strip some 25m wide survived running north of area 1B which contained no burials beyond a line marked both by the first discoveries made on the quarry edge and by the northern limit of the graves in the adjacent area 8AA. As already noted, the exposed top of the quarry had been walked for years on a daily basis by the eventual discoverer, Mr Jim Carter; had many other graves or major features been present they would not have gone unnoticed. A second burial, 2BB115, an unaccompanied crouched burial, was located adjacent to the stream channel 150m south-west of the cemetery; this was undatable, and while it may have been another outlier from the cemetery, it could as just as easily have been prehistoric in date.

# Sequence of development

The difficulty in precisely dating the graves makes the process of phasing or sequencing them and thus identifying the overall development sequence somewhat hazardous. One is therefore forced to apply simple pattern recognition and broad phasing information to attempt even a crude interpretation of the evolution of the cemetery.

The significance of a row or a cluster of graves is quite different if they can be shown to be contemporary. Although precise dating is not possible, generalised dating can be achieved through an examination of the grave assemblages. Only one grave contains material that is generally accepted to occur not later than the end of the fifth

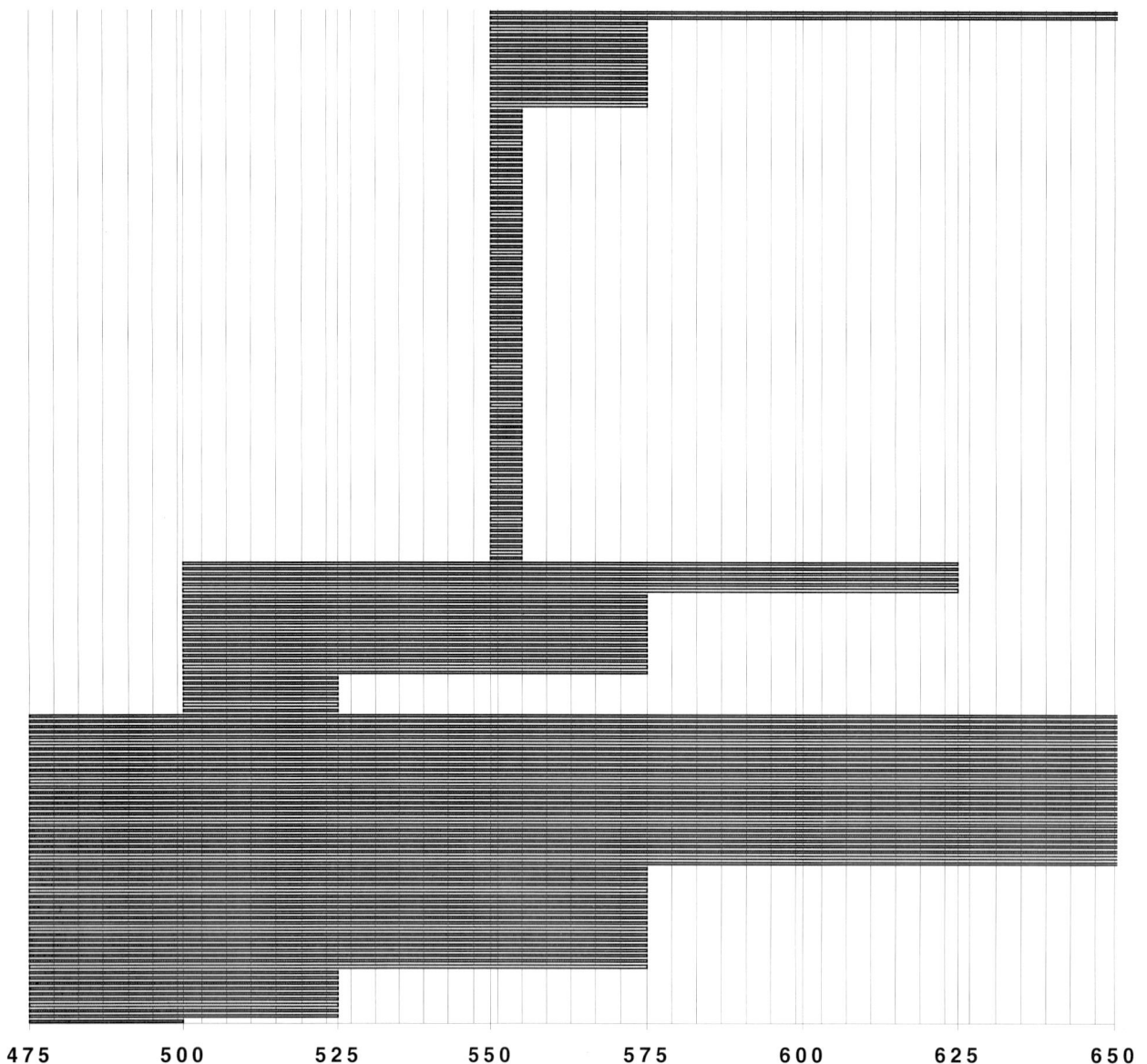

**West Heslerton: Inhumations Date Span**

| 475 | 500 | 525 | 550 | 575 | 600 | 625 | 650 |

*Figure 45: graves plotted according to maximum and minimum date range*

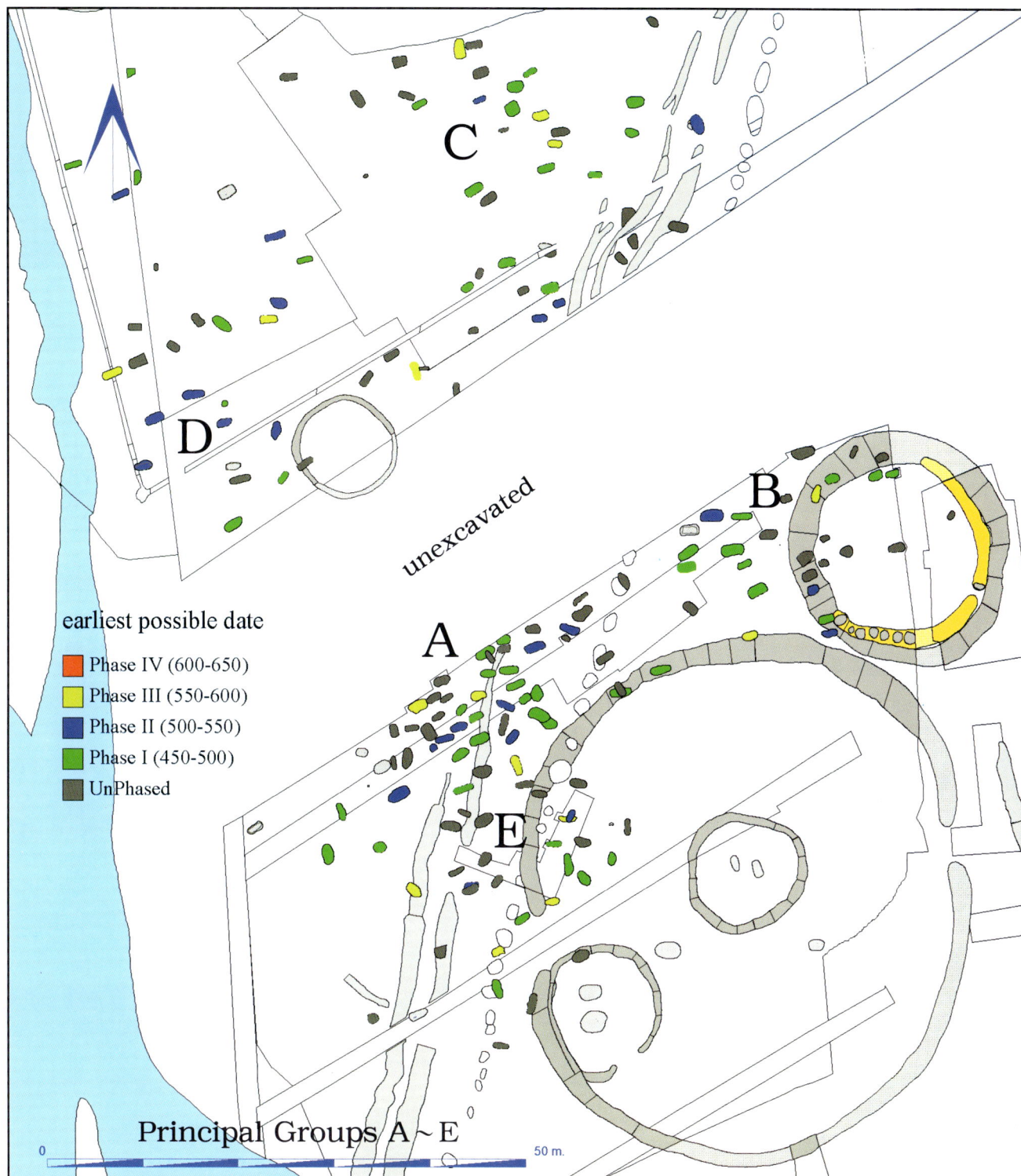

*Figure 46: distribution of the graves according to the earliest date (no graves dated solely to Phase IV)*

century, a class E1 spearhead from the disturbed grave G87. In addition, of the 104 graves for which a date range can be assigned, 57 contain assemblages that indicate a maximum date range from the late fifth to the end of the sixth century and 37 from the beginning of the sixth to the early seventh centuries, suggesting an overall date range for the whole cemetery between *c* AD 475 and *c* AD 650.

In order to provide a practical method for reconstructing the development sequence, each grave has been assigned a date range. A number of graves contained material which could only be imprecisely dated to the active life of the cemetery and others could not be dated at all. Each individual grave has been assigned minimum and maximum dates; these have been binary coded to identify the nine span ranges which cover the four phases, broadly identified with the late fifth, early sixth, late sixth and early seventh centuries. This method generates a series incorporating the nine phase combinations assigned to the graves and provides a basis for the examination of the development of the cemetery as a whole. The date span

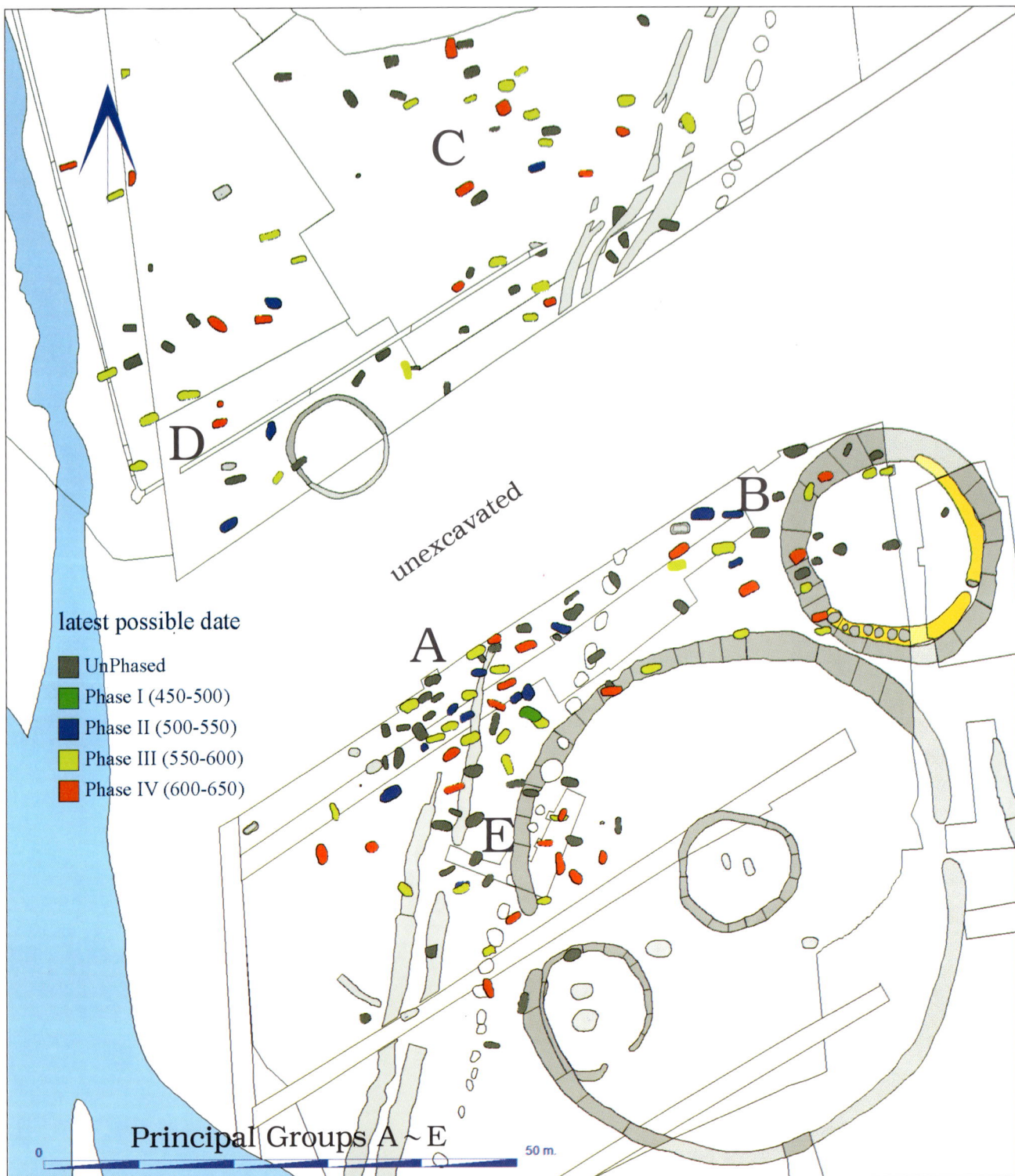

*Figure 47: distribution of the graves according to the latest date*

of the graves is expressed in Figure 45 above; for charting purposes, where no date span could be identified, a nominal date of AD 550-560 has been assigned to distinguish these entries from those dated by material that spans the duration of the use of the cemetery.

The relative infrequency with which graves intercut (there are only six examples: see below), provides little opportunity for clarifying these broad phases from within the cemetery itself. Imprecise as the dating is, it does provide a basis for establishing the development sequence.

From the 104 graves (57% of the total) to which a phase has been assigned, it is clear that the cemetery developed polyfocally rather than evolving from a single centre; only the cremations, which are few and undatable, exhibit a localised distribution along the south-eastern edge of the cemetery. This concentration may give some weight to the argument that the cremations are associated with an early phase in the development of the cemetery and were therefore localised in their distribution. However, if cremation continued as a rite throughout the life of the cemetery, the exclusivity of its distribution suggests that this

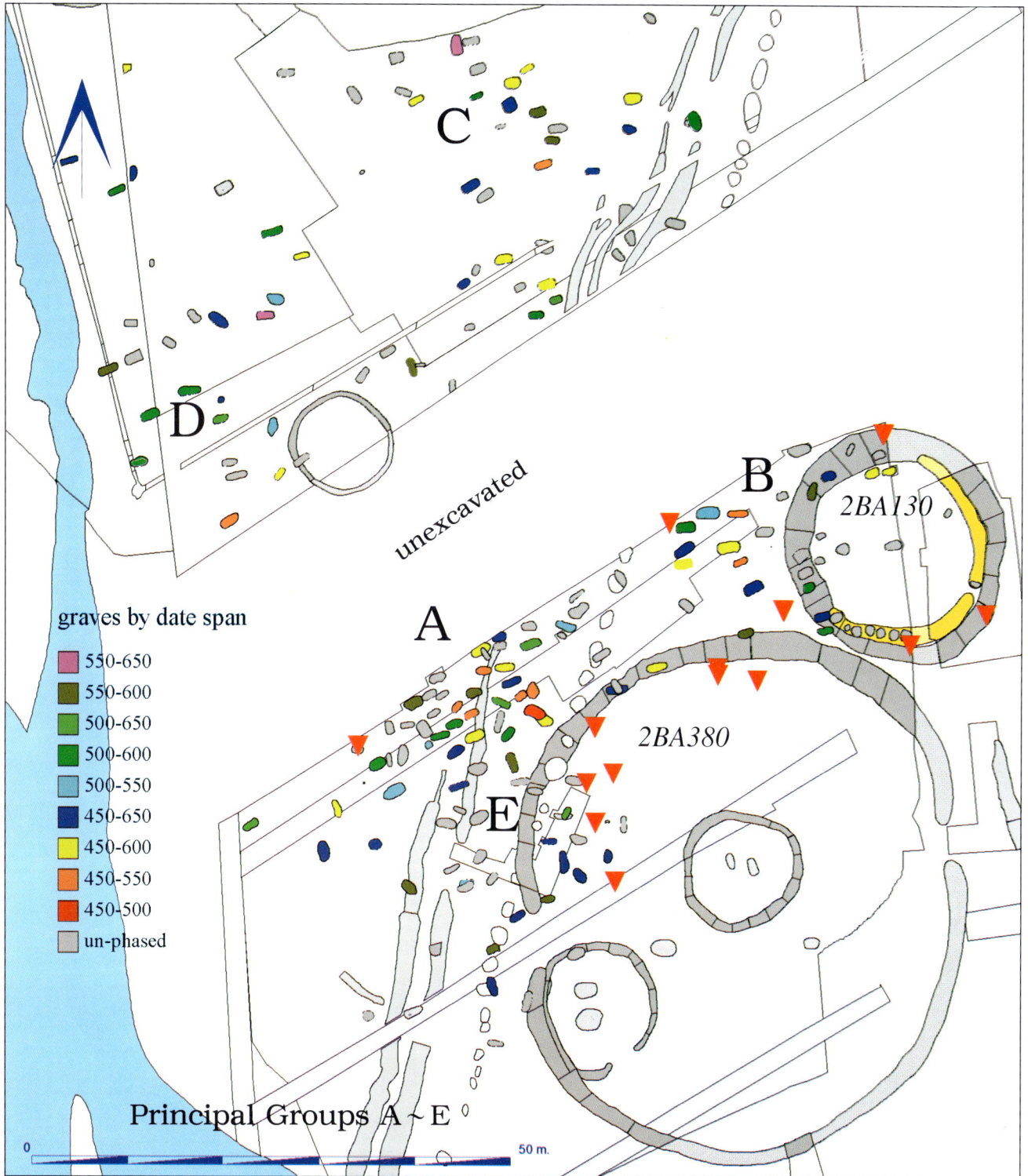

*Figure 48: distribution of the graves according to phase group (cremations as triangular symbols)*

area (in which, incidentally, it would have been most difficult to cut a grave pit) may have been reserved for cremation and as such have been identifiable to the Anglian population. The cremation distribution, restricted to the prehistoric enclosure and the larger of the barrows, also gives credence to the view that the prehistoric monuments were still generally visible at this time. The distribution of the graves cut into the ditches of barrow 2BA130 and enclosure 2BA380 clearly indicates that these were visible, and the distributions around the western entrance of the enclosure and to the north and west of barrow 2BA130

respect both these features (Fig 48).

The indications from the phase plans are that the cemetery develops from at least five centres, two on Site 1 (Groups C and D) and three on Site 2 (Groups A, B and E). As the site developed each group expanded, sub-groups were added and the gaps were filled. The polycentric nature of the distribution encourages one to suggest that each group relates to an individual extended family or kinship group. A generalised trend surface of the grave distribution reveals a number of concentrations, with the highest

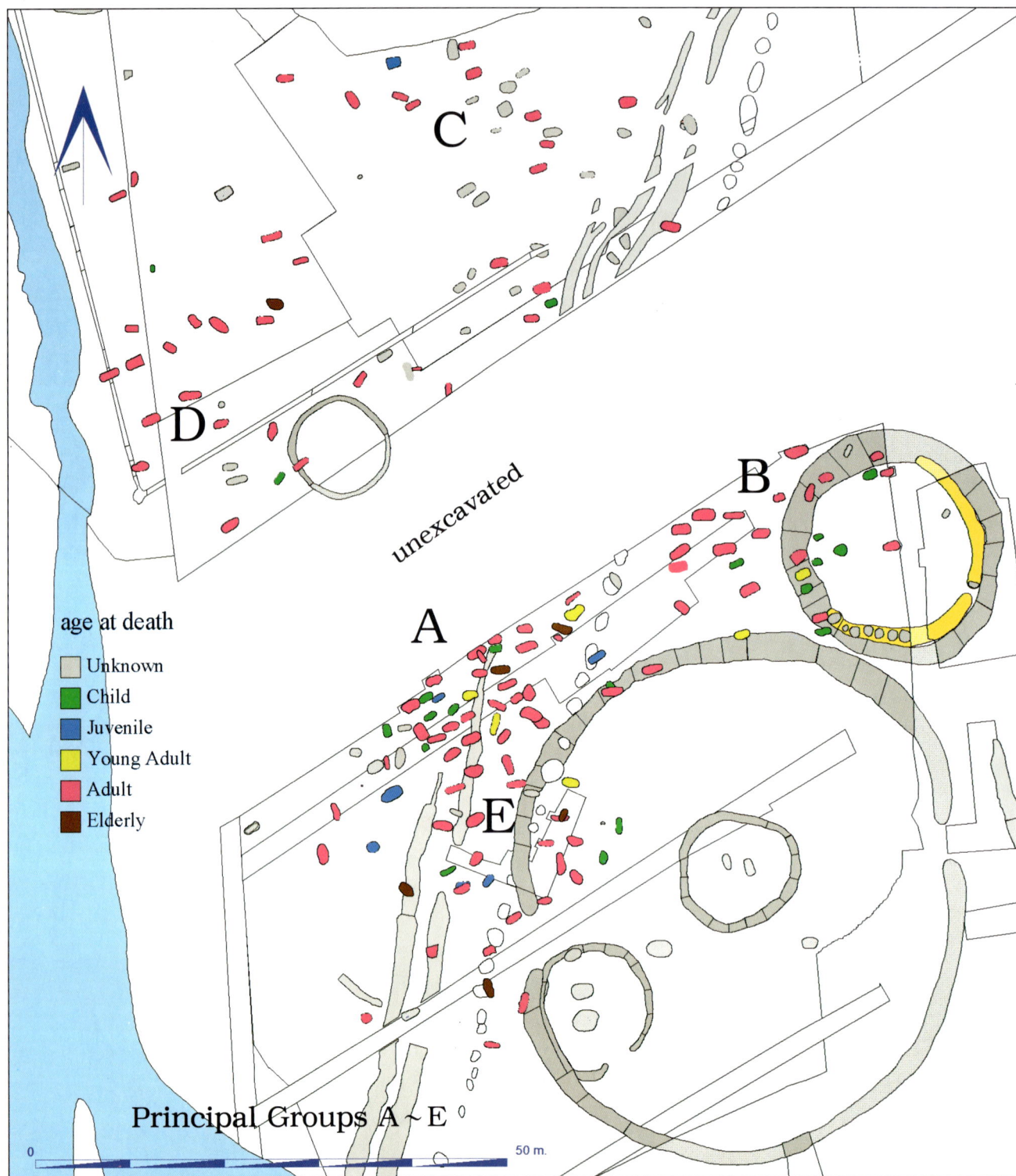

*Figure 49: distribution of the graves according to age at death*

concentration, Group A, in the western half of area 2BA, just south of the A64. This group also contains the highest number of early graves (Figs 46, 47).

If we examine the distribution by age then it is clear that the distribution within each group is fairly even, except in the case of Group C in area 1HE, an area in which bone survival was generally poor or nonexistent, and Group B which has a higher frequency of children than any other area (Fig 49).

The groups identified here, based initially upon the broad phasing of the graves, may hide other significant arrangements, in particular what appears to be a deliberate row of 'weapon burials' in group A (G72, G73, G74, G75) (Fig 50). The cluster in group A appears to sit on the north-east corner of another group, E, which covers a rectangular area extending to the south and west, aligned north-west to south-east, the southernmost edge of the rectangle running up to the entrance of the large enclosure 2BA380. It is unfortunate that so many graves in this extended group remain undated beyond the full range

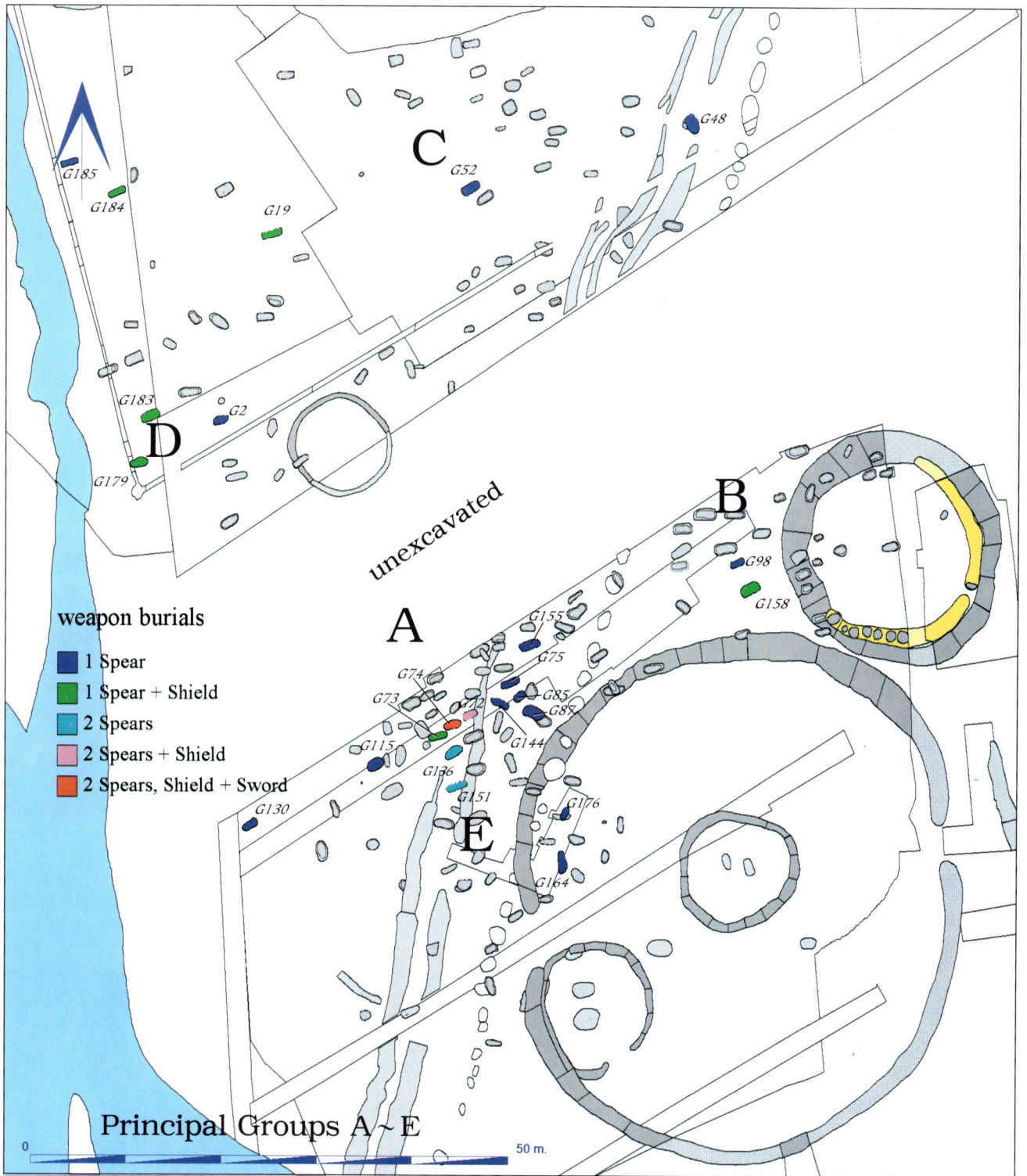

Figure 50: the distribution of weapon burials

available since the south-western edge of the group looks as though it may have respected some now lost boundary feature; only a few graves lay beyond this line, although the gap from here to the estimated edge of the stream channel was more than 15m.

If the date ranges are correct and linear and rectangular arrangements within the grave distribution in both Groups A and B are a result of deliberate placing, then the cemetery must have incorporated either a degree of long-term planning or exclusive ritual zones that were filled over a

long period of time. Whatever method we use to plot the overall distributions the picture is similar; burials of all phases occur over the whole of the cemetery area and the groups which emerge early in the use of the cemetery seem to continue throughout its life. Even though there are a number of later graves towards the edges, they also occur in the heart of the established groups.

One aspect of the distribution which may be of interest is apparent when the graves are plotted according to gender. In both Groups E and B a series of female graves

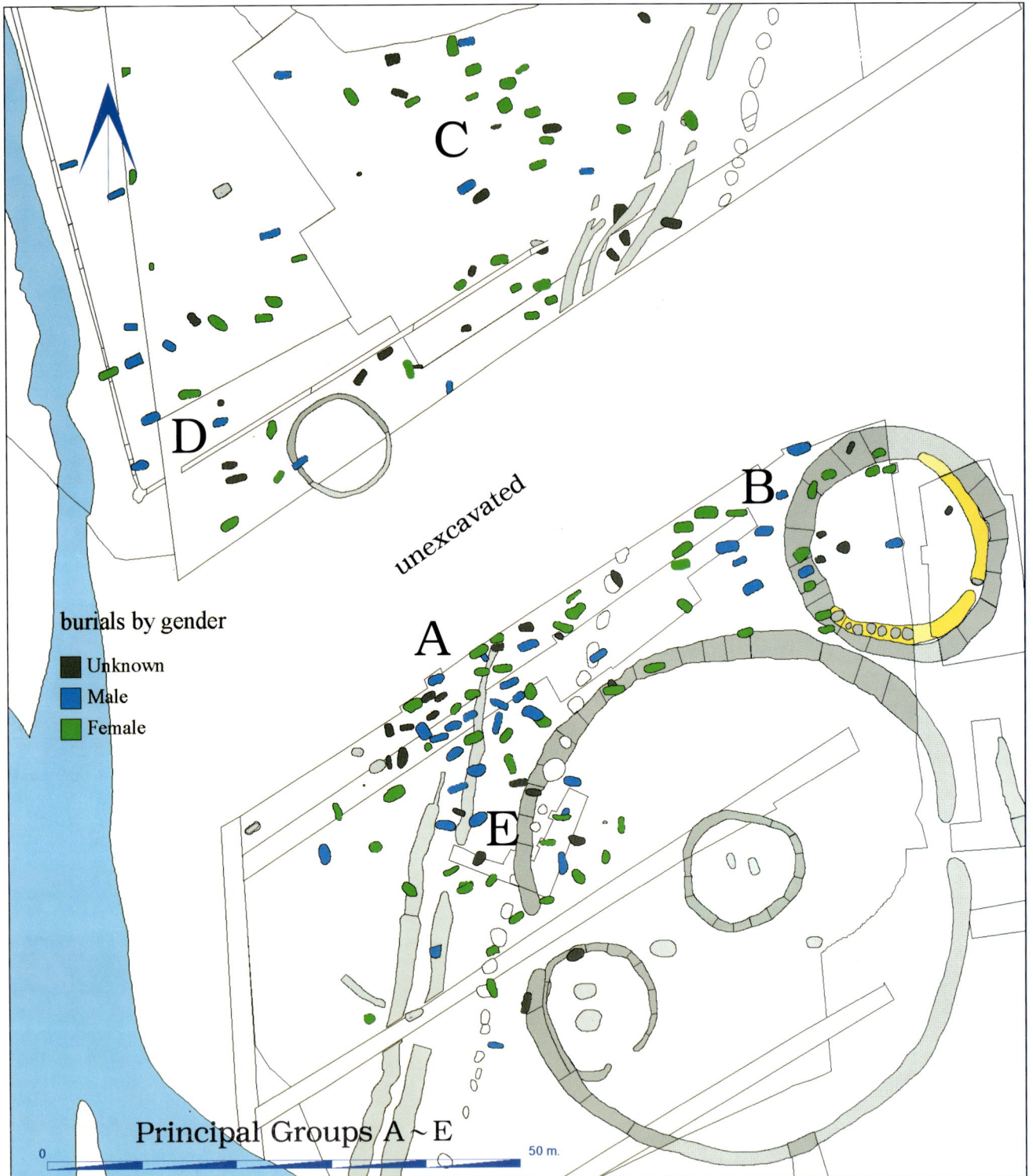

*Figure 51: distribution of the graves according to gender*

effectively enclose an area containing male graves; whether this is simply fortuitous is unclear and perhaps deserves examination in the light of other excavated cemeteries (Fig 51).

Adjacent pairs of graves within a single phase can be observed in a number of cases. Without much more precise dating it is difficult to argue the degree to which this may represent deliberate placement rather than evidence of what appears to be a relatively uniform polyfocal development sequence. Pairing of male/female graves within a phase can be observed in Group A: G154 (F) and G72 (M), G84 (F) and G85 (M); in Group E: G107 (F) and G164 (M); and in Group B: G76 (F) and G77 (M). Pairing of graves of the same gender can also be identified in a number of cases such as G76 and G72, both male 'weapon burials', and in Group B: G173 and G172, both female graves.

The polyfocal development observed at Heslerton raises important issues regarding the development and social reconstruction of Early Anglo-Saxon cemeteries.

# Aspects of burial practice

## Grave alignment

The question of grave alignment in Early Anglo-Saxon cemeteries has been discussed in detail by Rahtz (1978), and more recently by Hirst (1985) with particular reference to Sewerby. The evidence from West Heslerton is similar to that from Sewerby but contrasts with that from Norton, where grave alignments showed a more consistent pattern (Sherlock and Welch 1992). 50% of the graves at West Heslerton are aligned generally west–east with the head to the west; the remainder, however, are fairly evenly distributed round the points of the compass. Within the range 220 to 280⁰ there are two distinct peaks when the data is plotted, with more than 30 graves each aligned to both 270 and 250⁰ but fewer than 15 to 260⁰; when examined in relation to the plan there is no clear significance in this distribution. The distribution itself is likely to be biased by the data generation process, since measuring the grave alignment with any real precision was not possible, especially in view of the ill-defined nature of most of the grave cuts. Beyond the fact that the

west–east alignment is preferred in all phases, graves can be aligned at any angle. Within the cluster centred on 250⁰ there are twice as many female as opposed to male burials, and while this may be significant the reason is not clear. At Sewerby the sample size is smaller and the distribution is similar, only 1 out of the 12 burials in both westerly clusters is not female. If we accept that the westerly aligned graves are aligned on the setting sun then we could suggest that more females died in the winter than did the males. A more likely explanation is that the graph reflects the bias introduced by sexing by grave goods.

There is nothing to indicate that there is either an ethnic or social bias in the burial alignment overall; taking the one obviously distinctive group, the weapon burials, the alignments of the graves show the same general distribution as the sample as a whole. Hirst (1985) has suggested that the burial alignment was determined by individual religious belief and that the varied distribution at Sewerby

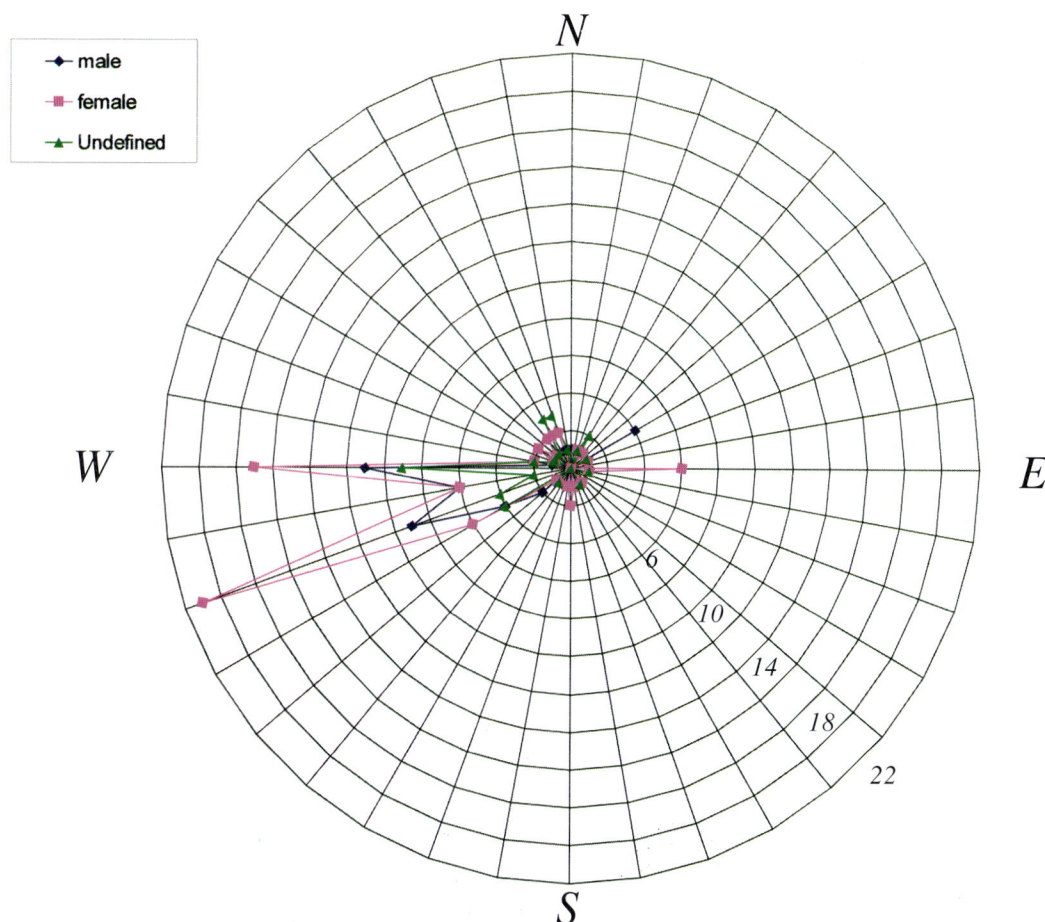

*Figure 52: radial plot showing the frequency of orientation of the burials by gender*

may reflect this. While this argument is quite acceptable, it raises important questions about how we interpret the grave clusters which feature at West Heslerton. If this clustering indicates kinship or family groups and the burial position is determined by individual belief, then it is difficult to reconcile the great variation within each cluster.

It is also difficult, when seeing only the below-ground view of the cemetery, to consider the other factors which may have determined grave alignment. The clusters identified here indicate a degree of planning and maintenance, and possibly in the case of the row of weapon graves a degree of the ritual planning of space. Certainly the alignment of some of the graves was determined by the prehistoric monuments, as in the case of the graves cut into the enclosure ditch, and other upstanding features may have restricted the use of parts of the cemetery. Many of the alignments may derive simply from the availability of space. Along the western side of the cemetery in Group E, the alignments of four out of six graves are generally to the north or the south rather than to the west; perhaps a trackway or slight barrier such as a hedge restricted alignment in this area next to the stream. The lack of any distinct correlation between the alignment of the graves with other factors indicates that the alignment was of less importance to the Anglian population than we tend to believe.

# Grave size

There is always a problem in attempting to assess the original depth of archaeological features in a plough-damaged and denuded landscape. At West Heslerton this situation is made more complex by the fact that in some areas the natural surface had clearly been eroded by plough damage while in others, although a clear buried soil horizon could not be identified, the ground level had risen as a consequence of the deposition of blown sand which had protected these areas from damage in recent times at least. Clearly any measurement of depth based on a simple addition of the depth of topsoil above the grave would produce spurious and certainly incorrect data. During excavation the depths recorded related to the point at which the grave first became clear and although any attempt to reconstruct the original depth in this environment would be fraught with difficulties, local differences within areas subjected to the same post-depositional change do show considerable variation which can be classified crudely if not in detail.

Excavated grave depth varies from the shallowest, effectively at the interface between the ploughsoil and the natural, to a maximum depth of 0.8m (G78). There is no correlation between the grave depth and the quantity or quality of the grave assemblage and there is likewise no patterning across the cemetery as a whole, other than the fact that the shallowest graves occur in the areas that we believe to have suffered most plough damage, a some-

what circular observation. When plotted against grave volume rather than depth there is a slight bias in favour of female graves but still no correlation with other attributes such as body position or grave assemblage.

# Coffins

In addition to body-stain features a number of graves contained staining which demonstrated the presence of a coffin while in one case, G86, a fragment of oak planking survived lying on top of the burial. Metal coffin fittings are not a characteristic feature of Early Anglo-Saxon coffins and it is not clear whether the coffins comprised simple arrangements of planks around the body or more elaborate constructions jointed, pegged or tied together. At West Heslerton the coffin stains were always fragmentary and showed a variable degree of survival; in no case could staining of a coffin cover be clearly defined above the burial during excavation. Where the side or head boards of the coffin could be isolated during excavation, increased staining at the base of the grave may owe its formation to the decay of both the coffin lid and the base as well as differential decay of the body and associated organic materials.

The survival of coffin stains was greatest in the most sandy parts of the site. Sites 1A and 8AA contained 11 graves showing clear evidence of coffins with a further 11 examples from site 2BA. This number is, however, unlikely to be a meaningful statistic given the variability in preservation in the graves in general, the frequent presence of less well defined organic staining suggesting that coffins were more frequent than the direct evidence suggests. There is no correlation between the presence of an identified coffin and the grave assemblage.

# Grave markers

The lack of intercutting graves, the clustering identified above, and the overall layout of the cemetery indicate that graves must have been marked in some way, even if only by a slight mound of soil. If we take the minimum date span of the cemetery as 125 years then it is unlikely that, without maintenance, a simple earth mound derived from the grave pit itself would have remained clearly visible. In no part of the cemetery was there any evidence for individual posts being used as grave markers or the type of four-post arrangements surrounding graves found in Kent and elsewhere in the south of England, nor of any Anglian ring ditches enclosing individual graves. The rectangular distribution of the graves in Groups B and E has already been observed, but there was no evidence to indicate what had influenced the distribution. In the north-eastern part of Area 2BA there was some indication that two graves may have been marked with stone cairns using Roman quern fragments (G79, G154) and in two other cases pottery vessels found high in the fills may likewise have served as markers (G77, above G168). The possibility that pots may have been placed at the surface above the graves is of some interest since if this were the case one is tempted to interpret the practice as the provision of foodstuffs after death.

# Intercutting graves

There are only six cases where graves intercut, assuming that we accept the interpretation of G118 above as a double burial. The rarity with which burials intercut in Early Anglo-Saxon cemeteries is both a benefit and a disadvantage. Whereas most graves remain undisturbed and intact where they have not been affected by post-depositional erosion through ploughing, there is little to help define the broad typologically derived date ranges. If graves of this period intercut more frequently the problem of the imprecision of the dating would probably be substantially resolved.

Intercutting graves were found in both the northern and southern parts of the cemetery, with one example in 1HE (G47/G49), one in area 1A (G14/G17) and further examples in areas 2F (G176/G177) and 2BA (G83/G87, G88/G106 and G149/G152).

In 1HE the explanation is quite obvious, since both burials also cut away a Beaker burial leaving only the vessel intact; these burials were clearly cut into a barrow. The intensive wind erosion coupled with plough damage in this part of the site had removed all trace of the monument; however, the presence of the Beaker and a gap in the later prehistoric boundary gullies running through the area provide adequate evidence to show that a barrow had originally been part of the landscape. The later burial, G49, a male aligned towards the south-east, was accompanied by a spearhead of Swanton's type C2/E2 and a knife, and had disturbed the burial of a female whose long-bones were distributed at the north end of the grave with a group of amber beads. The spearhead would generally be dated to the sixth century and the amber beads to the later sixth, and so a date late in the life of the cemetery can be assumed. This grave is the most easterly within the northern half of the cemetery and its location on the eastern side of Group C may result from pressure on the available space in the core area. Whether the supposed barrow was visible to any great extent at the time we cannot be sure. However, it would be surprising if these two graves were the only ones to take advantage of any already present mound, and we may therefore suggest either that any earlier monument had largely disappeared from sight by the time the cemetery became established or that the use of the barrows was deliberately avoided on account of superstition or respect.

The legs of a prone burial were contained in a narrow slot aligned west–east in the centre of area 1A (G17). The slot was less than 0.3m wide and it appeared almost as if the legs had been jammed into it; the feet may have been tied together. The remainder of the burial, that of an unsexed adult, had been removed by the cutting of grave G14 and thus it remains undated.

Using Swanton's dating for spearheads (Swanton 1973 and 1974), grave G87 would appear to belong to the fifth century, the only one to contain objects not classified as spanning a broader period. This grave was disturbed both by the cutting of grave G83 which contained an adult female and by later rig and furrow. The assemblage from G83 can be dated to within the period of the late fifth to the end of the sixth centuries. One can identify no external reason why these two graves intercut but they are on the edge of the cluster marked 2A, where the pressure on space appears to have been at its greatest.

In the centre of 2BA, in one of the initial sample areas 2F, a well furnished late sixth-century female burial, G177, accompanied by a cruciform brooch decorated with Style I panels and bearing a runic inscription on the reverse, was partially cut away by the burial of an elderly male G83 accompanied by a large bent spearhead of type E3 which have a date range extending into the seventh century. This grave must be among the latest in the cemetery and, with grave G87, demonstrates that weapon burials occurred throughout the life of the cemetery.

The remaining two instances where a direct stratigraphic relationship exists between graves offer little towards an enhancement of the dating. G149, which contained an unaccompanied adult male, was cut into G152 which could be dated anywhere in the period from the late fifth to the end of the sixth century. One aspect of this grave may be important. The head lay directly above a purse group related to the burial below, the condition of which was exceptional, perhaps on account of the altered localised environmental conditions following the insertion of the later burial. The child in grave G106, which cut G88, was accompanied by a pottery vessel and possibly a Roman coin, although this might have been residual; the lower grave cannot be precisely dated and the dating assigned covers the whole of the life of the cemetery.

# Grave form and burial position

Given the difficulty of distinguishing between the natural sand and the fills of most of the graves, the plan forms of the excavated features must to some degree be seen as an approximation, based not on clear differences in colour as much as on variations in the texture and density of the grave fill as opposed to the natural sand. Even allowing for a degree of excavator 'sculpting' it is clear that the graves were generally ovate and only broadly sub-rectangular in plan form, many being shallow and the bases not flat but scooped out. The implication is that the graves were not as carefully cut as we might anticipate and that they were simply suitably sized holes dug to take the burial; in fact, in a surprising number of cases the grave pit was insufficiently large to contain the burial fully within the base.

When we examine both the overall grave form and the placing of the burial in the grave, the evidence from West Heslerton indicates that the process of burial may not have been as careful as we tend to assume. The graves are neither neatly arranged nor neatly cut, and the body positions in some cases almost suggests that a hole was simply dug and the body thrown into the pit.

West Heslerton, like Sewerby and Norton, has instances of extended, crouched, flexed and prone burials; in addition there are both bound and multiple burials. The process of categorising the body position is not as simple as it may at first seem. The poor condition of the skeletal remains meant that often only fragments of bone and stains survived and sometimes not even these gave sufficient evidence to determine the body position with any accuracy. The tremendous variation in body position must include the results of post-depositional effects, although we can rarely identify these specifically; what we see is the final resting position of the body, which is not necessarily the same as its position when first placed in the grave (Fig. 53). In some cases it appeared that a burial on its side had slumped into a semi-prone position during decay. In many cases the position of the body appears to have been determined by no other factor than the shape and size of the grave.

# Extended burials

The most distinctive and perhaps the most deliberately placed of the burials were those laid out in an extended position with the torso supine and the legs extended, the well furnished female grave G78 representing a classic example of the type. These represent 14% of the total sample and 18% of the sample where body position could be determined. While the assemblages accompanying these extended burials do not show any unique attributes, it is probably significant that the two best furnished male and female graves both contain extended burials. There is some difficulty in examining the association between burial position and assemblage because a number of the graves considered flexed may in fact fall into the extended group. The distribution of cruciform brooches shows a bias towards inclusion with extended burials; of 11 graves containing cruciform brooches 5 were extended and 1 was assigned a flexed position with the torso supine, perhaps a loosely laid out extended burial; there were 3 accompanied bodies whose position was unclear. As a relative distribution within the cemetery as a whole this association must be significant.

# Crouched and flexed burials

There was a long-established tradition of both crouched and flexed burial in the prehistory of Eastern Yorkshire and it is not surprising that the rite continued into the Early Anglo-Saxon era. Margaret Faull's suggestion that the crouched burials with northerly grave alignments in cemeteries in Eastern Yorkshire represent native as opposed to continental Anglians, while offering an avenue of research, does not at present seem testable within the context of West Heslerton, where there is no distinctive association between burial position and the grave alignment (Faull 1974). At Norton, where 32% of the burials were crouched, the argument may be stronger, since the layout of that cemetery is quite different to that at West Heslerton.

Of the total number of burials, crouched and flexed burials make up 55% and 69% respectively of those where a position can be determined. The distinction between crouched and flexed burial is often difficult to ascertain; burials have been considered crouched when the legs are placed at an angle of less than $90^o$ to the torso. The poor survival of skeletal material has hampered the precision with which burials can be assigned to either class; however, the size of the sample is sufficient to indicate the general trend. The comparison between attributes based on gender is hampered by the fact that by virtue of the more frequent and more extensive assemblages associated with females they are over-represented in the sample as a whole. If we assign those burials for which a gender has not been assigned, whether by bone or by grave goods, to the male group, then gender-based statistics take on a more balanced appearance. The general frequency of accompanied to unaccompanied burials and the extensive nature of the female assemblages is such that this process of incorporation is unlikely to misrepresent the true picture. Flexed burials make up 54% of the female group and 51% of the male and unknown groups, with crouched making up 14% and 19% respectively, indicating a preference for crouched burial among the male and unknown burials. To a considerable extent the details of the burial position seem to owe more to the size of the grave than to any deliberate rite; it seems somehow absurd to imagine the members of the Anglian community considering whether to place a body with the legs flexed at less or more than $90^o$. What may perhaps be significant is the choice of whether to place the body on the left or the right side. In the case of burial on the right side the distribution is roughly even, with 21 males and unknown and 20 females. Burial on the left side was preferred less for females, with only 7 represented as opposed to 16 in the male and unknown group. This may not be particularly significant; however, the girdle hangers or 'keys of authority' and purses carried by some of the females were generally on the left-hand side, possibly for reasons now less obvious than simply right-handedness.

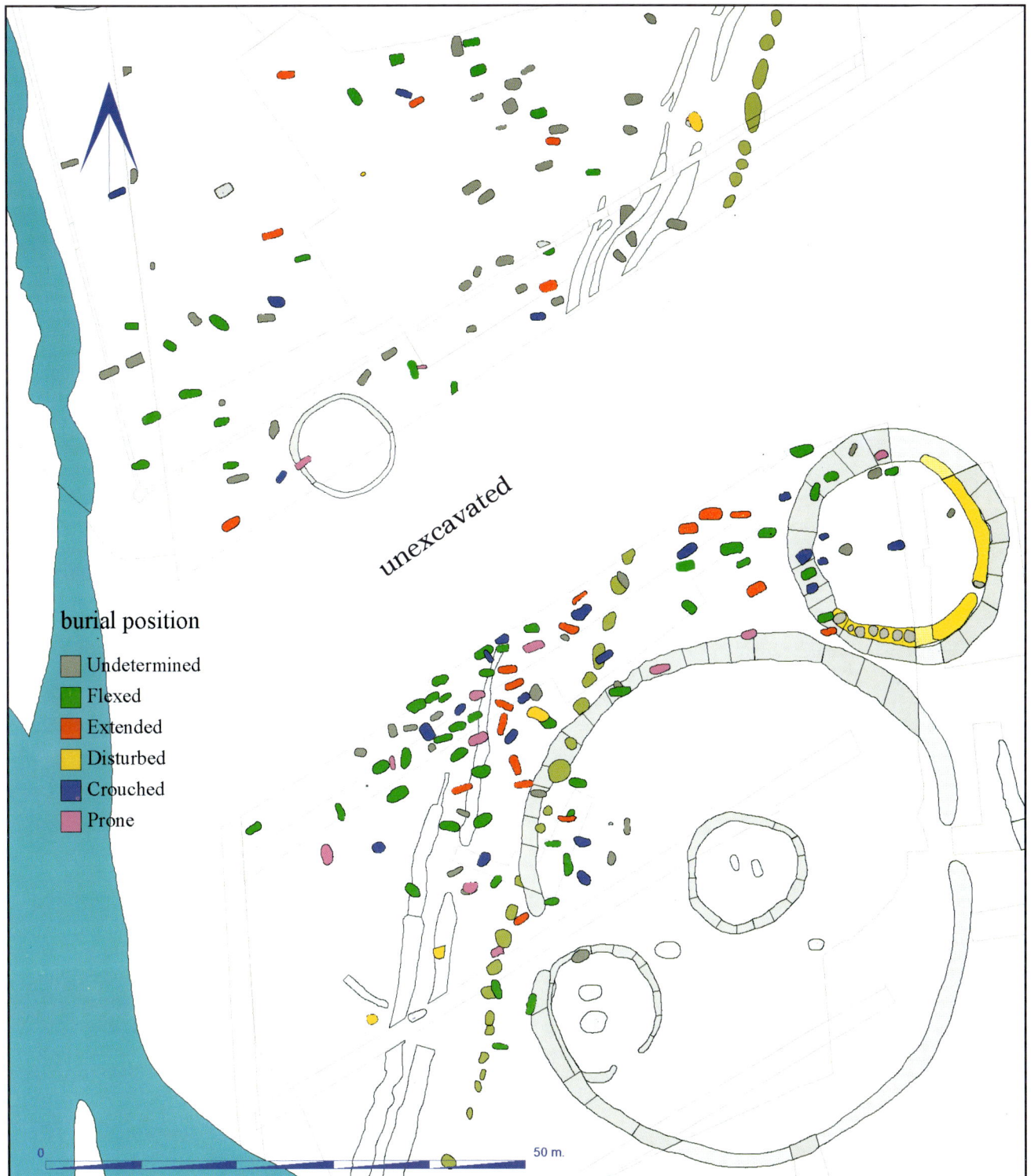

**burial position**

- Undetermined
- Flexed
- Extended
- Disturbed
- Crouched
- Prone

*Figure 53: plan showing the distribution of the graves according to burial position*

One distinction is clear, and may give some support to the theory that the crouched burials represent a distinct social group, and this is the fact that wrist-clasps, which occur in 27 graves, are absent in the case of the 12 crouched burials. Pader, in her analysis of the Holywell Row cemetery, has observed that wrist-clasps do not occur with extended burials, a situation almost the reverse of that observed here, indicating that we should not place too much stress on what appear in isolation to be distinctive characteristics (Pader 1982).

# Prone, bound and live burials

Prone burials seem to be a feature of the Northern Anglian cemeteries, with 3 at Sewerby, 7 at Norton and at least 12 at West Heslerton, a total of 22 from 3 cemeteries compared with 33 from 24 cemeteries in Britain as a whole (Harman *et al* 1981). Both Hirst and Sherlock and Welch (1985; 1992) have discussed the case for prone burial as a punishment, or for adulterers and witches in particular; whatever the case, the burials are not necessarily distinguished in other ways. The evidence from all three cemeteries suggests that at least some of these individuals may have been buried alive. Burial alive need not have necessarily been deliberate; comas and other medical conditions could have been mistaken for death. At Sewerby all were female; at Norton three were female and four male, and at Heslerton seven were female, three male and two of unknown sex. One male, one female and two of unknown sex were unaccompanied. The remainder were all accompanied, two of the female burials containing an unusually high status grave assemblage and one of the males a spearhead. At all three sites prone burial of one individual in a double or multiple grave occurs (see below). The grave orientations covered all points of the compass and the locations were distributed throughout the cemetery. It is unlikely that the count of 12 prone burials is a correct total since the poor bone survival and effects of animal burrowing in the graves make it likely that other examples went unnoticed. At Norton 5% of the burials were prone and at Heslerton 7%, making it a veritable den of witches if we are to accept this interpretation. The two female burials with high grave scores, G89 and G113, (see below) were both buried in fairly deep graves cut into the prehistoric enclosure ditch; G166 was unaccompanied and cut into the northern side of the enclosing ditch of barrow 2BA130 and another, G6, was cut through the suspected barrow ditch 1A10; the remainder show no particular distribution. Three at least were bound; G132 at the knees, G17 at the ankles (and partially cut away by a later grave), and G114 also at the feet. The position of the head and the hands in G113, G89, G6 and G70 all suggest live burial. Other possible examples include G16, which extended beyond the limit of excavation; the legs were bent up with the feet sticking out at the base of the ploughsoil. It was not possible to excavate the skull, and the bones of the torso had not survived. If the associations of these burials were in some other way distinctive, and at present this seems not to be the case, then they would make a more acceptable class; however, the range of grave goods is no different from that found elsewhere in the cemetery, and had it not been for the body position they would be invisible within the group as a whole. Clearly this is an aspect of the cemetery that deserves more attention than it is possible to give here. If these are indeed live burials there is a major distinction in ritual practices in the Northern Anglian region. Alternatively, some at least if not all of the positions achieved could result from care-free disposal of the remains; the character of the graves in general does not suggest that the burials were carefully laid out except in a very few cases and it may be that we grossly overemphasise the rituals associated with the burial process itself. We know nothing in detail concerning Early Anglo-Saxon beliefs and later documents such as Beowulf are concerned more with the extraordinary rather than the ordinary. One fact upon which everyone can agree is a belief in an afterlife, but we do not know at what point the spirit was thought to make the

transition from life to afterlife. If the afterlife began immediately at the point of death then perhaps the disposal of the earthly shell was of less importance than we might assume. To argue that the grave goods represent items needed in the afterlife is perhaps not as satisfactory as at first it seems; the males would have had a pretty thin time ahead, while the females may have been well dressed but had little else to carry them through an infinite existence.

# Multiple burials

Another feature of West Heslerton that also occurs at both Sewerby and Norton is the presence of multiple burials in the same grave. There are three examples of multiple burial as distinct from intercutting graves — G42, G101 and probably G118/G120 — although this was not recognised in the field. The last example is of particular interest because the upper of the two bodies, G118 (skeleton 2BA536), lay in a prone position. In this case, as in Sewerby Graves 44 and 45, both burials were of females, the upper burial surviving in poor condition although better than G120 (skeleton 2BA587) which was in fragmentary condition. During excavation this grave presented a problem because it was exceptionally difficult to define and the second burial was only isolated following the discovery of a latch-lifter buried at some distance to the south of the skeleton. At the time this arrangement was considered to represent two intercutting graves, although no edges could be defined, but on reflection it seems more likely that this represents another double burial like that at Sewerby, albeit on a much less grand scale. The pair of burials in grave G42 were represented only by the grave goods which again represent two females; unfortunately the evidence does not survive to indicate whether either was buried in a prone position. Grave G101 contained the burial of an adult female and a child of unknown sex, aged 5–6 years at death. The child lay in a crouched position facing the mother. This one at least does not defy interpretation and we can perhaps assume that here we are dealing with a mother and child, with the left forearm of the female extended as if placed upon the body of the child.

# Population and society

The interpretation of Early Anglo-Saxon cemetery data is fraught with difficulties, not least of which is our inability to provide precise dating of the grave assemblages and the frequently limited sample size. The advent of the 'New archaeology' more than 20 years ago focused scholastic efforts on theory generation largely directed towards social reconstruction, but this has not produced a solution to the problems of social reconstruction from Early Anglo-Saxon cemetery data, a situation exacerbated by the lack of associated settlement evidence. Arnold and Alcock have offered interpretations of the burials of Southern England and Bernicia respectively based on wealth scoring, while Pader has presented a case for social patterning derived from internal variations in burial practice and the distribution of grave goods at Holywell Row, Mildenhall, Suffolk (Arnold 1982; Alcock 1981; Pader 1982). The work in progress on the results from the excavation of the associated settlement at West Heslerton is of immense importance and we will have to return to compare and contrast in detail the impressions given by the cemetery with those from the settlement once that work is completed.

The Anglian cemetery was in use for a period of between 125 and 175 years, during which time an estimated 300–350 individuals were buried. The layout of the cemetery shows elements of long-term management and organisation which are reflected in the distribution plots based on a variety of criteria (Figs. 42-51). The conditions for the preservation of human skeletal material were very poor, but the specialists have gleaned a wealth of new data from the all too small scraps of bone. The study and extraction of ancient DNA from bone samples is now possible and one hopes that this form of research will be treated as a priority in any future work, since it is currently the only available method of demonstrating direct genetic links, and must be more reliable that working on impressions given from the excavations of sites such as West Heslerton. With the publication of a number of other major finds in the region we have seen, for the first time, a large body of relatively well excavated and recorded material, all of it from rescue excavations, come into the public domain, making possible the sort of inter-site as well as intra-site analysis of Northern Anglian material that is needed to enhance our knowledge of this period.

The interpretation of cemetery data draws upon a large number of variables. Some of them are factual, for instance the size or chemical composition of a brooch, but most are highly subjective; to some a gilded great square-headed brooch might be considered a beautiful and valuable item while to others it may be seen simply as an item of 'kitsch'. We have no idea what the processes were by which material is chosen, if indeed it is chosen, for inclusion with a burial. Are, for instance, the brooches and beads possessed by the female burials 'symbols of power' or more mundane dress fittings? The physical condition and longevity of the Anglian population is difficult to assess, and recent work at Spitalfields has indicated that the precision with which the age at death can be calculated is far smaller than we have tended to believe in the past (M Cox pers comm). We should therefore be careful before asserting too strenuously the short lifespan of the population, most of whom apparently died in early middle age (see M Cox's report on the human bones below).

If we are to attempt to identify social structure within the cemetery we need to be aware that there remain fundamental problems regarding precise sexing of the burials, difficulties in identifying native as opposed to foreign burials and modern perceptions of wealth and possession which may not be appropriate to Early Anglo-Saxon society. There are for instance two burials identified as female on osteological grounds although they were accompanied by weapons which would traditionally be accepted as indicative of a male burials (G164, G184). The presence of other weapon burials that were initially described as tall and gracile and possibly female demonstrates the need for DNA analysis to accurately sex these individuals. It is possible that the different stature of these individuals may reflect a different ethnic population; perhaps these burials represent the foreign (probably Scandinavian) component in the cemetery. Unfortunately there are no comparable differences amongst the burials interpreted as females.

There seem to be no specific indicators amongst the grave goods that could be used as ethnic indicators; most burials were accompanied by grave goods and there is no particular focus to those that might be considered poorly furnished. Regardless of how we interpret the migration of North European peoples into post-Roman Britain the lack of any evidence of contemporary non-Anglo-Saxon cemeteries or indeed settlements indicates that the native and migrant populations merged to become what we see as Anglo-Saxon communities. We have no evidence to show whether sites such as West Heslerton were established by an initial group of migrant North Europeans with a native component, or whether the migration continued through the life of the cemetery, introducing new blood into a gradually emerging Anglian society.

One of the most striking aspects of Early Anglo-Saxon cemeteries throughout lowland Britain is the degree to which Anglo-Saxon material culture is adopted almost exclusively so soon after the end of the Roman period. There has been a tendency to see this as a product of the total collapse of society and economy after the end of the Roman period; plagues and mass emigration have been invoked to explain the disappearance of the Roman Britons from the landscape. The appearance of Early Anglo-Saxon settlements on *de novo* sites may be interpreted as a demonstration of dominance by the migrant component in the population; however, this interpretation reflects a view of a thriving Roman Britain which suddenly stops in AD 410, a view not supported by the archaeological evidence. The documented date for the ending of Roman Britain in AD 410 has coloured archaeological interpretation for too long; we can argue that, in essence, Roman Britain was in a state of economic, climatic and almost certainly social decline for much of the fourth century. The appearance of Early Anglo-Saxon settlements in new locations may reflect the availability of new lands for settlement following the collapse of Roman land tenurial arrangements, the Early Anglo-Saxons grasping a new opportunity. In the Vale of Pickering; at least the principal Late Iron Age and Roman settlement complex, along the fen edge, shows signs of increasing wetness in the fourth century, making it less than suitable for continued settlement.

Taking a positive view the climatic, economic and social upheaval occurring during the declining decades of Roman Britain provided the perfect environment for the emergence of a new social order in Early Anglo-Saxon England. This need not be a new social order dominated by Anglian, Saxon or Jutish overlords. The widespread adoption of Anglo-Saxon material culture may reflect availability rather than dominance. The factory-based ceramic industries of Roman Britain indicate a consumer society based upon large-scale production, widespread trade networks and urban markets. Once these have disappeared a locally based substance economy is re-established; the migrant population were in a better position to lead this forward in contrast to the local population living in the shadow of four centuries of existence under the imperial arrangements of Rome.

# Social structure

Whether we interpret burial with grave goods in the context of a belief in an afterlife or some other belief system, the inclusion of grave goods can be interpreted in terms of the incorporation of disposable wealth. If we are to attempt to interpret social structure within a buried population, the combination of spatial arrangements and grave goods assemblages provides a starting point for such analyses.

The analysis of Early Anglo-Saxon cemetery data on a wealth scores basis is a widely used and logical approach. The tendency to see the graves as rich or poor or Anglian and native, however, is crude to say the least, and prejudges much about the formative years of English society. In a non-monetary economy it is the effort expended in the manufacture, collection or extraction of resources combined with their relative rarity that determines their value, so to give, for instance, all beads a value of 2 each, as Arnold has in his studies of burials in the South of England, disregards the degree of skill and effort that went into their manufacture (Arnold 1982, Arnold *et al* 1983). A rope inlay glass bead is, for instance, as difficult to manufacture as a cone beaker, and the rarity of such beakers in graves has encouraged people to assign them high score values (P Musgrove, 'Glassworks', pers comm). In the West Heslerton settlement fragments of glass vessels are not uncommon, and certainly occur more frequently than copper alloy brooches, highlighting perhaps the relative fragility of the glass but also the relative ease with which copper alloy can be recycled. The case of the beads is potentially very important; the inclusion of glass cullet in purse assemblages in a number of graves indicates that glass was collected and curated, possibly retained until it could be traded for beads. It is possible that the beads were used as a form of currency; in North Africa within the last century millefiori glass beads have performed exactly that function.

Figure 54 shows a trend surface generated on the basis of total number of objects in each grave; the effect of including bead numbers in the counts over-emphasises those graves with large bead groups and effectively suppresses those without bead assemblages. An alternative approach is to calibrate the grave goods totals to produce a more even trend, reducing the effect of the dominant bead assemblages (Fig 55). The method of calibration applied here is based upon the number of object types present with each burial, an approach similar to that used on the Norton material (Sherlock and Welch 1992). This approach minimises the risk of applying highly subjective values to each item. In this case each item has a score of 1 except in the case of the beads and wrist-clasps. Beads have been assigned scores according to quantity, so that 1–5=1, 6–50=2, 50–100=3, >100=4, and a pair of wrist-clasps has been given a value of 1 as has an individual clasp. This should not be viewed as anything other than a method of generating a generalised picture of the distribution of disposable wealth throughout the cemetery (Fig. 55). No attempt has been made to balance the resulting counts to remove the bias arising from the difference between 'female' and 'male' assemblages; the former frequently incorporating a greater range of material. Clearly there is a difference based on gender, and to attempt to accommodate this may

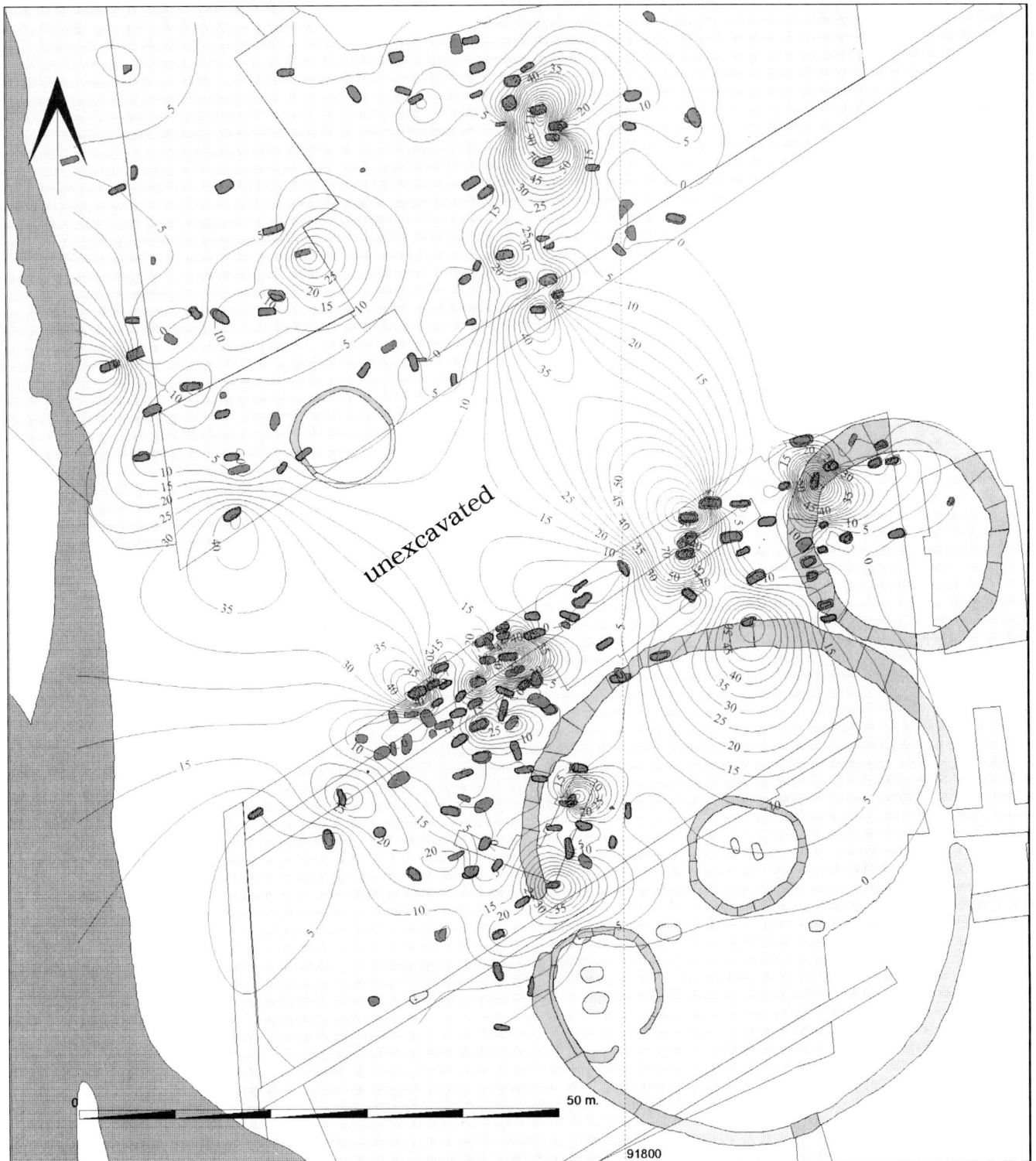

*Figure 54: plan showing a contoured trend surface based on the number of objects present statistics*

at the outset. There are, for instance, still questions regarding the degree to which grave assemblages can be used to accurately identify gender. The calibrated trend surface displayed in figure 55 does not indicate particular score concentrations greater than those generated by the density of the graves alone.

The scoring system adopted is quite simple and produces, we believe, an unbiased picture of what we may call 'types status'. One product of the method is that it tends to suppress the very great differences generated with more com-

plex systems. The evidence from the settlement does not indicate a massive variation in the overall status as represented in the structural evidence; rather, it indicates the contrary. The housing is of uniformly good quality and only in one area of the site do we see a clear change in the quality of the rubbish deposits, suggesting a settlement in which social stratification was represented by two clear levels, the comfortable and the more comfortably off. The clustering indicated using the calibrated number of types frequency seems to reflect the same polyfocal clusters demonstrated through the plots based

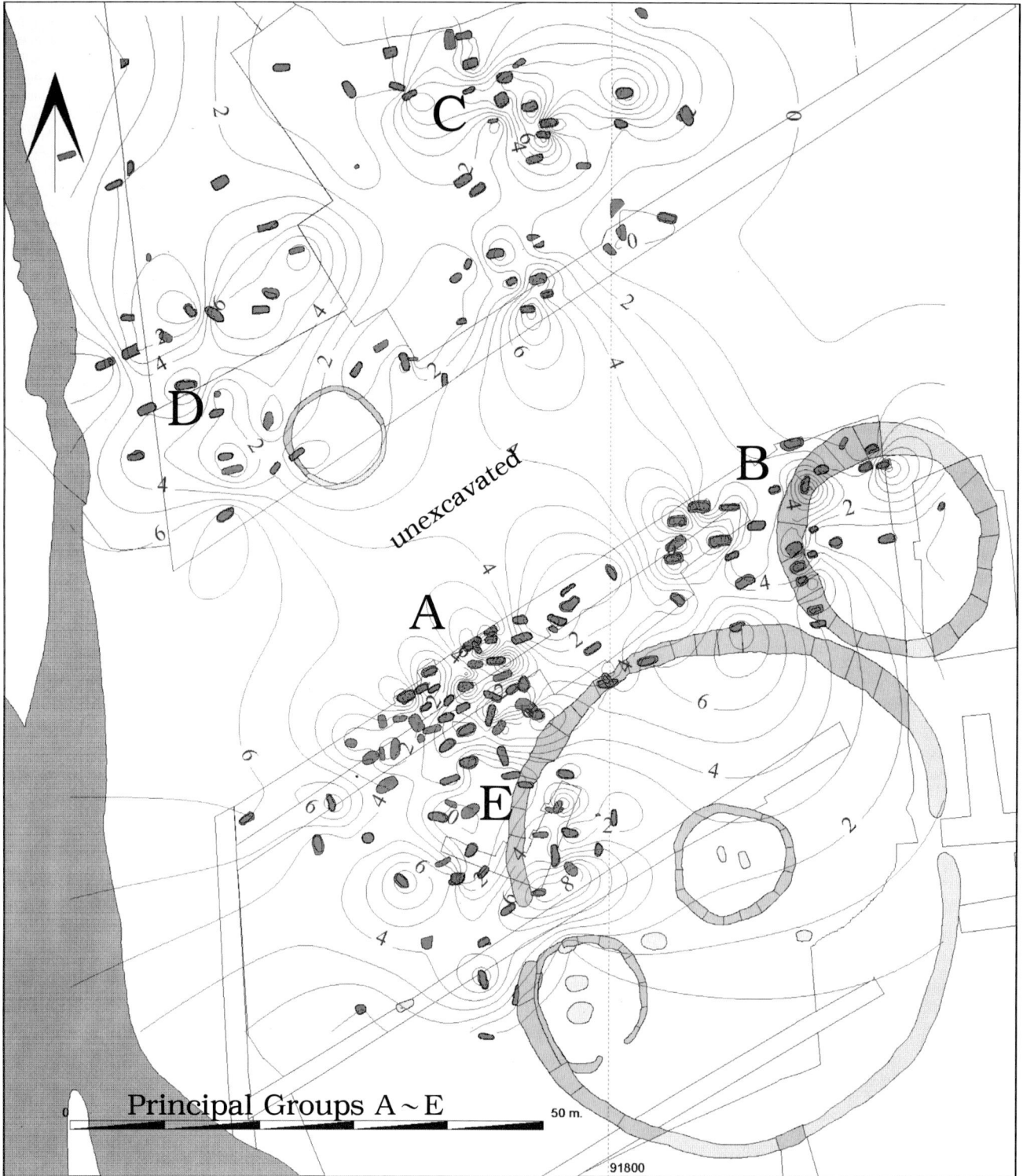

*Figure 55: Plan showing a contoured trend surface based on the number of types present statistics*

on chronological and other indicators. In the absence of high resolution chronological and guaranteed sexing data, any attempt to re-plot these data in relation to the calibrated types data could merely emphasise assumption rather than evidence.

Taken as a whole, the evidence from West Heslerton indicates that the cemetery developed from a series of focii centered on a major prehistoric monument complex. These focii may be indicative of kinship or family groups,

groups within which there was considerable variation in the level of disposable wealth as represented by the grave goods. Making some allowance for the area not examined in the centre of the cemetery, we can postulate that the cemetery may derive from between eight and fifteen groups. One of the challenges in analysing the excavated settlement will be to see whether this interpretation can be tested against the chronological, spatial and structural evidence from the early phase of the settlement.

# Anglian material culture

## Dress fasteners

### Brooches

65 graves contained at least one brooch or dress pin. Fourteen graves contained a single brooch or pin, 25 graves had 2, 25 had 3 and one grave produced 4. The styles of dress and method of fastening the various garments are discussed elsewhere in this volume, in the report on the textiles.

*Plate 38: digital scan of great square-headed brooch from Grave 123 (Scale 1:1)*

### Square-headed brooches

Three square-headed brooches were recovered from graves G14, G123 and G147. All accompanied adult females. Unfortunately, none of the associated grave goods are diagnostic in terms of date.

There were two gilded copper alloy great square-headed brooches from graves G14 and G123. Both have pieces of shaped sheet silver soldered to the upper corners of the headplate, around the side lobes, and around the foot terminal. The compositional elements of the brooch from G14 bear several similarities to the brooch from Londesborough Grave 6, E Yorks, classified as Group B1 by Leeds and Group XIV by Hines (Leeds 1949, 38–9, fig 59; Hines 1997, 107–111, pl 45a), but it also has much in common with those examples in Leeds' Group B8 and Hines' Group XXII, for example the corners of the upper headplates and the little side lobes on the footplate (Leeds 1949, 73; Hines 1997, 156–7, pl 86). The base of the bow was broken and repaired in antiquity by the application of two strips of copper alloy riveted to the front and back of the break. It was accompanied by a crude, undecorated funerary pot and some glass and amber beads.

The brooch from G123 has a similar shape and compositional elements to Mortimer's Driffield example, with its two studs on the bow and footplate and the downward-pointing triangle at the centre of the headplate, which Leeds placed in his group B8 (Mortimer 1905, 282, pl CIII, fig 828; Leeds 1949, 73, fig 120) However, it too has Group B1 features, a conclusion also reached by Hirst for the brooch in grave 19 at Sewerby, E Yorks, which is almost identical to the Heslerton example (Hirst 1985, 59–60, fig 39, pl IVB). Associated grave goods include a pair of openwork annular brooches and some glass and amber beads. Hines places the Sewerby brooch in his Group XXII (Hines 1997, 157–8, pl 82b).

Grave G147 produced a florid hybrid type with a square headplate with perforated corners, and a cruciform brooch-type foot, Leeds Type C2, a type well represented in the East Riding of Yorkshire (Leeds 1949, 79–82). It bears a very close resemblance to a brooch from Darlington, Co. Durham (Leeds 1949, pl 135). A second parallel from Fonaby in Lincolnshire has been dated to the latter part of the sixth or early seventh century (Cook 1981, 36–7, fig 13, pl II). The headplate bears similarities to an example from Mortimer's Driffield Group (1905, 282, pl CIII, fig 829). The associated assemblage includes Type B7 wrist-clasps, a simple iron penannular brooch, an undecorated flat copper alloy annular brooch and a bead necklace.

# Cruciform brooches

Twelve cruciform brooches were recovered from 11 graves: G62, G8, G12, G29, G177, G78, G84, G86, G95, G143 and G173. All accompanied adult females. A further fragment of copper alloy from Grave G83 may be part of a brooch. Unfortunately, the brooch from G8 was stolen shortly after it was found and could only be studied from a photograph. Grave G78 produced the only pair of cruciform brooches. In all cases, other forms of brooch were also present: pairs of annular brooches were associated with the cruciform brooches in graves G62, G29, G177, G86 and G173; an annular and a disc brooch accompanied the cruciform in grave G143; a small-long brooch and a Roman bow brooch in grave G12; a pair of small-long brooches in grave G95; a small-long brooch in grave G84; a small-long brooch and copper alloy dress pin in G8; and a pair of cruciform brooches, a small-long brooch, a copper alloy wire circlet and an annular brooch in grave G78.

*Plate 39: digital scan of a cruciform brooch from Grave 95. Aberg Group IV (Scale 1:1)*

*Plate 40: digital scan of the florid cruciform brooch from G29. Aberg Group V (Scale 1:1)*

The cruciform brooches have been classified according to Aberg's (1926, 28–55) groups:

**Group II** — Brooches with half-round knobs, foot without lappets, animal head with half-round nostrils, free or grown together below.

**Group III** — Brooches with half-round knobs, foot without lappets, animal head with scroll-shaped nostrils.

**Group IV** — Brooches with variously shaped knobs (Aberg 1926, 43, fig 70, 1–18); foot with lappets.

**Group V** — Brooches with knobs and nose parts greatly changed and generally decorated with animal ornament.

At Heslerton these are represented as follows: one from Group II, from grave G84; two from Group III, both from grave G78; eight from Group IV, from graves G62, G8, G12, G177, G86, G95, G143, and G173; and one from Group V from Grave G29.

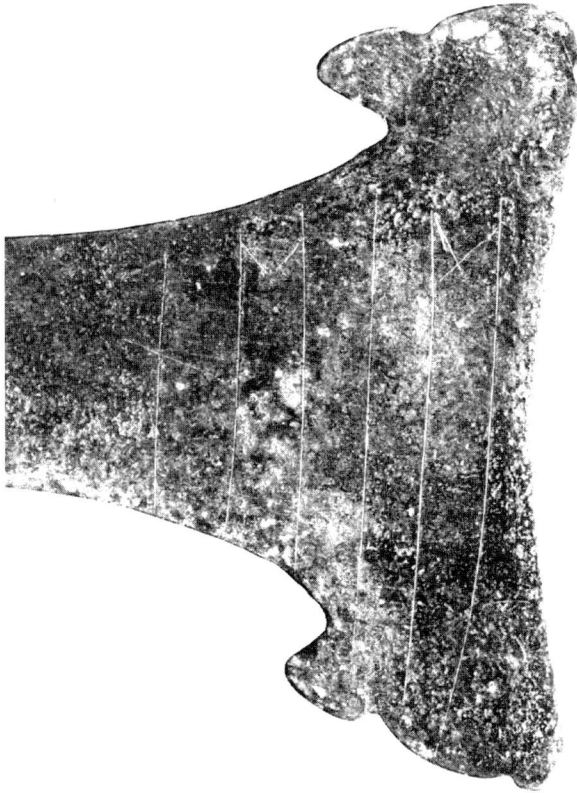

*Plate 41: digital scan of the runes on the back of a cruciform brooch from G177 (Scale 2:1)*

Ten of the brooches have cast half-round knobs; those in G62, G8, G95 and the pair in G78 have an integral knob at the top of the headplate, the two side-knobs having been cast separately. In graves G12, G84, G86, G143, and G173 these were cast as an integral part of the headplate. In three cases the knobs have nipples on the ends, G12, G84, G86. The brooch from G177 has flaring crescentic knobs and is decorated with panels of Style I ornament. The single example of a florid cruciform brooch comes from grave G29.

All of the Heslerton examples appear to be sixth-century in date. Typologically the earliest brooches are those without lappets from G78 and G84, while the latest include the example from G177, whose crescentic flaring knobs are considered to be a mid–late sixth-century development from the cast half-round knobs; and the florid brooch from G29, with its prominently browed mask, which also belongs to the mid–late sixth century (L Webster pers comm). The Group IV brooch from G12 is also considered to be a later development of this type, the nostrils beginning to change into animal heads at a late stage. This chronology is supported by the associated artefacts, the small-long brooches belonging to the first half of the sixth century (G8, G12, G78, G84), the Class B7, B12 and B13a wrist-clasps belonging to the late fifth–mid sixth century (G62, G12, G86, G143 and G173) and Class 13c and Class 18 clasps restricted to the sixth century (G95 and G177).

The brooch from G177 is of particular interest, as it has a runic inscription scratched along the back of the foot-plate. The runes spell out the word NEIM (R Page pers comm); as a word, this has no known translation. They may simply represent the name of the wearer, but it is possible that the runes were meant to be read individually, perhaps as a lucky charm. For example, runic inscriptions are not uncommon on weapons; some are personal names, others are associated with the warrior god Tiw, and one might assume that they were inscribed on weapons to ensure the support of the god in battle (Meaney 1981, 242). The fact that the runes are inscribed on the reverse of the brooch implies that their existence was known only to the wearer. Continental runic inscriptions on brooches are known from as early as the first century from sites in Denmark and Germany (Page 1987, 25–6). There are two runic inscriptions on the back of a disc brooch from the Buckland Anglo-Saxon cemetery; other English examples include a single rune scratched on a mid-sixth-century brooch from Sleaford in Lincolnshire and four runes on the reverse of a square-headed brooch from Wakerley in Northamptonshire (Evison 1987, 46–7).

# Small-long brooches

Seven graves contained a small-long brooch: G8, G12, G78, G84, G95 (pair), G97 and G154. Unfortunately the brooch in G8 was stolen before it could be studied. The seven that remain can be grouped according to Leeds (1945), the standard classification for small-long brooches. All of the brooches have catchplates with which to secure the iron pins. The original catchplate of the brooch in G97 was broken in antiquity; a replacement was soldered into place, part of it lapping onto the front of the brooch.

Six accompanied adult females, G8, G12, G78, G84 and G95; the others were buried with juveniles of eight or nine years of age, G97 and G154. What appears to be the

*Plate 42: digital scan of a small-long brooch from Grave 154 (Scale 1:1)*

fragment of the foot of a small-long brooch was recovered from the fill of grave G83.

The only pair is from Grave G95, of a type classified as small-long brooches of the square-headed variety (Leeds 1945); they are similar in shape to an example from Grave 72 at Linton Heath, Cambridgeshire (ibid, 63–6; fig 34f) which Leeds classifies as a square-headed imitation of the Kentish type, found as far north as Driffield (ibid, 65, fig 35). They were accompanied by a cruciform brooch, type B13c wrist-clasps, a bead necklace, knife, latchlifter and a bossed urn.

Two, from graves G12 and G97, are trefoil-headed, a type believed to have originated around AD 500 as a cheap variant of the cruciform brooch (Leeds 1945, 8). This is the largest and most widely distributed class of small-long brooch in England. The example from G12 is larger than the others from Heslerton and has a sub-triangular foot and no lappets (Leeds Class b). It was accompanied by a Roman bow brooch, a cruciform brooch, a bead necklace and a pair of Class 13a wrist-clasps, a type which had probably appeared by the end of the fifth century and was certainly present during the first quarter of the sixth century (Hines 1984, 107). The example from G97 is unusual in that it has a spatulate foot, barely wider than the bow at its terminal. It was accompanied by a pair of Type 18c wrist-clasps, a type restricted to the sixth century (Hines 1984, 107), a flat annular brooch and a D-sectioned annular brooch with five equidistant swellings resembling beads around its circumference.

The brooch from G84 is of the cross-potent variety of Leeds Class b with triangular foot, no lappets and bilobed angles on the headplate. This type is of continental ancestry and is the most widely represented type on the Continent (Leeds 1945, 6, 14). It was accompanied by an early cruciform brooch and a few glass beads.

The brooch from G154 is a cross-potent derivative of Leeds Class b(i), headplate with rebated upper corners, no basal notches, no perforations or lappets, and a triangular foot (Leeds 1945, 93). It was accompanied by a bead necklace and a small copper alloy disc brooch decorated with a central dot and ring surrounded by a row of stamped circles.

The fifth brooch, from grave G78, has a basically square headplate, the edges of which are scalloped and a trefoil-shaped foot. There are two perforated side lappets. It resembles an example from Brunnhem in Sweden whose lappets are decorated with an incised pair of concentric circles (Leeds 1945, 43, fig 27c; Reichstein 1975, 135, pl 72:4) The tri-lobed footplate is commonly a feature of the Kentish type of square-headed small-long brooches (Leeds 1945, 64, fig 34). It was accompanied by a pair of early cruciform brooches, a copper alloy wire circlet and a small 'bead-and-reel' annular brooch.

The missing brooch from G8 was accompanied by a cruciform brooch (also stolen), a bead necklace, a chatelaine complex and a complete pot.

No comprehensive study of the small-long brooch has been undertaken since Leeds' publication of 1945, and his work has been the subject of much recent criticism, largely directed at typological discrepancies, his underestimation of the correlation between small-long brooches and cruciform and square-headed brooches, and the fact that there is now a much larger corpus of material available (Cook 1981, 79; Hirst 1985, 59). All the Heslerton examples appear to belong to the first half of the sixth century (L Webster pers comm). The triangular foot is believed to supersede the crescentic foot, while those without lappets appear to be earlier than those with. The cruciform brooches which accompanied the small-long brooches seem to support this date: all have cast half-round knobs on the headplates, and two are without lappets.

# Annular brooches

One hundred and three annular brooches were recovered from 56 graves: G32, G36, G39, G40, G41, G43, G45, G47, G54, G55, G56, G60, G62, G5, G10, G22, G23, G25, G27, G28, G29, G180, G127, G68, G76, G175, G177, G78, G83, G86, G88, G89, G97, G100, G101, G107, G108, G110, G113, G114, G118, G119, G120, G123, G124, G132, G139, G140, G141, G143, G147, G152, G163, G165, G167, G173. A further three fragments were recovered from disturbed deposits.

The most common brooch type represented at Heslerton, and indeed in fifth- to seventh-century Anglian England, is the annular brooch. It would appear from the associated assemblages and the identification of the skeletal remains where this was possible, that all the annular brooches were buried with females. Those in graves G23, G123 and G124 were elderly ladies; those in graves G5, G10, G97, G100 and G108 were children. Five of the brooches, from G180, G89 and G118, are simple iron rings, perhaps a cheaper alternative to copper alloy.

Two main types of copper alloy brooch are represented, flat brooches and cast D-sectioned brooches; there are also two examples of round-sectioned brooches. Several of the flat brooches are slightly elliptical in shape, their diameters varying by a few millimetres. Three of them have openwork designs in the central area. Where pins were still present, all but five were of iron. In 52 cases the pins were simply looped around the brooch ring to hold them in place; in 4 cases the brooch ring had a narrower portion around which the pin was looped. Eight pins had been secured by a perforation in the brooch ring; 29 had a double pin emplacement and 7 a single emplacement. One of the brooches from G60 had a pin groove opposite the single emplacement. The three open-work brooches all had a copper alloy hinge and catch arrangement on the back.

Single annular brooches occur in eight graves where no other type of brooch is present, graves G42, G54, G22, G25, G28, G108, G114 and G120. Single annular brooches accompanied an iron dress pin in G5, a cruciform and a disc brooch in G143, an iron penannular brooch and a Type C2 square-headed brooch in G147, while a fourth accompanied a pair of cruciform brooches, a small-long brooch and a copper alloy wire circlet in G78. In 17 graves, a pair of annular brooches accompanied other types of brooches or a dress pin: four pairs are accompanied by an iron dress pin, G43, G45, G100 and G119; seven pairs by a copper alloy dress pin, G55, G60, G76, G175, G101, G124 and G167; five pairs by a cruciform brooch, G62, G29, G177, G86 and G173; and one pair by a small-long brooch, G97. A pair of openwork brooches accompanied a great square-headed brooch in grave G123; grave G140 contained an openwork fylfot brooch accompanied by a single annular brooch. The assemblage in grave G141 comprised an annular and penannular brooch and an iron dress pin. Three annular brooches were present in three graves, G36, G40 and G10; the third brooch in G36 was found during surface cleaning and is not certainly from this grave, although the excavator believed so at the time. Pairs of annular brooches alone occur in the remaining 21 graves, G89 and G118 (iron brooches), G180 (one iron and one copper alloy), G39, G41, G47, G56, G23, G27, G127, G68, G83, G88, G107, G110, G113, G132, G139, G152, G163 and G165 (grave G132 is included here although there was a third bead-and-reel annular brooch associated with the girdle complex in this grave).

Seventy-eight of the annular brooches are of the flat type (Leeds Type F), cut from a flat sheet of copper alloy with the exception of the undecorated pair from grave G56, which are composed of a curved strip of metal whose overlapping ends are secured by a rivet; grave 35 at Sewerby contains a similar pair (Hirst 1985, 131, fig 44), and further examples were recorded in graves 7, 18, 35 and 42 at Bergh Apton (Green and Rogerson 1978, 11–12, 18, 28,31; figs 69, 74, 84, 88).

Fifty-seven of the flat brooches have stamped or incised decoration, or a combination of both; 21 are undecorated. Two examples, from grave G127, have incised chevrons with stamped dot and ring. These have a parallel in grave 9 of the Driffield Group Barrow C44 (Mortimer 1905, 292, fig 878). Twenty-five are decorated with equidistant zones of incised transverse lines, ten of which have additional decoration comprising incised chevrons (four examples); stamped dots (two); stamped dot and ring (two) or stamped Vs (two).

The remaining 30 flat brooches have stamped decoration only. The commonest motif is a simple stamped dot,

*Plate 43: Digital scan of an annular brooch from Grave 177 (Scale 1:1)*

occurring around the inner and outer circumferences of the brooch ring in 10 examples, the outer circumference only in 1 example, and around the centre of the brooch ring in 2 examples. Seven of the brooches have stamped circles around their inner and outer circumferences, one has stamped Vs; four have stamped arcs, two with the decoration on both edges and two on the outer edge only; two have dot and ring decoration around the centre of the brooch ring; and the remaining three are decorated around both edges with the reverse-Z motif, probably representing the rune 'sigel'.

Two brooches are of circular section. The undecorated example from grave G22 was made from a length of round-sectioned copper alloy wire whose flattened ends were soldered together to form a ring; the second example, which accompanied the fylfot brooch in grave G140, has four equidistant bulbous swellings in the brooch ring, perhaps a representation of beads. The style of this brooch is similar to the bangle in grave G23, and indeed was originally thought to be a bangle on account of its large diameter. However, it was associated with fragments of an iron brooch pin and mineral-replaced woollen fabric. It is of course possible that the brooch was in fact fashioned from a bangle, the addition of an iron pin being a comparatively simple exercise.

Seventeen brooches are D-sectioned (Leeds Type G). Two are of shallow D-section with a row of stamped dots around the central ring which is divided into quarters by four zones of radiating lines, at which points the brooch ring is faceted to bring it into relief and is slightly wider than the rest of the ring, protruding a little into the centre. This form has a parallel in Sewerby Grave 29 (Hirst 1985, 130, fig 43) and is a type which most often occurs in graves of the second half of the sixth century. Seven examples are of the cast 'bead-and-reel' type; a further six have moulded ribbing, transversely grooved rings. Bead-and-reel ornament is known from native Celtic objects, but examples also exist in Scandinavia and Germany (Hirst 1985, 56). The two remaining examples are continuous D-sectioned rings which have been designed to resemble penannular brooches. One, from grave G28, has biting serpent heads at the 'terminals' and a ribbed 'body' decorated with stamped circles; the second, from grave G32 also has serpent head terminals, the 'body' of the serpent being decorated with zones of transverse lines. These have been found only in Kent, Northumbria, Yorkshire and Lincolnshire and probably belong to the late sixth and early seventh centuries (Hirst 1985, 56).

Three more unusual forms are represented at Heslerton. Grave G123 contained a matching pair of flat openwork brooches, decorated with stamped dot and ring around the centre of the brooch ring and along the arms of the internal cross. A flat, openwork fylfot or swastika brooch in Grave G140 was similarly decorated with stamped dot and ring. Leeds (1945, 52, fig 31) notes that these types are largely confined to the East Midlands. Where known examples can be dated, for example at Little Wilbraham, Cambridgeshire, and Woodstone, Huntingdonshire, all appear to belong to the sixth century, probably the latter half (Leeds 1945, 52). The openwork swastika brooches from grave 95 at Sleaford in Lincolnshire have also been dated to the late sixth century (Meaney 1981, 162). The swastika motif is also known on Anglo-Saxon pottery, and the shape itself has been variously thought to represent the power of the sun, the four winds, lightning and so on (Brewer 1981, 460).

Unfortunately, little detailed study has been undertaken for this type of brooch; Hines has suggested that annular brooches were in use from the last quarter of the fifth century until well into the seventh century (1984, 262–3). It is likely that the Heslerton examples date from the late fifth and throughout the sixth century, the two with zoomorphic decoration perhaps being a little later. Both were accompanied by small copper alloy buckles, 17 and 22mm wide respectively. Hirst (1985, 86) suggests that seventh-century buckles were generally narrower than sixth-century examples, reflecting the move towards narrower belts.

# Other brooches

A simple Iron Age or Roman bow brooch accompanied the female in grave G12 and was accompanied by a later Group IV cruciform brooch, a trefoil-headed small-long brooch and Type B13a wrist-clasps, placing the grave in the mid to late sixth century. Roman objects are not uncommon in Anglo-Saxon graves (White 1990, 125–152). A first-century broken bronze fibula brooch was found in grave 53 at Polhill, Kent, and a 'twisted and broken bow of an early Romano-British brooch' came from grave 10, Abingdon, Berkshire (Meaney 1981, 223–6, fig VI.hh). A further Roman fibula brooch was recovered from grave 67 at Portway, Hampshire (Cook and Dacre 1985, 42, fig 67). Two of the Heslerton graves contained Roman bronze coins. One, in G59, was too worn for iden-

tification; the second, from grave G106, is a coin of Victorinus (269–271). A fragment of a glass bangle of Romano-British type was contained within a bag in grave G26. Just to the north of the Heslerton Anglian settlement and cemetery is a Romano-British 'ladder' settlement running east–west along the 30m contour in the Vale of Pickering (Powlesland *et al* 1986, 159–160), and doubtless these items represent *objets trouvés* from the vicinity.

A single equal-armed brooch accompanying a female sub-adult was recovered from grave G122; no other brooch type was present. It is decorated with a single stamped dot in the centre of each arm. Hines believes this type to have a Norwegian source, the continental distribution being restricted to Norway and Sweden (Hines 1984, 374, Map 5.2), and comparable examples are dated up to about the middle of the fifth century; the English examples are all likely to belong to the sixth century, perhaps the end of the fifth century at the earliest (ibid, 158). According to Hines' distribution map (ibid, 374, Map 5.2), the equal-armed brooch is restricted to East Anglia and the Heslerton brooch is possibly the northernmost example found.

Two of the graves contained simple copper alloy disc brooches, G143 and G154. The example from G143 accompanied an adult female together with an annular brooch, a Group IV cruciform brooch, a bead necklace, Type B7 wrist-clasps and three iron latchlifters. It is 34mm in diameter with an iron pin and is undecorated. The second, from grave G154, accompanied a child of around nine years of age, together with a cross-potent small-long brooch and a bead necklace. This disc brooch is 27mm in diameter and is decorated with a slightly off-centre dot and double ring, with a row of stamped circles around the edge.

Dickinson places the manufacture of disc brooches between AD 450 and 550 (Cook and Dacre 1985, 79) and the Heslerton examples do not contradict this date; the presence of the small-long brooch and the single amber bead within a predominantly glass bead necklace in grave G154 may indicate that this is the earlier of the two graves.

Two penannular brooches, a simple iron example from G147, and one of cast copper alloy from grave G141, were recovered; both accompanied adult females. The iron brooch accompanied a florid square-headed brooch of Leeds Type C2, two annular brooches, a necklace of amber and glass beads and Type B7 wrist-clasps. The copper alloy penannular brooch was accompanied by an iron dress pin, an annular brooch, glass and amber beads and a wooden vessel. This example is 32mm in diameter, with an iron pin, and the terminals are simply decorated with an incised diamond with a dot outside each point.

A twisted wire circlet fastened with a slip knot in grave G78 may have functioned as a brooch. It was found on the left clavicle, and the proximity of the amber beads in this grave suggests that they may have been tied to it. This grave also included a pair of cruciform brooches and an annular brooch lying on the ribs, and a small-long brooch on the opposite shoulder to the wire circlet.

# Dress pins

Dress pins were present in 16 graves, G49, G45, G55, G60, G5, G8, G76, G175, G79, G100, G101, G111, G119, G124, G141 and G167. Seven of the pins are iron and the other nine are of copper alloy. Of the iron pins, two are spiral-headed (G43 and G119); one has a flattened head (G141); two have copper alloy *Klapperschmuck* suspended from them (G45 and G111); one has a perforated head and wire link which may originally have had a *Klapperschmuck* (G5); and one is plain (G100). Of the copper alloy pins, two have *Klapperschmuck* suspended from them (G175 and G167); one has a perforated head with a wire link (G55); two have faceted heads (G60 and G101); one has a flat trefoil-shaped head (G8); one is ring-headed (G76); and one is round-headed (G79). Only the shaft survives from the pin in Grave G124.

In all but two cases the pins accompanied adult females; those from Graves G5 and G100 were with juveniles. The pin was the only object apart from a pot accompanying the burial in Grave G79. Most of the others were associated with a pair of annular brooches. The exceptions are: G5, where only one annular brooch was present; the pin from G141 which was accompanied by an annular and a penannular brooch; and the trefoil-headed pin from G8, accompanied by a cruciform and a small-long brooch. Beads were present in all of the graves, with the exception of G79, with amber being the predominant type in all but two of the graves. Grave G76 contained 121 glass beads and no amber; Grave G5 contained five glass, four metal-in-glass and a rock crystal bead.

Most of the dress pins were found in a central position

*Plate 44: dress pin from G8 (Scale 1:1)*

on the chest and probably fastened a cloak or some other outer garment. Presumably they were cheaper than large cruciform or square-headed brooches but performed the same function. Unfortunately, little can be said about the typology or dating of these items and at Heslerton they appear in association with a variety of brooch types. A similar group of dress pins was recovered from Norton, Cleveland (Sherlock and Welch 1992, 41–2).

# Wrist-clasps

Twenty-seven of the graves at Heslerton contained wrist-clasps, G36, G39, G40, G45, G47, G50, G55, G60, G62, G12, G26, G27, G180, G66, G76, G177, G86, G87, G89, G95, G97, G119, G127, G143, G147, G152 and G173. All accompanied adult females, with the exception of the juvenile in grave G66 who was buried with a single clasp, and another in grave G97 who was accompanied by only one pair of clasps. Grave G76 contained a tiny simple hook and catch at one wrist which may have served as a cuff fastener. No other clasps were present. The wrist-clasps have been classified according to the system devised by Hines (1984 and 1993).

Nine of Hines' wrist-clasp types were encountered at West Heslerton, all of them from Group B:

**Type B7**: Graves G50, G55, G27, G89, G127, G143, G147 and G152. Rectangular plates with simple or no decoration, sewn to the garment. They were cut from very thin copper alloy sheet and therefore tend to be in a rather fragmentary state. Type B7 is the commonest form in England, accounting for around 40% of finds, but is rare in Scandinavia (Hines 1984, 72; 1993, 39–40). All of those from Heslerton have repoussé and sometimes additional stamped decoration. In all cases the repoussé decoration takes the form of dots, generally in vertical rows in the centre of the plate but occasionally around the edges as well. Three sets of Type B7 clasps have additional stamped decoration around their edges: the circle and triangle motif in grave G55; chevrons in grave G147 and simple dots in grave G27. Clasps of Type B7 are believed to have appeared towards the end of the fifth century, with the majority belonging to the sixth century, most being dated by association with cruciform brooches, for example, at Little Wilbraham, Sleaford and Nassington (Hines 1984, 74; 1993, 40–1). The clasps in Grave G147 were accompanied by a square-headed/cruciform hybrid brooch of Leeds Type C2, suggesting a mid-sixth-century date; the others are associated with annular brooches.

**Type B12**: Graves G40, G62, G180 and G86. Metal bars sewn to the garment with lugs (Hines 1984, 77–9; 1993, 46–9). This type occurs from the late fifth to mid-sixth centuries, the bars becoming progressively broader and flatter. Type B12 is one of the earliest examples of clasps sewn to the garment through projecting lugs (Hines 1984,

106). The Heslerton examples have simple decoration, the bars having three or four zones of horizontal lines, sometimes with incised crosses between them (graves G40 and G86). The projecting lugs on the clasps from G180 and G40 are decorated with dot and ring motifs. Clasp 1HE46GQ from grave G62 has a central zone decorated with a four-petalled floral motif (broken); this is identical to a clasp found in Grave 30 at Linton Heath in Cambridgeshire (Hines 1984, 388, fig 2.42). This form, with the T-shaped bar, has a largely East Anglian distribution, the hitherto most northern outlier occurring at Fonaby, Lincolnshire (Hines 1993, 46). The other clasps from grave G62 are paralleled by the single clasp from Grave 2 at Westgarth Gardens, Suffolk (West 1988, 20, 41, fig 57). The cruciform brooches in Graves G62 and G86 suggest a date in the late fifth to mid-sixth century.

**Type B13a**: Graves G36, G50, G12, G26, G66, G152 and G173. Rectangular plates with applied bars, sewn to the garment (Hines 1984, 80; 1993, 49–50). They are the second most common wrist-clasp type in England. A few Type B13a belong to the fifth century but most fall within the sixth century, where they are associated with cruciform and great square-headed brooches. Where the applied bars are still extant, the decoration on the Heslerton examples consists of zones of horizontal lines. The plates are undecorated with the exception of the examples in grave G36, which have small stamped arcs around the edges, and the clasp in grave G26 which has the stamped triangle and ring motif, common on Type B18a clasps, around the edges. The bars were applied with tin-lead solder. The cruciform brooches in G12 and G173 support a sixth-century date.

**Type B13c**: Graves G39 and G95. Rectangular with applied plates with repoussé decoration, sewn to the garment (Hines 1984, 81–2; 1993, 51–2). Examples of type B13c all appear to occur well within the sixth century and have been dated elsewhere by association with florid cruciform, small-long and swastika brooches. All the Heslerton examples were silvered. At first the worn silvering was believed to be traces of solder but XRF analysis carried out by the Ancient Monuments Laboratory confirmed the presence of both silvering and tin-lead solder. In all cases the swirling repoussé decoration was very worn.

**Type B18a**: Graves G45, G47, G50 and G177. Bars with conjoined knobs, sewn to the garment; Style I ornament on bar; frequently gilded (Hines 1984, 88; 1993, 59). There is no close dating evidence for Type B18a clasps (Sleaford-Londesborough type), although at Sewerby they are associated with a developed florid cruciform brooch dated to the mid-sixth century (Hirst 1985, 139), and at Heslerton with a cruciform brooch of similar date in Grave 2F103. The Heslerton examples all have six conjoined roundels and incorporate the triangle and ring motif characteristic of this type, either as part of the casting with the perforations as the 'ring', or as incised deco-

ration. (Hines 1984, 88). The bars in all cases are decorated with a rectangular panel comprising interlocking S-shaped scrolls and bordered at either end with a Style I eye. The clasps from G45 and G47 are gilded.

**Type B18b**: Grave G50. Bars with conjoined knobs, sewn to the garment; spigots on the outer two roundels or perforations between the roundels for fastening to the garment (Hines 1984, 88; 1993, 59). Type B18b appears to belong to the first half of the sixth century. The single example from grave G50 has six conjoined roundels instead of the usual four and has two projecting loops for attachment to the garment.

**Type B18c**: Graves G83 and G97. Bars with conjoined knobs, sewn to the garment; no spigots (Hines 1984, 88–9; 1993, 59–60). Type B18c is probably derivative of Type B18b, although the two overlap chronologically in the first half of the sixth century. It is a type common in northern England (ibid 1993, 60; fig 114). All of the Heslerton examples have five conjoined roundels. The set from G83 have bars decorated with zones of horizontal lines, while the bars on the clasps from G97 have a row of six dot and ring motifs separated by horizontal lines.

**Type B19**: Grave G119. Cast rectangular plate/bar, sewn to the garment. Type B19 belongs to the late fifth to mid-sixth centuries (Hines 1984, 91; 1993, 62–3). The only set of this Type at Heslerton, from grave G119, had five dot and triple ring motifs on the plate and eight dot and single ring along the bar.

**Type B20**: Graves G60 and G152. Cast plate/bar with lugs or a shaped rear edge, sewn to the garment. Type B20 also belongs to the late fifth to mid-sixth centuries (Hines 1984, 92; 64–5). The gilded clasps from G60 have ladder decoration on the bar and Style I crouching beasts on the plate; those from G152 comprise four conjoined triangles with the triangle and circle motif and the bars are decorated with stamped crosses separated by zones of horizontal lines.

*Plate 45: digital scan of a pair of wrist clasps from Grave 177 (Type B18a) (Scale 1:1)*

Not all the clasps were matching pairs. The female in grave G152 was accompanied by one pair of Type B20 clasps and a second pair comprising both Type B7 and B13a clasps. Non-matching Type B12 female clasps occurred in grave G40 while grave G62 contained non-matching Type B12 male clasps, with an extra, broken Type B12 female clasp contained within a purse. Grave G26 contained a Type B13a female clasp within a purse but none at the wrists. All five wrist-clasps in grave G50 were of different types (B7, B13a, B18a and B18c) and, interestingly, were incorporated in a bead necklace together with a scutiform pendant. Another unusual use for wrist-clasps was noted by Colebrook in grave 43 at Fonaby, Lincolnshire. Here, four clasps 'lay on the forehead with a leather-like substance attached to two of them' (Cook 1981, 42–3, fig 43).

Three graves contained silvered clasps, G39, G95 (Type B13c) and G26 (Type B13a). Three contained gilded clasps, G45, G47 (Type B18a) and G60 (Type B20). XRF surface analysis of the clasps from grave G60 showed that they had been fire-gilded, which involves the amalgamation of gold with mercury, the application of the amalgam to the surface, and the heating of the piece to drive off the mercury, leaving the gold in place. Gilded clasps tend to have a lower lead content than the others; lead was known to have a detrimental effect on the gilding process and it would appear that low-lead alloys were deliberately selected for the purpose of gilding (N Blades pers comm).

Wrist-clasps are widespread in Anglian areas of England, occurring from the late fifth to late sixth centuries. Dating on typological grounds has been rejected by Hines (1984, 107) but Types B7, B12, B13a, B19 and B20 had probably all appeared by the end of the fifth century, and all were certainly present during the first quarter of the sixth century; Types B13c and B18 are restricted to the sixth century. The particular dress style in which wrist-clasps were used to fasten the cuffs appears to have gone out of fashion by the end of the sixth century. In England they seem to occur only with female burials, although in Scandinavia they appear to have been worn by both sexes.

*Plate 46: reconstuction of Anglian female dress (by Coral Sealey, English Heritage Education Service)*

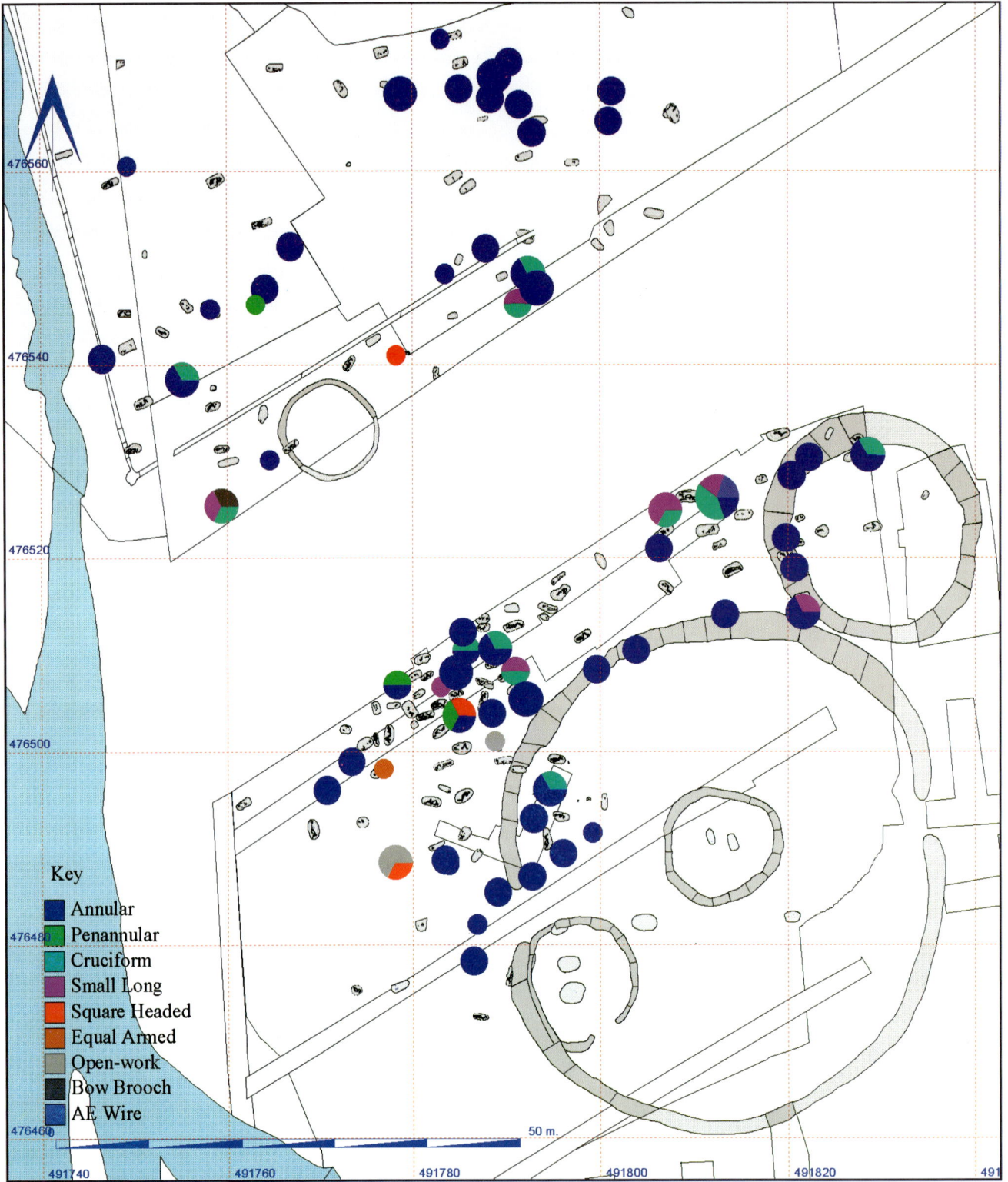

*Figure 56: The frequency and distribution of brooches by type*

# Beads, pendants and other items of adornment

## Beads

A total of 2133 beads were recovered, 2126 from 73 graves and a cremation and a further 7 from within the cemetery area, although these could not be assigned to particular graves. Of the total, 67.91% are amber (62 graves), 22.73% monochrome glass (50 graves and a cremation), 3.66% polychrome glass (29 graves), 4.98% metal-in-glass (13 graves), the remainder being made up of stone (2 graves), shell (2 graves), jet, rock crystal, copper alloy, iron, silver (5 graves), antler and bone (all occurring in single graves).

Nine graves contained a single bead, G39, G25, G71, G82, G91, G152, G153, G159 and G162. The small bone bead in G71 is the only case of a bead accompanying a male burial, and it was located in the area of the waist where it appears to have been associated with a belt. In five cases the bead was the only object accompanying the body: G82, an elderly female; G91, G153 and G162, who were young children; and G159, a young adult female. Twenty-four strings contained between 2 and 10 beads; 14 between 11 and 20; 8 between 21 and 40; 8 between 41 and 60, 3 between 61 and 80; 1 between 81 and 100; the remainder in excess of 100. The majority of the bead strings were comparatively short and were not necklaces as such; rather, they were worn as festoons across the chest in single or, occasionally, double strands, between a pair of brooches. Examination of the mineralised textile often shows evidence of the thread used to string the beads being wound around the brooch pins, for example the disc brooch in G154 (see P Walton Rogers' textile report below). In two cases, G143 and G173, the strings were attached to copper alloy wire rings which were held in place by a brooch pin. The larger bead strings in G45, G47, G76, G86, G95, G113, G141 and G167 were hung around the neck, often as double strands or as two strands converging into one, generally with the larger and polychrome beads as centre-pieces. Precise stringing arrangements were rarely easy to determine due to the extensive animal disturbance which had taken place in many of the graves. In two cases, including G62 and G26, beads were contained within purses along with fragments of glass cullet.

The classification system for the beads has been based upon that adopted at Sewerby (Hirst 1985, 62–70) with the addition of several categories to take account of particular types found at West Heslerton. They are as follows:

## Group A: monochrome glass, 481 beads from 50 graves and a cremation; 3 disturbed

### Type A1: annular beads

**Type A1a:** medium annular beads, 5–11mm in diameter: 1 bead from cremation G194 and 3 from surface scatters; 291 beads from 31 graves, G36, G60, G62, G63, G8, G12, G22, G27, G28, G29, G68, G76, G84, G86, G92, G95, G96, G101, G107, G110, G111, G117, G118, G123, G127, G139, G141, G143, G154, G163, G167. All the Type A1a beads accompanied adult females with the exception of G117 and G118 who were sub-adult, and G154, a child. The most common colour is translucent dark blue, occurring in 22 graves and accounting for just over 75% of this type. Large quantities of dark blue beads in relation to other colours seems to be the norm with this type, and can be seen, for example, at both Fonaby and Sewerby (Cook 1981, 81; Hirst 1985, 64). Opaque red is the second most frequent colour encountered, accounting for almost 13% and occurring in nine graves. Opaque yellow and white each make up around 12% of the Type A1a assemblage and were found in 11 and 18 graves respectively. Black, opaque and translucent turquoise, opaque green and colourless glass beads were found in smaller proportions. Interestingly, all of the green glass beads, together with at least half of the white, yellow, red, black and turquoise beads occurred in one grave, G76. Dark blue beads of this type were imported from the sixth century BC and are common on many Iron Age and Roman sites. They persisted into the eighth century AD and are therefore of little use for dating purposes (Guido 1978, 66–8). Opaque yellow annular beads were common during the Iron Age between about 250 BC to AD 50 and green also occurs during the Romano-British Iron Age (Hirst 1985, 64); the other colours are less common on Romano-British and Roman sites (Hirst 1985, 64).

**Type A1b:** medium double-segmented annular beads: five beads from five graves, G23, G26, G28, G107 and G118. There are two each of dark blue and turquoise and one red bead. None of the graves with this type contained more than 12 beads overall, and the associated types tend to be rather fine, for example, polychrome beads in G118 and G28, large globular beads in G107 and silver herringbone-decorated beads in G26; only one or two amber beads are present in these assemblages. All were

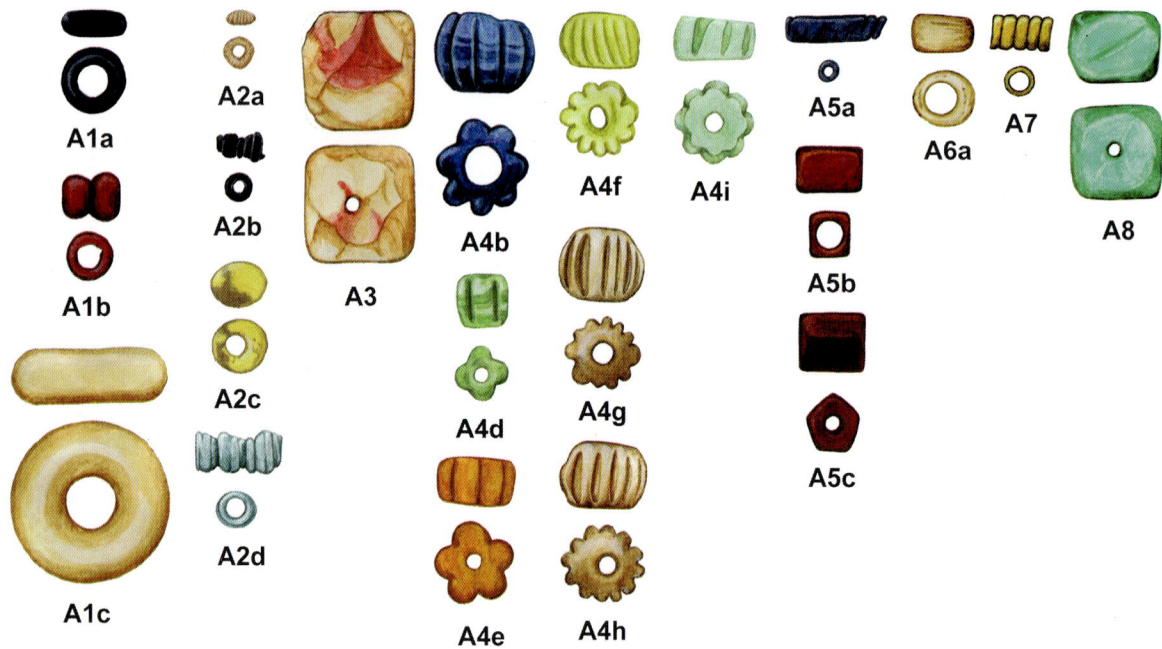

*Plate 47: glass beads types A1–A8 (Scale 1:1)*

buried with adult females with the exception of G118, a sub-adult.

**Type A1c:** Large annular beads, >11mm in diameter: 12 beads from 8 graves, G8, G12, G25, G95, G110, G119, G141, G152. Six are translucent green, four colourless, and two translucent turquoise. All accompanied adult females. Those in G25 and G54 occurred as single beads. The other six bead assemblages all contained large numbers of amber beads. Other associations include polychrome beads in G8, G12, G95 and G119; and metal-in-glass in G119 and G141.

**Type A2: globular or 'barrel' beads**

**Type A2a:** Small beads, 2.4–4mm in diameter: 3 beads from 2 graves, G111 and G141. One bead is of colourless glass; two are pale blue. The other beads in the two adult female grave assemblages comprise only amber and monochrome glass beads.

**Type A2b:** Small segmented beads: 18 beads from 1 grave, G141, an adult female. All are black in colour. The other beads in this assemblage include 13 metal-in-glass, 41 amber, 10 dark blue cylinder beads and 5 other monochrome glass beads.

**Type A2c:** Medium beads: 49 beads from 18 graves, G42, G60, G62, G12, G22, G23, G24, G26, G27, G76, G86, G95, G107, G117, G127, G147, G163 and G167. All accompanied adult females with the exception of the child in grave G24 and sub-adult in grave G117. There is a wide range of colours: 15 dark blue, 9 white, 9 turquoise, 8 red, 4 yellow, 3 black and 1 brown. Associations include amber beads in all but four of the assemblages; polychrome beads in 11 of the assemblages; and metal-in glass beads in graves G86 and G167.

**Type A2d:** Medium double-segmented beads: the single example of this type, turquoise in colour, comes from grave G22, an adult female. It was accompanied by nine other monochrome glass beads and a stone disc bead. Segmented beads are common in both Roman and pre-Roman contexts both here and on the Continent (Guido 1978, 92–93).

**Type A3: bicone beads**

The single, colourless example from a large necklace in grave G167 was accompanied by metal-in glass beads, dark blue cylinders, a sub-melon bead, other monochrome beads and a large quantity of amber beads.

**Type A4: sub-melon and melon beads**

Seventeen melon or sub-melon beads were present in ten of the graves. All the assemblages containing this type included both monochrome and polychrome glass beads as well as amber beads, with the exception of grave G41 which was accompanied only by amber beads and a silver biconical bead. Sub-melon beads do not occur in association with metal-in-glass beads, but dark blue cylinders of Type A5a, which usually occur in association with metal-in-glass beads at Heslerton, were present in graves G42 and G167. All were buried with adult females with the exception of graves G117 and G154, a sub-adult and a child respectively. While melon beads occur on the Continent as early as the third century BC, they are unknown in pre-Roman Britain, and appear to be restricted to the first and second centuries; they reappear during the post-Roman period but can generally be distinguished from the earlier examples as they tend to be less well made (Guido 1978, 100). The various sub-types occurring at Heslerton are as follows:

**Type A4b:** 7-lobed: Two pale green translucent beads from grave G42 and a dark blue example from G28.

**Type A4d:** 4-lobed: One colourless example from grave G117, a sub-adult.

**Type A4e:** 5-lobed: This is the commonest type within the Group A4 beads from Heslerton, nine examples occurring in five graves, G8, G22, G143, G154 and G167. Five are opaque yellow, two opaque white and two turquoise.

**Type A4f:** 10-lobed: The single example, from grave G175, is pale translucent green in colour.

**Type A4g:** 11-lobed: a single pale translucent green bead from grave G42.

**Type A4h:** 12-lobed: a single pale translucent green example, also from grave G42.

**Type A4i:** 8-lobed: a single pale blue-green example from grave G41.

## Type A5: long cylinder beads

**Type A5a:** narrow circular section: 45 beads from 11 graves: G42, G47, G50, G5, G177, G86, G89, G101, G141, G167 and G180. All of these narrow cylinders are of drawn dark blue glass with the same slightly fibrous appearance common in metal-in-glass types. They occur in Britain during the Roman period and beyond. Fourth- and fifth-century examples are known from Lankhills in Winchester and there are sixth- and seventh-century occurrences in Frankish cemeteries on the Continent (Guido 1978, 95). All the Heslerton examples accompanied adult females, with the exception of grave G5, a child. Eight of the 11 bead assemblages also contained Group B metal-in-glass beads; all contained amber beads, except G5 which was accompanied by a rock crystal bead. The only polychrome beads occurred in grave G42, which also produced four sub-melon beads.

**Type A5b:** square or rectangular section: 29 beads from 8 graves, G43, G5, G177, G86, G114, G127, G132 and G167. The wide variety of colours comprises 8 opaque yellow, 7 opaque white, 6 opaque red, 2 opaque yellow-green, 1 dark blue, 4 turquoise, and 1 green with faint hints of red. All of the assemblages included amber beads with the exception of G5 and five contained metal-in-glass beads. Polychrome beads were present in G43, G114 and G127; rock crystal in G5; jet and stone in G132 and a sub-melon bead in G167. Most British examples date to the third and fourth centuries (Guido 1978, 96). All accompanied adult females except G5, a child, and G132, a sub-adult.

**Type A5c:** pentagonal section: there are three examples, two opaque red and one opaque white, from graves G68 and G117. Both assemblages are associated with both monochrome and polychrome glass beads and amber

beads. A single example of this type in opaque red glass was found at Sewerby (Hirst 1985, 66).

## Type A6: short cylinder or drum-shaped beads

**Type A6a:** circular section: 3 beads from 3 graves, G62, G22 and G96. The example from G62 is opaque yellow, the other two opaque white. All accompanied adult females.

## Type A7: spirally-wound beads

Two beads from two graves, G24, opaque yellow; and G141, black. The assemblage from G24 includes monochrome and polychrome glass and a shell; G141 comprises monochrome glass, blue cylinders, metal-in-glass and amber beads.

## Type A8: square-sectioned with faceted corners

The single example accompanied the adult female in G12. It is translucent pale blue in colour and the associated bead assemblage includes polychrome and monochrome glass and amber.

# Group B: metal-in-glass beads, 106 beads from 13 graves

These drawn beads have layers of metal foil sandwiched between two layers of colourless glass and they have a somewhat fibrous appearance. Their origins, distribution and mode of manufacture have been the subject of a study by G C Boon (1977). Gold-in-glass beads originated in the Near East and large quantities are known from Egypt and the Sudan; there was a production centre in Rhodes of Hellenistic date. Examples with silver foil first appear during the Roman period. British and continental examples of both types occur from the second to fourth century in Roman Britain, and persist throughout the fifth to seventh centuries, with examples from West Stow Heath, Abingdon and Haslingfield (Guido 1978, 94). They are common in Migration period cemeteries of the fifth and sixth centuries. Finds from Birka, York and Dublin indicate that they remained popular during the Viking period (Cook 1981, 81). Three main sub-types are present at Heslerton, single globular or barrel beads, segmented beads and cylindrical beads; the first two occur with both silver and gold foil and the cylinders are of gold foil only. Metal-in-glass beads occur in 13 of the Heslerton graves, G40, G50, G62, G5, G180, G177, G86, G119, G132, G141, G167 and G172. Six of the associated assemblages contain dark blue cylinders of Type A5a, all contain amber with the exception of grave G5, and only G62 and G119 have associated polychrome glass beads. Almost half of the total of 106 metal-in-glass beads are from G50, 51 beads in a 70-bead necklace; in contrast, only 2 metal-in-glass beads were incorporated in the 167-bead necklace in G86. The beads accompanied children in graves

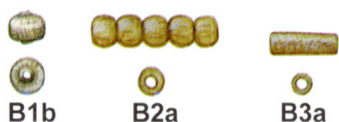

*Plate 48: metal-in-glass beads types B1–B3 (Scale 1:1)*

G5 and G172, a sub-adult in G132 and adult females in the other graves.

## Type B1: singular globular or 'barrel' beads (these are derived from Type B2)

**Type B1a:** gold foil: 32 beads from 6 graves, G40, G50, G5, G177, G132 and G172.

**Type B1b:** silver foil: 14 beads from 4 graves, G5, G177, G119 and G141.

## Type B2: segmented beads

**Type B2a:** gold foil: 44 beads from 6 graves, G50, G62, G89, G132, G141 and G167.

**Type B2b:** silver foil: 13 beads from 4 graves, G180, G177, G86 and G167.

## Type B3: long circular-section beads

**Type B3a:** gold foil: 3 beads from 2 graves, G5 and G86. These are the equivalent of the Type A5a dark blue cylindrical beads.

## Group C: polychrome glass beads, 78 beads from 29 graves

### Type C1: spiral-decorated beads

**Type C1a:** annular beads: three beads from three graves: G68, G76 and G127. Two are opaque yellow with red spirals; one, from G127, is turquoise with red spirals. All accompanied adult females and the associated bead assemblages include monochrome glass and amber beads in all cases, together with further polychrome types in both G68 and G76.

**Type C1d:** circular-section cylinder: a single opaque red bead with a white spiral trail was the only item accompanying the burial of a child in grave G91.

### Type C2: wave-decorated beads

**Type C2a:** large annular beads: eight beads from six graves, G60, G12, G68, G92, G95 and G119. Four of these are black with white waves, one black with yellow waves, two translucent blue with white waves and one translucent green with white waves. Black beads with white waves are the most common of this type at Schretzheim in Germany where they are dated to the sixth and seventh centuries (Hirst 1985, 68), although one should be wary of applying continental dating to English material. All of the Heslerton examples accompanied adult females and all the associated bead assemblages include monochrome glass and amber beads; all but G119, which had a metal-in-glass bead, contained further examples of polychrome beads.

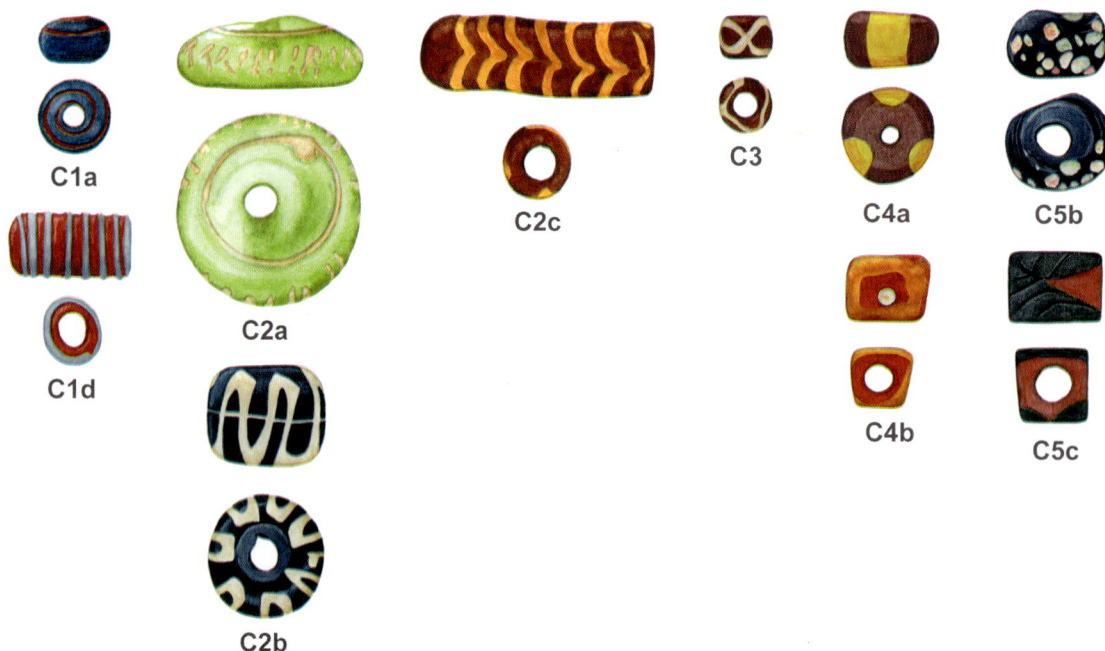

*Plate 49: polychrome glass beads types C1–C5 (Scale 1:1)*

**Type C2b:** large 'barrel' beads: two beads from two graves. The example from G14 is black with red and yellow waves; the bead in G114 is black with white waves. Both are the only polychrome bead in assemblages otherwise composed of amber beads, with a single red bead of Type A5b occurring in grave G114.

**Type C2c:** circular-section cylinder: four beads from two graves. The two-year-old child in grave G153 was accompanied by a single opaque red bead with yellow waves. The other three examples all come from grave G163, an adult female. These comprise two opaque white beads with turquoise waves which have all but dissolved out, and an opaque red bead whose waves have disappeared altogether. The associated bead assemblage includes monochrome glass and amber beads, and eight further polychrome beads.

### Type C3: double swag and spot decorated beads

28 beads from 12 graves, G62, G12, G24, G27, G28, G29, G76, G117, G118, G123, G124 and G163. This is by far the most prolific polychrome type in the Heslerton cemetery. Fifteen are opaque white with turquoise swags in various stages of deterioration, 5 of these have red spots and 1 has turquoise spots. Nine are opaque red with white swags and spots, one dark blue with dissolved swags, and three are black with white swags and spots. Grave G163 contained eight examples of this particular type. All accompanied adult females with the exception of the sub-adults in G117 and G118 and the child in G24. The associated bead assemblages all include amber, except G24 and G76; all include monochrome glass beads and six include examples of other polychrome types. G62

was the only instance of a Type C3 bead occurring in association with a metal-in-glass bead. At Schretzheim too white beads are commonest, and are thought to belong to the second half of the sixth century, persisting into the seventh (Hirst 1985, 68).

### Type C4: spot decorated beads

**Type C4a:** annular beads: five beads from three graves, G8, G76 and G154. Three are opaque red with yellow spots and two are opaque white, one with red spots and one with red and green spots. All are associated with monochrome glass, other polychrome types and amber beads. The Sewerby examples are opaque yellow or green with red spots. Beads of this type have been dated to the second half of the sixth century at Schretzheim (Hirst 1985, 68).

**Type C4b:** square-section beads: three beads from two graves, G60 and G62. All three are opaque red with yellow swirls; two have white spots and one has green spots. Both graves also included monochrome glass and amber beads and further polychrome types.

### Type C5: speckled beads

**Type C5b:** 'barrel' beads: the single example from G60 is black with red and turquoise speckles and is associated with other polychrome types together with both monochrome glass and amber beads. Two tapering barrel beads in dark blue glass with red, green and yellow speckles were found at Sewerby and similar beads from Schretzheim have been placed in the second half of the sixth century (Hirst 1985, 68).

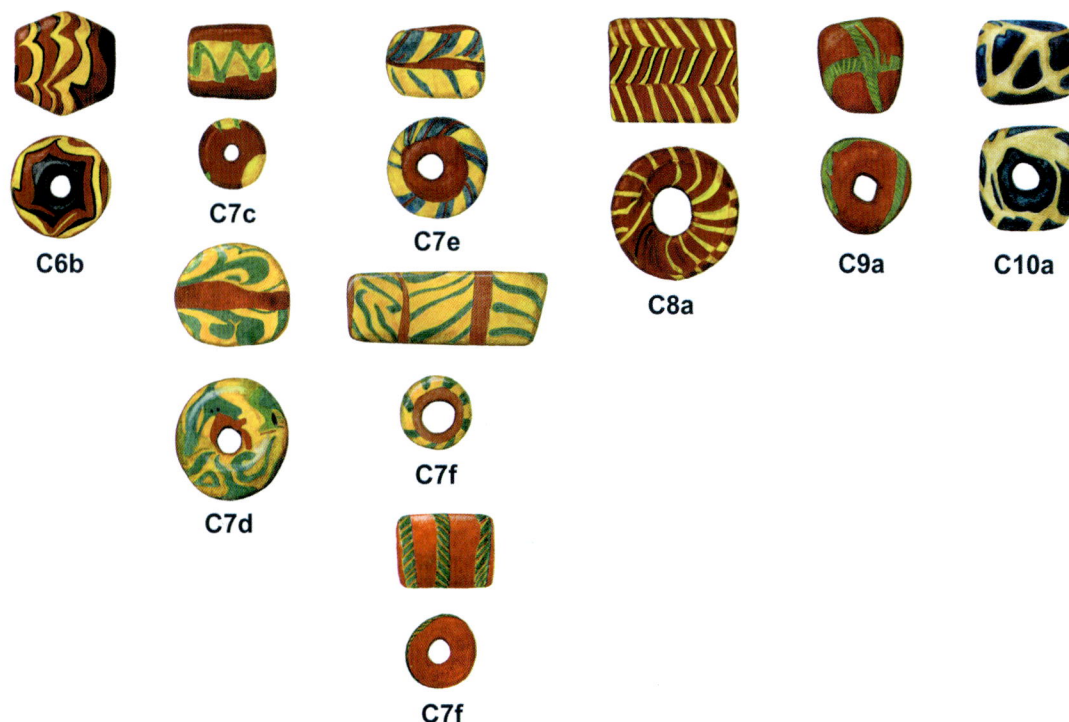

*Plate 50: polychrome glass beads types C6–C10 (Scale 1:1)*

**Type C5c:** square-section beads: a single example accompanied the infant in grave G121. It is yellow with black speckles and is associated with a polychrome bead of type C7c and 19 amber beads.

### Type C6: horizontal-striped beads

**Type C6b:** 'barrel' beads: one example from grave G29 is black with yellow, red and white stripes and is associated with monochrome glass and amber beads and six other polychrome beads.

### Type C7: beads with decorative bands

**Type C7c:** circular-section cylinder with vertical bands: one example from the grave of an infant, G121, is opaque red with yellow bands containing black waves. It is associated with a Type C5b polychrome bead, amber and monochrome glass.

**Type C7d:** 'barrel' beads with encircling bands: seven beads from two graves, G43 and G60. Five are opaque red, two of those have a plain pale green central band, one has yellow bands with black trails, and the other two have a yellow and black central band. A single black bead has a red, yellow and black band with white spots, and an opaque yellow example has red bands. Both bead assemblages include monochrome glass and amber beads and further polychrome types.

**Type C7e:** annular beads with encircling bands: the single example from G29 is opaque red and has yellow bands enclosing dark blue diagonal lines.

**Type C7f:** circular-section cylinder with encircling bands: four examples, all from grave G60. All are opaque red with yellow and black bands.

### Type C8: beads with herringbone decoration

**Type C8a:** circular-section cylinder: four beads from four graves: G42, G43, G13 and G92. Three are opaque red with yellow herringbone decoration; the fourth, from G42 is black with red and yellow herringbone.

### Type C9: beads with random trails

**Type C9a:** circular-section cylinder: three beads from three graves, G42, G8 and G27. All are opaque red; one has green trails, one has yellow, and the third has both green and yellow trails.

### Type C10: Beads with outlined edges

**Type C10a:** square-section beads: the single example of this type is from grave G175. It is black in colour and the edges are outlined in white. A sub-melon bead and five amber beads are in association.

## Group D: amber beads, 1442 beads from 62 graves; 4 disturbed

Twelve graves with beads contained amber beads only; 11 graves contained no amber. Where amber was present, either on its own or in combination with other bead types, 4 graves contained Type D1 only, 1 contained Type D2 only, and 27 graves had Type D3 only. All four types were present in three of the graves. Monochrome, polychrome and metal-in-glass beads are all found in association with amber. It is not possible to determine whether the raw material was imported from the Baltic or whether it was collected from the Lincolnshire or East Anglian coast or the other side of the North Sea. Meaney states (1981, 67) that amber beads appear to be restricted to the sixth century and are only found in quantity in mid- to late sixth-century graves; 20 of the Heslerton graves contained large quantities of amber or were predominantly amber, and the associated assemblages seem to support this hypothesis: these are G43, G45, G47, G49, G180, G177, G113, G114, G119, G120, G123, G132, G139, G141 and G167. The assemblages in G86, G95, G127, G147 and G173 may have a date closer to the mid-sixth century on account of their wrist-clasps and cruciform brooches. Graves with a single amber bead were thought to be early burials at Holywell Row, Suffolk, Abingdon, Berkshire and at Petersfinger, Wiltshire (ibid). At Heslerton, such graves include G39, G13, G23, G66, G82, G118, BA915 and G159. A few examples show signs of the perforation having been rebored.

**Type D1:** disc beads: 178 beads from 27 graves, G36, G40, G45, G47, G50, G60, G62, G63, G8, G12, G23, G28, G29, G180, G177, G78, G86, G95, G100, G101, G108, G139, G141, G147, G154, G167 and G173.

**Type D2:** wedge-shaped beads: 105 beads from 17 graves, G36, G43, G45, G47, G49, G50, G60, G62, G8, G12, G27, G68, G82, G86, G95, G113 and G123.

**Type D3:** 'barrel' beads: 5 disturbed; 1143 beads from 54 graves, G36, G39, G40, G41, G42, G43, G45, G47, G49, G50, G55, G60, G62, G63, G13, G14, G27, G29, G180, G66, G68, G175, G177, G86, G89, G92, G96, G100, G101, G107, G108, G110, G111, G113, G114, G117, G118, G119, G120, G121, G122, G123, G124, G127, G132, G139, G141, G143, G147, G159, G163, G167, G172 and G173.

**Type D4:** long convex bicone beads: 16 beads from 8 graves, G60, G62, G27, G177, G86, G95, G127 and G147.

*Plate 51: beads of amber and other non-glass types. Types D–J  (Scale 1:1)*

## Group E: jet bead

Although jet is not commonly found in graves of this period, where datable examples exist they tend to belong to the second half of the sixth century (Hirst 1985, 70), and this date is supported by the large quantity of amber found in association with the only jet bead from Heslerton. However, jet occurs naturally on the East Yorkshire coast and would have been readily available in the area during the entire period of the cemetery.

**Type E1:** disc bead: a single bead from grave G132, an adult female. This grave also contained a chalk drum-shaped bead.

## Group F: rock crystal bead

The earliest dated example of a rock crystal bead comes from grave 843 at Mucking, Essex; most belong to the second half of the sixth century (Meaney 1981, 77). However, the necklace accompanying the Heslerton example comprised only monochrome glass and metal-in-glass, with no amber. The crystal was probably imported; in Britain it occurs mainly in the Highland Zone (ibid).

**Type F1:** bicone bead: a single colourless quartz bead from grave G5, accompanying a child.

## Group G: ceramic bead

**Type G2:** circular-section cylinder: a single example accompanied the sub-adult in grave G117.

## Group H: stone beads

**Type H1:** disc bead: a perforated slate disc from grave G22, an adult female.

**Type H2:** circular-section cylinder: a chalk bead from grave G132.

## Group I: metal beads

**Type I1a:** a ring of sheet copper alloy was incorporated in the necklace from G167.

**Type I1b:** a corroded iron washer-like bead was found beneath the skull in grave G113. The bead impressions in the surface corrosion on either side imply that it was part of the necklace.

**Type I1c:** fragments of at least three and possibly four beads of silver foil with repoussé herringbone decoration from grave G26. The only known parallel comes from the cemetery at Norton, Cleveland (Sherlock and Welch 1992, 44; pl 15).

**TYPE I2:** four graves each contained a pair of silver hemispherical beads, G41, G28, G113 and G163. The latter three each comprise a pair of hollow rounded cones perforated at the narrowest end and were probably joined at their mouths to form large biconical beads. All are 15–19mm in diameter and 6.5–11mm tall. Those in G28 are decorated with four equidistant arcs with internal vertical line, those in G113 have four pairs of concentric arcs and those in G163 have three arcs with internal vertical line. The pair in G41 are slightly different. They are made of silvered copper alloy and are true hemispheres, each with a small perforated loop on the outside edge for suspension from a necklace, either as a pair of bell-like beads or as a larger biconical bead; these examples are undecorated.

### Group J: antler and bone beads

**Type J1:** a bead fashioned from an antler tine was incorporated in the necklace from G113.

**Type J2:** a bone bead or toggle was found at the waist of the male buried in grave G71.

### Group K: shell beads

The fragmentary remains of two shells were found in graves G62 and G24. These are assumed to have been beads. Shell beads are known from Portway, Hampshire (Cook and Dacre 1985, 87, fig 42).

# Pendants

## Scutiform pendants

Three of these pendants were found at Heslerton in graves G50, G55 and G139. The broken example from G50 is of copper alloy with two perforations for suspension, decorated with a ring of repoussé dots around the outer circumference with a second row of dots around the boss. It was incorporated in a necklace of glass and amber beads which also included five wrist-clasps worn as pendants. No other grave goods were present. The example from G55 is of sheet silver and the central boss is surrounded by a poorly executed pair of eight-point stars composed of tiny stamped dots, with a ring of dumbell-shaped motifs between the stars and around the outer edge. There are two perforations for suspension. It was found on the chest in association with a plain sheet silver disc, a pair of annular brooches, a copper alloy dress pin, six amber beads, Type B7 wrist-clasps and a possible purse. Grave 5 at Fonaby, Lincolnshire, contained a small bronze scutiform pendant accompanied by a plain bronze disc, both perforated (Cook 1981, 18–19, fig 4). The example from G139 is of silvered copper (XRF); it is decorated

*Plate 52: digital scan of silvered copper scutiform pendant from G139 (Scale 2:1)*

with a ring of stamped dots around the outer circumference and with a seven-point star composed of tiny stamped dots around the central boss. The suspension loop, which was soldered onto the back of the pendant, is absent. It was incorporated in a necklace of amber beads with a single blue glass annular bead. Accompanying grave goods included a pair of annular brooches, a pair of girdle hangers, six latchlifters and a purse with ivory ring.

This type of pendant is also known during the Migration Period in Denmark and Norway, with a single example of this period from Sweden, and Hines (1984, 221–4) suggests the area on either side of the Skagerrak as the point of origin at some time around the beginning of the fifth century. Scutiform pendants in England generally belong to the sixth century and were widespread in Anglian areas between 500 and 560, although they do occur as late as the seventh century, for example at Shudy Camps in Cambridgeshire (Hines 1984, 227; Hawkes and Meaney 1970, 44–55). They are also found in Christian-period graves (Meaney 1981, 162). The silver example from Sewerby grave 35 is dated to the early sixth century (Hirst 1985, 70; 131, fig 44) and the four from Norton in Cleveland (three silver and one copper alloy) are also believed to belong to the sixth century (Sherlock and Welch 1992, 42–4; 153–4, fig 47; 169; 172, fig 56). The three grave assemblages at Heslerton suggest a similar date.

Scutiform pendants appear to be a feature of female graves and are thought to represent miniature shields. They may have had amuletic significance. Model shields and other weapons are known from the Iron Age and Roman periods as well as in Germanic graves on the Continent (Meaney 1981, 159).

# Other disc pendants

There are, in addition to the two scutiform pendants, four other circular pendants; all accompanied adult females. One, a plain iron disc with a suspension loop from grave G132, was incorporated in a glass and amber necklace which also included a jet and a chalk bead; this grave also contained a pair of annular brooches, three latchlifters, and a purse associated with a walnut amulet. Grave G111 contained a bronze (XRF) pendant with an applied silver disc and two perforations for suspension. This was associated with a short string of glass and amber beads and an iron dress pin. Grave G55 contained a plain sheet silver disc as well as a scutiform pendant of the same material. It has two large perforations for suspension. The fourth pendant, from grave G86, is quoit-shaped and is of copper alloy, decorated in relief with entwined beasts; there are two perforations for suspension. The associated assemblage includes a cruciform and a pair of annular brooches, a necklace of over 150 glass and amber beads, Type B12 wrist-clasps, 4 latchlifters and a purse. All four, by association, belong to the sixth century.

# Bucket pendants

Four graves produced copper alloy bucket pendants, G177 (at least 9), G152 (13), G167 (12) and G172 (4). All accompanied relatively rich adult female burials, with the exception of G172, a child. The pendants in G172 may have been suspended from a fine copper alloy wire necklet which disintegrated on excavation. Those in G177 were associated with a fragment of cabled cord while those in G167 had a narrow leather thong running through the loops of the pendants. Traces of white powder within the pendants may be the remains of solder.

Each pendant comprises a strip of copper alloy folded into a cylinder and soldered onto a disc base, with a narrow folded strip of copper alloy soldered to the inside of the cylinder to form a handle. They are small in size, with a maximum height and diameter of 8mm. Their association with the wrist-clasps in G177 and G152, and the cruciform brooch in G177 and girdle hangers in G152, would appear to place them in the mid-sixth century.

These miniature buckets are known from fourth-century contexts in Schleswig-Holstein and southern Denmark; they occur in 15 female burials at Preetz in Schleswig-Holstein, and also from third- and fourth-century cemeteries of the Cernjachov culture in South Russia and Rumania (Hines 1984, 306; Meaney 1981, 166). There are several examples from English sites, including Holywell Row, Lakenheath, Westgarth Gardens and Morningthorpe in Suffolk; Nassington in Northamptonshire; Sleaford in Lincolnshire; and Driffield in Humberside (Hines 1984, 306; West 1988, 37, fig 83). Re-

cent excavations at Norton, Cleveland, have added a further 16 to the corpus (Sherlock and Welch 1992, 44). None of the English examples is positively dated early in the fifth century but some are certainly sixth-century. Hines believes that so peculiar a form could only have appeared in England as a result of direct influence from the Schleswig-Holstein/southern Denmark area between the late fourth and early sixth centuries (Hines 1984, 13).

Mortimer encountered bucket pendants in two of his burials. The child in Barrow C38/22 of the Driffield Group had under the chin '…several cylindrical or drum-shaped pieces, inside which were small tongues of bronze arranged in a row on their ends, side by side. From the position in which they were found they seem to have been fastened together by a thin, flat piece of bronze…' (Mortimer 1905, 281, fig 802). The arrangement of the bucket pendants in grave C44/6 at Cheesecake Hill has much in common with those found on the breast of the woman in Heslerton G167: Mortimer writes, 'on the breast were 92 beads in contact with a crescentic article....The shell of this…had been made of very thin bronze. Its lower and convex edge had been set round with a row of hollow, drum-shaped studs of bronze, standing on their ends, about a quarter of an inch in height and diameter....These drum-like studs were close together, and the interior of each contained the remains of an arrangement of small thin strips of bent bronze' (Mortimer 1905, 291, fig 873). This crescentic arrangement is very clear on the X-radiograph of the pendants from Heslerton grave G167, and the position of the pendants in grave G177 suggests a similar arrangement. One of the assemblages from Norton was found above and around the skull, suggesting that they may have adorned a veil (Sherlock and Welch 1992, 44).

Bucket pendants may be symbolic of the larger bronze-bound wooden buckets. These larger vessels were probably used to replenish drinking cups, and Meaney believes they should be considered as amulets (1981, 168).

# Beaver tooth pendant

The single example of an animal tooth is a beaver incisor (S Payne pers comm) from grave G113. It was enclosed in a copper alloy mount at the root end, both tooth and mount being perforated. It accompanied a young adult female and was incorporated in a necklace which included, in addition to 57 amber beads, a silver biconical bead and a piece of an antler tine fashioned into a bead; there was also a pair of annular brooches. At her waist were four iron latchlifters, a pair of copper alloy girdle hangers and one of two walnut amulets recovered from the cemetery.

Perforated boar tusks have been found at Wheatley and at Cassington I, Purwell Farm, Oxfordshire, and in Germanic graves on the Continent; two were recovered from the Heslerton Anglian settlement and will be discussed in the report on that excavation (Powlesland *et al* forthcoming). There is documentary evidence for the use as amulets of the teeth of dogs, horses, wolves and foxes (Meaney 1981, 136–7). Meaney also cites six instances of beaver teeth, all from late graves: Wigber Low, accompanying an adult female; an adult female in an isolated triple grave between the sites of Ducklington and Yelford, Oxfordshire; two from Marina Drive, Dunstable, Bedfordshire, accompanying an infant and an eight-year-old child; the Christian cemetery at Burwell, Cambridgeshire, accompanying a woman and child; and Bidford, Warwickshire. Continental examples include a tooth from Schretzheim in Wurttemberg and a beaver paw and two teeth from Villey-Saint-Etienne (ibid). Meaney proceeds to suggest that beaver teeth may have been worn to ward off dental decay and to encourage the growth of strong teeth, the industrious beaver being renowned for its strong, powerful incisors.

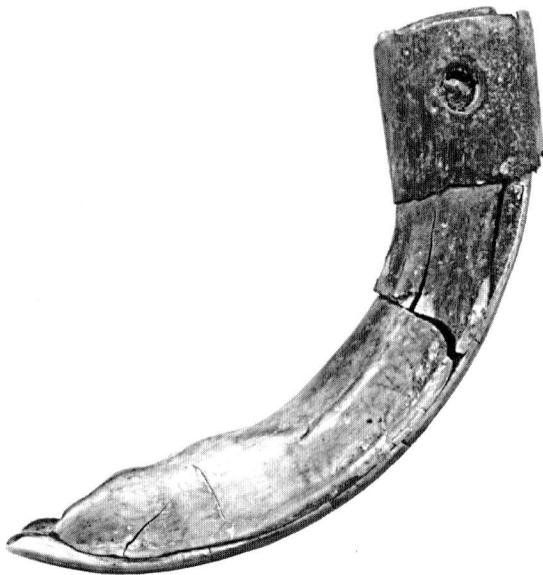

*Plate 53: digital scan of a Beaver tooth pendant from G113 (Scale 2:1)*

# Necklets

A brass necklet which had been badly fragmented by ploughing was recovered from within and around grave G100, which contained the burial of a five-year-old female accompanied by a pottery vessel, a pair of annular brooches, an iron dress pin, two amber beads and a knife. The necklet is crescentic in shape and is constructed in two parts which fasten at the back of the neck. Both sections are made from a round-sectioned strip of metal, flattened into a long broad terminal at one end. The opposite end of one piece is bent to form a hook which

fastens through a perforation at the end of the second piece. The terminals are decorated with stamped circles around the edges and have a number of perforations along the lower edges from which pairs of *Klapperschmuck* were suspended from loops of copper alloy wire. These triangular-shaped spangles have traces of tinning on their surfaces.

A similar necklet was recovered from Bergh Apton Grave 50 (Green and Rogerson 1978, 35 and 76, fig 91). This was constructed from a flattened circlet of metal, with a smaller round-sectioned portion bent into a hook at either end which fastened through a perforation at either end of the main ring. Three perforations in the broadest part of the necklet may have held decorative studs or spangles. In this case the burial was that of an adult male and it was accompanied by a Type C1 spear. Further 'metal collars' have been found at Market Overton II in Leicestershire, Ipswich in Suffolk and Emscote, Warwickshire (Owen-Crocker 1986, 56).

A second necklet was found in grave G172, also of a child. The fine copper alloy wire, curved into a hook at either end for fastening, was so fragile that it disintegrated on excavation. The four bucket pendants found in association are thought to have been suspended from this wire.

# Bangles and an anklet

Bangles were recovered from graves G23 and G76. The elderly female in G23 wore a continuous round-sectioned copper alloy ring with three equidistant 'swellings'. The bangle from G76, the grave of an adult female, is a strip of ovoid-section copper alloy wire coiled into a circlet. A fragment of a Roman glass bangle was found in a purse in grave G26 in association with another piece of glass cullet and several fragments of copper alloy; these items probably represent *objets trouvés*.

The female in grave G12 wore a coiled copper alloy wire anklet.

# Finger rings and an ?earring

A silver wire finger ring with a spirally wound bezel and a knot on either side accompanied the female in grave G113. A second ring comprising a simple coil of copper alloy wire was found in a possible purse accompanying the female in grave G127.

Fragments of silver wire with a slip knot were recovered from grave G23, to the side of the skull, which suggests that the object is an earring.

# Belt fittings and girdle complexes

## Buckles and associated belt fittings

Fifty-five graves produced 62 buckles, G31, G32, G33, G42, G45, G47, G52, G59, G8, G10, G12, G13, G19, G21, G22, G27, G186, G28, G29, G30, G179, G181, G182, G184, G185, G71, G73, G74, G175, G176, G77, G89, G93, G95, G101, G103, G108, G109, G115, G121, G123, G126, G128, G130, G132, G136, G137, G144, G150, G151, G160, G164, G167, G168 and G173. A further five graves produced possible buckles, G39, G88, G96, G114 and G127.

Eleven of the buckles are copper alloy, the rest are iron. Buckles were the only objects accompanying the burials in graves G31, G33, G137 and G168. Two buckles were recovered from graves G45, G184, G73, G175 and G136, and there were three in G74, where at least two appear to be associated with the shield and spears rather than with a belt around the waist.

The 11 copper alloy buckles accompanied 2 unsexed burials, 3 males and 6 females, including a sub-adult. Five of them are small, less than 20mm in length; the other six range from 24–28mm in length. Eight are D-shaped, one ovoid and one sub-circular. The example from G132 was covered in organic remains and could not be examined. All have a simple copper alloy pin wound around the buckle loop.

The 51 iron buckles and 5 possible buckles accompanied 21 adult males, 20 adult females, 8 unsexed adults, a male and an unsexed sub-adult and 2 female and 2 unsexed children. One accompanied the horse burial and is assumed to be associated with a leather bridle. Six of the buckles are up to 20mm in length, 24 are 21–30mm in length, 16 exceed 30mm, with the two largest, from G29 and G150 over 50mm; the others are too fragmentary to measure. Four, all possible buckles, are circular, three are sub-circular (including one possible buckle), six are D-shaped and 36 are ovoid. The others are too fragmentary to categorise or they were covered in organic material which could not be disturbed.

Many of the buckles show traces of the leather belts that they fastened. Six of the copper alloy buckles are attached to copper alloy belt plates, one to an iron belt plate. Four iron buckles have copper alloy plates and ten have iron plates. These were all attached to the belts with one or two copper alloy or iron rivets. Two graves produced additional decorative belt mounts. The iron buckle in G71 was accompanied by two silvered copper alloy rectangular plates, with a single perforation at each end. A teardrop-shaped copper alloy stud is thought to have been mounted on the belt from G101.

Unfortunately, none of the buckles is diagnostic in terms of date.

## Purses

Evidence for the presence of bags or purses was encountered in 16 female graves, G39, G42, G62, G8, G24, G26, G86, G107, G108, G111, G127, G132, G139, G152, G163 and G167.

The fragmentary remains of ivory purse rings were found in graves G107, G139, G152, G163 and G167, all adult females. The ring would have formed the mouth of a bag which would remain closed when the ring lay against the hip (MacGregor 1985, 111, fig 62). During the Roman period, ivory reached the Roman Empire via Red Sea trading posts, while later post-Roman ivory seems to have a Byzantine source. The ivory purse rings found in graves of the pagan period are thought perhaps to have come from the fossil tusks of mammoths, since previous trade had been disrupted, few other exotic imports are present, and the affluent Frankish graves of the period contain no ivory (ibid, 38–40).

Fragments of copper alloy tubing with organic remains, leather where identifiable, may represent purse mounts. These are present in six graves, G43, G8, G24, G86, G108 and G140, and accompany children in graves G24 and G108.

Copper alloy lace tags are present in 11 of the graves, G39, G8, G86, G107, G111, G127, G132, G139, G152 and G167, and may represent the ends of drawstring closures for bags.

In two cases staining in the pelvic area and the location of some of the accompanying grave goods indicated the presence of bags or purses. The dark organic staining in grave G62 marked the location of a bag which contained four beads, a shell, a fragment of glass cullet, a broken Type B12 wrist-clasp, fragments of copper alloy and small wire links. A similar area of staining in G26 contained glass and silver foil beads, a fragment of glass cullet, part of a Romano-British glass bangle, a broken Type B13a wrist-clasp and assorted fragments of sheet copper alloy.

Associated with the bag in grave G107 is a strange rectangular object which has been variously interpreted as a purse lid, a comb case and a belt fitting. It comprises a dot-and ring decorated copper alloy plate with three tubular sides. One short side comprises a silvered copper alloy bar with rounded ends, each pierced by a copper alloy rivet. At this end of the object a 10mm square has been cut from the plate. Unfortunately, the entire object is covered in a complex arrangement of organic material which prevented its detailed examination. The overall dimensions of 78 x 30mm are inaccurate, taken as they were from the X-ray, but nevertheless they seem far too small to represent a comb case.

# Chatelaine

Only one chatelaine, in the true sense of the word, was found in grave G22. This comprises an iron ring and up to 20 figure-of-eight chain links which would have been worn around the waist. In this case, no items such as latchlifters or girdle hangers were suspended from the chatelaine, which belonged to an adult female.

# Girdle hangers

Three pairs of girdle hangers were recovered from three graves, G113, a young adult female; and G139 and G152, both adult females; all are from comparatively rich assemblages. All are flat-sectioned.

The pair in grave G113 are undecorated except for the moulded shaft ends which are perforated for suspension. They are 150mm long and have closed hooks. The pair in G139 were originally attached by iron rivets to a curved strip of copper alloy and are non-matching. One exists as the shaft only, with moulded decorative bands at the top. The second is undecorated but has two perforated side lobes in the bottom third of the flat-sectioned shank which continues for a further 7mm below the open double hook. It is 135mm long. The pair in G152, also 135mm long, have closed double hooks decorated with stamped dots. The flat-sectioned shafts swell out in the lower third and taper towards the top where they were attached to a curved strip of copper alloy. All are accompanied by iron latchlifters.

Girdle hangers usually occur in pairs, suspended from the waist, and occur from the later fifth century until possibly as late as the seventh century. The Heslerton examples all appear to belong within the sixth century. They are thought to represent keys, symbolic of the woman's role as 'keeper of the household' (Meaney 1981, 170). Bunches of keys were commonly worn by Roman matrons.

Further fragments of girdle hangers have been recovered from the associated Anglian settlement at Heslerton (Powlesland and Haughton, forthcoming).

# Latchlifters

Forty-two, and possibly 43, iron latchlifters, some in fragmentary condition, were recovered from 15 graves, G39, G43, G45, G8, G86, G107, G113, G118, G119, G132, G139, G143, G152, G167 and G173.

Latchlifters are typically sixth-century in date, worn at the waist by females. Only three graves, G39, G120 and G119, contained single latchlifters, the example in the last grave being much larger than all the others. Pairs were found in graves G8 and G152, three in G43, G45, G107, G132, G143 and G173, four in graves G86, G113 and G167, and two sets of three in G139. Those in graves G113, G139 and G152 were accompanied by a pair of copper alloy girdle hangers. At least 18 had curved C-shaped terminals, 2 had straight-sided hooked terminals, 1had an S-shaped terminal, 1 was L-shaped and the remainder were slightly curved at the ends. The example in G119 is 227mm long; all the rest are between 115mm and 195mm in length.

# Walnut amulets

Two walnut amulets were recovered from the cemetery. Both accompanied young adult females and were suspended from the waist in association with a purse and iron latchlifters, and in Grave G113 with a pair of copper alloy girdle hangers as well. Both graves contained amber necklaces which included more exotic beads and pendants, a beaver tooth, an antler bead and a pair of silver hemispheres in the case of Grave G113 and a chalk bead, jet bead and iron disc pendant in the case of grave G132. Both walnuts were enclosed within copper alloy cradles, two hoops of sheet copper alloy at right-angles to each other, and had a pair of copper alloy *Klapperschmuck* suspended from the base. The walnut from G113 had three perforations at the top and that from G132 had an iron pin through its centre.

Although walnut amulets appear to be unique to Heslerton, similar objects have been recorded elsewhere. An 'oak apple enclosed in two bronze hoops with an iron bolt running through it longitudinally' was found in Grave 3 at Little Wilbraham, Cambridgeshire, a wooden coil in a silver cradle was found in Grave 18 at Welbeck Hill, Lincolnshire, and a second flat wooden coil in a bronze cradle with a suspension loop came from Grave 41 on the same site (Meaney 1981, 60–61). A similar item consisting of possible oak wood wound around a central bronze rivet, was recorded as a possible amulet from Grave 4 at Fonaby, Lincolnshire (Cook 1981, 83). The burial in Sewerby Grave 54/29 had at her waist a narrow strip of oak wood wound around a central bronze pin with traces of sheet bronze, presumably from a cradle, on the surface (Hirst 1985, 90, 142). All have been dated by association to the late sixth and early seventh centuries.

The significance of these objects is uncertain. The Little Wilbraham example was accompanied by a Roman spoon bowl corroded onto a copper alloy girdle hanger, and White suggests that this is in imitation of the strainer spoons and crystal balls found in rich Kentish female graves of the period (Southworth 1990, 142–3). Certainly the copper alloy bindings are similar to those found around crystal balls. Nuts may also have been symbolic of new life. Both Heslerton burials were of young females whose married status is implied by the presence of chatelaines; perhaps the walnuts were worn as fertility charms. Oak was considered to be sacred to Thor, while *Juglans* sp. (walnut) is derived from *Jovis glans* or *Iuvens glans*, thus Jupiter's nuts (Grieve 1985, 842), so walnuts may also have had a religious significance. The walnut was dedicated to the goddess Artemis by the ancient Greeks who saw it as a symbol of wisdom, fertility and longevity. Walnuts do not appear to have been imbued with any particular medicinal properties, although later herbalists claim that infusions of walnut husks and kernels would ward off plague and expel worms and poisons (Gerard 1633, 1440–1).

The walnut is not a native British species, and the date of its introduction to this country is a matter of some debate. Grieve states that there is a general belief that it was introduced in the second half of the sixteenth century (Grieve 1985, 842); however, Gerard, writing in 1597 and 1633, implies that by then it was already well established, saying that 'the Walnut tree groweth in fields neere common high-wayes, in a fat and fruitfull ground, and in orchards' (Gerard 1633, 1440).

The Romans certainly imported the nuts from Persia and presumably exported them to other parts of the Empire, but more interestingly, walnut pollen grains have occasionally been found 'in the soils beneath Iron Age camps' (Dimbleby 1978, 31), suggesting that the tree itself was present in this country at that time. Therefore the Heslerton walnuts may not be as 'exotic' as one might imagine.

# Knives

Eighty-six knives were recovered from 78 graves, G32, G34, G36, G39, G40, G43, G45, G47, G48, G51, G55, G59, G60, G61, G64, G8, G13, G16, G19, G21, G22, G23, G25, G27, G28, G30, G179, G180, G181, G182, G183, G84, G185, G71, G72, G73, G74, G75, G76, G176, G77, G83, G86, G88, G90, G93, G94, G95, G98, G100, G103, G105, G107, G112, G115, G118, G119, G120, G122, G123, G124, G126, G127, G130, G136, G138, G141, G144, G150, G151, G152, G155, G157, G158, G160, G163, G164 and G173.

Knives appear to be evenly distributed between males and females, although it was not possible to determine the sex of some of the burials. Twenty-three knives accompanied adult males, 24 accompanied adult females and 7 accompanied unsexed adults, 6 belonged to sub-adults including 2 males and 2 females. and 2 belonged to children, one of them male. Nine were buried with unaged females on the basis of associated finds, and two with unaged males. Four burials are both unaged and unsexed.

Knives were the only accompanying object in nine graves, G34, G51, G61, G64, G94, G105, G112, G138 and G157. Four graves contained two knives, G77, G130, G150 and G151, all males except for the unsexed G77; two graves had three knives, G16, a male, and G107, a female. Of the intact knives, eight are less than 100mm in length, fifteen are 101–110mm, four are 111–120mm, twelve are 121–130mm, ten are 131–140mm, three are 141–150mm, two are 151–160mm and three are 161–170mm. There is no correlation between knife size and the sex of the burial, where this is known.

The majority were found at the right hip where, presumably, they were suspended from a belt. Nine, all belonging to women, were associated with iron suspension loops, four belong with girdle complexes, and one was apparently contained within a bag. Only two knives were located at the right hip, with a further two lying in the small of the back and another placed just beyond the skull. Forty-eight show traces of a leather sheath and at least four appear to have had pelt sheaths, with the fur to the inside. Sixty-two of the tangs have the mineralised remains of horn on them; one may be either horn or bone. The horn has been identified by Jacqui Watson as possible cattle in six cases and sheep or goat in one example. Three knives have been identified as having wooden handles, willow or poplar for the example in G27, maple in the knife from G77 and ash for the knife in G157. Whetstones were present in two instances, G77 and G150.

Since knives are the only object type from the cemetery which also features prominently in the contemporary settlement, it was decided to include detailed discussion of the complete Heslerton knife assemblage in the report on the settlement excavation (Powlesland and Haughton, forthcoming), so that the entire group can be examined in relation to a number of metalworking furnaces together with smelting and other metalworking debris dating from the earliest settlement to the Middle Saxon period.

## Whetstones

Whetstones were found in two graves, G77 and G150. A fragment of a whetstone accompanied the burial in G128 and a further fragment was found in the fill of G147, although it is not clear whether this accompanied the body or was simply residual material.

## Tweezers and other toilet implements

Tweezers were found in association with eight burials: six are copper alloy, graves G2, G22, G180, G77, G83 and G161, and two are iron, G26 and G130. Those in graves G77, G130 and G161 were accompanied by little awl-like implements, perhaps used to clean beneath the nails. Short pins with helmeted and other heads occur with tweezers at Birka and have been interpreted as toilet sets (Evison 1987, 84). Four accompanied adult females, two adult males, and the other two were with unsexed adults. The pair of objects in G161 are the only grave goods.

## Weapons
## A sword from grave G74

*by Brian Gilmour*

This sword was found complete with the mineralised remains of its scabbard and a simple copper alloy pommel still in place. The blade was very heavily corroded but although clearly in poor condition preliminary examination indicated that under the encrusted remains of the scabbard there was at least some iron surviving along most of its length. Allowing for the scabbard remains the length of the sword was approximately 900mm by 50mm wide and the blade appeared to be parallel-sided along most of its length. In sectional profile the blade would appear to be flattened or very slightly convex in form. It is difficult to date closely on stylistic grounds but its burial context and overall form would suggest a date somewhere between the fifth and early seventh century.

Radiography showed the blade to be pattern-welded along its central part although the detail was not clear enough for reproduction in this report. The type of pattern was very unusual and took the form of a snake running down the centre of the blade. The pattern seems to have been the same on either side of the blade, although from radiography it would seem that on one side much of the pattern has been lost to corrosion.

The wiggly snake pattern, reconstructed here in diagrammatic form (Fig 57), has not been seen among the many pattern-welded swords of the Anglo-Saxon period so far identified in this country and appears to be the earliest yet identified anywhere. Two examples of snake patterns on swords from mainland Europe have been illustrated, one from Vehmaa on the west coast of Finland (Lepääho 1964, 69, Taf 32) and another from Nijmegen in Holland (Ypey 1982, 366, Abb 15), although these are both later and date to between the ninth and eleventh centuries. In both these later examples the snake pattern is much coarser and appears on one side of the sword only, in each case with a variant of the much commoner herringbone type of pattern on the other side of the blade.

Two wedge-shaped transverse sections extending approximately halfway across the width were cut from the upper part of the blade. One section (Fig 59) was cut approximately 100mm down from the hilt an one side, whereas the second (Fig 60) came from near the centre of the other side. These were taken from either side of the blade to allow an overall composite transverse view to be achieved. Metallographic examination showed the blade to be constructed from five main parts hammer-welded together. The two cutting edges had been welded onto either side of a three-part central piece. This central piece consisted of two surface pieces which would have given rise to the snake pattern on the surface after suitable polishing and etching, and a plain core piece on either side of which the snake pattern pieces had been welded. Both the cutting edges and the snake pattern pieces were also found to be made of several parts (Fig 58a, b).

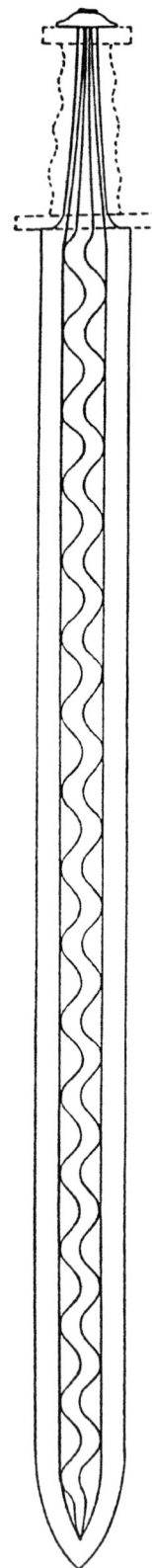

*Figure 57: simplified reconstruction of the sword blade showing the snake pattern*

Unetched, a scattering of mostly small slag inclusions could be seen across both sections. These showed up as both two-phase, medium and darker grey inclusions probably of fayalite (iron silicate) in a glassy matrix, and three-phase inclusions in which a pale grey phase, probably wustite (iron oxide) was also visible. Some large, mainly three-phase slag inclusions were congregated along the positions of the welds where they had become entrapped during the hammer-welding together of the different parts of the blade.

The structure of the blade became clearer after etching the mounter sections with nital, 2% nitric acid in alcohol (Figs 59, 60). Each of the cutting edges had originally consisted of a sandwich of three parts, a piece of medium to high carbon steel welded between two pieces of low carbon iron. In one section each of these three parts (a, b, and c in Fig 59) had partly survived, whereas in the other section only the central steel part (d in Fig 60) and a small fragment of one outer low carbon iron part (e) remained of the cutting edge.

In both cases the steel central parts of the welded-on cutting edges showed a quenched structure, although one was bainitic rather than martensitic. The steel cutting edge of one section (Fig 59) appeared to show a less completely quenched structure with some free ferrite (alpha iron) showing in a very variable grain structure (ASTM 1–7), largest towards the weld boundaries with the outer pieces (b) and (c) where the carbide gave a rather feathery bainitic or pearlitic appearance which was difficult to resolve optically. Vickers micro-hardness values of 281 HV 0.1 near the fine-grained centre and 294 HV 0.1 towards the weld boundary were obtained for this piece. The structure would suggest a carbon content of about 0.5% for this piece.

The steel central cutting edge part (d) of the other section, which came from near the centre of the sword, showed a more completely quenched structure. Virtually no free ferrite was visible in a fairly uniform feathery bainitic structure which gave micro-hardness values between 424 and 488 HV 0.1.

It seems probable that the steel in both edges is more or less the same (a medium carbon steel with approximately 5% carbon) and that the different appearance is the result of ineffective quenching near the hilt of the sword. The bainitic structure would suggest that this sword blade has been slow or slack quenched in a liquid such as oil with a lower thermal capacity than water, which would tend to produce a faster quenched and harder martensitic structure in a medium carbon steel such as this. The cutting edge pieces between which the steel was welded consisted of a low carbon iron with (originally) no more than about 0.1% carbon, although there was a fairly diffuse zone near the weld marking the diffusion across the weld of some of the carbon from the steel centre of the cutting edge sandwich. A fairly typical micro-hardness value of

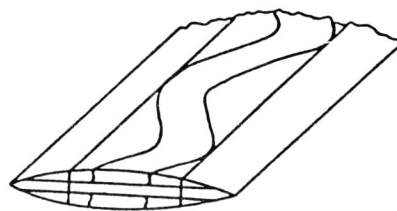

*Figure 58a: three dimensional view to show the main parts of the sword blade*

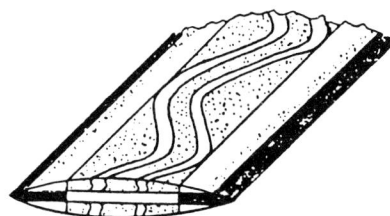

*Figure 58b: three dimensional view to give the impression of the effect of final polishing and etching of the sword blade*

158 HV 0.1 was obtained from one (b) of these low carbon iron edge pieces.

The main welds between the cutting edges, pattern-welded surface pieces and the plain central core in between were also marked by narrow white lines which were highlighted in places by thin grey pearlitic lines (Figs 59, 60). Examination by electron probe microanalysis (EPMA) showed these white lines to be locally enriched in cobalt and nickel, an enrichment effect caused by oxidation of the surface of the iron during welding. The pearlitic lines along the welds bear no relation to the pearlitic content of the metal and appear to indicate the use of a carbon-based flux to counter the deleterious effects of oxidation during welding.

On both sections the plain central core piece (f) of the blade was clearly visible (Figs 59, 60). This piece consisted of iron, in this case a very variable medium to large grain (ASTM 2–6) ferrite with some streaks of pearlite visible in places and gave micro-hardness values of 176 and 180 HV 0.1. These values are rather high for what appears to be a plain iron piece but the increased hardness (plain iron usually gives a micro-hardness value of about 100–120 HV) and the occasional pearlitic streaks are indicative of a slight enrichment by phosphorus (possibly up to about 0.2%) for this plain central core piece. EPMA analysis showed the phosphorus content to be rather variable rising to approximately 0.5% where the ferrite grain size was at its largest.

The folded appearance of the snake pattern surface strips is clearer on one section than on the other and shows that the snake pattern has been achieved by using a twist-

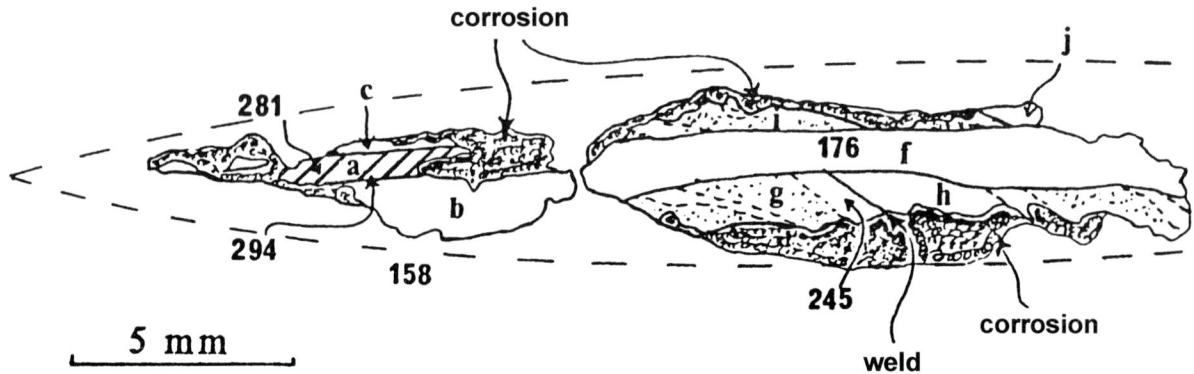

*Figure 59: sketch showing the main components and vickers micro-hardness values from a section near the hilt of the sword*

ing process. The alternating darker and paler banding also shows that each of these surface pieces was itself made of three main parts (g–j in Fig 59 and k–m in Fig 60). The pale bands consisted of very large grain ferrite (ASTM1) with Neumann banding (dislocation lines) visible, showing that some forging work on the blade was carried out when the temperature of the blade had fallen below the normal forging temperature range of about 950–1050'C.

Micro-hardness values ranging between 245 and 309 HV 0.1 were obtained from these pieces. These greatly increased hardness values over those expected of a plain iron together with the very large grain size of these bands is suggestive of a fairly high phosphorus content, probably within the range 0.5–0.8%, for these parts.

By contrast, the grey bands in these snake pattern pieces consisted of a low carbon iron which appeared as a fine grain (ASTM8) ferrite and pearlite with a carbon content of little more than approximately 0.1%. Micro-hardness values in the range of 220 to 236 HV 0.1 were obtained for these bands, rather higher than expected (approximately 120–180 HV) although the reason for this is not clear and may indicate the presence of a small amount of another alloying element apart from phosphorus.

These rather complex-seeming surface pieces appear to have been made by first of all welding a bar of low carbon iron along its length to a similar-sized bar of high phosphorus iron. Next, this new bar was either forged out longer then folded in the middle and forged together so that the low carbon iron was in the middle of the resulting sandwich, or the new bar was cut in the middle and the two pieces forged together to give the same effect.

A separate bar was probably prepared by welding together a much smaller bar of high phosphorus iron to a bar of low carbon iron. A similar piling process to that described above would appear to have been followed, although in this case it seems to have been repeated to give a laminated bar (b) predominantly consisting of low carbon iron

but with several alternating thin bands of high phosphorus iron within it.

A new laminated bar (c) would then appear to have been prepared by taking a sandwich bar of type (a) and along its length welding it between two rather thinner bars of type (b). These bars would have been welded together in such a way that the laminations all lay along the same two sides of the resulting bar (c).

The central bar of this new bar (formerly bar a) is the part that resulted in the snake pattern. This snake pattern was achieved by twisting then counter-twisting the laminated bar (c) alternately by approximately $45°$, each twist and counter-twist resulting in one curve in the pattern. Final polishing and etching of the blade would have revealed the snake pattern (Fig 58a, b). The even character of the pattern also suggests that an intermediate flattening hammer was used in the final forging out of the blade.

The later snake pattern sword blade from Nijmegen may have been made by much the same twisting and counter-twisting process, although this is not certain from the illustration, whereas the snake on the pattern-welded blade from Vehmaa seems certain to have been given its distinctive profile by a corrugating process, the snake then forming an inlay, with the 'valleys' of the corrugations of the snake pattern being filled with short lengths of the more familiar twisted pattern welded pieces. This is quite a different process from that used for the Heslerton sword and possibly the Nijmegen blade as well. However,, the coarser snake patterns on both these later swords are perhaps more likely to have been made using an inlay technique.

There are several references to snake patterns on sword blades from early Norse literature (discussed in Davidson 1962), the clearest of which comes from Thidrick's Saga in which the sword Ekkisax is described as follows:

> The blade is well polished and marked with gold and if you set the point down on the earth, it

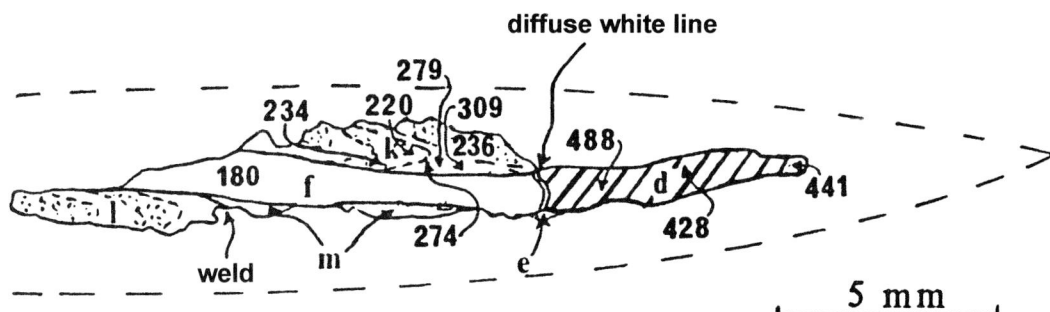

*Figure 60: Sketch showing the main components and vickers micro-hardness values from a section near the centre of the sword blade*

seems as if a snake runs from the point and up to the hilt, gleaming like gold. But if instead you hold it upwards, then it seems as if the same snake runs from the hilt and up the point, and it moves as if alive.

(Davidson 1962,166)

Davidson equates this and other more obscure allusions to snake patterns to the more familiar herringbone form of weld pattern (Davidson 1962, 166), although the snake pattern on the Heslerton sword shows that the description of the sword Ekkisax is actually quite a good description of one rare type of pattern-welded sword.

**Acknowledgements**
I would like to thank Chris Salter of the Oxford University Research Laboratory for Art and Archaeology for his help with the EPMA analysis, and Frank Craddock for his advice on the practical smelting of blades such as this.

# Shield bosses

Eight burials, all adult males, were accompanied by shields or, more correctly on account of their size, bucklers: graves G19, G72, G73, G74, G158, G179, G183 and G184. Typologically, all of the iron bosses appear to belong broadly to the sixth century; six belong to Dickinson Group 2 and two (from G72 and G158) to Dickinson Group 3 (Dickinson and Härke 1992, 13–7). All have disc apices, with the exception of the boss in G72 which has a rod apex, and all were secured to the shield board by five iron flange rivets. The flange rivets and the broad disc apex of the boss in G184 all had applied silvered discs. Seven shield grips survived; two are flat with expanded terminals, one is straight and strap-like, while the others are flanged. All appear to be short grips within Härke's Type I, although it is impossible to be sure due to their often fragmentary nature (ibid, 24–7).

All but two of the shields (in G19 and G158) had disc-headed board studs or mounts, ranging from two to five

in number and placed between the boss and the outer edge, presumably securing the leather covering over the shield board. Traces of such a covering are preserved between the boss and board on the shields from graves G19, G179, G184, G73, G74 and G158. The shield in G184, in addition to its silvered apex and flange rivets, had two pairs of copper alloy board studs with applied silver discs. A parallel for the silvered discs may exist from Mortimer's Driffield Group Barrow C35, burial 5, which produced two silvered rivet heads, although the excavator did not at the time associate them with the shield (Mortimer 1905, 277, fig 763).

The wood from which the shield boards were constructed has been identified by Jacqui Watson of the Ancient Monuments Laboratory. The shields from G19 and G184 are of willow or poplar, those in G72, G73 and G74 are of lime, G183 has a maple board, and the shield in G179 is constructed of either lime or maple. The board from G158 is of unknown timber. Lime or linden shield boards are mentioned in the early English poem *The Battle of Maldon* (trans Alexander 1977), when '[Bryhtnoth] bade them brace their linden-boards aright'.

All eight shields were accompanied by a spear, or two spears in the cases of G72 and G74, which also contained a sword. The spear types represented belong to Swanton's groups B1 (G72), C2 (G19, G72), C3 (G183), D1 ( G158), E2 (G179 and a pair in G74), and H2 ( G73).

# Spears

A total of 28 spears were recovered from 20 graves. Four of the graves, G72, G74, G136 and G151, contained two spears. All have been classified according to Swanton's Type Series (1973 and 1974), although they do not always fit happily within a particular group. The two most commonly occurring types are Types C2, five examples from G19, G185, G72 and G136 (two examples), and E2, seven examples from G2, G179, G184, G74 (two examples), G130 and G144. There are two each of Types C1 (G98 and G151) and D1 (G158 and G164) and single examples of Types B1 (G72), C3 (G183), D3 (G115),

E1 (G87), E3 (G176), H2 (G73), and K2 (G85). The remaining five cannot be placed with certainty within an individual sub-group. Two of those belong somewhere within Series C (G151 and G155); one to Series C or D (G52), and one falls between Groups C2 and E2 (G75). Six of the spears had ferrules, graves G179, G183, G185, G73, G151 and G158.

Type B1 spears are relatively rare in England, but their use spanned the pagan period, and the form is derived from the pre-migration Roman Iron Age tradition (Swanton 1973, 38). They were a thrusting weapon, a stout socketed spike without lateral blade parts. A date in the late fifth or first half of the sixth century is suggested for the example in grave G72, which was accompanied by a Type C2 spear and a shield boss with low, straight-sided cone.

Leaf-shaped spears are represented by Swanton's Series C and D, the two insular developments from the leaf-shaped blade of the pre-migration period. The blades are generally lentoid in cross-section. Series C has an increasing proportion of blade to socket length, Series D an increasing proportion of socket and shank length. (Swanton 1973, 48–9). Type C1 is fairly common but there are few datable examples; such examples as exist suggest an early phase in the settlements (Swanton 1973, 79). Type C2 occurred throughout the pagan period while Type C3 appears to have been a sixth-century development, lasting into the seventh century. Type D1 also spans the pagan period and D3 persists throughout the sixth century. The accompanying shield bosses in graves G19, G72, G183 and G158 imply a date during the sixth century for four of the spears; the others cannot be dated with any precision.

Series E blades, generally lozengiform in cross-section, are the angular equivalent of Series C. Type E1 is believed to belong to an early phase; there is little evidence to suggest that many examples belonged to even the sixth century (Swanton 1973, 79). They tend to occur in poorly furnished graves with little additional dating evidence. Type E2 occurs during the sixth century, but most examples belong to the seventh century and the type persists beyond the pagan period; the spears in G179, G184 and G74 can be dated to the sixth century on the basis of the accompanying shield bosses. Type E3 is fairly common, but once again, datable examples are rare; most belong to the sixth and seventh centuries (Swanton 1973, 83). The example from G176 had been bent before deposition.

Series H, angular blades characterised by a concave curve above the angle, have a long history in the Germanic north (Swanton 1973, 106–7). They are commonly found in sixth century contexts. Type K2 have narrow leaf-shaped fullered blades and, while chronological evidence is poor, the latest examples appear to belong to the latter part of the fifth and early sixth centuries (Swanton 1973, 133).

Where mineral-replaced wood has survived in the shafts of the spears and ferrules, it has been identified by Jacqui Watson of the Ancient Monuments Laboratory. Nine are hazel, five are willow or poplar, four are mature ash, three are alder, and the remaining seven of unknown wood. Spears of ash are mentioned in *The Battle of Maldon* (trans Alexander 1977), where '[Bryhtnoth] raised the shield board, shook the slim ash-spear', and the ash is an important tree in Scandinavian mythology, Yggdrasil being the ash tree whose roots and branches bind together Heaven, Earth and Hell.

There is no apparent correlation between the occurrence of ferrules and spearhead type or the wood utilised in the shaft.

# Vessels
## Pottery vessels

Pottery of this period is notoriously difficult to date, most being simple, undecorated vessels, but all the Heslerton pots appear to belong within the broad range of late fifth to early seventh centuries. All are hand-built from sandy clay, sources of which are known in the immediate vicinity, although the oolite-tempered vessels may have originated elsewhere. Current examination of the assemblages from the settlement by the Anglo-Saxon Pottery Studies Group in Lincoln will in the future provide more detailed information on the raw material sources; this will be included in the report on the settlement excavations (Powlesland *et al*, forthcoming). Sixteen burials were accompanied by pottery vessels, G40, G1, G8, G13, G14, G29, G66, G77 (three vessels), G79, G83, G90, G95, G100, G106, G110 and G116. There was also a series of cremations. The fabric types are as follows:

**Type I:** calcite inclusions
**Type II:** calcite and mica/biotite
**Type III:** sand
**Type IV:** oolitic limestone
**Type V:** sand and calcite
**Type VI:** straw or dung-tempered

**Grave G40**, Type I: small bowl of irregular baggy shape with a slightly flattened base; orange-brown in colour, with a few patches of grey. The dissolved inclusions appear to have comprised coarse calcite grit together with organic material, probably straw. The rim diameter is 109mm, the height 98mm and the wall thickness *c*5mm.

**Grave G1**, Type III: approximately half of an almost hemispherical bowl, 100mm tall with a rim diameter of 119mm and wall thickness of 8-10mm. The sandy fabric is black with brown surface patches, and appears to have had a fairly high organic content.

**Grave G8**, Type III: intact almost hemispherical bowl

of black sandy fabric with a burnished surface; 119mm tall with a rim diameter of 141mm and wall thickness of 6mm.

**Grave G13,** Type III: eight body and base sherds from a round-bottomed possible funerary vessel placed at the feet; dark grey in colour with a brown inner surface; a wall thickness is 6mm.

**Grave G14,** Type I: fairly crude and irregular bucket-shaped vessel of black fabric with a brown surface. Its vesicular appearance is due to dissolved calcite inclusions; 116mm tall with a rim diameter of 113mm, base diameter of 98mm and wall thickness of *c*8mm.

**Grave G29,** Type II: about three-quarters of a shouldered bowl, now reconstructed, with slightly flaring rim whose neck is decorated with four incised horizontal lines. The very friable fabric is dark grey in colour with calcite and dissolved calcite inclusions along with some mica; the surface has been burnished; 126mm tall with a rim diameter of 114mm, base diameter of 72mm, wall thickness of 6mm and base thickness of 9mm.

**Grave G77,** Three pots were present in this grave:
**(i) (2B96AA-AK; AS–BB;BD)** Type II: over 20 rim and body sherds comprising about half of a slightly carinated bowl of reddish-brown sandy fabric with a dark grey core; calcite and micaceous inclusions as well as a small quantity of grog. Wall thickness is 7mm.
**(ii) (2B95AA–AB;AD–AE)** Type III: three bodysherds and a rim from a second vessel of dark grey sandy fabric and a wall thickness of 7mm.
**(iii) (2B96AP–AR)** Type VI: three sherds comprising around half of a very small pottery cup of very light brown to grey fabric. The inclusions appear to have been chopped straw. Rim diameter is *c*60mm and wall thickness is 4mm.

**Grave G79,** Type III: nine rim and body sherds from a bowl of reddish sandy fabric with a burnished, soot-stained outer surface; rim diameter is *c* 100mm and wall thickness is 7–9mm.

**Grave G83,** Type I: around four-fifths of a fairly large wide-mouthed globular bowl of grey fabric with a red-brown surface. Its vesicular appearance is due to the dissolved calcite inclusions. The rim, which is slightly out-turned, has a diameter of 154mm; base diameter is 81mm and wall thickness is 8–9mm; overall height is 147mm.

**Grave G90,** Type III: almost complete sub-biconical wide-mouthed bowl of black sandy fabric with patches of brown on the burnished surface. The pot is 102mm tall with a rim diameter of 133mm, base diameter of 70mm and wall thickness of 6mm.

**Grave G95,** Type II: intact biconical urn of grey sandy fabric with patches of brown on the burnished outer sur-face, and with calcite and micaceous inclusions. The rim is slightly out-turned. The vessel is decorated with seven central horizontal bosses, above each of which is an incised triple arc, or *stehende Bogen,* design. Five incised horizontal lines encircle the neck of the vessel with a further three lines below these round *c* one-fifth of the circumference only. Wall thickness is 8.5mm; the vessel stands 241mm tall with a rim diameter of 114mm, base diameter of 99mm and a maximum girth of 203mm. It is closely paralleled by a vessel from Heworth, North Yorkshire (Kennett 1989, 35, fig 33).

**Grave G100,** Type I: intact wide-mouthed shallow bowl of smooth black fabric with patches of brown; calcite inclusions; 84mm tall with a rim diameter of 152mm and wall thickness of 5.5mm.

**Grave G106,** Type III: most of a small globular bowl with a slightly out-turned rim and a flat base. The sandy fabric is black with patches of brown on the surface; 92mm tall with a rim diameter of 98mm, base diameter of 53mm and maximum girth of 107mm. Wall thickness is 5mm.

**Grave G110,** Type I: small biconical urn with out-turned rim; the sandy fabric is black with grey-brown patches on the burnished surface, and has calcite inclusions. It is decorated with twelve small bosses around the middle; between these and the rim is a zone of three comb-impressed chevrons bordered by a single incised horizontal line above and three horizontal lines below. It is 137mm tall with a rim diameter of 122mm, base diameter of 54mm and maximum girth of 148mm; wall thickness is 6–8mm.

**Grave G116,** Type V: around half of a small sub-biconical bowl with slightly out-turned rim. The black fabric contains calcite and large rounded sand inclusions; the outer surface is burnished. The vessel is 77mm tall with a rim diameter of *c*94mm, base diameter of 41mm and a maximum girth of 92mm; wall thickness is 5mm. A further five graves contained sherds which may represent disturbed funerary vessels, either from the inhumations or from earlier cremations, or are simply residual material.

**Grave G2,** Type I: large body sherd with mica and dissolved calcite inclusions, on top of which lay the tweezers.

**Grave G7,** Type II: two body sherds from a bowl of grey-brown sandy fabric with some dissolved and micaceous inclusions; wall thickness of 10mm.

**Grave G66 (i)** Type I: rim and body sherd from a hand-built bowl of grey-brown fabric with calcite inclusions, most of which have dissolved; rim diameter is *c*150mm and wall thickness is 7.5mm.
**(ii)** Type I: rim sherd and ten body sherds from a flat-

based bowl of brown sandy fabric with dissolved calcite inclusions; smooth surface; rim diameter is c145mm and wall thickness is 8mm.

**Grave G81**, Type III: rim sherd from a carinated bowl of black sandy fabric, decorated with three horizontal lines around the neck. Wall thickness is 3mm for the rim and 7mm for the body.

**Grave G170**, Type I: body sherd of black fabric with a burnished surface and calcite inclusions. Wall thickness is 9.5mm. There were also two body sherds of black sandy fabric with a brown, burnished surface and quartzite inclusions; wall thickness is 9mm.

Several cremation vessels were recovered; most had been badly disturbed by ploughing:

**G189: 2B56AA**, Type I: much of a hand-built pot (base missing) of black sandy fabric with patches of brown on the surface. The calcite inclusions have dissolved. The rim is slightly out turned and wall thickness is 7mm.

**G196: 2C4**, Type I: much of a large, heavy vessel, now partially reconstructed. The corky fabric is dark grey with patches of brown on the rough surface; the inclusions are calcite. Although the pot has suffered some post-depositional flattening, rim diameter is at least 200mm and it stands 210mm tall. It was accompanied by two fragments of sheet copper alloy and a copper alloy round-headed stud.

**G88: 2BA17AD**, Type I: 17 sherds comprising around half of a hand-built bowl with straight sides and a slightly rounded base. The fabric is grey-brown in colour with small calcite inclusions and the vessel stands 80mm tall with a rim diameter of around 110mm.

**G187: 2BA18AC,AD,AG**, Type I: 23 body sherds from a hand-built cremation vessel. The fabric is black with a brown outer surface and has calcite inclusions, most of which have dissolved. Wall thickness is 12mm.

**G188: 2BA19AA-AB,AD**, Type I: fragments of a hand-built cremation vessel of black fabric with a brown outer surface. The calcite inclusions have dissolved. Wall thickness is 6.5mm.

**G189: 2BA56AC**, Type III: large body sherd of burnished grey-brown sandy fabric with a wall thickness of 7–9mm.

**G190: 2BA58AE,AF,AT,AW**, Type III: 30 rim and bodysherds from a cremation vessel of sandy fabric with a dark grey core and red surface. The rim is flattened. Wall thickness varies between 7mm and 11mm.

**G192 (10AF–AK)**, Type VI: over 50 sherds from a fairly large cremation vessel of smooth sandy fabric with a black

core and brown surfaces. The chopped straw inclusions (?derived from animal dung) have been fired out. There are also straw impressions on the surface. The pot has a slight shoulder and flattened rim. Overall dimensions are impossible to determine due to the fragmentary nature of the pot and the fact that much of it has been lost to the plough. Rim diameter is at least 200mm and wall thickness is 10mm. There was also a small body sherd of black fabric (103AL) with calcite and quartzite inclusions, decorated with an excised horizontal line and a single stamp with a circular cross motif. Wall thickness is 7mm.

**Pit G193 ( 3AA–AG;143AA,AE,AF)**, Type I: 12 body sherds and fragments from a hand-built cremation vessel of black fabric with a brown, slightly burnished surface. Most of the calcite inclusions have dissolved. Wall thickness is 9mm.

**G193: 2BA341(55AF–AM)**, Type I: 0ver 50 sherds from a large cremation vessel, bucket-shaped with a flat base. The fabric is dark grey with a smooth brown outer surface and dissolved calcite inclusions. The overall dimensions are impossible to determine as the rim and much of the base are missing, but the pot was at least 260mm tall with a wall thickness of 8mm and base thickness of 12mm.

**G194: 2BA1076AA**, Type I: 20 rim and body sherds from a hand-built cremation vessel of reddish-grey sandy fabric with a few calcite inclusions. It is well finished and has a smooth surface and flattened rim. Wall thickness is 5–7mm.

**G195: 2BA1177AB,AE–AG,AJ**, Type IV: 36 sherds from a hand-built cremation vessel of black fabric with a red surface. Its vesicular appearance is caused by the oolitic inclusions having dissolved. It appears to be a fairly large vessel but is likely to have been subjected to some post-depositional flattening as it is not well fired. It has a flat base and straight sides with a wall thickness of 6-7mm and a base thickness of 10mm.

Parts of two vessels reocovered from the base of the blown sands in the north-eastern part of 2BA and not directly associated either with an inhumation or cremated bone may have been grave markers.

**2BA1150AA**, Type I: around 30 sherds comprising around a quarter of a small hand-built round-bottomed bowl of grey-brown fabric with calcite inclusions and a fairly large fragment of chalk. The surface has been smoothed. The pot stands around 70mm tall, wall thickness is 7mm and the base thickness is 10mm. Three sherds from a second vessel are also present, one of which appears to have a handle, only the base of which survives. The fabric is grey-brown with calcite inclusions, most of which have dissolved, and some mica. Wall thickness is 8mm.

**2BA1159AA**, Type III: an almost complete wide-mouthed globular bowl with a flat base. The black sandy fabric has patches of brown on the surface. The vessel is 97mm tall with a rim diameter of 127mm, base diameter of 78mm and wall thickness of 5mm.

Finally, sherds from other Anglian vessels, not certainly related to inhumations or cremations, were found within the cemetery area:

**Ditch 2BAM38 (1125AA)**, Type I: much of a round flat-based bowl uncovered during machining. The fabric is black with a grey-brown soot-stained surface, with calcite inclusions, most of which have dissolved, as well as some organic material. Rim diameter is 135mm, body diameter is 145mm and base diameter is 95mm. The wall thickness is 9.5mm and base thickness is 13mm.

**Ditch 2BAM130 (i) (1070AA)**, Type I: black body sherd of sandy fabric with calcite inclusions; wall thickness is 8mm.
**(ii) (1113BA)**, Type I: grey-brown body sherd with dissolved calcite inclusions and a wall thickness of 7mm.

**Pit 2BA164 (165AK)**, Type III: rim sherd from a small carinated bowl of black sandy fabric. Wall thickness is 9mm and rim thickness is 5mm.

**Posthole 2BA1046 (1047AB, AC)**, Type I: five black to brown body sherds with calcite and organic inclusions and a wall thickness of 9mm.

**Undefined context 2BA1074 (1075AQ)**, Type II: Black-brown rim sherd with calcite, mica and fired-out organic inclusions, with a wall thickness of 9mm.

**Spit 2BA2 (i) (2BL)**, Type I: rim sherd from a bowl of black fabric with a slightly burnished surface and calcite inclusions, most of which have dissolved. It is slightly carinated with an out-turned rim and wall thickness of 4.5mm.
**(ii) (2CT)**, Type I: a base sherd from a bowl of grey-brown fabric with dissolved calcite inclusions. There are grass impressions on the outer surface only. The base diameter is around 90mm and thickness is 5mm.
**(iii) (2CU)**, Type I: rim sherd from a hand-built burnished bowl of grey-brown sandy fabric with a few calcite inclusions. Wall thickness is 6mm.

**Spit 2BA598AH**, Type III: rim sherd from a bowl of grey-brown sandy fabric with some quartzite inclusions and a wall thickness of 8.5mm.

**Spit 2BA945 (i) (AY)**, Type II: base from a flat-bottomed bowl of grey-brown sandy and slightly micaceous fabric with a base thickness of 14mm and wall thickness of 9mm.
**(ii) 945BB**, Type III: Burnished bodysherd of grey-brown sandy fabric with a wall thickness of 8mm.

**SPIT 2BA1066 (i) (AX, BP)**, Type I: two rim sherds of grey-brown fabric with calcite inclusions, most of which have dissolved. Wall thickness is 9–10mm.
**(ii) 1066AY**, Type I: burnished body sherd of black fabric with calcite inclusions and a wall thickness of 9mm.

# Wooden vessels

Wooden vessels were recovered from 11 graves, G32, G47, G16, G27, G30, G69, G101, G121, G122, G128, and G141, with a further three possible vessels from graves G108, G129 and G132; one was found at the base of the ploughsoil on Area 2F and presumably belongs to one of the graves here. They accompanied unaged females in G32 and G47, adult females in G27, G101 and G141, an adult male in G16, children in G108, G121, G128 and G129, sub-adults in G122 and G132, and unsexed and unaged burials in G30 and G69.

There are only two stave-built wooden vessels. The first, a copper alloy-bound yew bucket, was found during preliminary work on the cemetery in Area 2F and had been disturbed by the plough; indeed, a furrow ran straight through it. It is 84mm tall and 85mm in diameter and comprises ten staves held together by two vertical and three encircling copper alloy bands, secured by tiny copper alloy rivets. The base, now missing, was recessed into a groove in the staves. A similar vessel from Norton, Cleveland, was associated with a Type H2 spear (Sherlock and Welch 1992, 194–6; fig 66). There are two further examples of copper alloy-bound stave-built yew buckets from graves 48 and 54 at Portway, Hampshire (Cook and Dacre 1985, 36, fig 61; 40, fig 65).

The second stave-built bucket is also of yew but was bound with iron hoops, now broken and badly corroded, and an iron handle attached to the bucket by chain links. It was found in the isolated grave G30 and was accompanied by a leather belt decorated with tiny filigree stud-heads. It was impossible to determine its size from the fragmentary remains, but it perhaps resembled the iron-bound wooden bucket from grave 66 at Westgarth Gardens, Suffolk (West 1988, 37; 65, fig 83).

A hoop of copper alloy with stamped decoration was found at the left shoulder of the female in grave G132 and may represent the binding of a wooden vessel although no wood remains survived. There were brassica seeds within the hoop (R Scaife, pers comm). A similar item comprising a stamp-decorated copper alloy hoop around organic material was found between the shoulder and wall of grave 67, Portway, Hampshire (Cook and Dacre 1985, 67; fig 67).

Vessel repairs take the form of copper alloy staples and pieces of sheet copper alloy folded over the rim and secured by copper alloy rivets. Fragments of sheet copper alloy which are thought to represent vessel repairs come from graves G108 and G129, although no organic material survived.

Where there are wood remains surviving in contact with repairs, this has been identified by Jacqui Watson of the Ancient Monuments Laboratory. The vessel in G32 is made of alder and the wood was 4mm thick. Those in G47 and G121 are either willow or poplar, 4mm and 6mm thick respectively. Four vessels, from G16, G27, G69 and G122 (4–5mm thick), are maple; two are maple or lime, G101 (4mm thick) and G141, and the vessel in G128 is maple or birch. All are lathe-turned.

All the brooches in the associated assemblages are annular, with the exception of the equal-armed brooch in G122. Two of the graves, G101 and G141 also had dress pins.

It is possible that other wooden vessels were buried in the Heslerton graves, but those which had not been repaired have presumably disappeared from the archaeological record.

# Horse-fittings
## Snaffle bit

A simple iron snaffle bit and a buckle, which is assumed to have fastened a leather bridle, accompanied the burial of a young mare who had been decapitated and placed in grave G186 with her head between her legs. Grave 10 at Garton Slack, East Yorkshire, produced two bridle bits (Mortimer 1905, 250, figs 659–60); these accompanied a male sub-adult.

# Chemical analysis of the copper alloys

by Nigel Blades

## Introduction

Sixty-nine copper alloy artefacts from the pagan Anglian cemetery at West Heslerton, North Yorkshire, were quantitatively analysed. These included a large number of annular brooches, a smaller number of more ornate brooch types such as cruciform and square-headed, several wrist-clasps and other miscellaneous copper alloy artefacts such as rings, pins and some wire and sheet. A much larger number of objects had initially been selected for analysis, including much more sheet and wire. Unfortunately, due to corrosion, the quantitative analyses of many of these objects were unreliable, since corrosion can deplete one metal at a greater rate than another, as in the process of dezincification, where zinc is lost from a brass at a greater rate than copper. Consequently, it is not possible to deduce the original composition of an artefact from its corroded composition, and so this report is based on the analyses of uncorroded or only slightly corroded objects.

I would like to thank Dominic Powlesland and Christine Haughton of the Heslerton Parish Project for their assistance in providing information and illustrations and with sampling of the artefacts. I would also like to thank Elizabeth Hartley of the Yorkshire Museum for allowing access to finds in her care.

## Methods

Quantitative analysis was carried out at Royal Holloway and Bedford New College, University of London, using inductively coupled plasma spectrometry (ICPS). The elements sought were: copper, zinc, lead, tin, nickel, arsenic, bismuth, antimony, phosphorus, sulphur, cobalt, chromium, manganese, vanadium, cadmium, silver and gold. The technique necessitates the removal of a small sample from the object, typically 5–10mg, which is dissolved in aqua regia (3 parts hydrochloric acid:1 part nitric acid) and the resulting solution pumped into the ICPS system. Sampling is carried out either by drilling or, in the case of sheet metal, by cutting away a small piece. This must then be filed clean of corrosion products to expose unaltered metal. These measures ensure that a sample of the core metal is obtained, which can be assumed to represent the original composition of the artefact.

## Nomenclature

The alloy names used in this report follow the guidelines set out by Bayley (1991):

Bronze: an alloy of copper and tin. Zinc, if present, is at a level of less than one third the tin.

Brass: copper with zinc. Tin, if present, is at a level of less than one quarter the zinc.

Gunmetal: an alloy of copper with both tin and zinc as alloying components.

'Leaded': this term is applied to any of the above containing more than 4% lead.

## Analysis

The alloy composition of the artefacts (ie the relative proportions of the major metals zinc, lead and tin) was depicted on a series of ternary diagrams, one each for the annular brooches, other brooches, wrist-clasps and miscellaneous other finds. These are obtained by plotting the relative percentages of the major components zinc, tin and lead on a triangular graph, where each of the apices represents a maximum for that alloying metal. Thus, a point plotted at the zinc apex indicates an alloy of copper with zinc, containing no lead or tin, while a point in the centre of the triangle represents an alloy with equal amounts of zinc, tin and lead (Fig 61).

It should be noted that this method plots relative compositions, not absolute ones; thus two coincident points do not necessarily contain the same amounts of each alloying metal, but they do have these present in the same ratio. However, by only plotting alloys with similar copper content on any particular graph, it can be ensured that coincident points are reasonably similar in composition.

# Results

The ternary diagram (Fig 61) show the compositions of the annular brooches, other brooches, wrist-clasps and miscellaneous other finds respectively. It can be seen that the alloys used in these four groups are broadly similar, but with some differences. The annular brooches, 31 in number and the largest group of artefacts of any one type, fell mostly into the gunmetal category, sometimes with high lead levels. The other brooch group, of only seven finds, were more tin-rich, being largely bronzes rather than gunmetals. The wrist-clasps were gunmetals, with generally small lead additions, as was the miscellaneous group (consisting of the other finds from the site).

Overall, 56% of the West Heslerton artefacts were gunmetals and the remaining 44% bronzes. It is quite striking that none of the alloys are brasses. This is a pattern repeated throughout the pagan Anglo-Saxon period; although zinc is commonly present in these copper alloys, it is very rarely the major alloying metal. Indeed, it is quite uncommon to find any simple binary alloys, except tin bronzes. The dominant alloy type is one of copper with significant proportions of each of zinc, lead and tin. The general consensus is that this state of affairs is accounted for by the recycling of copper alloy, often many times over, from various sources, including a large amount of Roman metalwork. This would presumably result in brasses being mixed with bronzes to give a gunmetal-type alloy, like those we find at West Heslerton.

# Discussion

Recycling is thought to be prevalent at this time because of the lack of new metal. Scarcity would encourage the use of a diverse range of sources, including Roman copper alloy objects and coinage. The levels of the precious metals silver and gold in the West Heslerton finds, as at other Migration Period sites, are generally higher than are found in Roman alloys (in a study of late Roman brooches of English provenance, Bayley found that the average silver level was ~0.1%; J Bayley pers comm). The average silver level at West Heslerton was ~0.2%, with values of 0.3–0.4% quite common. Gold also occurs at heightened levels at West Heslerton: 0.01% is very common, ~0.1% occurs frequently, and in one wrist-clasp there is a highly exceptional 0.84% gold. Such a gold level is probably due to erratic recycling (ie melting down a gold object with copper alloy scrap), but it is just possible that it may have been added to give a blackened surface colouring, as in the Japanese technique of *Shakudo*.

These heightened precious metal levels could reflect a change in the copper sources being exploited; or perhaps the same sources were being used, but no effort was made to remove the precious metals from the copper. Alternatively, increased silver content could occur because of the recycling of debased late Roman 'silver' coinage,

which would contain only a few percent of silver. Subject to corrosion, this would take on the appearance of base copper alloy, and might easily be recycled as such. Gold could be introduced into the copper alloys by recycling of gilded Roman objects such as brooches.

# The nickel-arsenic correlation

Figure 62 is a plot of nickel v arsenic. As can be seen, there is quite a clear correlation between these two elements. Figures 63 and 64 show the relationship between zinc and nickel and arsenic. While it is hard to see any correlation in Figure 63, Ni v Zn, there is some correlation between arsenic and zinc, Figure 64, with the lower zinc finds tending to be predominantly low in arsenic, whereas those with more zinc contain more arsenic. Figures 65 and 66 show that high levels of gold only occur in artefacts low in nickel and arsenic.

If this is true then this a fascinating result, since arsenic, and nickel, which correlates with arsenic, are unlikely to have been associated with zinc geologically, yet they correlate with this metal; they are more likely to have been associated with copper. The implication, therefore, is that they were introduced with copper, but this must have contained zinc, ie have been a brass or brass-like alloy, and this was used in the making of the artefacts at West Heslerton, thus representing the use of recycled metal.

Many of the wrist-clasp and brooch pairs from West Heslerton had identical compositions (within the limits of analytical precision), indicating that they had been made at the same time using the same charge of metal, a not entirely surprising result. However, this appears to have been confined to objects occurring in pairs; non-identical artefacts, even those found in the same grave, do not appear to have been made from the same metal. This is consistent with copper alloy manufacturing, or perhaps craft would be a better word, being carried out on a very small, domestic scale at this time.

It may be that production was on a larger scale, as at Helgo in Sweden (Lamm 1973, 1980) where an extensive workshop complex, with many mould remains contemporary with, and producing brooches and other small cast items similar to those from West Heslerton, has been excavated. However, such remains are rare in England (for one of the few examples, see Jones 1975). A single mould fragment was recovered from the settlement at West Heslerton (C Haughton pers comm).

Four of the wrist-clasps (comprising two identical pairs from grave 1HE343) not only were made of the same metal, but had rather unusual composition consisting of ~1% tin with ~0.8% lead, very little of anything else, and the balance made up of copper. Such a composition is explained by the fact that these artefacts had been gilded. X-ray fluorescence (XRF) surface analysis revealed that the gold had been applied using mercury in a fire-gilding process (see Oddy 1980 for a description of the method). Such a process requires an alloy low in lead, otherwise a reaction occurs, with the lead 'sweating out' and forming disfiguring white spots on the surface of the object. The 1% of tin in the clasps would have facilitated their casting; pure copper is a very poor casting metal, being prone to excessive gassing which results in a pock-marked surface.

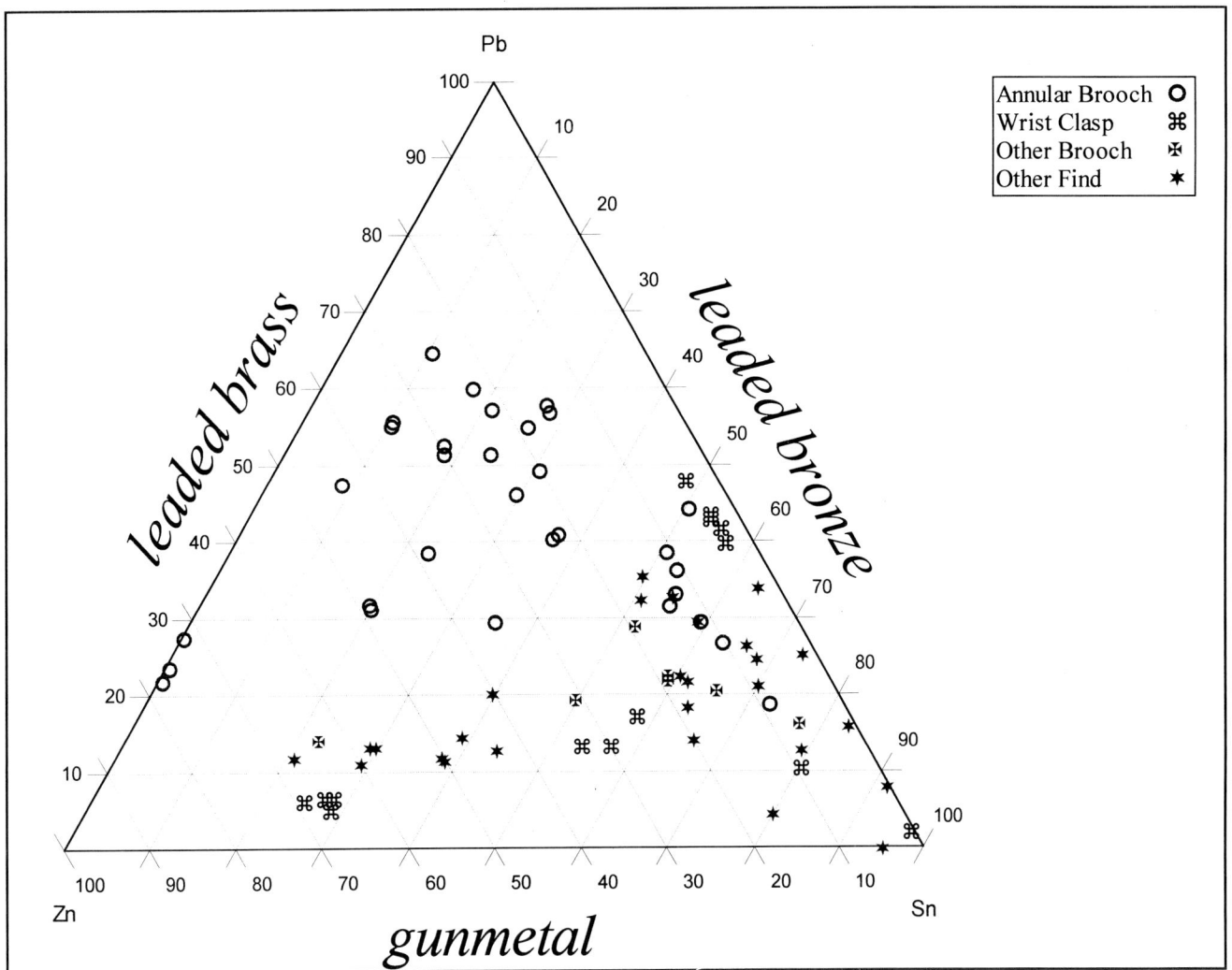

*Figure 61: ternary diagram showing the different ratios of zinc, lead and tin in the copper alloy brooches, wrist-clasps and other objects*

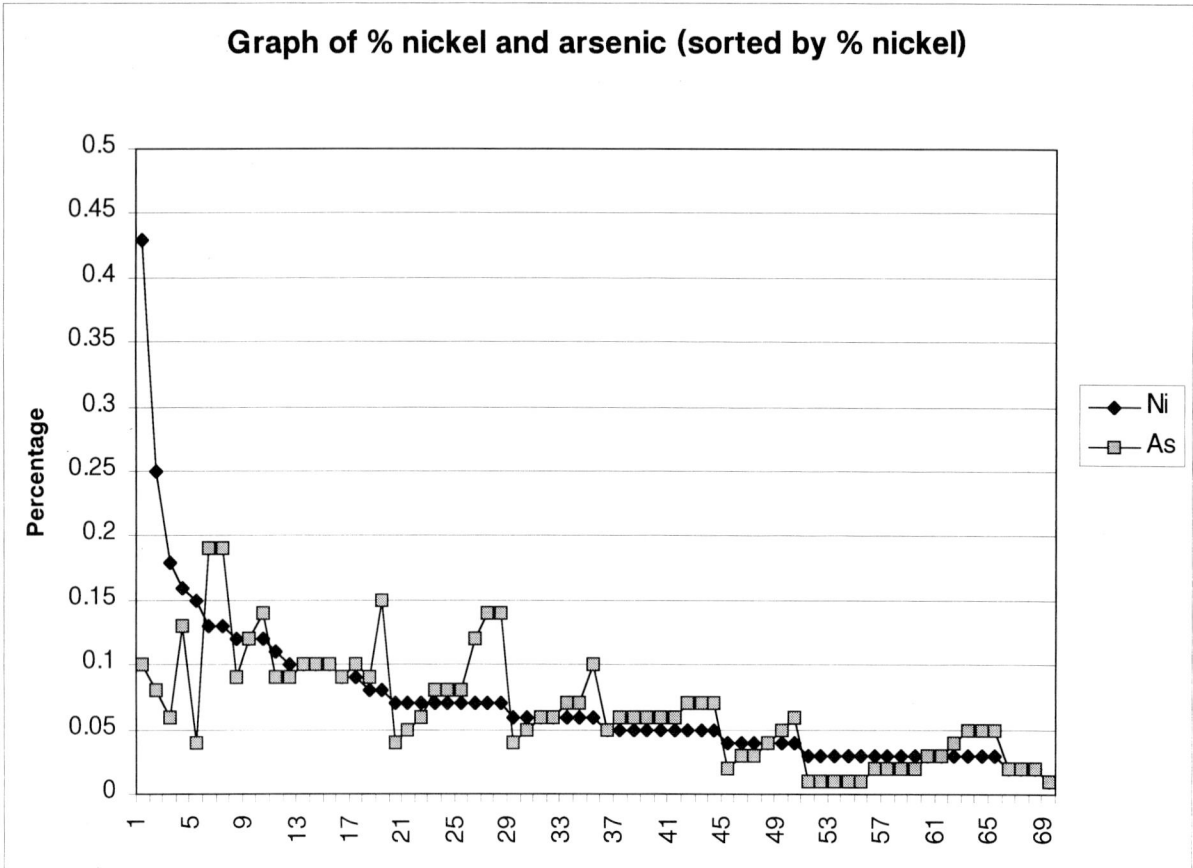

*Figure 62: plot of nickel v arsenic*

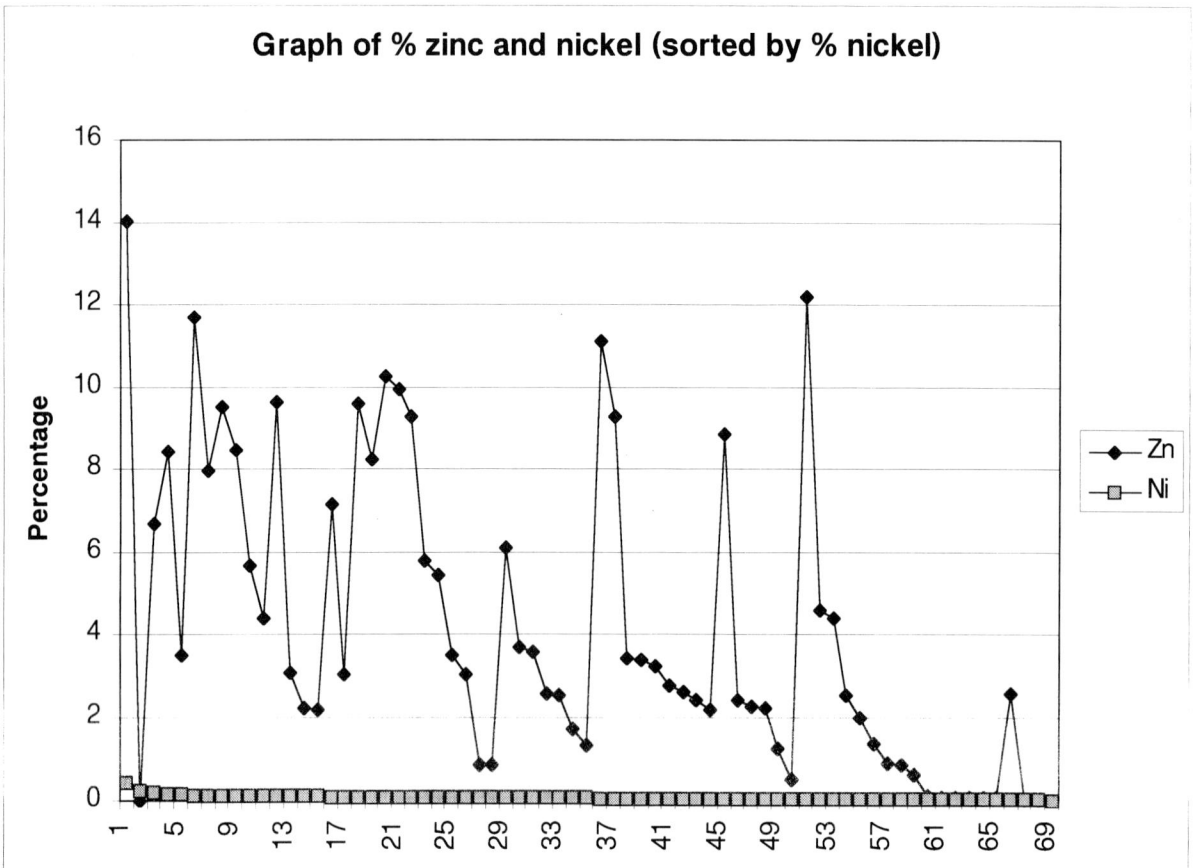

*Figure 63: plot zinc v nickel*

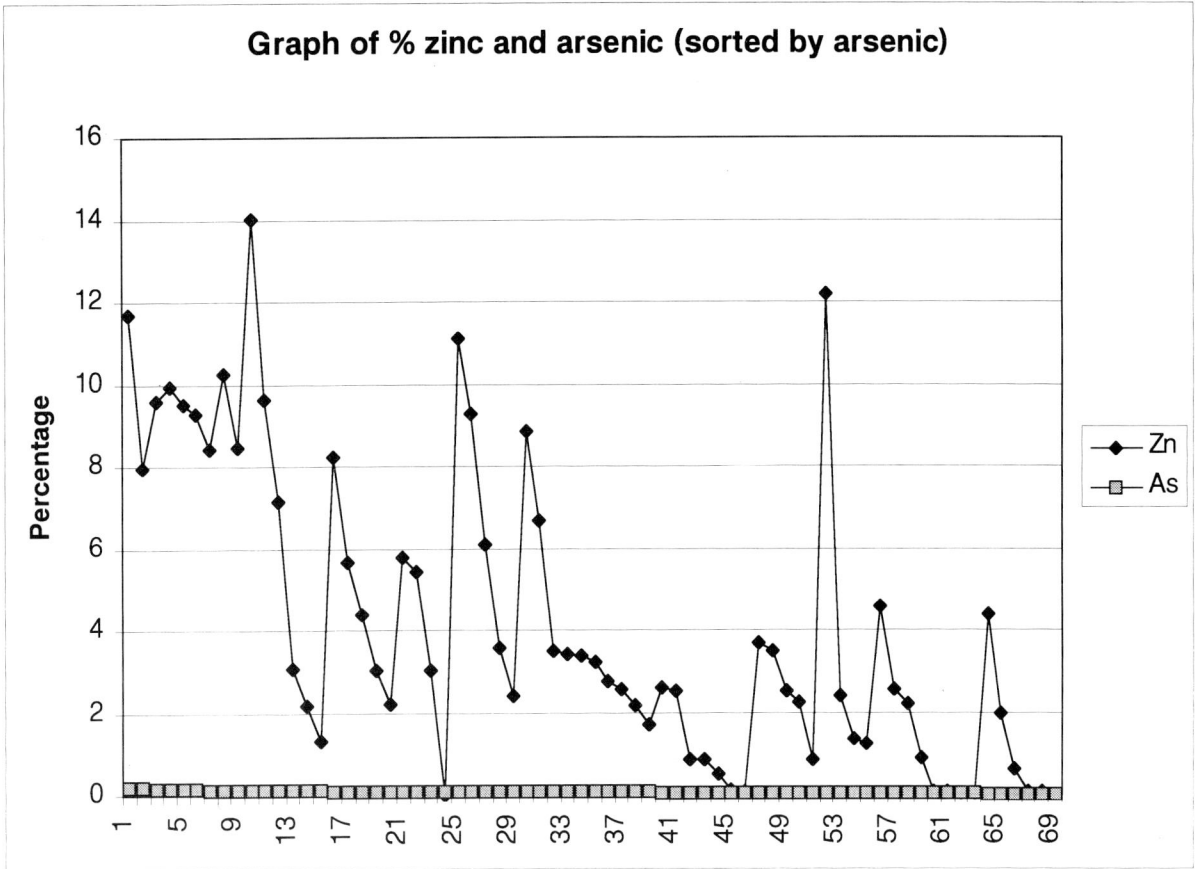

*Figure 64: plot of zinc v arsenic*

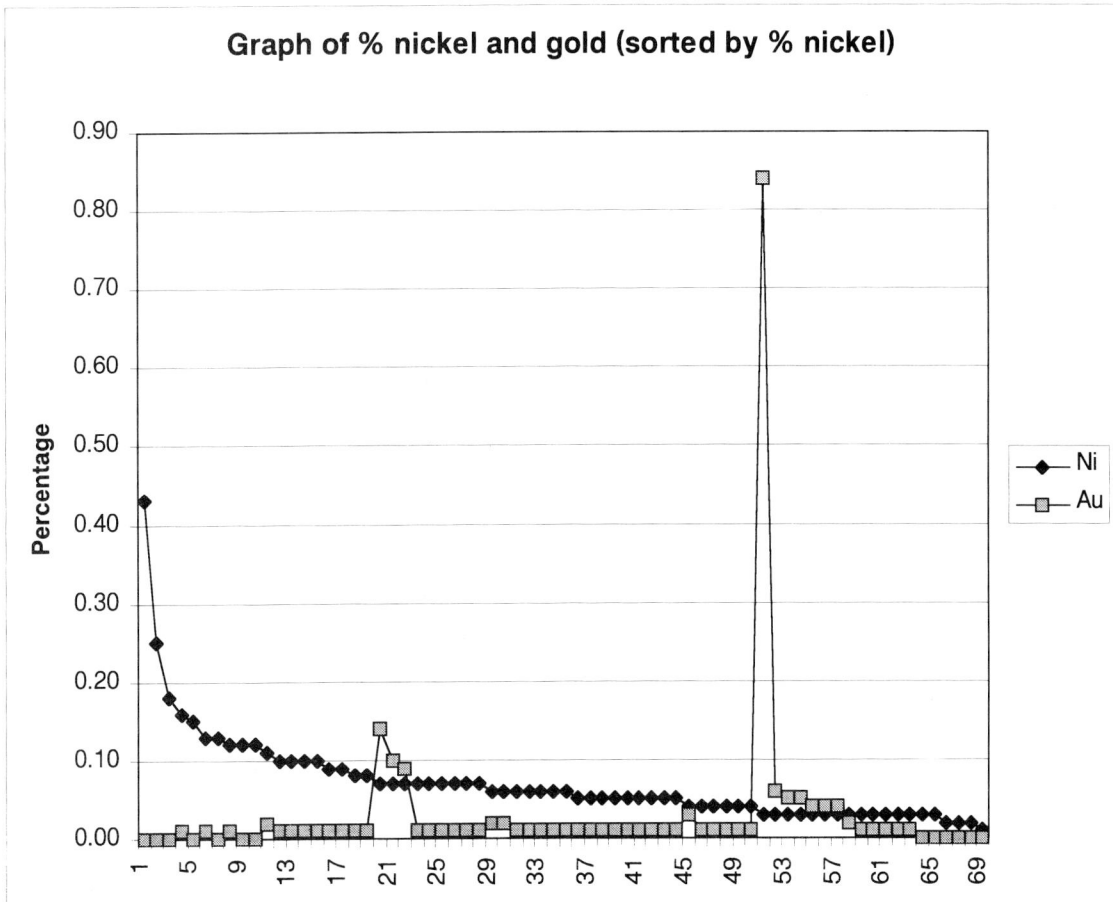

*Figure 65: plot of nickel v gold*

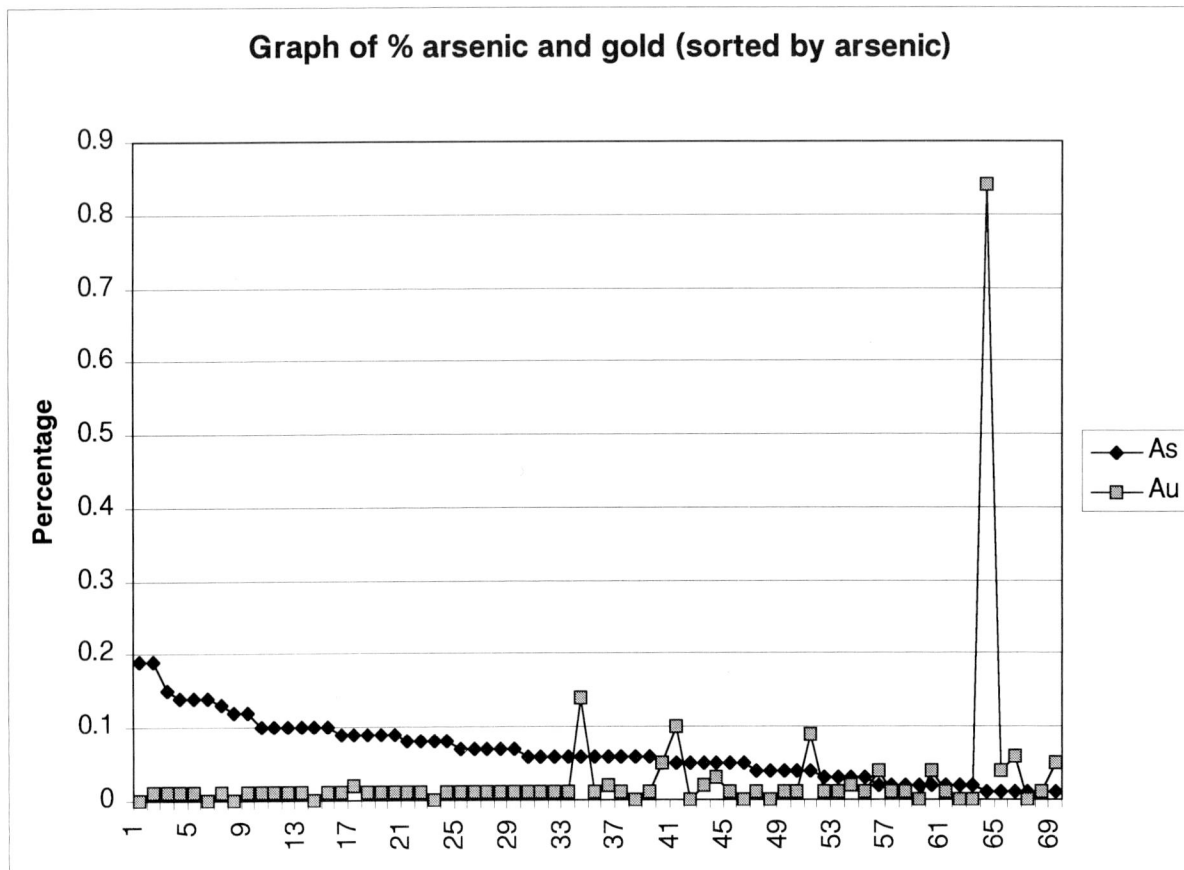

*Figure 66: plot of arsenic v gold*

| ARTEFACT | SITE | AREA | CONTEXT | OBCODE | Sample | Cu | Zn | Pb | Sn | Fe | As | Bi | Cd | Sb | Co | Ni | Cr | P | S | Mn | Ag | Au | V | Total |
|---|---|---|---|---|---|---|---|---|---|---|---|---|---|---|---|---|---|---|---|---|---|---|---|---|
| RING | 1 | HE | 46 | GX | 234 | 86.21 | 1.25 | 2.87 | 9.51 | 0.08 | 0.03 | 0 | 0 | 0.11 | 0 | 0.04 | 0 | 0.01 | 0.11 | 0 | 0.11 | 0.01 | 0 | 100.34 |
| RING | 1 | HE | 12 | CA | 235 | 82.38 | 2.24 | 1.57 | 7.34 | 0.13 | 0.04 | 0 | 0 | 0.07 | 0 | 0.04 | 0 | 0 | 0.16 | 0 | 0.16 | 0.01 | 0 | 94.14 |
| RING | 1 | HE | 12 | CC | 236 | 78.3 | 11.69 | 2.05 | 3.6 | 0.19 | 0.19 | 0.02 | 0 | 0.07 | 0.01 | 0.13 | 0 | 0.11 | 0.12 | 0 | 0.11 | 0.01 | 0 | 96.6 |
| BUCKLE | 1 | HE | 12 | DL | 237 | 85.79 | 6.08 | 3.05 | 5.96 | 0.17 | 0.07 | 0 | 0 | 0.08 | 0.01 | 0.06 | 0 | 0 | 0.09 | 0 | 0.11 | 0.01 | 0 | 101.48 |
| BUCKLE PIN | 1 | HE | 12 | DL | 238 | 77.19 | 9.53 | 1.75 | 4.57 | 0.18 | 0.14 | 0.01 | 0 | 0.07 | 0.01 | 0.12 | 0 | 0.08 | 0.12 | 0 | 0.08 | 0 | 0 | 93.85 |
| BUCKLE | 1 | HE | 12 | EE | 239 | 87.43 | 0.84 | 1.28 | 7.96 | 0.38 | 0.05 | 0.01 | 0 | 0.15 | 0.01 | 0.03 | 0 | 0.05 | 0.24 | 0 | 0.1 | 0 | 0 | 98.53 |
| RIVET FRON STRAP-END | 1 | HE | | CW | 240 | 73.72 | 11.12 | 2.55 | 5.72 | 0.36 | 0.07 | 0.01 | 0 | 0.08 | 0.01 | 0.05 | 0 | 0.24 | 0.16 | 0 | 0.11 | 0.01 | 0 | 94.21 |
| ANNULAR BROOCH | 1 | HE | 14 | CR | 241 | 82.99 | 3.03 | 5.13 | 5.15 | 0.49 | 0.08 | 0 | 0 | 0.11 | 0 | 0.07 | 0 | 0.07 | 0.12 | 0 | 0.15 | 0.01 | 0 | 97.4 |
| ANNULAR BROOCH | 1 | HE | 14 | CQ | 242 | 80.07 | 5.42 | 5.48 | 4.58 | 0.28 | 0.08 | 0 | 0 | 0.08 | 0 | 0.07 | 0 | 0.06 | 0.13 | 0 | 0.16 | 0.01 | 0 | 96.42 |
| ANNULAR BROOCH | 1 | HE | 12 | CI | 243 | 78.29 | 8.47 | 1.94 | 5.18 | 0.6 | 0.12 | 0.02 | 0 | 0.04 | 0 | 0.12 | 0 | 0.12 | 0.07 | 0 | 0.14 | 0 | 0 | 95.11 |
| ANNULAR BROOCH (GILDED) | 1 | HE | 12 | CE | 244 | 83.48 | 7.14 | 1.46 | 4.91 | 0.18 | 0.1 | 0.02 | 0 | 0.1 | 0 | 0.09 | 0 | 0.01 | 0.11 | 0 | 0.1 | 0.01 | 0 | 97.71 |
| ANNULAR BROOCH | 1 | HE | 11 | BX | 245 | 81.76 | 3.21 | 7.97 | 5.22 | 0.19 | 0.06 | 0.01 | 0 | 0.13 | 0 | 0.05 | 0 | 0.02 | 0.17 | 0 | 0.13 | 0.01 | 0 | 98.93 |
| ANNULAR BROOCH | 1 | HE | 11 | BY | 246 | 83.66 | 3.42 | 8.4 | 5.37 | 0.2 | 0.06 | 0.01 | 0 | 0.08 | 0 | 0.05 | 0 | 0.15 | 0.07 | 0 | 0.02 | 0.01 | 0 | 101.5 |
| ANNULAR BROOCH | 1 | HE | 43 | FS | 247 | 80.59 | 1.34 | 3.26 | 8.45 | 0.67 | 0.03 | 0 | 0 | 0.15 | 0 | 0.03 | 0 | 0 | 0.21 | 0 | 0.17 | 0.02 | 0 | 94.92 |
| ANNULAR BROOCH | 1 | HE | 43 | FT | 248 | 78.89 | 3.7 | 2.09 | 7.97 | 0.51 | 0.04 | 0 | 0 | 0.13 | 0 | 0.06 | 0 | 0.02 | 0.21 | 0 | 0.12 | 0.01 | 0 | 93.75 |
| ANNULAR BROOCH | 1 | HE | 24 | EL | 249 | 82.56 | 3.5 | 2.34 | 5.69 | 0.37 | 0.04 | 0 | 0 | 0.08 | 0.01 | 0.15 | 0 | 0.03 | 0.1 | 0 | 0.13 | 0 | 0 | 95 |
| ANNULAR BROOCH | 1 | HE | 16 | DB | 250 | 85.59 | 8.43 | 2.17 | 4.92 | 1.05 | 0.13 | 0.01 | 0 | 0.1 | 0.02 | 0.16 | 0 | 0.03 | 0.35 | 0 | 0.11 | 0.01 | 0 | 103.08 |
| ANNULAR BROOCH | 1 | HE | 16 | DN | 251 | 87.03 | 3.39 | 2.41 | 7.06 | 0.23 | 0.06 | 0 | 0 | 0.13 | 0 | 0.05 | 0 | 0.2 | 0.2 | 0 | 0.12 | 0.01 | 0 | 100.69 |
| ANNULAR BROOCH | 1 | HE | 26 | FA | 252 | 80.51 | 5.67 | 3.43 | 6.32 | 0.43 | 0.09 | 0.01 | 0 | 0.11 | 0.01 | 0.12 | 0 | 0.22 | 0.13 | 0 | 0.14 | 0.01 | 0 | 97.2 |
| ANNULAR BROOCH | 1 | HE | 11 | FB | 253 | 84.84 | 7.97 | 1.3 | 3.4 | 0.18 | 0.19 | 0.01 | 0 | 0.08 | 0 | 0.13 | 0 | 0.13 | 0.09 | 0 | 0.11 | 0 | 0 | 98.43 |
| LARGE PIN | 1 | HE | 43 | FU | 254 | 88.08 | 1.71 | 3.98 | 5.51 | 0.22 | 0.06 | 0 | 0 | 0.13 | 0 | 0.06 | 0 | 0.06 | 0.15 | 0 | 0.1 | 0.01 | 0 | 100.07 |
| WRIST CLASP (MALE) | 1 | HE | 43 | FO | 255 | 92.26 | 0.06 | 0.7 | 1 | 0.03 | 0.01 | 0 | 0 | 0.06 | 0 | 0.03 | 0 | 0 | 0.02 | 0 | 0.12 | 0.05 | 0 | 94.34 |
| WRIST CLASP (FEMALE) | 1 | HE | 43 | FO | 256 | 99.87 | 0.06 | 0.81 | 0.99 | 0.05 | 0.02 | 0 | 0 | 0.12 | 0 | 0.03 | 0 | 0 | 0.07 | 0 | 0.11 | 0.04 | 0 | 102.17 |
| WRIST CLASP (MALE) | 1 | HE | 43 | FP | 257 | 93.1 | 0.07 | 0.82 | 1.02 | 0.01 | 0.02 | 0 | 0 | 0.11 | 0 | 0.03 | 0 | 0.05 | 0.05 | 0 | 0.11 | 0.04 | 0 | 95.43 |
| WRIST CLASP (FEMALE) | 1 | HE | 43 | FP | 258 | 93.65 | 0.06 | 0.8 | 1.06 | 0.04 | 0.01 | 0 | 0 | 0.1 | 0 | 0.03 | 0 | 0.01 | 0.06 | 0 | 0.11 | 0.06 | 0 | 95.99 |
| WRIST CLASP | 1 | HE | 20 | EH | 259 | 90.8 | 0.63 | 0.7 | 5.4 | 0.03 | 0.01 | 0 | 0 | 0.12 | 0 | 0.03 | 0 | 0.04 | 0.12 | 0 | 0.16 | 0.84 | 0 | 98.88 |
| WRIST CLASP | 1 | HE | 46 | GR | 260 | 83.38 | 0.49 | 6.04 | 6.04 | 0.38 | 0.05 | 0 | 0 | 0.05 | 0 | 0.04 | 0 | 0.03 | 0.12 | 0 | 0.14 | 0.03 | 0 | 96.79 |
| SLIP LOOP | 1 | HE | 46 | GY | 261 | 81.02 | 2.41 | 4.59 | 7.18 | 0.18 | 0.07 | 0 | 0 | 0.17 | 0 | 0.05 | 0 | 0.34 | 0.15 | 0 | 0.09 | 0.01 | 0 | 96.26 |
| ANNULAR BROOCH FRAGMENT | 1 | HE | | FD | 262 | 69.25 | 0.09 | 24.1 | 6.82 | 0.08 | 0.05 | 0 | 0 | 0.16 | 0 | 0.03 | 0 | 0.05 | 0.15 | 0 | 0.09 | 0.05 | 0 | 100.87 |
| TWEEZERS | 1 | A | 12 | AA | 166 | 81.68 | 9.29 | 2.1 | 4.61 | 0.13 | 0.07 | 0 | 0 | 0.13 | 0 | 0.05 | 0 | 0 | 0.06 | 0 | 0.07 | 0.01 | 0 | 98.2 |
| ANNULAR BROOCH | 1 | A | 17 | AA | 167 | 80.25 | 1.33 | 7.01 | 7.57 | 0.1 | 0.1 | 0 | 0 | 0.21 | 0 | 0.06 | 0 | 0 | 0.23 | 0 | 0.06 | 0.01 | 0 | 96.93 |
| CRUCIFORM-HEADED PIN | 1 | A | 31 | CS | 168 | 81.55 | 2.16 | 2.15 | 7.38 | 0.17 | 0.06 | 0 | 0 | 0.11 | 0 | 0.05 | 0 | 0 | 0.07 | 0 | 0.07 | 0.01 | 0 | 93.78 |
| FLAT BROOCH | 1 | A | 34 | AC | 169 | 82.36 | 2.56 | 2.98 | 8 | 0.13 | 0.06 | 0 | 0 | 0.15 | 0 | 0.06 | 0 | 0.01 | 0.05 | 0 | 0.07 | 0.02 | 0 | 96.45 |
| FLAT BROOCH | 1 | A | 34 | AC | 170 | 83.37 | 2.51 | 3.01 | 7.89 | 0.13 | 0.05 | 0 | 0 | 0.16 | 0 | 0.06 | 0 | 0 | 0.03 | 0 | 0.09 | 0.02 | 0 | 97.32 |

Table 5: chemical composition of the copper alloys from areas 1HE, 1A, 1B, 2B, 2C and 2F

| ARTEFACT | SITE | AREA | CONTEXT | OBCODE | Sample Code | Cu | Zn | Pb | Sn | Fe | As | Bi | Cd | Sb | Co | Ni | Cr | P | S | Mn | Ag | Au | V | Total |
|---|---|---|---|---|---|---|---|---|---|---|---|---|---|---|---|---|---|---|---|---|---|---|---|---|
| WIRE | 1 | A | 34 | AD | 171 | 49.79 | 1.73 | 4.34 | 8.63 | 0.41 | 0.03 | 0.01 | 0 | 0.18 | 0 | 0.01 | 0 | 3.62 | 0.36 | 0.01 | 0.08 | 0.04 | 0 | 69.24 |
| FIBULA BROOCH | 1 | A | 50 | AB | 173 | 79.99 | 0 | 4.32 | 10.33 | 0.01 | 0.08 | 0.01 | 0 | 0.95 | 0 | 0.25 | 0 | 0.17 | 0.01 | 0 | 0.07 | 0 | 0 | 96.19 |
| ANKLET FRAGMENT | 1 | A | 50 | AC | 174 | 28.56 | 0.29 | 4.4 | 22.97 | 0.49 | 0.13 | 0.02 | 0 | 0.32 | 0 | 0 | 0 | 0.2 | 0.93 | 0 | 0.08 | 0.02 | 0 | 58.41 |
| SMALL-LONG BROOCH | 1 | A | 50 | AD | 175 | 80.68 | 0.88 | 2.17 | 10.2 | 0.09 | 0.02 | 0.01 | 0 | 0.12 | 0 | 0.03 | 0 | 0 | 0.07 | 0 | 0.08 | 0.01 | 0 | 94.36 |
| WRISTCLASP | 1 | A | 50 | AF | 176 | 79.29 | 4.38 | 1.96 | 8.28 | 0.13 | 0.01 | 0.01 | 0 | 0.1 | 0 | 0.03 | 0 | 0.1 | 0.04 | 0 | 0.08 | 0.01 | 0 | 94.42 |
| CRUCIFORM BROOCH | 1 | A | 50 | CG | 177 | 87.02 | 2.23 | 3.34 | 5.95 | 0.17 | 0.02 | 0.01 | 0 | 0.12 | 0 | 0.04 | 0 | 0 | 0.03 | 0 | 0.08 | 0.01 | 0 | 99.02 |
| GREAT SQUARE-HEADED BROOCH1 | 1 | A | 86 | AB | 178 | 82.67 | 3.03 | 1.89 | 4.84 | 0.29 | 0.09 | 0.01 | 0.12 | 0.01 | 0.09 | 0 | 0 | 0.09 | 0 | 0.07 | 0.07 | 0.01 | 0 | 93.21 |
| ANNULAR BROOCH | 1 | B | 8 | AC | 179 | 85.78 | 0 | 0.04 | 8.21 | 0.12 | 0.01 | 0.01 | 0 | 0.15 | 0 | 0.01 | 0 | 0.03 | 0.04 | 0 | 0.07 | 0 | 0 | 94.47 |
| ANNULAR BROOCH | 1 | B | 10 | AC | 181 | 81.16 | 2.22 | 3.7 | 6.29 | 0.61 | 0.09 | 0.01 | 0 | 0.14 | 0.01 | 0.1 | 0 | 0 | 0.13 | 0 | 0.08 | 0.01 | 0 | 94.55 |
| BANGLE | 1 | B | 10 | AE-AF | 182 | 79.03 | 5.77 | 1.68 | 5.77 | 0.3 | 0.08 | 0.01 | 0 | 0.12 | 0.01 | 0.07 | 0 | 0.01 | 0.11 | 0 | 0.07 | 0.01 | 0 | 93.04 |
| ANNULAR BROOCH | 1 | B | 10 | AK | 183 | 81.35 | 2.16 | 3.61 | 6.42 | 0.62 | 0.1 | 0.02 | 0 | 0.16 | 0.01 | 0.1 | 0 | 0.02 | 0.12 | 0 | 0.08 | 0.01 | 0 | 94.78 |
| CYLINDER FRAGMENTS | 1 | B | 12 | AG | 184 | 56.77 | 0.1 | 1.43 | 16.62 | 0.13 | 0.05 | 0.01 | 0 | 0.3 | 0 | 0.01 | 0 | 0.73 | 0.5 | 0 | 0.09 | 0.04 | 0 | 76.78 |
| ANNULAR BROOCH | 1 | B | 15 | AA | 185 | 64.87 | 0.03 | 0 | 2.25 | 0.31 | 0.02 | 0.01 | 0 | 0.09 | 0 | 0.03 | 0 | 0.17 | 0.17 | 0.01 | 0.08 | 0.01 | 0 | 68.05 |
| ANNULAR BROOCH | 1 | B | 15 | AA | 185 | 76.52 | 8.23 | 1.76 | 6.28 | 0.25 | 0.09 | 0.02 | 0 | 0.13 | 0 | 0.08 | 0 | 0.21 | 0 | 0 | 0.08 | 0.01 | 0 | 93.66 |
| WRISTCLASP (CAST BAR) | 1 | B | 17 | AN | 186 | 86.18 | 4.57 | 1.82 | 7.31 | 0.14 | 0.02 | 0.01 | 0 | 0.12 | 0 | 0.03 | 0 | 0 | 0 | 0 | 0.08 | 0.01 | 0 | 100.29 |
| WRISTCLASP (PLATE) | 1 | B | 17 | AN | 186 | 37.32 | 0.12 | 0.5 | 22.3 | 1.06 | 0.05 | 0.01 | 0 | 0.21 | 0 | 0.01 | 0 | 3.46 | 0.28 | 0.01 | 0.07 | 0.01 | 0 | 65.41 |
| ANNULAR BROOCH | 1 | B | 101 | AX | 187 | 80.39 | 3.59 | 3 | 5.64 | 0.98 | 0.07 | 0.01 | 0 | 0.15 | 0.01 | 0.06 | 0 | 0.02 | 0.11 | 0 | 0.08 | 0.01 | 0 | 94.12 |
| ANNULAR BROOCH | 1 | B | 101 | | 188 | 81.69 | 2.74 | 2.84 | 7.51 | 0.46 | 0.06 | 0.01 | 0 | 0.16 | 0 | 0.05 | 0 | 0.02 | 0.07 | 0 | 0.09 | 0.01 | 0 | 95.71 |
| ANNULAR BROOCH | 1 | B | 104 | AW | 189 | 84.91 | 3.08 | 3.24 | 6.71 | 0.13 | 0.1 | 0.01 | 0.01 | 0.13 | 0.01 | 0.1 | 0 | 0.04 | 0.12 | 0 | 0.08 | 0.01 | 0 | 98.68 |
| CRUCIFORM BROOCH | 1 | B | 105 | BB | 190 | 82.78 | 1.97 | 2.86 | 9.1 | 0.14 | 0.01 | 0.01 | 0 | 0.13 | 0 | 0.03 | 0 | 0 | 0.08 | 0 | 0.08 | 0.04 | 0 | 97.23 |
| ANNULAR BROOCH | 2 | B | 26 | G | 191 | 62.39 | 9.82 | 1.92 | 4.93 | 0.36 | 0.12 | 0.02 | 0 | 0.09 | 0.07 | 0.3 | 0 | 0.9 | 0.35 | 0 | 0.11 | 0 | 0 | 81.38 |
| ANNULAR BROOCH | 2 | B | 26 | F | 192 | 80.55 | 2.6 | 3.42 | 9.04 | 0.15 | 0.05 | 0.02 | 0 | 0.14 | 0 | 0.05 | 0 | 0 | 0.05 | 0 | 0.07 | 0.01 | 0 | 96.15 |
| ANNULAR BROOCH | 2 | B | 27 | G | 193 | 75.8 | 14.02 | 1.72 | 3.65 | 0.26 | 0.1 | 0.01 | 0 | 0.11 | 0.08 | 0.43 | 0 | 0.16 | 0.16 | 0 | 0.07 | 0 | 0 | 96.57 |
| BINDING | 2 | B | 40 | AA | 194 | 88.84 | 9.63 | 2.17 | 7.31 | 0.35 | 0.1 | 0.01 | 0 | 0.15 | 0.01 | 0.1 | 0 | 0 | 0.28 | 0 | 0.03 | 0.01 | 0 | 108.99 |
| BINDING | 2 | B | 40 | AA | 194 | 73.97 | 0.22 | 0 | 4.11 | 0.35 | 0.04 | 0.01 | 0 | 0.12 | 0 | 0.06 | 0 | 0.23 | 0.13 | 0.01 | 0.09 | 0.01 | 0 | 79.35 |
| SHEET FRAGMENT | 2 | B | 42 | AX | 195 | 75.28 | 0.27 | 3.82 | 11.04 | 0.05 | 0.04 | 0.01 | 0 | 0.2 | 0 | 0.03 | 0 | 0.23 | 0.27 | 0 | 0.07 | 0.04 | 0 | 91.35 |
| BINDING | 2 | B | 54 | AA | 196 | 54.36 | 0.56 | 1.88 | 4.69 | 0.1 | 0 | 0.01 | 0 | 0.16 | 0 | 0 | 0 | 2.29 | 1.29 | 0 | 0.09 | 0.01 | 0 | 65.44 |
| BINDING | 2 | B | 54 | AB | 197 | 50.83 | 0.74 | 2.44 | 6.72 | 0.16 | 0.01 | 0.01 | 0 | 0.18 | 0 | 0 | 0 | 2.76 | 1.15 | 0 | 0.09 | 0.01 | 0 | 65.1 |
| ANNULAR BROOCH | 2 | B | 58 | AS | 198 | 82.12 | 4.37 | 2.79 | 4.85 | 1.12 | 0.09 | 0.02 | 0 | 0.13 | 0.01 | 0.11 | 0 | 0.11 | 0.06 | 0 | 0.07 | 0.02 | 0 | 95.87 |
| BELT FITTING | 2 | B | 55 | AB | 199 | 14.11 | 0.84 | 10.55 | 19.58 | 1.33 | 0.11 | 0.02 | 0 | 0.2 | 0 | 0.02 | 0 | 8.13 | 0.3 | 0 | 0.05 | 0.03 | 0 | 55.28 |
| RING | 2 | B | 58 | BR | 201 | 79.62 | 8.84 | 2.07 | 6.63 | 0.24 | 0.06 | 0.01 | 0 | 0.16 | 0 | 0.04 | 0 | 0 | 0.02 | 0 | 0.08 | 0.01 | 0 | 97.78 |
| WRISTCLASP | 2 | B | 58 | BV | 202 | 61.14 | 1.99 | 1.37 | 4.59 | 0.17 | 0.09 | 0.03 | 0 | 0.15 | 0 | 0.03 | 0 | 1.04 | 0.08 | 0 | 0.1 | 0.01 | 0 | 70.79 |
| BANGLE | 2 | B | 91 | EG | 203 | 83.29 | 2.53 | 3.27 | 8.75 | 0.22 | 0.04 | 0.01 | 0 | 0.17 | 0 | 0.03 | 0 | 0 | 0.05 | 0 | 0.09 | 0.01 | 0 | 98.46 |
| RING-HEADED PIN | 2 | B | 91 | EL | 204 | 78.38 | 2.42 | 3.13 | 8.8 | 0.22 | 0.03 | 0.01 | 0 | 0.18 | 0 | 0.04 | 0 | 0.09 | 0.06 | 0 | 0.1 | 0.01 | 0 | 93.47 |
| ANNULAR BROOCH | 2 | B | 91 | GW | 205 | 58.14 | 0.13 | 27.76 | 8.61 | 0.12 | 0.05 | 0.01 | 0 | 0.19 | 0 | 0.03 | 0 | 0.01 | 0.09 | 0 | 0.07 | 0 | 0 | 95.21 |

*Table 5 (continued): chemical composition of the copper alloys from areas 1HE, 1A, 1B, 2B, 2C and 2F*

| ARTEFACT | SITE | AREA | CONTEXT | OBCODE | Sample | Cu | Zn | Pb | Sn | Fe | As | Bi | Cd | Sb | Co | Ni | Cr | P | S | Mn | Ag | Au | V | Total |
|---|---|---|---|---|---|---|---|---|---|---|---|---|---|---|---|---|---|---|---|---|---|---|---|---|
| ANNULAR BROOCH | 2 | B | 91 | GT | 206 | 65.47 | 0.02 | 22.16 | 8.45 | 0.07 | 0.02 | 0 | 0 | 0.14 | 0 | 0.02 | 0 | 0 | 0.07 | 0 | 0.06 | 0 | 0 | 96.48 |
| ANNULAR BROOCH | 2 | B | 91 | GT | 206 | 63.38 | 0.02 | 21.74 | 8.07 | 0.1 | 0.02 | 0 | 0 | 0.17 | 0 | 0.02 | 0 | 0 | 0.05 | 0 | 0.07 | 0 | 0 | 93.64 |
| BUCKET BINDING | 2 | | | | 207 | 76.69 | 2.55 | 0.73 | 12.89 | 0.23 | 0.02 | 0 | 0 | 0.16 | 0 | 0.02 | 0 | 0.15 | 0.12 | 0 | 0.07 | 0 | 0 | 93.63 |
| CRUCIFORM BROOCH | 2 | F | 13 | AA | 209 | 77.43 | 12.18 | 2.73 | 4.31 | 0.41 | 0.03 | 0.01 | 0 | 0.18 | 0 | 0.03 | 0 | 0.01 | 0.03 | 0 | 0.08 | 0.01 | 0 | 97.44 |
| CYLINDERS | 2 | F | 13 | AF | 210 | 63.58 | 1.38 | 3.49 | 5.77 | 0.11 | 0.06 | 0.03 | 0 | 0.08 | 0 | 0 | 0 | 0.38 | 0.08 | 0 | 0.08 | 0 | 0 | 75.04 |
| ANNULAR BROOCH | 2 | F | 13 | DA | 211 | 90.19 | 0.85 | 2.82 | 4.62 | 0.41 | 0.05 | 0.01 | 0 | 0.14 | 0 | 0.07 | 0 | 0 | 0.14 | 0 | 0.08 | 0.1 | 0 | 99.48 |
| ANNULAR BROOCH | 2 | F | 13 | AD | 212 | 82.68 | 0.84 | 2.81 | 4.47 | 0.43 | 0.04 | 0 | 0 | 0.14 | 0 | 0.07 | 0 | 0.02 | 0.09 | 0 | 0.09 | 0.09 | 0 | 91.77 |
| ANNULAR BROOCH PIN | 2 | F | 13 | AD | 213 | 81.03 | 6.69 | 0.72 | 5.87 | 0.18 | 0.06 | 0 | 0 | 0.1 | 0.01 | 0.18 | 0 | 0 | 0.05 | 0 | 0.08 | 0 | 0 | 94.97 |
| WRISTCLASP (MALE) | 2 | F | 13 | AE | 214 | 80.44 | 9.94 | 0.97 | 4.02 | 0.28 | 0.14 | 0.01 | 0 | 0.13 | 0.01 | 0.07 | 0 | 0 | 0.01 | 0 | 0.08 | 0.01 | 0 | 96.11 |
| WRISTCLASP (FEMALE) | 2 | F | 13 | AE | 215 | 84.19 | 9.61 | 0.72 | 4.08 | 0.3 | 0.15 | 0.01 | 0 | 0.14 | 0.01 | 0.08 | 0 | 0 | 0.07 | 0 | 0.08 | 0.01 | 0 | 99.45 |
| WRISTCLASP (MALE) | 2 | F | 13 | DD | 216 | 77.82 | 10.25 | 0.91 | 3.66 | 0.3 | 0.12 | 0.01 | 0 | 0.12 | 0.01 | 0.07 | 0 | 0.05 | 0.08 | 0 | 0.09 | 0.01 | 0 | 93.5 |
| WRISTCLASP (FEMALE) | 2 | F | 13 | DD | 217 | 79.68 | 9.3 | 0.94 | 3.96 | 0.3 | 0.14 | 0.01 | 0 | 0.13 | 0.01 | 0.07 | 0 | 0.01 | 0.05 | 0 | 0.08 | 0.01 | 0 | 94.69 |
| FRAGMENTS | 2 | C | 4 | AA-AC | 218 | 75.7 | 5.87 | 1.82 | 4.87 | 0.15 | 0.16 | 0.02 | 0 | 0.15 | 0 | 0.07 | 0 | 1.1 | 0.1 | 0 | 0.08 | 0.01 | 0 | 90.1 |
| ANNULAR BROOCH | 1 | B | 105 | | 219 | 84.84 | 3.5 | 1.93 | 7.14 | 0.4 | 0.06 | 0.01 | 0 | 0.24 | 0 | 0.07 | 0 | 0.01 | 0.11 | 0 | 0.13 | 0.14 | 0 | 98.58 |

Table 5 (continued): chemical composition of the copper alloys from areas 1HE, 1

# Conservation

by Jacqui Watson

## Introduction

The material from this Anglo-Saxon cemetery has been examined as three different groups:

a: group excavated by J Dent, conserved at the York Archaeological Trust laboratory and the organic material examined in the Yorkshire Museum.

b: group excavated by the Heslerton Parish Project team (HPP), and conserved at York Archaeological Trust by Margaret Brookes.

c: group excavated by HPP and conserved and examined at the Ancient Monuments Laboratory of English Heritage

This discussion covers only the material conserved by the Ancient Monuments Laboratory. The discussion on the mineral-preserved organic material is mainly confined to the non-textile components preserved on the metalwork, the textile is reported on seperately in this volume by P Walton Rogers. This section includes all the objects from the cemetery with non-textile organic material. The detailed catalogue entries relating to the individual objects have been integrated with the other evidence in the calalogue volume, Volume ii of this report.

## Examination and conservation

The metalwork came into laboratory in two forms, either as single objects or as metal/organic complexes in soil blocks. The latter was necessary because many metal grave goods were found corroded together with organic material which could not be separated for conservation purposes, and needed detailed examination before being dismantled.

All ironwork and the soil blocks were X-rayed. In the case of the blocks, the radiographs were used to locate the position of metalwork and some dense organic materials such as ivory and bone. Other materials including glass beads with a high metal content are also X-ray opaque and can clearly be seen on an X-radiograph, the different colours often represented by varying shades of grey. Amber, on the other hand, is X-ray transparent and many examples were less dense than the surrounding sand. This means that it is often possible to locate amber beads as dark grey or black shapes on a radiograph. X-radiographs cannot be used as an accurate placing of all objects in a soil block because the cone-shaped beam enlarges items any distance from the plate, and some items were found to be up to 15% larger on the plate. Stereo X-radiography was used with some success on some of the smaller blocks to separate objects at different levels. Unfortunately it could not be used on the larger blocks as one has a narrow separating distance between the two plates of around 70 mm.

Xero-radiography was attempted at the Royal Marsden Hospital on the soil block from Grave G143 which contained brooches and part of a bead necklace. This technique produced a print which did not enlarge the objects and enhanced the edges of features. This was useful in order to see all the items in the block clearly, but other enhanced features in the soil matrix were difficult to interpret.

The soil blocks were excavated in the laboratory, making 1:1 plans or taking photographs to record the position of all items, along with the extent and nature of any preserved organic material. The process is the same as excavating on site but there is of course more time for recording. All objects were examined, using a binocular microscope to detect any remains of organic material preserved in the corrosion layers, and the details have been recorded in the accompanying catalogue.

Many members of the conservation section worked on this material including the author, Bridget Ibbs and Colin Slack. We were assisted by students from the Institute of Archaeology, University College London: Kirsty Bell, Paul Benson, Emily Ford and Mary Scott; at Durham,

Liz Beresford and Judy Greenfield; and at Cardiff, Anthony Read.

Objects were cleaned using various mechanical techniques, such as hand tools and airbrasive for the ironwork, leaving any areas of preserved organic material. All the objects have been put into dry passive storage, rather than using any water- or solvent-based stabilisation processes, in order not to interfere with either their metallographic structures or damage the associated organic material. Consolidants also have not been used as these limit the range of specialist examination techniques that can be used, such as the scanning electron microscope for identification purposes. This means that the objects continue to be very fragile and can withstand little handling or transportation.

# Organic material associated with the metalwork

In damp conditions most metals will corrode and the resulting corrosion products will stain any adjacent organic material. When buried, organic material impregnated with metal salts cannot readily be broken down by soil microorganisms, and over long periods this material will become chemically altered by these minerals (Keepax 1975). The acid sandy soils at West Heslerton, especially in association with inhumations, have provided a particularly aggressive environment for the metalwork, and have promoted the large-scale preservation of organic material for study.

Mineral-preserved organic material is more common on ironwork as this metal corrodes more rapidly than copper, lead or silver alloys. Iron-preserved organic material is heavily impregnated with corrosion and in some cases the whole structure has become replaced by iron salts and the organic component dissolved away. On the other hand organic material preserved by copper corrosion still resembles the original material, which is sometimes stained green; this mainly applies to bone or ivory. In a few instances copper corrosion has replaced the organic material. Hard animal tissue such as bone, ivory and horn is usually poorly preserved because of the acid environment, and in the case of horn is only seen preserved in iron corrosion products. Textiles, especially woollen ones, are often extensively preserved, sometimes exhibiting both replaced and coated states on one sample.

Fresh and waterlogged organic materials are identified by examining their microscopic structures and this is also possible for mineral-preserved examples. It has been possible to distinguish between most materials such as horn, bone, wood, leather and textile with the aid of a hand lens or low-powered incident light microscope. For the most part the identification of wood species was done by observing either thin sections of lightly coated mate-

rial or gold coated specimens in the Scanning Electron Microscope. Where the latter technique has been used a sample number is quoted in the catalogue.

A large variety of organic materials were recognised and these are best discussed under their object types, along with any comments on reconstruction. It should be noted that the quality of preservation of organic material was highly variable. In some cases the iron corrosion was highly crystalline which made replication of the diagnostic features poor. Others were formed in powdery corrosion and have produced some of the classic structures which have been reproduced in this report. At the moment it is difficult to know if the form of preservation is due to variable soil conditions across the site or as a result of factors purely local to an individual object. A summary of this organic material is presented in two tables: Table 6 includes the brooches, buckles, purse groups and girdle hangers, while Table 7 covers shields, spears, knives and vessels.

# Brooches

Most of the brooches are made of copper alloy with iron pins. Due to the preferential corrosion of the iron, most of the preserved organic material is to be found in the iron oxides. For the most part this is mainly textile, but skin and undiagnostic tissue are common. Many of these objects are associated with a black mass, which on examination appears to be soil consolidated by a root mass. Any textile or tissue that may have caused this has deteriorated beyond recognition.

# Buckles

Thirty-seven buckles were examined, the majority of which were iron and therefore had the remains of leather belts and adjacent garments preserved on them. On three examples skin was also preserved on the reverse.

# Purses

It is possible to identify seven definite purse groups, from G107, G113, G132, G139, G152, G163 and G167. Most were lifted as discrete assemblages and excavated in the laboratory. Nearly all had traces of leather, some quite extensive, over the metalwork, which would suggest that the purses were made from this material. Most had textile associated which appeared to be inside the leather; this could have been a lining fabric or individual pieces of textile. Several sets of iron girdle hangers were found tied together with plied or plaited cords, and in two examples (G132, G152) the knots were also preserved.

At least five of these purses had elephant ivory rings, G107, G139, G152, G163 and G167, but some were very

|  | Brooches | Buckles | Purses | Girdle hangers |
|---|---|---|---|---|
| copper alloy | 72 (60)* | 6 [3] |  | 3 |
| iron | 9 | 24 [6] |  | 9 |
| lace tags |  | 6 | 7 |  |
| amulets |  |  | 2 | 2 |
| textile | 70 | 18 [3] | 6 | 9 |
| cords |  |  |  | 2 1? |
| leather | 1 | 21[5] | 6 | 7 |
| skin | 14 | 2 [1] |  |  |
| pupae | 7 |  |  |  |
| insect eggs | 1 |  |  |  |
| ivory |  |  | 4 | 3 |
| random organic | 6 | 1 |  |  |
| no organic | 7 | 4 [2] |  |  |
| Total | 81 | 29 [8] | 8 | 9 |

\* number of brooches with iron pins
[ ] material conserved at York Archaeological Trust

*Table 6: summary of organic material associated with brooches, buckles, purse groups and girdle hangers.*

poorly preserved. It is therefore possible that there might originally have been more but that they have not survived.

On the purse from G152, the leather originally enclosed the ivory ring and it would not have been visible in use. This may also have been the case for the other examples, which makes it very hard to understand why they used elephant ivory for this purpose, especially as this is the only object type made from this material commonly found in the Anglo-Saxon period. Two purses, from G113 and G132, had walnut shell amulets which were probably suspended on the outside. Both the amulets were bound in a cage of four copper alloy strips, with triangular copper alloy spangles suspended from the base. The walnut from G132 has been pierced with an iron pin through its centre. The walnut shell from G113 appears to have had holes drilled through the top, which may indicate that it was used as a pomander, but there was nothing inside it.

Several of the purses included sets of copper alloy lace tags attached to leather strips, possibly used to suspend the purse from a belt and also to fasten the opening.

Graves G86, G173 also contained sets of girdle hangers, but it is difficult to say whether they were originally in purses or not.

# Shields

Eight sets of shield fittings were examined and all but one had organic remains. Of those with organic remains, all were leather-covered. Most appear to have lime shield boards, with a couple of examples in maple and willow or poplar. These woods are commonly used for shield boards and lime is noted in the historical literature.

Three of the shield bosses (G179, G183 and G184) appear to have been recessed into the front of the shield board. Four of the shields (G73, G74, G179 and G183) appear to have grips made from separate pieces of wood to the shield board, which were inserted between the shield board and the boss and held in place by the iron grip (Härke 1981). The grip from G19 has been bound with leather.

# Sword

There is one sword from the site (G74), and this has mineral-preserved organic material relating to the hilt and scabbard. The hilt appears to be made up of three pieces of horn which roughly correspond to the pommel, grip and guard sections. These can clearly be recognised by the change in grain orientation, the grain of the grip lies along the length of the tang and the other two lie perpendicular to it. The scabbard appears to be made from lime lathes lined with fleece. Originally there may have been an outer leather covering, which probably also served to hold the scabbard together, but no evidence for this remains.

# Spearheads

Spearheads and ferrules from 28 spears were examined. Nearly all had the remains of the hafting representing the traditional range of wood species for this function. Hazel (nine), alder (three), and willow or poplar (five) very probably represent the local coppices which provided long straight poles suitable for spear shafts. In fact one or two examples could clearly be seen to have been made from young trunks rather than mature timber. Three others that could not be identified should be added to this group, as they exhibited enough features to suggest that they were made from these four species. Only four spears appear to have ash shafts, three of which were made from mature timber.

| | Shields | Spearheads/ferrules | Knives | Vessels |
|---|---|---|---|---|
| Wood | 3 [4] | 17 [9] | 2 [1] | 7 [7] |
| ash | 3 [2] | 1 | | |
| alder | | 1 [2] | | |
| birch | | | | 2? |
| hazel | | 7 [3] | | |
| lime | 1? [4] | | | 1? |
| maple | 1 | 1? | 1 | |
| oak | | | 2 | |
| willow/poplar | 1 [1] | 4 [2] | [1] | 1 [1] |
| yew | | | [3] | |
| not identifiable | | | | |
| horn | | | 35 [28] | 1 |
| bone | | | [1] | |
| leather | 4 [4] | 3 | 39 [15] | 2 [1] |
| pelt | | 1 | 2 [1] | |
| pupae | | | 2 | 1 |
| textile | 2 | 3 | 8 [1] | |
| random organic | 2 | 3 | | |
| no organic | | [1] | 1 [1] | 3 |
| Total | 4 [5] | 19 [10] | 45 [32] | 14 [8] |

[ ] = material conserved at York Archaeological Trust

*Table 7: summary of organic material associated with shield fittings, spearheads, ferrules, knives and vessel mounts.*

Two of the ferrules appear to have the remains of leather strips around the top of the socket which may have been part of a carrying strap. A few appear to have the remains of textile or fleece preserved on them but it is uncertain whether such materials were used to protect the metalwork (possibly from rusting?) or if they are all that remains of adjacent clothing such as the possible 'raised thread decoration' from G164.

## Knives

A total of 77 knives have been examined from the site, and as can be seen in Table 7 the majority of them have horn handles and leather sheaths. Where the evidence for the handle was preserved, only four were not made from horn, and three of these were of wood and one of bone. In three examples the horn handle has an internal T-shaped section and is mounted on a rectangular sectioned tang. It is difficult to suggest a reason for this unless it was to insert some other material, such as a wooden splint, in order to make the handle a tight fit. However, no additional organic material was found in order to support this idea.

None of the leather sheaths had a grain pattern preserved, so it was not possible to identify the types of leather used. The leather sheath on the knife from G157 is possibly decorated. There are two examples where awls were also housed in the sheath (G130 and G161), possibly aligned along the back of the knife blade. On the knife from Grave

G152 it was possible to see the construction of the sheath as the stitching holes remain down the blade edge and along an extended flap at the handle, very similar in shape to the scabbard patterns from medieval London, (Cowgill *et al* 1987, 116, 118, 133, 156, 158).

Most of the sheaths appear to cover the handle as well as the blade. The knife from G184 seems to have a fleece or pelt scabbard.

## Vessels

Some 22 mounts were examined, most of which had wood remains preserved on them, a variety of species were represented. Most were thought to be mounts or repairs for lathe-turned vessels, which has been confirmed by the orientation of the grain (Morris 1982). Some of the staples are probably repairs as they are usually attached to wood with a cross-section or tangential surface. These are the weakest areas on a vessel as the wood splits along the grain through them.

There are three groups of bucket fittings; all have traces of preserved yew, which is commonly used for this purpose. Some of the staples may be part of grave coverings rather than vessels (G179 and G184), because of the thickness of the wood and the use of oak and ash.

Three of the mounts have preserved leather on them rather than wood, which may suggest that these are from purses.

# Necklaces

Several soil blocks contained fragments of bead necklaces in addition to metalwork and organic material. During the course of excavation it has been possible to identify different stringing arrangements. Most were single strands of beads, frequently with random arrangements of amber and coloured glass, but there were at least two examples of a double strand of beads being pinched together by a single bead, G110 and G141.

In several instances there was evidence to suggest that the strings of beads were worn between a pair of brooches rather than around the neck. It has been possible to pick up traces of the cord being looped around the brooch pin on some annular brooches; 2BA976AW (G163) is a particularly good example.

There were groups of copper alloy bucket pendants which appear to have been grouped together into circles, G152 and G167. In the group from G167 it is possible to see that they were threaded onto a thin leather thong which held them tightly in a circle. The group from G152 are less well preserved, but in addition to being arranged in a circle the centre is made up of two copper alloy cylinders. Another group was found in G172, but it was not possible to suggest how they were arranged.

# Other organic material

In addition to the organic material associated with specific objects, random organic material like straw and in one case rush seeds (G40) has been found on a number of objects. Such materials were probably used to line the graves or placed on top of the body before burial. In G86 slivers of plant material were found on a number of the brooches which may have been part of a wreath or bunch of flowers or herbs placed on top of the body. Unfortunately it was not possible to identify them.

# The textiles

by Penelope Walton Rogers

## Introduction

The clothes in which the West Heslerton Anglo-Saxons were buried have mostly decomposed over the centuries. All that is left of them now are small, poorly preserved fragments of textile adhering to brooches, clasps and other metal grave goods. This is a common condition among early Anglo-Saxon cemeteries, which tend to lie on the types of light, free-draining soils which offer little protection to organic materials. Nonetheless, it has been shown by other authors that scattered patches of remains such as these can make a useful contribution to the study of early dress and textiles.

The corpus of early Anglo-Saxon textiles is already large. Elisabeth Crowfoot has studied similar remains from 91 cemeteries, barrows and single graves, representing 850 burials of the fifth to seventh centuries (and has generously provided the author with a table of her published and unpublished work). Five further groups reported by Henshall (1959), Janaway (Arnold *et al* 1983) and Walton (1992, 1998, forthcoming) add 102 graves with textile to the list. Much of this data has been used by Bender Jørgensen for an outline of the main fabric-types of the Anglian, Saxon and Kentish regions, within a larger survey of European textiles (1989, 1991, 1992). In addition, some of the evidence has been used in the reconstruction of early Anglo-Saxon dress (Cook 1974; Owen 1976; Owen-Crocker 1986; Vierck 1978).

The West Heslerton cemetery has some significant contributions to make to these studies. First of all, the textile collection is large — certainly the largest in the Northumbria-Deira-Lindsey region — and this has allowed a comparison between burials of differing age, sex and status. Secondly, improved techniques of microscopy have led to better identification of fibres, so that wool and linen fabrics can be distinguished in a way that has not been possible with other cemeteries. Thirdly, a three-way exchange between archaeologist, conservator and specialist has allowed the maximum evidence for costume to be retrieved. The author is

therefore indebted to Dominic Powlesland and Christine Haughton at West Heslerton and to Jacqui Watson of English Heritage for background information on the site and the grave goods.

## Collecting the data

The textile remains were studied over the period 1978 to 1991, in the early years at the Yorkshire Museum and more recently at the laboratory of York Archaeological Trust. Weave, yarn type and thread-count were identified using a hand-lens or a low-power (x10, x20) binocular microscope. Altogether, 97 out of approximately 250 excavated graves yielded traces of textile or fibre.

The fibres in the textiles were identified by two different means. The few which were well preserved were examined with a high-power (x400) transmitted-light microscope, fitted with polarising analyser. Wool fibres were identified by their cuticular scale-pattern, and the plant stem fibres, flax and hemp, by the central channel, or lumen, and cross-markings, mineralised fibres and fibre casts (for the distinction between flax and hemp see Körber-Grohne 1967, 161–5) . The quality of the evidence could not, of course, be identified by this means, as transmitted light would not pass through them. Instead, scanning electron microscope (SEM) photographs, which show the surface detail of the fibre, were prepared by J Watson and J Webb at the English Heritage Laboratory. These photomicrographs show the scale pattern of wool (Plate 54a) and the surface cross-banding of plant stem fibres (Plate 54b, 54c). The SEM work has contributed 63 to the number of the identifications, so that altogether 81 out of 150 textiles have been given a fibre identification, much more than for any other Anglo-Saxon cemetery.

Few of the remains were large enough to allow sampling for dye analysis. Those that were, the diamond twill from grave G29, the tabby weave from G100 and the diamond twill and headdress with braid from G123, were exposed to the usual tests for natural dyes. These consist of extraction into solvents, followed by absorption spectrophotometry and, where necessary, thin-layer chromatography (Walton and Taylor 1991). Only the headdress gave satisfactory results. A red dye of the madder/bedstraw class was detected by spectrophotometry, and thin-layer chromatography showed the main component to be strongly defined purpurin without any alizarin. This suggests a native bedstraw (*Galium verum L.*), or one of the wild madders (*Rubia* spp.), as the source of the dye, rather than cultivated dyers' madder (*Rubia tinctorum L.*), which yields alizarin as well as purpurin (Taylor 1990, 1157). It is likely that the process of decay and mineralisation has destroyed any dyestuff originally present in the other samples.

The details of individual finds appear in the grave inventory. A grave-by-grave summary, together with an interpretation of the costume evidence, is given in Table 9.

# The quality of evidence

How representative is the surviving material? Since only textiles in the vicinity of metal artefacts have been preserved, the better furnished graves, especially those of women with several dress fasteners, are more fully represented than the poorer ones; and at least 150 graves have yielded no evidence of textiles at all. The range of fabric-types discussed below may not, therefore, include those worn by the poorer levels of West Heslerton society; also, women's dress is better represented than men's.

Has the process of decay favoured some fabrics over others? Buried textiles may be subject to several forms of physical and microbiological attack, depending on the nature of the burial environment. At West Heslerton the sandy soils would have allowed water to drain freely through the graves, providing a moist but not waterlogged environment, subject to seasonal fluctuations of temperature. Such conditions would promote the fungi and aerobic bacteria which attack natural-fibred textiles (Cooke 1990, 9; Janaway 1985, 30). Where metal goods were in the grave, however, moisture would cause copper and iron salts to be released. The copper salts in particular would inhibit microbiological attack, so that a small area of original textile might be preserved intact in the immediate vicinity of the artefact (Jakes and Sibley 1983, 37; Jakes and Sibley 1984a, 23). Other research has suggested that plant fibres are more likely to be preserved in these circumstances than animal fibres (Janaway 1985, 30; 1989, 21), but at West Heslerton both wool (eg G29, G110, G180) and flax (eg G22, G103, G175) seem to have been preserved by their association with copper alloys. Alternatively, the metal salts from corroding artefacts might act in concert with the process of physical decay: they might form a cast of the deteriorating textile, or impregnate it as it decayed, forming a mineral replacement of the original (Jakes and Sibley 1984b, 421; Janaway 1989, 21). At West Heslerton casts and mineralised remains — sometimes called pseudomorphs — were mainly of iron, occasionally of copper (Plate 54). There was no evidence that flax pseudomorphs (eg G60, G78, G100) were better preserved than wool (eg G47, G95, G113) or *vice versa*.

In summary, if there is a bias in the survival of the different fibre-types at West Heslerton, it is not an obvious one.

# The main textile types

A summary of the main textile types from West Heslerton cemetery is given in Table 8. Only those textiles with complete records of weave, spin and thread-count have been used for this table. In counting up totals, the same textile occurring twice in the same grave has been treated as one piece, so that a garment fastened by two brooches is counted only once.

Altogether, 150 textiles were recorded in full detail. These may be divided into whole cloths, from which the main garments have been made, and braids or plaits, which have been used as cuffs, belts and decorative borders.

# Whole cloths: weave and yarn-type

The 129 whole cloths are in the typical weaves of the Anglo-Saxon period. Fifty are in tabby weave (syn. plain weave) and 79 in 2/2 twill (Fig 67a, b). At least ten of these 2/2 twills have been woven in such a way as to produce a diamond or chevron effect (Fig 67c). All textile fragments are, however, very small and it is likely that the reverses of some diamond/chevron twills have been missed and their numbers underestimated.

Yarn in these textiles may be Z-spun, that is, produced by turning the spindle clockwise, or S-spun, by turning the spindle anti-clockwise. Z-spun in warp and weft (ZZ) is the more common, with 98 examples, but Z-spun in one direction and S-spun in the other (ZS) has been noted in 27 fabrics. In addition, in one twill, from grave G146, the yarn is S-spun throughout (SS), and in one tabby, from G152, the yarn has been plied (Z2S). In three examples, from G2, G23 and G113, Z and S have been alternated in singles or pairs, to give the fabric a very subtle striped or checked effect — a technique called spin-patterning (Fig 67d).

Bender Jørgensen (1989, 1991) has taken these technological features of weave and spin and has

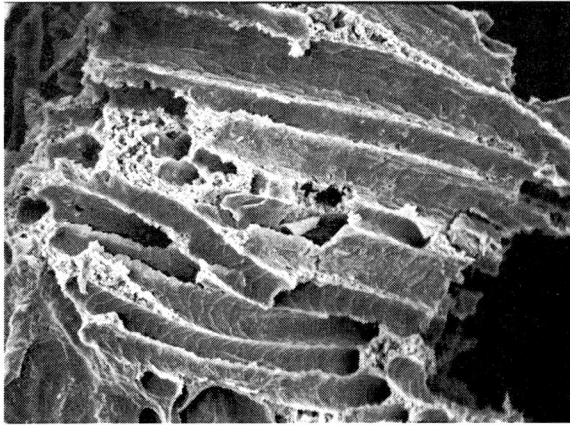

54a. casts of wool fibres from plied threads binding gir-dle-hanger (G152:2BA909AI) and latch-lifter (G152:2BA909AK)

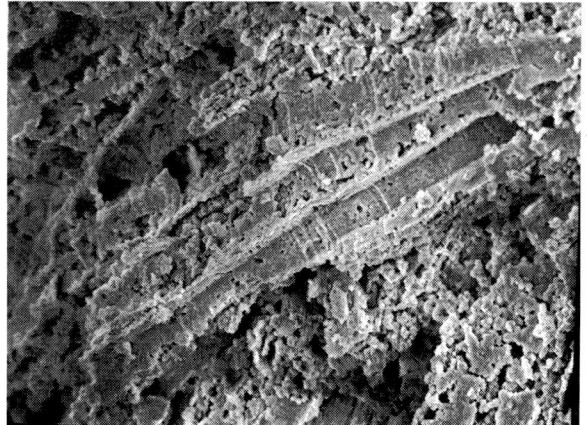

54b casts of flax fibres from tabby on square-headed brooch (G147:2BA880AI)

54c. Mineralised flax/hemp fibre from tabby on iron pin (G100:2BA146AG)

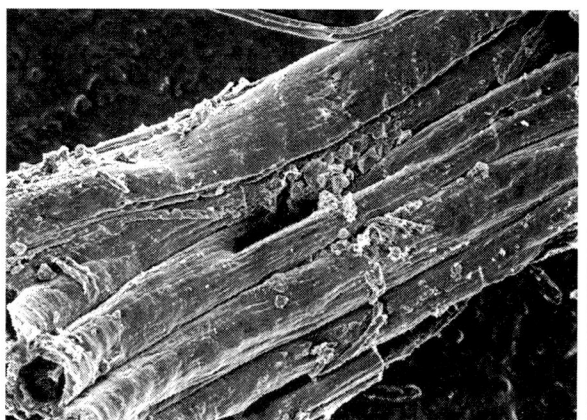

54d mineralised and abraded animal fibre, the pattern thread from the tablet band with wrist clasp (G47:1HE316DM)

*Plate 54: SEM photographs of fibres from West Heslerton cemetery*

constructed graphs to show the main textile-types of different regions of Europe at different times. When the West Heslerton material is displayed in the same format (Fig 68a), the pie-graph shows a striking resemblance to that of Bender Jørgensen's Anglian group (Fig 68b) and is distinctively different from the Kentish collection (Fig 68c). Recent research (Walton 1992, Walton Rogers 1998) has shown that the difference between the Anglian and Kentish groups is more likely to reflect a difference in date, rather than geography, the Anglian cemeteries with textile being on the whole earlier than the Kentish. However that may be, the work with graphs shows that the West Heslerton material is typical of the Anglian region in the fifth and sixth centuries in its range of types. The contribution of the present study is to add fibre identifications to these textile-types.

# Whole cloths: fibres

Fibre identifications were possible in 72 of the 129 whole cloths: 47 proved to be wool and 25 linen (all textiles made from plant stem fibres such as flax or hemp are classified here as linens). On average, the linens are finer

than the textiles of wool, although there is considerable overlap (Fig 69a, b). Twills are more commonly wool and tabbies more often linen, but linen twills and wool tabbies are also present (Table 8). Neither thread-count nor weave can therefore be used as a guide to the iden-tity of the fibre.

One particular yarn combination may, however, be a significator of the fibre. Of the 27 textiles with yarn spun ZS, 16 have been identified as wool and none as linen. Out of a number of ZS textiles from cemeteries studied by Crowfoot, 22 have also been identified as wool, with only one uncertain piece, from Finglesham, Kent, which may be of flax (Crowfoot 1958, 36). In other words, a ZS yarn combination in a mineralised textile of this date is likely to indicate that the fibre is wool. If that is so, then the figures for the West Heslerton whole cloths can be readjusted to 58 wool, 25 linen and 46 not identified.

| Textile Type | Wool | Linen | Not Identified | Totals |
|---|---|---|---|---|
| Tabby ZZ | 5 | 18 | 19 | 42 |
| Tabby ZS | 4 | 0 | 2 | 6 |
| Tabby Spin-patterned | 1 | 0 | 0 | 1 |
| Tabby Plied yarn | 1 | 0 | 0 | 1 |
| 2/2 Twill ZZ | 24 | 5 | 24 | 53 |
| 2/2 Twill ZS | 8 | 0 | 6 | 14 |
| 2/2 Twill Spin-patterned | 0 | 0 | 1 | 1 |
| 2/2 Twill SS | 0 | 0 | 1 | 1 |
| Diamond or Chevron 2/2 ZZ | 0 | 2 | 1 | 3 |
| Diamond or Chevron 2/2 ZS | 4 | 0 | 3 | 7 |
| **Sub Totals** | 47 | 25 | 57 | 129 |
| Tablet Braids | 5 | 4 | 10 | 19 |
| Other Braids | 0 | 0 | 2 | 2 |
| **Totals** | 52 | 29 | 69 | 150 |

*Table 8: the main textile-types in the West Heslerton cemetery (includes only textiles for which full details could be recorded)*

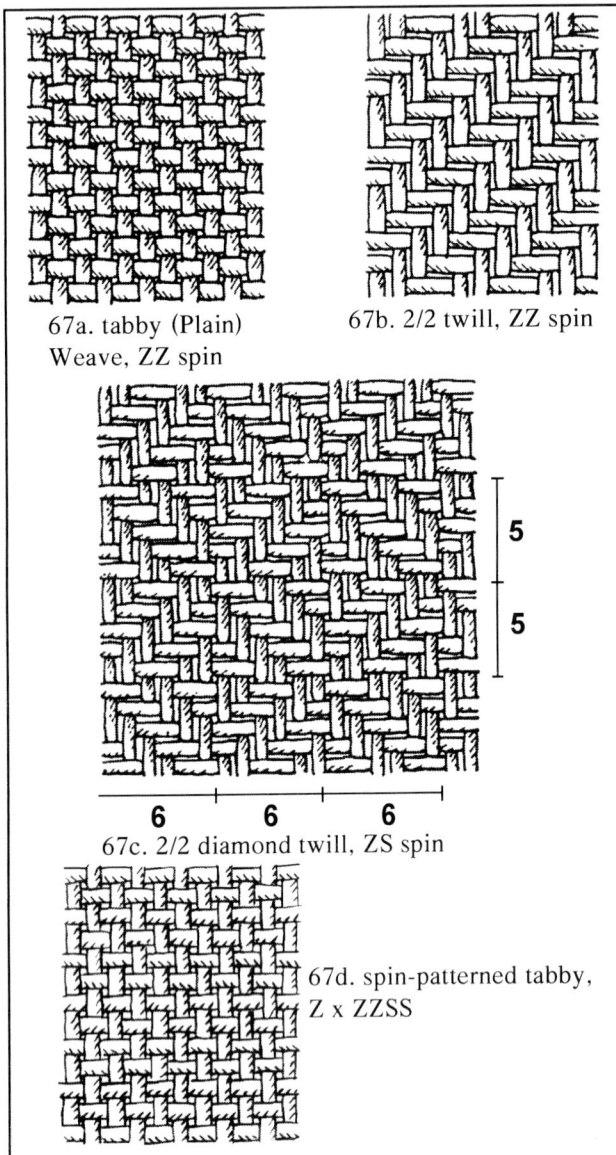

67a. tabby (Plain) Weave, ZZ spin

67b. 2/2 twill, ZZ spin

67c. 2/2 diamond twill, ZS spin

67d. spin-patterned tabby, Z x ZZSS

*Figure 67: the structure of the textiles from the West Heslerton cemetery*

# Whole cloths: a summary of types

## Wool twill

The most common textile type in the West Heslerton graves was wool twill without any form of patterning. These textiles range from coarse (8 x 6 threads per cm) to fine (18 x 18 per cm), but most are medium weight fabrics (9 x 9 to 12 x 12 per cm). Some of them have a matted surface, which appears to be a deliberate finish (G95, G113, G152). The nap of these soft-finished twills is patchy, which may be a result of wear, or of microbiological attack during burial.

Most of the wool twills are ZZ, with a proportion ZS (Table 8). One of the finer ZZ examples, from G152, has a relatively wide tablet-woven border (Fig 71b; see below, tablet braid type 1b). This is the only example of a wool twill with a surviving selvedge. Fringes are more common, in a variety of techniques: on the ZS twill from G124, Z-spun threads have been left hanging loose; in other graves the Z-threads have been twisted into plied cords (G43, G86), or into cords and plaits (G62, Fig 73b). A more elaborate bound wool fringe in grave G139 was mixed up with a group of textiles in association with a purse, and may be a cut-off fragment kept inside the purse, or a fringe from the purse itself.

Wool twills of this sort were a common clothing fabric through much of north-west Europe from the Late Iron Age to the tenth century (Bender Jørgensen 1986, 343-361; 1989 *passim*). They were generally made with ZZ or ZS spinning, ZZ being the more common in the Anglo-Saxon cemeteries contemporary with West Heslerton (Crowfoot 1978, 1985a, Walton 1989, 334). Selvedges in such twills might be woven in the form of a hollow tube or tablet-woven in the manner of the selvedge from G152. In the fifth and sixth centuries the tablet-woven type was generally narrower than in earlier periods: Nockert has ascribed this to the introduction of more complicated braid patterns, which were woven separately and then stitched on to the cloth (Walton 1991, 82). The relatively broad selvedge from G152 is therefore unusual in the fifth to sixth centuries and may represent a throw-back to the deep borders of *Prachtmanteln*, large wool twill rectangles with borders and fringes, which were worn in the continental homelands of the Anglo-Saxons in the Roman Iron Age (Schlabow 1965, 1976).

## Linen tabby

Linens made from Z-spun yarn in tabby weave are the second most common fabric-type. Most are made from flax, but some may be hemp (eg G122). They are found in both medium and fine qualities, although the thread-count does not always reflect the weight of the fabric:

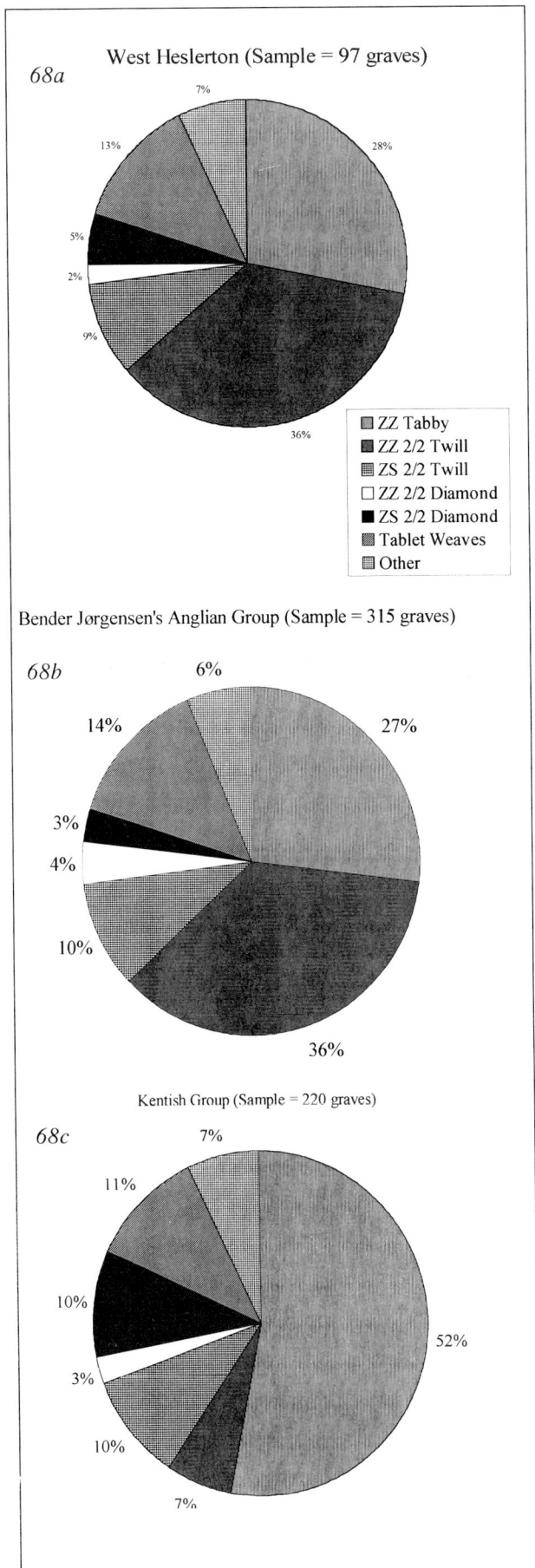

West Heslerton (Sample = 97 graves)
68a
7%
13%
28%
5%
2%
9%
36%

ZZ Tabby
ZZ 2/2 Twill
ZS 2/2 Twill
ZZ 2/2 Diamond
ZS 2/2 Diamond
Tablet Weaves
Other

Bender Jørgensen's Anglian Group (Sample = 315 graves)
68b
6%
14%
27%
3%
4%
10%
36%

Kentish Group (Sample = 220 graves)
68c
7%
11%
10%
3%
10%
7%
52%

*Figure 68: the realtive frequency of different textile types. Figs 68b and 68c after Bender Jørgensen 1989*

some of the pieces with low counts are made from light, fine yarns, woven into open-weave fabrics (eg G78) — making a semi-transparent material suitable for head-veils (see below).

The flax plant was grown in Britain as early as the Bronze Age, although there is only sketchy evidence for its use in textile manufacture before the Late Iron Age (Hedges 1980, 20–1). Romano-British supplies of linen may have been obtained locally or imported from flax- and hemp-growing regions such as the Rhone Valley (Wild 1970, 15, 17). Linen production probably became more common among the Germanic tribes both inside and outside the Empire's boundaries during the Roman Iron Age (Schaefer 1945, 1768). Bender Jørgensen has noted in her survey of cemeteries of the fifth–eighth centuries that ZZ tabbies, mainly linen, account for between a third and a quarter of the remains from Anglian and Saxon England and from Saxon Germany (1989, 148–50), while in Kent, Belgium and Normandy the proportion is even higher (ibid, 152). There is little reason to suppose that the West Heslerton linens were anything other than a common fabric-type, locally made.

## Wool tabby

There are ten examples of wool tabby, with two ZS tabbies assumed to be wool. Some of these pieces should not perhaps be included under whole cloths: one may in fact be a selvedge border of a diamond twill (G29); a second is a coarse strip wrapped around an iron shield grip and may have been a tape (G179), such as that used to bind the shield-grip from grave 62 at Bury St Edmunds, Suffolk (Crowfoot 1988, 14). Leather had been used in the same way to bind the grip with skeleton G19 (Watson forthcoming). Nevertheless, at least two of the wool tabbies are ordinary garment material (G119, G23).

There are other oddities among the wool tabbies. One example, on the front of a shoulder brooch from G143, looks like, and is in the same position as, the open-weave linen tabbies believed to be head-veils — although this is the only example of wool being used in this way. A second, a densely ribbed fabric made from strong plied yarn, has been constructed so that one system of threads completely covers the other (G152): this fabric was found with a leather purse with an ivory purse ring (Watson forthcoming) and may represent the purse lining. Three other wool tabbies were found only at the waist or hip and in association with iron purse rings (G119, G124) or chatelaines (G22). These, too, may be purses, bags, or bag linings.

Finally, there is a spin-patterned wool tabby from G23, which has loose twists of wool on the surface, probably the remains of a tufted pile. The textile lies on the outer face of an annular brooch with the pile facing outwards: in this position it may represent a cloak or a cover of some sort.

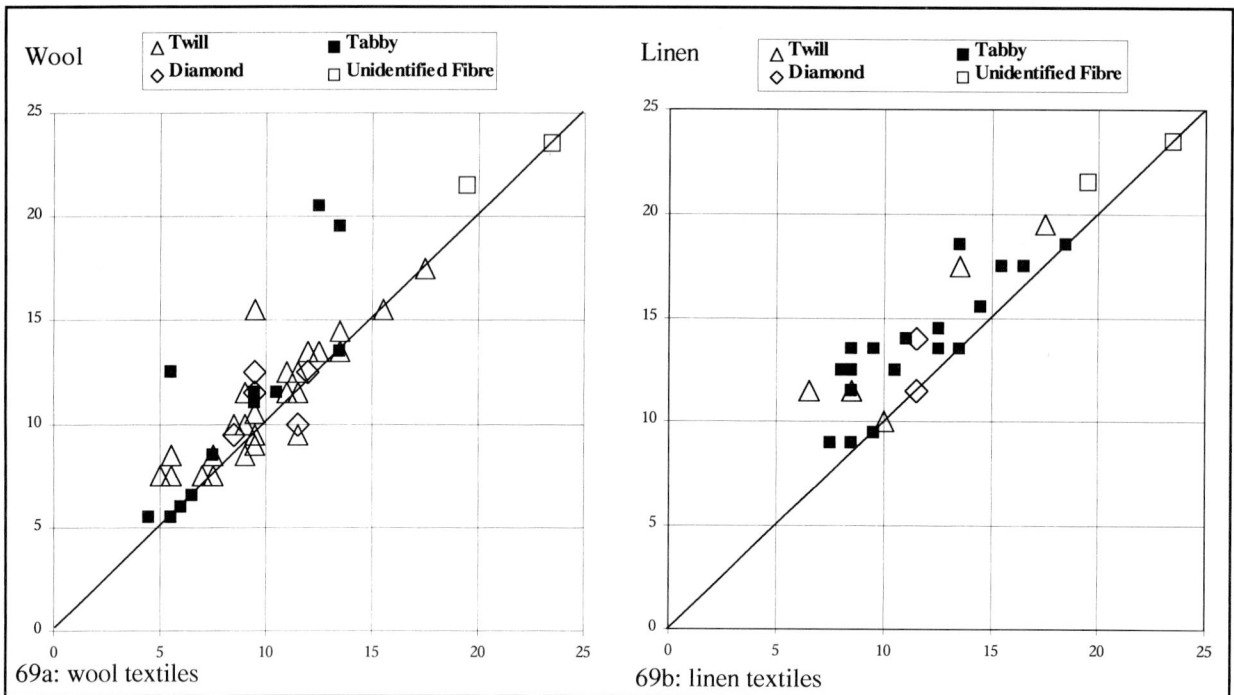

Figure 69: weave, thread-count and fibre in the West Heslerton textiles

Most piled textiles are likely to have been cloaks or rugs, the pile being worked into the ground during weaving or sometimes stitched in afterwards (Walton 1989, 335–6). They are not common finds and some are probably traded goods, possibly associated with a degree of social status. Anglo-Saxon examples include two relatively fine pieces with looped pile from Sutton Hoo, Suffolk, and Broomfield Barrow, Essex (Crowfoot 1983, 443–4), and coarser examples from Banstead Down, Surrey (Crowfoot 1976, 69) and possibly also Bergh Apton, Norfolk (Crowfoot 1978, 104–5). These are on simple tabby or twill grounds. The spin-patterning of the West Heslerton piece seems unusual, although a later example from tenth-to eleventh-century York had a stitched pile on a diamond twill ground (Hedges 1982, 114): this, like the West Heslerton piece, would have had a shaggy outer face and a patterned inner face.

The source of these piled fabrics is uncertain. Ireland and Iceland are known to have exported piled cloaks at a later date and Frisian traders dealt in them (Guðjónsson 1962), although the Viking Age piled fabrics from York may have been locally made copies of the traded goods (Walton 1989). It is difficult to suggest whether the West Heslerton example is native Anglo-Saxon or an import, but whatever the case, the fine weave and the spin-patterning suggest a garment of some quality.

## Linen twill

There are only four examples of linen twill, one very fine (G47) and three of medium quality (G71, G78, G103). One of these has a tubular selvedge, although poorly preserved (G78). Linen twill was not a common fabric-type at any period in British history, but occasional examples have been identified in other Anglian

cemeteries such as Welbeck Hill, Lincolnshire, Wakerley, Northamptonshire, Mucking, Essex (E Crowfoot pers comm for unpublished information on these sites), and Spong Hill, Norfolk (Crowfoot and Jones 1984, 22, 24); there is only one example from the Saxon region, from Blacknall Field, Wiltshire (E Crowfoot pers comm), but others may be hidden among the number of ZZ twills for which no fibre identification has been possible.

## Patterned fabrics

Bold colour changes in stripes and checks are only rarely a feature of early Anglo-Saxon textiles. Patterns in the surviving material are generally subtle textured effects, produced by manipulating the weave or by varying the yarn.

At West Heslerton one wool tabby is spin-patterned (the piled fabric from G23, described above): it has Z-spun yarn in one direction and two Z-spun alternating with two S-spun in the other. A twill of unidentified fibre from G2 has the same arrangement of yarns. A third twill, from G113, is an irregular mixture of Z and S yarns in warp and weft — assumed to be a part of a pattern, although it is difficult to perceive the overall effect.

Spin-patterning has a long heritage and was a relatively common technique in Hallstatt Eastern Europe and La Tène Western Europe (Bender Jørgensen 1989, 145–8). The best preserved examples from Iron Age Denmark (Hald 1980, 88, 91, 190) show how the technique could be used to give subtle shaded effects, sometimes supported by colour changes in the yarn, although there is no evidence for a colour change in the West Heslerton examples. Spin-patterning had become less common by

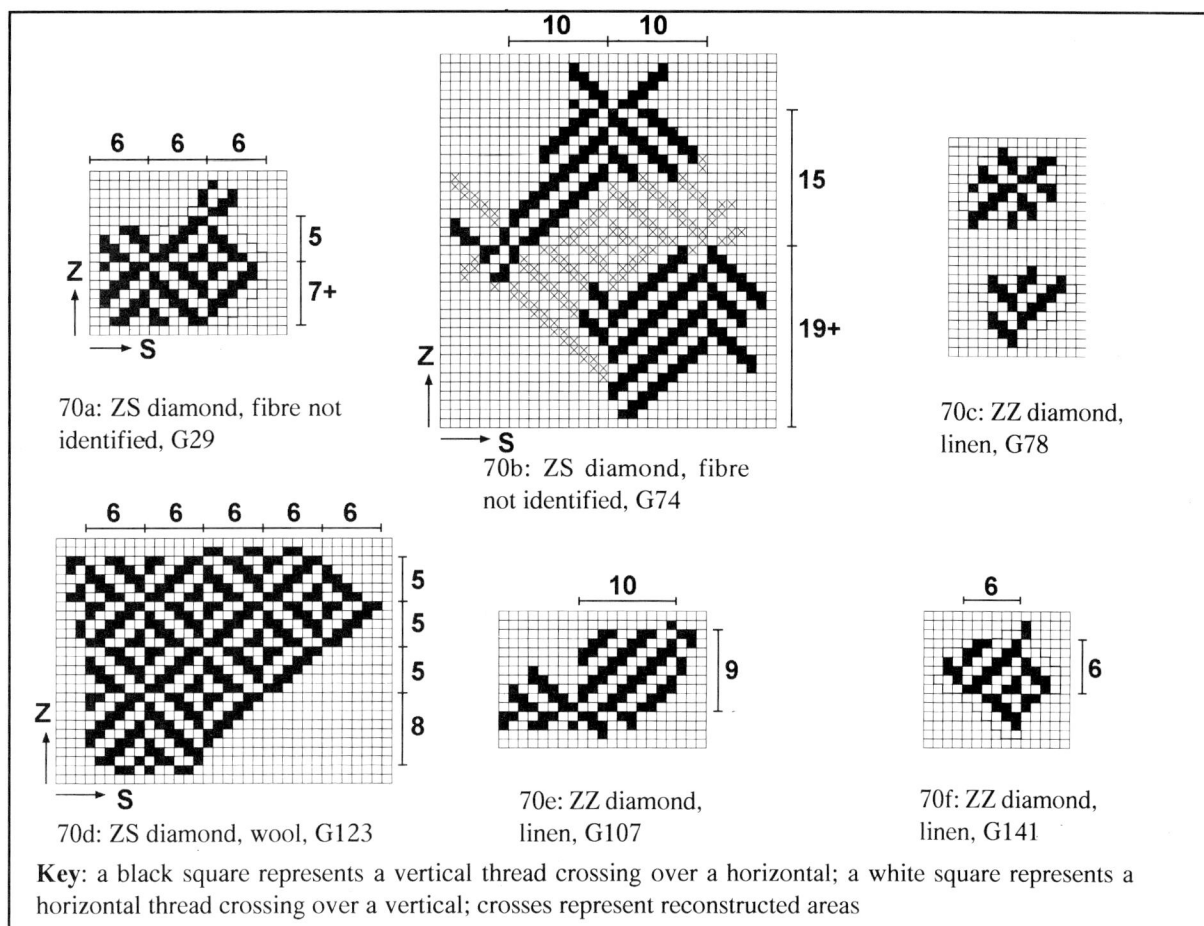

70a: ZS diamond, fibre not identified, G29

70b: ZS diamond, fibre not identified, G74

70c: ZZ diamond, linen, G78

70d: ZS diamond, wool, G123

70e: ZZ diamond, linen, G107

70f: ZZ diamond, linen, G141

**Key**: a black square represents a vertical thread crossing over a horizontal; a white square represents a horizontal thread crossing over a vertical; crosses represent reconstructed areas

*Figure 70: the pattern repeats in 2/2 diamond twills from West Heslerton cemetery*

the Migration Period, but there are scattered examples from Anglo-Saxon cemeteries such as Sewerby, East Yorkshire (Crowfoot 1985, 52); and from cemeteries of the upper Rhine, where they are more commonly of linen (Bender Jørgensen 1991, 19). A well-preserved example of white spin-patterned linen forms the ground of an embroidered tunic in which the seventh-century queen, Bathilde, was buried at Chelles in France (Laporte 1982; Anon Rouen museum catalogue 1985, 138). Two of the three West Heslerton examples are relatively fine and in graves with silver goods (G23, G113), suggesting a degree of wealth. The technique of spin-patterning is, however, simple to do, merely requiring two weft bobbins with different yarn, and there is no reason to see these fabrics as exotic in any way.

Patterning at West Heslerton more commonly took the form of twill weaves worked in diamonds and perhaps chevrons. There are at least ten examples: four in wool (ZS), two in linen (ZZ) and four of unidentified fibre (1 ZZ, 3 ZS). If all the ZS examples are assumed to be wool, then the figures are seven wool, two linen and one unidentified. Because the fragments are so small, it is often difficult to determine the pattern repeat (Fig 70). In three examples, however, the diamond pattern appears to be particularly small (Fig 70a, d, f).

Diamond and chevron patterns were a common feature

of twills of the Iron Age, Roman, Anglo-Saxon and Viking periods. They occur in wool and linen, in a range of thread-counts and with a wide variety of pattern units. It might be expected that the small size of the surviving fragments would bias the record towards small pattern units, but such is not the case — a great range of pattern repeats have been recorded by Bender Jørgensen in her surveys, some of them quite large (eg 1986, 309). The small, regular repeat of the diamond twills in wool from G29 and G123 and in linen from G163 have no obvious parallels in contemporary cemeteries. There is, however, a similar diamond twill from seventh- to eighth-century Orsett, Essex (Crowfoot 1985b, 15), and three identical wool examples from Viking Age York (Walton 1989, 339; 1990, 64). York lies near the western edge of the old kingdom of Deira, in which West Heslerton is situated: it is possible, therefore, that these especially small diamond patterns were a local tradition.

## Tablet-woven bands

The whole cloths from West Heslerton are in general fairly standardised in appearance and structure. The narrow bands on the other hand are more varied. Nineteen tablet-woven bands in seven different techniques have been identified, as well as two tubular braids described separately below; in addition there are several examples of poorly preserved corded remains (eg G45, G147), which may once have been tablet bands. All the tablet bands from West Heslerton are medium to fine, from 10 warp cords per cm to 16 per cm. Most have been worked from strong plied yarn (Z2S), to withstand the strain which is placed on the warp during weaving, although singles yarn (Z) has been used in the example from G176. Only two bands, the cuff from G47 and the headdress braid from G123, have been preserved in their complete width of 27mm and 9mm respectively; but most of the bands used as cuffs must have been over 25mm wide, to accommodate the width of the cuff fasteners (wrist-clasps).

In its simplest form, a tablet-woven band consists of several parallel cords held together by a crossways weft thread (Fig 71a). Such braids are constructed by threading a deck of tablets, flat, square plates with a hole at each corner, with individual warp threads, one thread per hole, four per tablet. As the deck of tablets is rotated, each tablet twists its own cord of four threads; a weft thread woven back and forth with each 1-turn of the tablets holds the whole together as a flat band.

## Type 1a: non-patterned bands

If tablets are threaded alternately from opposite sides, the alternate cords in the band will twist Z and S (Fig 71a). Since all the tablets are being turned as one deck, the alternating Z and S cords give a neat chevron effect, each pair of cords meeting with regular Vs. This is the most common type from West Heslerton. There are seven examples, of which two are wool (both from G147) and one linen (G60).

## Type 1b: selvedge braid

If the tablets are threaded from opposite sides in groups, rather than alternately, the cords are formed in groups of Z and S. This is the case with the braid edging the fine wool twill from G147, where the cords are arranged in groups of five (Fig 71b). Although the outside edge of this border braid is absent, its construction does not resemble that of the starting borders from Blewburton Hill, Berkshire (Henshall 1959), and Fonaby, Lincolnshire (Crowfoot 1981, 97), or the closing borders from Spong Hill, Norfolk (Crowfoot and Jones 1984, 20), Broomfield Barrow, Essex (Crowfoot 1983, 469–70), and Coombe, Kent (Crowfoot 1967, 21), and it is assumed to be a selvedge (side border). Other, tentatively identified tablet woven selvedges have been recorded at Swallowcliffe Down, Wiltshire (Crowfoot 1989, 116), and Finglesham, Kent (Crowfoot 1958, 17). None of the complete border braids is more than 8 cords wide. The best preserved area of the West Heslerton piece is 20 cords (= 20 mm) wide and was almost certainly originally wider (see above, Wool twill).

## Type 2a: warp-patterned bands worked on 2-hole tablets

If tablets are threaded with differently coloured yarns and manipulated separately or in groups, a host of designs may be produced. In the case of the tablet band from G62, two shades of yarn, light and dark, form a chevron design in the warp (Fig 71c). The cords in this braid lie in groups of S and Z, but the twists are staggered, so that S and Z cords meet with a Y instead of a V. This is characteristic of a band in which alternate tablets have been separated into a second deck: one deck is rotated, the weft passed, the other deck rotated, and the weft returned. The cords in this band are each made up of only two strands, indicating that only two holes were threaded in each tablet. A second band, that bordering the headdress in grave G123, may have been of a related type. In its present state it has outer borders, each with two wool warp cords of type 1a. In the middle is a decayed area in which the wool weft is clear, but there are also traces of a linen warp, which passes over the weft in places. It is not clear whether this band has been brocaded, with the pattern carried by a weft thread floating on the surface of the weave; or warp-patterned, the pattern formed by differently coloured yarns in the warp. From comparison with a better preserved braid from Laceby, Lincolnshire (E Crowfoot 1956b), the latter seems the more likely.

## Type 2b: twill-effect tablet bands

Two of the bands have an obvious twill effect, the twill being warp-faced and the weft obscured. Unfortunately, one is heavily mineralised and the other is a narrow fold over the pin of a brooch — neither can be dissected to identify the weave. The first, one of the wool bands from G152, appears to be a double weave of some sort: the twill diagonals on front and back run in opposite directions, which is not possible with a simple weave. The second, a linen fragment from G113, from its surface appearance seems to be woven in 2/1 twill (Fig 71d): the high warp count and some twists toward one side suggest it is made by tablet-weaving, rather than as a whole-cloth technique.

## Type 3: band with pattern in weft-wrapped hair

One fragment of band, from the gilded wrist-clasp DP from grave G47, has a central panel patterned in a weft-wrapping technique, within borders of plain tablet weaving of type 1a. Much of the surface of the decorative panel is abraded, but one small area has survived as shown in Figure 6e. The pattern is in two shades of brown and is built up as follows: a single coarse animal fibre (Plate 54d) is wrapped several times around adjacent groups of warp thread, so that a rectangle of colour is built up before moving on to the next block. The exact passage of the ground weft, which is sandwiched in the middle of the band, is not clear: it may be a 'passive' weft, as de-

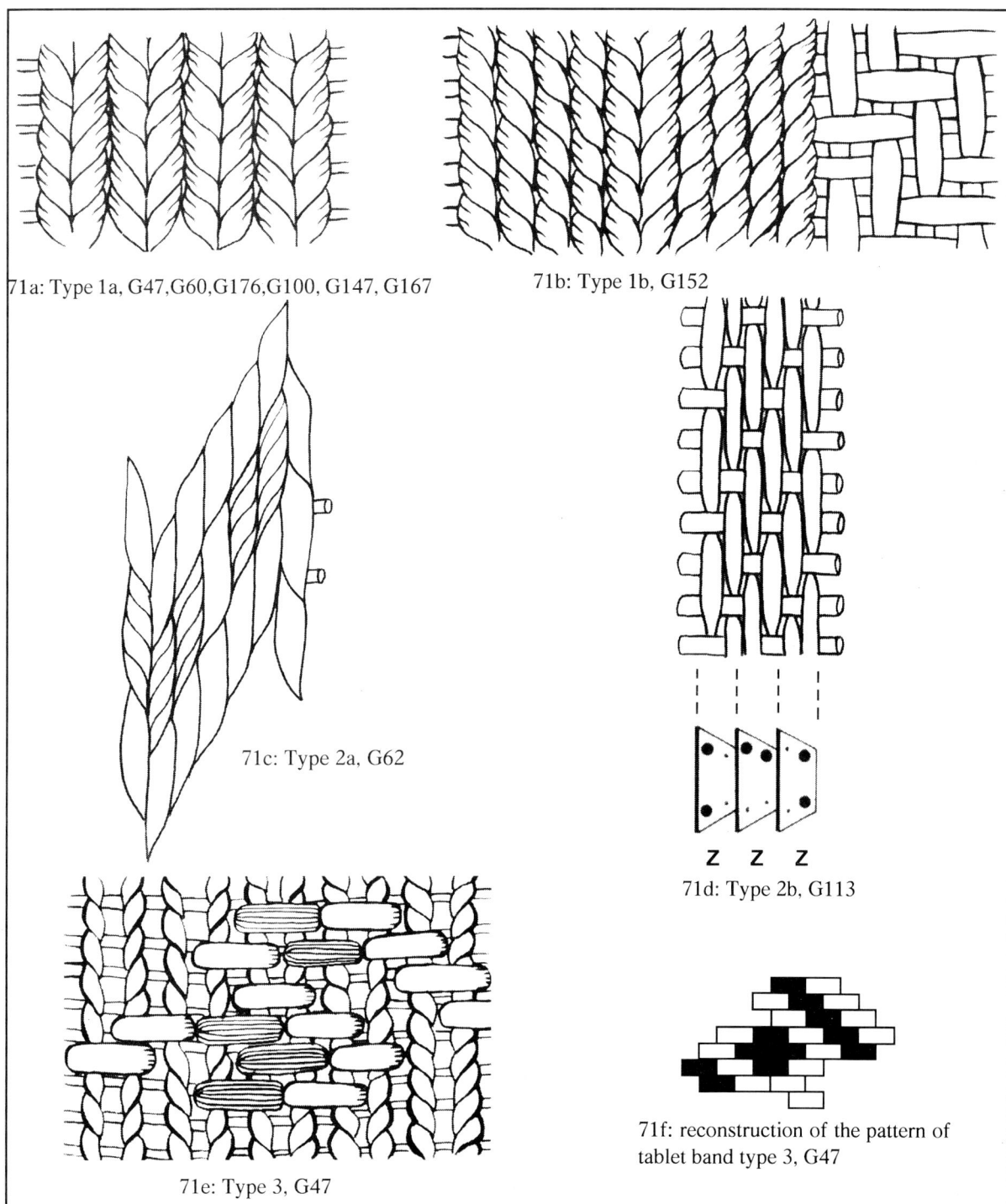

71a: Type 1a, G47,G60,G176,G100, G147, G167

71b: Type 1b, G152

71c: Type 2a, G62

71d: Type 2b, G113

71e: Type 3, G47

71f: reconstruction of the pattern of tablet band type 3, G47

*Figure 71: tablet-woven bands from West Heslerton*

scribed by Nockert (1991, 86), which only comes into operation at the borders. The wrapping thread passes right around each pair of grouped warp threads, so that the pattern is the same on front and back. Using information from both faces, a part of the pattern can be reconstructed as shown in Figure 6f.

## Tablet-weaving in context

The craft of tablet-weaving can be traced back to the Bronze Age in northern Europe. Most of its basic forms were established by the end of the Roman Iron Age, but the Migration Period saw fresh designs and new variations of patterning techniques, in both Scandinavia and England. It is therefore not difficult to find parallels for the West Heslerton bands in other cemeteries of the north.

Types 1a and 1b are the simplest form. The use of mixed Z- and S-cording, either singly or in groups, is not just a matter of design, but essential to make the braid lie straight. In Anglo-Saxon cemeteries type 1a is the most numerous, but in Norway and Sweden it is outnumbered by patterned weaves (Nockert 1991, 91).

72a: warp-patterned band form Laceby, Lincs. after Crowfoot 1956b, fig.3.

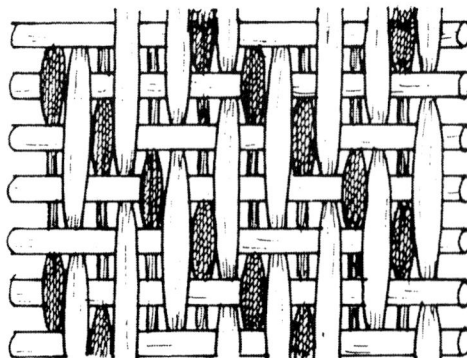

72b: double-faced 3/1 tablet weave, after Collingwood 1982, fig. 142. Note how the twill diagonal on the front face (pale threads) runs in the opposite direction to the twill diagonal on the back (dark threads), a feature which can be seen in the braid from West Heslerton G152.

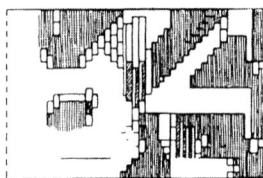

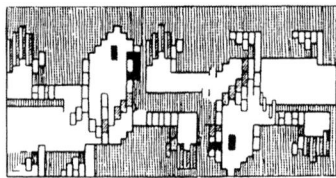

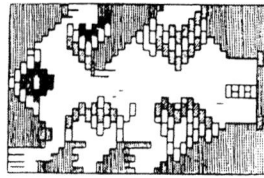

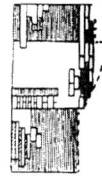

72c: the pattern field of a tablet-woven braid from Evebø Eide, Norway, worked in weft-wrapped horsehair, after Dedekam 1925. Compare with the small fragment form West Heslerton, Fig 71f above.

Figure 72: tablet-woven bands from other sites mentioned in the text

The braid from G62, type 2a, is in a technique suitable for simple diamond and chevron patterns. The method of dividing the tablets into two decks and turning one deck, then the other, can be seen in a diamond-patterned linen braid from Cambridge (E Crowfoot 1951, 28–30). In that example 4-hole tablets have been used, allowing a 3-colour design; and the tablet cords are alternately S- and Z-twist (Fig 72a). A closer parallel is a chevron-patterned wool braid from Migration Period Snartemo, Norway (Dedekam 1925, 42–4), worked, like the West Heslerton piece, in two colours, with two holes threaded in each tablet and with tablet cords in groups of Z and S. The basic technique continued to be used in England in later centuries (E Crowfoot 1951). The pattern of the Laceby-like band from G123 is also likely to have been some simple geometric design, although it is not possible to determine its precise nature.

The double-faced weave from G152 is almost certainly double-faced 3/1 twill (Fig 72b), forms of which have been recorded in England and Scandinavia from the Roman Iron Age to the Viking period (Collingwood 1982, 223–316). One example from an Anglo-Saxon cemetery at Sibertswold Down, Kent (Crowfoot 1990, 49, 53), has narrow lengthways bands of the weave, separated by single cords of ordinary 4-hole tablet weaving. More commonly the weave was used for free-hand designs in which different colours on front and back exchange places as the design requires. Stylised animal shapes in the fifth- to sixth-century finds from Norway and more fluid plant motifs with gold brocade in the tenth-century girdle of

St Cuthbert at Durham (G Crowfoot 1956a, 435–8) are just some of the variations. None of the early Anglo-Saxon examples shows a complete motif, but the boundaries between one colour and another were found in a braid from Morning Thorpe, Norfolk (Crowfoot 1987, 173).

Tablet-woven 2/1 twill was less common, although this, too, first appeared in the Roman Iron Age at Dätgen, Germany (Collingwood 1982, 222); there are two further examples from Migration period Vestrum and Snartemo II, Norway, but most Anglo-Saxon examples of 2/1 twill (eg Crowfoot 1978, 100) are thought to be from whole cloths rather than tablet bands. 2/1 twill can be worked by 2-hole tablet-weaving, either plain or with simple 2-colour pattern effects (Collingwood 1982).

The tablet band with wrapped-weft pattern, type 3, from G47, is the most significant in the group. This type is limited to the Migration period and seems to be essentially a Scandinavian technique. Margareta Nockert has noted 18 examples from Norway and 10 from Sweden, with an uncertain number from Denmark (1991, 91); but in England there are only three other examples, two from Snape, Suffolk, and one from Barrington, Cambridgeshire (E Crowfoot pers comm), in all the 96 cemeteries with textile. Hines (1984) has suggested the presence of a Scandinavian element in the Anglian population, on the basis of his study of wrist-clasps and other metalwork. These four tablet-woven bands with animal-hair decoration, all from Anglian cemeteries, tend to confirm this view.

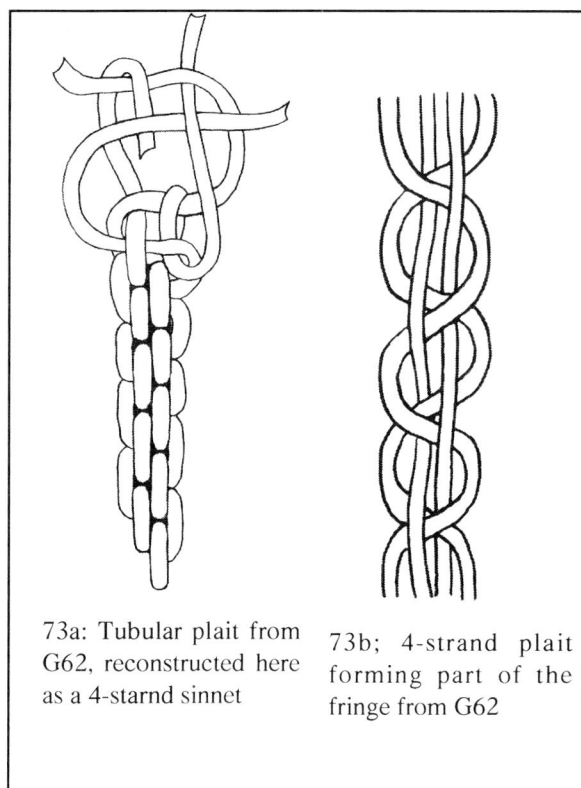

73a: Tubular plait from G62, reconstructed here as a 4-starnd sinnet

73b; 4-strand plait forming part of the fringe from G62

*Figure 73: plaits and fringes from West Heslerton*

The West Heslerton fragment of type 3 band is small in comparison with the well preserved Norwegian and Swedish examples, but it would appear to be one of Nockert's type 1, which has rectangular panels of patterning in horsehair within borders of ordinary 4-hole tablet-weaving. The wrapping technique is probably only a part of a design which would have included soumak technique and weft-faced 2/2 broken twill within the pattern rectangles. The designs within the panels of the Scandinavian bands are stylised animals, birds and human figures (Fig 72c). While elements of both design and weave can be traced back to Near Eastern sources, the final product seems to be distinctively Scandinavian. Nockert sees later soumak-brocaded bands, such as one from St Cuthbert's tomb (G Crowfoot 1956a, 454), as an Anglo-Saxon development of the Nordic technique (Nockert 1991, 92). The West Heslerton band represents a stepping-stone between the two, a band of Scandinavian style being worn in England as part of a typically Anglian costume.

## Tubular plaits

Two narrow tubular plaits, 3.5mm in diameter, were recovered from the pelvic region of the woman's body in grave G62. Both were knotted at the lower end and the yarn frayed out below the knot. It seems likely that these represent the ends of a belt knotted at the waist, with the ends left hanging down. The braids were too heavily mineralised to allow dissection of the technique, but the surface matches that of a 4-strand chain plait (also called a 4-strand sinnet with right and left crowns: Ashley 1944, 479) (Fig 73a). Several different types of plait are known

from Anglo-Saxon England. Their mineralised state often makes it difficult to analyse their construction, but one found between two layers of textile on a disc brooch from grave 845 at Mucking, Essex, has a similar surface appearance (E Crowfoot pers comm).

A simpler 5mm wide braid, a 3-strand plait made from three 3-ply cords, with a neatly knotted bobble at one end, was found below the waist of another woman, from G132. This was in association with a purse and latchlifters and may represent a suspension cord for one of these items, or the belt to which they were tied. Other narrow plaits or braids were used to string beads (G163), in the manner of the plied cords described below.

## Cords for beads and binding

Cords were found running through beads (G28, G123, G167) and other objects used in necklaces (G50, G176, G113), although leather thongs were also used to string bucket pendants in graves G152 and G167 (Watson forthcoming). Cords might be 2-plied, 3-plied, or cabled (cabled cords are plied yarns twisted together into a multi-strand cord: eg G28, G176). Cords were also frequently wrapped around the pins of annular brooches (G23, G68, G176, etc) with beads nearby; this suggests that the beads were hung in festoons between brooches rather than around the neck. Watson has also noted the use of single beads to pinch together a double row of beads into one, in G110 and G141 (Watson forthcoming). Two of the cords were found to be made from plant stem fibres, and wool is unlikely in the rest of the material, as it is too elastic for stringing beads.

Cords were also used to bind objects together. In grave G89 they held copper-alloy girdle hangers together, in G95 and G111 they bound iron objects, perhaps latchlifters, and in the best preserved example from G152 girdle hangers and latch-lifters were neatly bound for part of their length by an S-plied cord knotted at one end. The handle of the knife from G161 also seems to have been given a whipped binding of cord.

Some single threads and cords may have been used to suspend objects from the belt. In G22, G78, G110, G132, G86, G163, single threads (Z or S) and plied cords (Z2S) were knotted around suspension rings, in at least one case the suspension ring belonged to a pair of tweezers (G22).

## Animal skins

Remains of animal fibre were found on the blades of seven knives, the sockets of two spearheads, the outer face of a shield boss and on part of an iron buckle. The scale patterns on these fibres were not well enough preserved to allow identification of the species of animal. The fibres on the spearhead from G75, however, were arranged in weakly twisted curls, resembling the fleece side of a sheepskin. Similar locks of wool may be seen on woven piled fabrics (see above, Wool tabby), but there is no evidence of a ground weave over a considerable area of the spearhead from G75 and the identification as sheep-skin seems more likely. The fibres on the knife blade from G130 are smooth, straight and uniformly fine (20–30 microns diameter). Such fibres are unusual in sheep's wool — unless perhaps in the fleece of a young lamb. Some other animal pelt may have been used here. These skins appear to have been used mainly as covers or sheaths for the knives and weapons in men's graves (see below, Men's costume).

## Reconstructing the costume

Anglian dress has already been reconstructed in general outline by other authors (Vierck 1978, Owen 1976, Owen-Crocker 1986). Typically, women wore a sleeved underdress with a tubular overgown fastened at the shoulders; men wore belted tunics and trousers. In the West Heslerton graves the usual range of Anglian dress-fasteners, generally arranged in the usual position on the body, suggests that the men and women of West Heslerton were for the most part wearing the traditional style of dress. The small fragments of textile from the graves can therefore be used to fill in the detail of this clothing.

Of the 97 West Heslerton burials with textile or fibre remains, one was a cremation (G120) and five had only sparse remains of little use in reconstructing dress: this leaves 91 inhumations with useful evidence. The report on the human bones identified 3 of the 91 as male burials, 14 as female and 11 as juveniles of 15 years or under.

Two of the burials identified as female (G114, G164) are at odds with the typically male grave goods (spearhead, knife and buckle); other more tentative sex identifications from G184 and G83 are also contradicted by the artefact evidence. While the notion of cross-dressed Anglo-Saxons is intriguing, for the student of costume it is more important to know whether the person buried was wearing conventional male or conventional female attire. For this reason, graves with the usual accoutrements of Anglian women — paired annular brooches and wrist-clasps — necklaces, girdle hangers and latch-lifters, have been identified in Table 9 as (female) and graves with a spearhead, shield boss or sword as (male). In counting numbers, the artefact evidence has been given precedence over the palaeopathology. Altogether 16 male burials with textile have been identified and 48 female; at least four of the juvenile burials were also accompanied by female grave goods (G5, G10, G100, G97).

Before dealing with individual items of dress, some general comments may be made. First of all, a complete suite of garments could be all linen (G78), or all wool (G86, G143) or, more commonly, a combination of the two (G47, G141, G147 etc). Secondly, men and women seem to have had access to the same types of cloth and there is

no evidence that either sex had a greater preference for patterned fabrics or finer materials than the other. Decorative braids and edgings, however, were only found in female graves, while animal skins were only identified with certainty in male graves. Finally, patterned fabrics seem to have been a little more common in graves with large numbers of grave goods, while juveniles were generally buried in plain fabrics: this may indicate that patterned textiles are some reflection of social rank. Women with obviously valuable jewellery also seem to have had access to finer fabrics, although two of the finest examples occurred in graves with only one artefact (G34, G109). There is therefore no clear-cut correlation between quality of textile and social status.

## Women's tubular gowns

The tubular gown consisted of a large cylinder of material which the woman could step into, pull up to her armpits and then fasten with brooches at the shoulders (Owen-Crocker 1986, 28–39). This garment is similar to the wool *peplos* seen on vase-paintings of classical Greece. It seems to have reached northern Europe either before or during the Iron Age (Hald 1980, 359–61). The Greek *peplos* was made from two rectangles which could be open down the sides or stitched into a closed tube; and it might be worn with the upper edge folded outwards and downwards for a cape-like effect. A complete tubular gown from Iron-Age Huldremose, Denmark, was rather long for a woman's dress (1.68m long x 2.64m circumference), which may indicate that it, too, had been folded over at the top (Hald 1980, 360–3). The same style of garment, without the fold-down cape, can be seen in Roman sculptures representing Germanic women, the garment generally fastened at the shoulders with two brooches, and sometimes, in Rhineland funerary sculptures, with a third central brooch holding the front of the gown to an inner garment (Wild 1968, 202–3, 1985, 394). The Anglo-Saxons evidently brought these styles of dress with them from the continent (Vierck 1978, 245ff). In England the tubular gown was to be replaced, probably by a simple overtunic, in the Conversion period (Owen-Crocker 1986, 99–100), while in Scandinavia it was to continue and in some areas to develop into a closer fitting garment fastened with looped shoulder-straps (Geijer 1938, 139–40, 153–5; Hägg 1974).

At the time of the West Heslerton burials, the tubular gown seems to have been still loose and flowing. The paired shoulder brooches, usually annulars, which would have clasped the top edges of the gown have sometimes slipped to one side as a result of the loose nature of the gown — as, for example, in grave G55, where an annular brooch has fallen against the woman's face.

The materials of the tubular gown have been identified from the remains pinned by the shoulder brooches (Table 9). These show that the gown might be made from linen or wool, in tabby or twill, plain or, less commonly, patterned. The brooches clasped the front and back edges of the gown in such a way that one loop of cloth would pull towards the hinge of the brooch and the other towards the pin tip. This can be seen most clearly in the brooches from G5 and G147.

In some instances it is a fold of cloth which has been clasped, which may indicate that the upper edge of the gown was folded down to form a cape, in the manner of the *peplos* (G5, G127). In most cases, however, there was no cape. In graves G23, G29, G78, the selvedge of the cloth has been clasped and in others a braided border has been worked along the upper edge of the gown. The child in G100 wore a linen tabby gown with a plain tablet band along the top edge; the young woman in G113 wore a spin-patterned linen twill edged with a narrow braid or plait; the wool twill gown in G163 may also have had a plait as an upper border; and the twill gown from G62 was edged with a chevron-patterned band.

There was a more unusual arrangement of the gown in grave G78. Here there was a small-long brooch on the right shoulder, an annular on the left and a pair of matching cruciform brooches on the lower chest. The textiles are particularly well preserved in this grave and show that an inner gown of linen diamond twill has been clasped only on the right shoulder by the small-long brooch. Over this is an unpatterned twill, with a distinctive selvedge which is clasped by the annular brooch on the left shoulder and then reappears pinned back to the undergown by the cruciform brooch under the right breast. The edge of the gown may be reconstructed as running diagonally between the left shoulder and the right breast and, presumably, disappearing under the woman's right arm. The second cruciform brooch also seems to pin an outer layer of plain twill to the undergown. Crowfoot (1985a, 49, 54) found a similar arrangement in an early sixth-century burial at Sewerby (grave 12), where a gown of twill had been fastened on the right shoulder with a cruciform brooch and then also pinned by a pair of cruciforms lower down the body. Hirst (1985, 46–8) tentatively suggested that this might represent a gown fastened on one shoulder and passing under the opposite arm, an arrangement which seems highly likely in view of the West Heslerton evidence. In the Sewerby grave, however, the fourth brooch on the opposite shoulder appeared to fasten a cloak, although at West Heslerton the fourth brooch incontrovertibly fastened the undergown.

Greek vase-paintings and Roman sculptures also show the tubular gown fastened with one or two belts, over which the garment has been arranged in decorative folds. The woman in G173 certainly seems to have worn a belt over her gown, as the same textile which was clasped by the annular brooches at her shoulders is also on the back of the iron buckle at her waist. The knotted braid girdle in G62 also most probably fastened the outer gown. In other burials, however, the arrangement is not so clear.

In burial G175 the belt buckle holds a different material from that fastened by the shoulder brooches; and in G123, G108, G143 the textile fastened by the annulars is on the front of the buckle. Of course, the loose folds of the tubular gown may have fallen on to the front of the buckle, but all the evidence taken together tends to suggest that the belt sometimes fastened the underdress. In these instances the outer gown may have been left hanging straight down from the shoulders or may have been fastened by a second belt without a buckle, perhaps a knotted braid like that in grave G62.

## The underdress

Remains of an inner garment were found as a second layer behind the borders of the tubular gown on the shoulder brooches and also in association with braided cuffs on the wrist clasps. This sleeved undershirt or underdress seems to have been adopted in the colder climate of the north for wear with the tubular gown. A sleeved undergown can be seen in Roman sculptures from the Rhineland, the sleeves sometimes turned back into cuffs (Wild 1985, 393; Owen-Crocker 1986, 31). It was a Scandinavian and Anglian fashion to fasten braided cuffs with wrist-clasps.

The underdress at West Heslerton was made in the same range of linen and wool textiles as the tubular gown. The young woman in grave G113 wore a tabby underdress which, in the small area preserved, was heavily folded. This is reminiscent of the pleated linen undershifts from ninth- to tenth-century Birka, Sweden (Geijer 1938, pl I; Hägg 1974, 26–34), although there is no evidence for a garment of this type in any of the other West Heslerton graves. Whether the inner garment was belted separately from the outer gown has been discussed above. The presence of a belt would in itself suggest that the garment was of some length, rather than a short undershirt. The cuffs on the sleeves of the underdress were often tablet-woven, occasionally in decorative techniques. The woman in grave G47 wore a fine wool twill underdress with cuffs fastened with gilded wrist-clasps and at least one cuff patterned in a Scandinavian technique (see above, tablet-woven band type 3). Plain tablet-woven cuffs were also found on a fine tabby underdress in G60, a twill in G176 and a linen tabby in G147.

## Headdress or veil

It is very common to find remains of linen tabby on the outer face of brooches from Anglo-Saxon cemeteries. These have been interpreted as evidence for a veil or shroud. At West Heslerton similar remains were recorded in at least 15 women's graves, almost all on brooches from the shoulder region. There is no evidence for a shroud anywhere else in these graves and on balance it seems more likely that the remains represent a head-veil hanging down to the shoulders. In G78 the veil may have been a little longer than elsewhere: the same linen tabby which is on the shoulder brooches is also on the top half of two cruciform brooches lower on the chest. The tabby

*Plate 55: a scene from the Franks' casket, a whalebone box, probably made in Northumbria in the second half of the seventh century, now in the British Museum. Note the two central figures, wearing voluminous cloaks: the head-covering may be a head-veil tucked into the cloak (reproduced with kind permission of the trustees of the British Museum)*

is mainly on the front, but on one cruciform it is also tucked round on to the back, where it is gathered by a sewing thread running horizontally through the weave. This most probably represents the lower edge of a veil which reaches down to about two inches above the elbow.

The fabrics of the veils are often fine and loosely woven, to give a semi-transparent material; they are usually linen, although there is one example in wool (G143). In a few cases the linen tabby is more densely woven and these heavier linens are more commonly found in folds or pleats (eg G25, G113), although the gathered veil from G78 is one of the lighter pieces. There is no evidence for these veils being pinned and they were presumably allowed to flutter open, to reveal the brooches beneath.

In burial G123 the remains of a lightweight tabby were found on the skull itself. A folded edge of the weave runs horizontally across the temple and over the ear and is edged by a narrow tablet-woven band. The tabby proved to have been dyed a deep red colour, with wild madder or bedstraw; the band also showed a trace of the same dye, although this may have bled from the tabby. A strand of hair had been pulled back across the temple, behind the braid, while the rest of the hair seems to hang downwards. Is the red tabby the upper part of a head veil

or is it some other kind of headdress? Unfortunately no trace of the same textile is detectable on the shoulder brooches in the grave, although the lightweight character of the weave is typical of the veils in other graves.

Roman sculptures usually depict Germanic women with heads uncovered or with a length of cloth, either a veil or the edge of a cloak, over the head. A gemstone from 1st-century France, however, shows the veil held in place with a headband or circlet (Owen-Crocker 1986, 52); a headband crossing the forehead was also worn by Kentish women in the sixth century; and documentary sources suggest that the headband, *binde*, was worn at a later date over a textile headdress (Owen-Crocker 1986, 50–53, 142, 207). A manuscript illustration of the early eleventh century (BM MS Cotton Claudius Biv fol. 76) shows women wearing a wimple-like headdress with a headband across the forehead. It is dangerous to impose the styles of the later period on to the earlier, since there was a considerable change in women's dress in the seventh century, with the coming of Christianity; but the angle of the band in the manuscript illustration is much like that on the woman in G123 and the length of the wimple-like headdress in the manuscript matches most of the evidence from cemeteries, for a veil reaching the lower shoulders, but rarely any further.

Veil material in most of the graves looks either natural

or white and so the colour of the headdress in G123 may have some bearing on the status of the woman. Among the Romans purple was considered a prestigious colour and both red and purple continued to be associated with rank long after the decline of the Roman empire. A Frankish queen, for example, was buried in a suite of red and purple garments, including a long red veil (Werner 1964, 212–5), while Gisela, Charlemagne's daughter, was described by Angilbert as having veils which 'glow with purple threads' (Angilbert *Carmen de Carolo Magno*, line 232, MGH 1880). In Scandinavia reds and purples have proved to be more common in princely burials than in other graves (Walton 1986, 38–40, Walton 1991). In England there is less evidence for the use of dyes among the early Anglo-Saxons, but by the eighth century aristocratic women who took to the religious life were expected to give up brightly coloured veils for more sombre ones (Aldhelm *De Virginitate* 58, MGH 1919) and there seems to have been a correlation between strong colours, especially purple-reds, and luxury.

The dye used for the West Heslerton red was from a native plant (see above, Collecting the data) and not from the more usual species of madder, *Rubia tinctorum*. *R. tinctorum* is a richer source of dyestuff and was used for the same colour in earlier and later periods. It was originally a native of Asia Minor and its cultivation may not have reached far into the north by the Migration Period. Similar wild madder/bedstraw dyes have been identified in textiles from Migration Period Denmark (Walton 1988b, 154–5) and their use in the fifth to sixth centuries is probably a reflection of the few long-distance trade routes, by which *R. tinctorum* could reach the north.

## Women's cloaks and shawls

Remains of a fourth garment were found in 14 graves, in each case lying outside all the other textiles, including the veil. In one instance this garment was fastened by a square-headed brooch at the throat (G147), in another the cloth was probably pinned by a cruciform brooch in the same position (G29), and in a third it seemed to be fastened by a central annular brooch (G143). Other graves in which this fourth garment has been identified do not include any brooch suitable for fastening (eg G152, G107). In some graves the garment covered all the grave goods, including those arranged near the knees (eg G113). This outer garment is most likely to have been a cloak or shawl, in some cases quite voluminous. It was sometimes fastened at the front by the central brooch but in other graves it may have been wrapped around the body or laid over it as a cover.

The fabrics of these cloaks and shawls are wool or linen twill, frequently patterned and often finer than the other garments; some may have had fringed borders (G62, G124, G86). Three of the wool twills are heavier than the others and have been soft-finished (see above, Wool twill, G113, G147, G152). The piled fabric from grave

G23 is probably also from a cloak (see Wool tabby, above): it was found on the outer face of an annular brooch, outside the remains of a wool tabby overgown.

The evidence for cloaks and shawls in the early Anglo-Saxon period has been rather sketchy, in part because of a confusion with shrouds. Owen-Crocker (1986, 48–50) has listed some of the evidence and the West Heslerton remains confirm that heavy cloaks and more lightweight shawls could be worn with a brooch at the front and with the head-veil tucked in. This may be the style of dress illustrated on the seventh-century Northumbrian Franks' Casket, where women are depicted in an ankle-length dress, with the head and upper body enveloped in either a large hooded cloak, or, more probably, a veil tucked inside a cloak (Plate 55). The fine lightweight nature of much of the cloak/shawl material at West Heslerton is unexpected, although another fine diamond twill was also worn over all the other garments at Sewerby, East Yorkshire (Crowfoot 1985a, 54). In most cemeteries where cloak material has been identified, such as Castledyke, Humberside, heavier materials seem to have been more common (Walton Rogers 1998).

## Bags and other accessories

The textile lining for a leather purse, G143, and other remains of bags or purses from G22, G119 and G124 have been described above (Wool tabby): these items, together with other goods kept at the waist or hip, consistently lie outside the tubular gown and under the cloak. Belts were usually of leather, although at least one textile braid, G62, is likely to have been worn knotted around the waist (see above, Women's tubular gowns). The binding of latchlifters and girdle hangers with cords, and the stringing of beads as festoons between shoulder brooches, have also been described (Cords for beads and binding). Some of the copper-alloy bucket pendants suspended from these necklaces were stuffed with textile or fibre, those in grave G113 with fine linen tabby and those in G117 with raw plant fibre. All of these accessories are from women's graves.

## Men's costume

The dress of the West Heslerton men is more difficult to reconstruct. Textiles were recovered from 16 male graves, most commonly from the backs of buckles in the region of the waist. Here the textile may represent a tunic or trousers. In no case were remains found on the front of a buckle, in the manner of the women's graves. The man in grave G74 had two buckles, fastening two different fabrics, perhaps the tunic and the trousers. The diamond twill on one is reminiscent of the diamond twill trousers from Thorsbjerg, North Germany, and from Damendorf, Southern Schleswig (Hald 1980, 328–30). In grave G176 another diamond twill against the back of a buckle just below the waist was also on a spearhead lying on the man's chest. This suggests that the diamond twill is in this instance from a tunic, which reaches down to the hips at least. The fabrics of the other garments fastened by buckles are medium and fine, twills and tabbies, in linen and wool.

Coarser textiles were found on other metal grave goods in the male graves, where they may represent wrapping fabrics. In grave G72, for example, a spearhead lay well away from the body, above the man's head, and appeared to be wrapped in a coarse twill, 8 x 7 threads per cm. In grave G176 an even coarser twill lay over the socket of the spear, but in this instance the spear lay on the man's chest with the tunic material, as described above, close up against the blade of the spear: the coarse twill may, therefore, be another wrapping fabric, or a cloak in which the spear shaft happens to be enveloped. Another coarse twill from grave G183 lies between the body and the shield and spear, as either a cloak or a blanket. Remains of animal skins were mainly found with weapons or knives, where they may represent sheepskin-lined sheaths. Animal skins are likely to have been used for winter cloaks (Owen-Crocker 1986, 118), although the only evidence for their use in this way at West Heslerton comes from G181, where a possible fragment of fleece lay alongside a man's buckle at his waist.

## Summary and conclusions

The materials from which the main garments have been made are relatively standard types. A simple range of wool and linen fabrics have been used, with patterning confined to a few well-known techniques. The tablet bands used for cuffs and other edgings show a greater range of designs, but many of these, like the full-size fabrics, are typical Anglo-Saxon products. Most of the West Heslerton textiles, whether whole cloths or bands, could have been woven near at hand, using locally grown wool and flax: the small pattern repeat of some of the diamond twills in particular may have been a speciality of the Yorkshire Anglians. Weaving would have been on the warp-weighted loom, which at this date could produce particularly wide pieces of cloth (Hoffmann 1974, 280–1), suitable for the voluminous overgown and shawl: weights from this loom have been recovered from most Anglo-Saxon settlements, including West Heslerton village. The native madder or bedstraw used to dye the red headdress could also have been collected from nearby fields or hedgerows. Only a single example of a piled cloak may not have been made locally and one braid has been shown to be almost certainly of Scandinavian origin.

The styles of dress at West Heslerton are typical of the period and the region, but it is evident that the details could be varied, presumably to suit fashion, personal taste, social status or the weather. Veils might be thin and light or heavy and gathered into folds. Shawls and cloaks might be fine and patterned or thick, plain, matted fabrics. Outer gowns were mostly fastened on both shoulders, but might also be fastened on only one. The main garments for men

and women could be made from any of the available fabrics and, amongst women especially, braids and plaits could be used to give an individual look. Colour-patterning was obvious in some of the tablet bands and dyes were no doubt used in other garments besides the red head veil. Altogether, the West Heslerton evidence has shown that the traditional Anglian costume was not a strict form of dress, but one which, within a general framework, could allow an infinite number of variations.

| Grave | Sample | Skeleton | Sex (Gender) | Fibre | Weave | Spin | Count | Position of textile in grave | Costume interpretation | Objects with textile | Objects without textile |
|---|---|---|---|---|---|---|---|---|---|---|---|
| 2 | | 001A 00012 | (male) | not ident. | 2/2 spin-patterned | Z x Z&S | 10-11 x 9-11 | On both faces of a spearhead, to right of right shoulder. Yarn in one direction Z, in other spin-patterned ZSSZS | A medium-weight spin-patterned twill of uncertain function | iron spearhead (AC) | copper alloy tweezers |
| 5 | a | 001A 00017 | juvenile (female) | not ident. | tabby | ZZ | 10 x 9-10 | On the back of one of the annular brooches | Tubular gown is obviously made from medium-weight twill. Another garment in tabby weave was worn, perhaps an underdress | copper alloy annulars (AA, AN), iron objects | |
| 5 | b | | | not ident. | 2/2 | ZZ | 9-10 x 9-10 | Two folds pierced by pin of annular brooch, one fold at hinge, other towards tip | | | |
| 8 | a | 001A 00031 | female | not ident. | 2/2 | ZZ | 9-11 x 8-10 | On fragmented iron objects, at waist | Garment of medium-weight twill. Fine, open weave may represent head-veil | iron objects (CV,CZ,DD,DF), a cruciform-headed | 2 iron buckles, iron knife, iron ?latch-lifter, pottery vessel, necklace of amber, glass, & |
| 8 | b | | | not ident. | ?tabby | ZZ | ? | Fine open-weave textile on outside of head of pin (CS) at throat | | | |
| 10 | | 001A 00034 | juvenile (female) | not ident. | ?2/2 | ZS | ? | Fold of textile along one edge of buckle | None | iron buckle (AC) | 3 copper alloy annulars, frags copper alloy wire |
| 12 | a | 001A 00050 | female | not ident. | Ribbed tabby | ZS | 20 x 14 | On back of cruciform brooch(CG) at throat, outside twill and cord | Inner garment of medium-weight twill, with beads worn over it. Cruciform brooch pins a fine ZS tabby, possibly the border of the cloth. Comparison | copper alloy cruciform brooch (CG) | copper alloy annular, copper alloy small-long brooch, pair wrist-clasps, copper alloy fibula brooch, iron buckle, glass & amber necklace |
| 12 | b | | | not ident. | 2/2 | ZZ | 10 x10 | On back of cruciform brooch (CG), behind ribbed tabby | with other graves suggests the twill is the tubular gown and the ZS fabric is the border of the cloak | | |
| 12 | c | | | not ident. | cord | ?ZZ3S | - | Plied cord sandwiched between ribbed tabby and twill | | | |
| 14 | a | 001A 00073 | gender unknown | flax hemp | tabby | ZZ | 12 x 9 | On back of gilded square-headed brooch (AB) | None | gilded (copper alloy) square-headed brooch (AB) | pottery vessel, glass and amber necklace |
| 14 | b | | | not ident. | 2/2 | ZS | 10-11 x 8 | | | | |
| 22 | a | 001B 00008 | probably adult (female) | not ident. | tabby | ZZ | 22 x 20 | In several folds on buckle | Garment of fine tabby fastened with belt. Possibly a bag of ribbed wool (ZS) fabric. The ribbed linen tabby is of uncertain function, perhaps a belt | iron buckle, copper alloy tweezers, iron knife (AB,AT,AU), iron 'belt' & chatelaine (AS) | small copper alloy annular, glass & slate necklace |
| 22 | b | | | flax | ribbed tabby | ZZ | 12-16 x 9 | On one side of tweezers | | | |
| 22 | c | | | not ident. | threads | Z | - | Threads wrapping ring of tweezers | | | |
| 22 | d | | | not ident. | ribbed tabby | ZS | 20-22 x 12-14 | On two fragments of iron belt fittings and on part of chatelaine and perhaps on knife | | | |
| 23 | a | 001B 00010 | elderly (female) | wool | Tabby with ?pile | Z x Z x Z & S (ZZSS) | 14-16 x 12-14 | Spin-patterned textile with loose threads on surface, probably from pile. Over front of annular brooch at neck | A tubular gown of wool tabby pinned by annular brooches (ribbed effect on annular brooches may indicate border of cloth). | copper alloy annular (235), iron knife (240) | 2nd copper alloy annular, copper alloy bangle, silver earring, 3 beads |
| 23 | b | | | not ident. | tabby | ZZ | 10-14 x 8-10 | In folds or pleats on back of annular brooch; brooch probably pinned this. Also on knife, at waist | Beads worn as festoon between brooches. Cloak of plied fabric, worn pile-outwards | | |
| 23 | c | | | not ident. | cord | ? | - | Several Z-spun threads, probably originally plied together, over pin of annular brooch | | | |
| 25 | | 001B 00015 | adult? (female) | not ident. | tabby | ZZ | 18 x 10 | In folds or pleats over front and back of annular brooch | Possibly remains of a full veil | copper alloy annular brooch (AA) | glass bead, iron knife |

*Table 9: catalogue of textile and costume evidence.*

| Grave | Sample | Skeleton | Sex (Gender) | Fibre | Weave | Spin | Count | Position of textile in grave | Costume interpretation | Objects with textile | Objects without textile |
|---|---|---|---|---|---|---|---|---|---|---|---|
| 27 | a | 001B 00101 | (female) | not ident. | ?2/2 | ZS | 12 x 9 | On ?front of annular brooch (AX) below jaw | None | iron knife (AV), copper alloy annular (AX) | 1 copper alloy wrist-clasp, iron pin, iron buckle brooch, iron buckle, wooden cup, 2nd copper alloy annular, amber & glass necklace |
| 27 | b | | | not ident. | ? | ZZ | ? | Traces of textile on the face of knife blade (AV). | | | |
| 28 | a | 001B 00104 | adult (female) | flax | tabby | ZZ | 18-20 x 12-16 | In folds on front of annular brooch (AW) | Fine linen tabby may be remains of veil | copper alloy annular (AW), glass bead | iron knife, copper alloy buckle, copper alloy frags, copper alloy penannular brooch, 5 glass beads, silver bell |
| 28 | b | | | not ident. | cord | Z2S2S | - | Cabled cord 1.5mm diameter inside glass bead | Beads strung on cabled cord | | |
| 29 | a | 001B 00105 | (female) | not ident. | 2/2 diamond | ZS | 8-9 x 8-10 | In large loose folds on front of annular brooch (BC) and also on broach pin. On back of cruciform brooch (BB), but not pinned by it | An undergown of coarse tabby fastened with iron annular brooch. Tubular gown of wool diamond twill with tabby-woven border, pinned by pair of annular brooches. Outside this, a finer twill, probably a shawl fastened by the cruciform brooch.   A further medium-weight twill outside the tubular gown, of uncertain function | copper alloy cruciform (BB), 2 copper alloy annulars (BC,BD), amber & glass necklace, iron annular | iron pin, 2 iron buckles, pottery vessel |
| 29 | b | | | wool | tabby | ZS | 12 x 6 | Looping around pin of copper alloy brooch (BD) possibly border of diamond twill | | | |
| 29 | c | | | not ident. | 2/2 | ZZ | 16 x 12 | In association with cruciform brooch (BB) | | | |
| 29 | d | | | not ident. | tabby | ZZ | 10 x 7 | On both sides of iron annular brooch, in folds | | | |
| 29 | e | | | not ident. | 2/2 | ZZ | 10 x 9 | On pin of annular brooch (BC)outside ZS diamond twill | | | |
| 32 | | 001HE00002 | ?female | not ident. | tabby | ZZ | 18-20 x 16 | Loose on top of pin of penannular brooch (AA) | None | copper alloy penannular brooch (AA) | iron knife, iron buckle, wooden vessel |
| 33 | | 001HE00003 | juvenile-gender unknown | ?wool | 2/2 | ZZ | 14 x 12 | In loose folds lapping around edges of buckle (AQ) at lower chest. | Loose garment of medium-fine, ?wool twill, fastened above waist with belt | iron buckle (AQ) | none |
| 34 | | 001HE00004 | female | not ident | tabby | ZZ | 20 x 16 | Loose in association with knife (AT) at waist | None | iron knife (AT) | none |
| 40 | a | 001HE00010 | female | not ident. | ?tabby | ZZ | ? | Poorly preserved remains now detached from brooch (BE) | None | copper alloy annular (BE),copper alloy wrist-clasp (BJ) | 2 further annulars, 2nd wrist-clasp, iron knife, amber & glass necklace |
| 40 | b | | | not ident. | ?tablet braid | Z2S x ? | ? | Now detached from wrist clasp (BJ) | | | |
| 41 | | 001HE00011 | female | not ident | ? | ZS | ? | On back of annular brooch (BZ) at hinge of pin | Possibly remains of tubular gown fastened by annular brooch | copper alloy annular (BZ) | 2nd annular, necklace of amber, glass & silver |
| 42 | a | 001HE00012 | (female) | not ident. | Fringe & ?braid | Z2S | ? | Remains of tablet braid or fringe diagonally over pin of annular brooch (CE) definite fringe parallel to pin | None | copper alloy annulars (CE, CI) | 2 amber & glass necklaces, 3 copper alloy rings links, copper alloy ?purse mount, 2 iron buckles, iron ?pin, 3 iron latch lifters, iron knife, iron ring |
| 42 | b | | | not ident. | ? | ZS | ? | On front of pin of brooch (CI) | | | |
| 45 | a | 001HE00014 | (female) | not ident. | 2/2 | ZZ | 20 x 14 | On back of buckle (CS), on upper chest, close to annular brooches | A garment of medium-fine twill,leather strap with buckle lies over this, below throat. A sleeved garment probably with tablet-woven cuffs. | copper alloy wrist-clasp (CO), iron buckle (CS) | 2 copper alloy annulars, iron buckle, 2 amber necklaces, iron pin, 2 copper alloy pins with spangles, iron knife, iron... |
| 45 | b | | | not ident. | ?tablet weave | Z2S x ? | ? | Corded remains on back of wrist clasp (CO) | | | |

*Table 9:(continued) catalogue of textile and costume evidence*

| Grave | Sample | Skeleton | Sex (Gender) | Fibre | Weave | Spin | Count | Position of textile in grave | Costume interpretation | Objects with textile | Objects without textile |
|---|---|---|---|---|---|---|---|---|---|---|---|
| 47 | a | 001HE00016 | (female) | wool | 2/2 | ZZ | 18 x 18 | On wrist-clasp (DM) in association with tablet woven braid type 3 | A sleeved undergown of fine wool tablet-woven cuffs, at least one of which is patterned. Over this a tubular gown of coarser twill, fastened at right shoulder by annular brooch DP (and presumably also at left shoulder by annular brooch DN). A third garment of fine linen twill was worn, perhaps a shawl | copper alloy wrist-clasps (DM, DO), copper alloy annulars (DN), (DP) | copper alloy buckle, wooden cup, amber & glass necklace, iron knife, iron ring |
| 47 | b | | | flax | 2/2 | ZZ | 20 x 18 | In association with annular brooches at shoulders (DN, DP) but probably not pinned by them | | | |
| 47 | c | | | not ident. | 2/2 | ZZ | 10 x 10 | At right shoulder on back annular brooch (DP) at hinge | | | |
| 47 | d | | | not ident. | ?tablet band type 1a | Z2S x Z2S | 13 warp cords and 12 weft | Tablet woven band at 30 mm wide from back of wrist-clasp (DO) | | | |
| 47 | e | | | coarse animal fibre | ?tablet band type 3 | Z2S x Z2S & I | ?13 warp cords and 12 weft | Patterned band attached to fine wool twill (above) with wrist-clasp (DM) | | | |
| 50 | | 001HE00020 | (female) | not ident. | cords | Z2S | | 3 plied cords running between holes of one of the copper alloy objects at neck | Necklace strung on three cords | necklace of glass, amber and copper alloy objects (FH) | none |
| 54 | | 001HE00024 | gender unknown | not ident. | 2/2 | ZZ | 11 x 10 | In association with pin of annular brooch (EL) | None | copper alloy annular (EL) | none |
| 55 | | 001HE00025 | (female) | not ident. | tabby | ZZ | 10 x 10 | On lower edge of lower jaw with impression of an annular brooch in the weave) | A loose gown of medium-weight tabby, a fold of which has fallen against the woman's face | lower jaw | copper alloy wrist-clasps, iron knife, iron ring, glass vessel sherd, copper alloy pin & link, copper alloy annulars, 6 amber beads, 2 silver medallions |
| 60 | a | 001HE00043 | (female) | not ident. | tabby | ZZ | 20 x 16 | In association with gilded wrist-clasp (FO), at wrist and perhaps also on pin of annular (FS) at shoulder | Sleeved underdress probably of fine tabby, with linen tablet woven cuffs fastened with clasps. Another garment (possibly the tubular gown) of a heavier weight of tabby | gilded copper alloy wrist-clasps (FO), copper alloy annulars (FS,FT) | amber & glass necklace, iron knife, copper alloy pin |
| 60 | b | | | flax | tablet braid type 1a | Z x Z2S | 9 warp cords and 10 weft | In association with 4 gilded wrist clasps | | | |
| 60 | c | | | not ident. | tabby | ZZ | 13 x 13 | Originally with annular (FT) at right shoulder | | | |
| 62 | a | 001HE00046 | (female) | wool | 2/2 | ZZ | 9-12 x 8-10 | On back of both wrist-clasps(GP,GR). On back of annular brooch (GV), behind finer twill and tablet braid (see below). Variable thread-count may be due to distortion or may represent two similar fabrics | An inner garment or garments of medium-weight wool twill, with an outer garment of finer twill. Two Possible interpretations:- (I) if all the medium-weight twills are from one garment, then it is probably a sleeved underdress, fastened with a belt of tubular braid at the waist. Over this a tubular gown of finer twill fastened by annular brooches and edged with a patterned band. Function of the fringe not clear. More probably:- (ii) if the medium-weight twills are from two garments the sleeved underdress and the tubular gown, then the outer gown was edged by the patterned band. The fine twill would then be from a cloak (presumably fastened by the cruciform brooch) of which a fringed corner has caught behind the annular brooch. A veil of medium-weight linen tabby was also worn. | copper alloy wrist-clasps (GP,GR), copper alloy cruciform (GT), copper alloy annulars (GV,GW), copper alloy folded object (GY) | amber & glass necklace, copper alloy ring, copper alloy wire ring, copper alloy link |
| 62 | b | | | not ident. | 2/2 | ZZ | 14 x 13 | In folds on back and front annular brooches (GV,GW). Outside coarser twill (see above) | | | |
| 62 | c | | | not ident. | ?tablet band type 2a | Z x ? | 10 warp cords x 9-10 weft | Tablet band with chevron pattern on back of annular brooch (GV) | | | |
| 62 | d | | | not ident. | Cords and plaits | Z2S and Z | - | Fringe of cords and plaits diagonally over pin of annular brooch (GV). All very fine and probably related to finer twill | | | |
| 62 | e | | | not ident. | tubular plait | Z | | Two lengths of braid, both with an overhand knot at one end, on back of wrist-clasp (GR) between clasp and coarser twill. This clasp was on its own in pelvic region, not at wrists | | | |
| 62 | f | | | flax | tabby | ZZ | 13 x 9 | On front of annular brooch(GV), at left shoulder | | | |

*Table 9:(continued) catalogue of textile and costume evidence*

| Grave | Sample | Skeleton | Sex / (Gender) | Fibre | Weave | Spin | Count | Position of textile in grave | Costume interpretation | Objects with textile | Objects without textile |
|---|---|---|---|---|---|---|---|---|---|---|---|
| 68 | a | 002B 00026 | adult (female) | not ident. | 2/2 | ZZ | 10 × 9 | On front of iron pin of annular brooch (F) | Beads probably worn as a festoon between brooches | copper alloy annular (F) | glass & amber beads, frags of 2nd annular |
| 68 | b | | | not ident. | cord | Z2S | - | Over pin of annular brooch (F) | | | |
| 68 | c | | | not ident. | cord | Z3S | - | Originally in association with annular brooch (F) | | | |
| 71 | | 002B 00055 | gender unknown | flax | 2/2 | ZZ | 10-11 × 10-11 | In association with belt fitting (AB, AC) at waist | None | copper alloy belt fitting (AB,AC) | iron knife, iron buckle |
| 72 | a | 002B 00084 | male | not ident. | 2/2 | ZZ | 8 × 7 | Over socket of iron spear-head (AF), above and to right of man's head | The coarse twill, well away from the body, may be a wrapping fabric for the spear | iron spearhead (AG), iron knife (AG) | iron shield boss & studs, 2nd iron spearhead |
| 72 | b | | | not ident. | 2tabby | ZS | ? | On one face of knife (AG) at left waist | | | |
| 73 | | 002B 00068 | adult (male) | not ident. | ?2/2 | ZZ | ? | On one side of blade of knife (AG) at left waist | None | iron knife (AG) | iron spearhead & ferrule, iron shield boss, 4 shield discs & grip, iron buckle |
| 74 | a | 002B 00085 | adult male | not ident. | ? | ZZ | ? | On back of buckle(AF) | Garment of medium-fine diamond twill | iron buckle (AF), | iron sword, iron shield boss, grip & studs, 2 iron spearheads, 3rd iron buckle |
| 74 | b | | | not ident. | 2/2 diam | ZS | 12 × 14 | On back and sides of buckle(AP) below waist | fastened by belt below waist. Second garment fastened by separate belt | copper alloy & iron buckle (AP) | |
| 75 | | 002B 00075 | adult (male) | not ident. | fibres | - | - | Curls of weakly twisted fibre(no ground weave visible) on socket of spearhead (AA) by head | Probably remains of a sheepskin | iron spearhead (AA) | iron knife |
| 76 | a | 002B 00091 | (female) | not ident. | ?2/2 | Z × ? | 12 × 12 | On pin of ?buckle (AU) | Garments of at least two different twills. | iron ?buckle (AU), | copper alloy fastener, iron |
| 76 | b | | | not ident. | 2/2 | ZS | 14 × 12 | Possibly the same as above. On both sides of iron object(BA) | Relationship to each other not clear. | iron object (BA), copper alloy wire | ring-headed object, glass necklace, copper alloy |
| 76 | c | | | not ident. | 2/2 | ZZ | 9 × 7 | On front of annular brooch (GW). Perhaps also on back | | bracelet (EF), copper alloy | bangle, copper alloy ring-headed pin |
| 78 | a | 002BA00100 | adult female | flax | 2/2 diam | ZZ | 12 × 12 | Pinned by small-long brooch (AD) at right shoulder and by cruciform brooches (AA,AB) on lower chest. On both cruciforms the diamond twill is inside a second fabric, which, on brooch (AA), is clearly the plain twill | An undergown of diamond twill pinned by the small-long brooch on the right shoulder. An overgown of simple twill, with a selvedge which is clasped by the annular brooch on the left shoulder. The selvedge runs diagonally across | copper alloy cruciform (AA), copper alloy cruciform (AB), copper alloy wire ring (AC), copper alloy brooch (AD), copper alloy small annular (AE) | none |
| 78 | b | | | flax | 2/2 | ZZ | 12 × 7 | Twill with tubular selvedge pinned by annular brooch (AE) at left shoulder. On cruciform brooch (AA) below right breast, the tubular selvedge runs diagonally down the back of the brooch and is pinned to the diamond twill behind | body and is pinned back to the undergown below the right breast, by a cruciform brooch. It may also be pinned to the undergown by the cruciform under the left breast. | | |
| 78 | c | | | flax | tabby | ZZ | 14 × 12-14 | Fine, gauzy linen textile over shoulder brooches (AD, AE) and over top half of brooches on lower chest (AA, AB). On AA a fold of the material laps round on to the back and in this area is gathered by a horizontal running thread | A long, gauzy linen veil, gathered towards the lower edge, hangs down over the other garments to just above the elbows | | |
| 78 | d | | | not ident. | threads | Z | - | Threads wrapped around wire (AC) | | | |

*Table 9:(continued) catalogue of textile and costume evidence*

| Grave | Sample | Skeleton | Sex (Gender) | Fibre | Weave | Spin | Count | Position of textile in grave | Costume interpretation | Objects with textile | Objects without textile |
|---|---|---|---|---|---|---|---|---|---|---|---|
| 83 | a | 002BA00022 | adult (?female) | not ident. | ?2/2 | ZS | 12 x 10 | Poorly preserved remains in association with handle (AA) | A garment of twill with a fine tabby veil. | handle (AA), copper alloy annular (AB), copper alloy annular (AC) copper alloy | copper alloy annular, copper alloy tweezers, copper alloy frag |
| 83 | b | | | not ident. | ?tabby | ?ZZ | ? | Fine textile over annular brooch (AB) | | | |
| 84 | | 002BA00445 | gender unknown | not ident. | 2/2 | ZZ | 11 x 11 | On front of cruciform brooch at left of neck | None | copper alloy cruciform (AH) | copper alloy small-long brooch, beads |
| 86 | a | 002BA00921 | adult (female) | wool | 2/2 | ZZ | 7 x6 | On back of cruciform brooch (AI) at right shoulder inside ZZ twill; also on front of wrist-clasp (AQ) at waist | An inner gown of coarse wool twill. A gown of medium wool twill fastened at right shoulder with cruciform brooch. A fringed cloak of fine wool (ZS) twill fastened by annular brooch at centre chest and covering arms at waist. Purse chatelaine lies over them tubular gown | copper alloy wrist-clasps (AC AQ, AM AN), copper alloy cruciform brooch (AI), copper alloy annular brooches (AJ, AK), gilded copper alloy pendant (AL), purse-group & chatelaine (BF-BK) | tweezers, wrist-clasp, iron objects |
| 86 | b | | | wool | 2/2 | ZZ | 9-10 x 8-10 | On front and back of cruciform brooch (AI) and under purse-group (BF-BK) | | | |
| 86 | c | | | not ident. | ?2/2 | ZS | 16 x 14 | Behind annular brooch (AJ) at centre chest, on front of wrist-clasps (AM,AQ) at waist | | | |
| 86 | d | | | wool | fringe | Z2S | - | Fringe of plied threads, lying above ZS textile (above) on back of annular brooch (AJ). Pin pierces fringe | | | |
| 86 | e | | | not ident. | thread | Z | - | Z-spun thread wrapped 3-4 times around ring of annular brooch (AK) | | | |
| 86 | f | | | not ident. | thread | S | - | S-spun thread between suspension holes of gilded pendant (AL) | | | |
| 86 | g | | | not ident. | thread | ? | - | At securing hole of wrist-clasp (AQ) | | | |
| 88 | a | 002BA00285 | adult (female) | not ident. | ? | ZZ | ? | Poorly preserved remains of loose weave on iron ring (AC) by thighs | Poorly preserved but probably tubular gown of medium-weight ZZ fabric pinned by annular brooch, with finer veil over top. | iron ring (AC), copper alloy annular (AS) | iron knife, copper alloy annular, Roman coin |
| 88 | b | | | not ident. | ? | ZZ | ? | Loop of this fabric pinned by annular brooch (AS) at left shoulder | | | |
| 88 | c | | | not ident. | ? | ZZ | ? | Finer fabric on front of annular brooch (AS) | | | |
| 89 | a | 002BA00078 | adult female | not ident. | ?tabby | ZZ | 6 x 6 | A coarse-fibred textile on front, back and sides of buckle (AH) | Loose garment of coarse fabric fastened with belt | iron buckle (AH), copper alloy girdle-hanger (BH) | iron annulars, copper alloy wrist-clasp |
| 89 | b | | | not ident. | threads | Z | ? | Three parallel threads on the square foot of girdle-hanger (BH) | A wrapping thread binding the girdle-hanger, or remains of a fringe | | |
| 93 | | 002BA00149 | ?adult gender unknown | not ident. | 2/2 | ZZ | 10 x 12-14 | On back of buckle (AE) at waist. Strap is leather | Garment of medium weight wool twill, fastened with leather belt. | iron buckle (AE) | iron knife |
| 95 | a | 002BA00226 | adult female | wool | 2/2 | ZZ | 10-8 x 8 | Pinned by square-headed brooch (EF) at left neck; also in contact with iron object (DA) on left shoulder | Unclear. Perhaps a tubular gown of coarse wool twill, pinned by smaller brooch (EF). Cloak of matted wool twill pinned by cruciform brooch (EE). Beads as festoons between brooches (EE) and (FK). Linen tabby veil over brooches, but buckle appears to lie over the veil fabric | iron objects (BG,CT,DA,DC,DI,D N), iron buckle (DB), copper alloy cruciform (EE), copper alloy small square-headed brooches (EF,FK) | copper alloy wrist-clasps, beads, iron fragments, copper alloy plate |
| 95 | b | | | wool | 2/2 | ZZ | 12-14 x 12 | Matted textile pinned by cruciform brooch (EE) at left neck; and in association with square-headed brooch(EF) and iron object (BG) | | | |
| 95 | c | | | flax | tabby | ZZ | 12-14 x 10-12 | In two layers behind buckle (DB); also on front of square-headed brooch (EF) | | | |
| 95 | d | | | not ident. | tabby | ZZ | 7-8 x 8 | On front of cruciform brooch (EE) | | | |
| 95 | e | | | not ident. | threads | Z | - | Parallel threads - probably a binding - on iron fragments (DI). | | | |
| 95 | f | | | not ident. | cords | S-ply | - | On back of cruciform brooch (EE) at hinge. | | | |
| 95 | g | | | not ident. | cords | Z2S | - | On front of small square-headed brooch (FK) | | | |

*Table 9: (continued) catalogue of textile and costume evidence*

| Grave | Sample | Skeleton | Sex / (Gender) | Fibre | Weave | Spin | Count | Position of textile in grave | Costume interpretation | Objects with textile | Objects without textile |
|---|---|---|---|---|---|---|---|---|---|---|---|
| 97 | | 002BA00153 | juvenile (female) | flax | tabby | ZZ | 12 x 8-10 | Poorly preserved remains pinned by annular brooch (AA) and perhaps by small-long brooch (AC); in association with wrist-clasp (AI) | Grave disturbed | copper alloy annular (AA), copper alloy small-long brooch (AC), copper alloy | copper alloy wrist-clasp |
| 100 | a | 002BA00148 | young juvenile (female) | flax hemp | tabby | ZZ | 14-16 x 12 x 14 | Pinned by iron pin (AG) below chin and by both annular brooches (AI,AJ) at neck | Tubular gown of linen tabby, edged with tablet-woven braid, and pinned at shoulders by annular brooches. Centre of gown held in place at throat by pin with spangle | iron pin with copper alloy spangle (AG), copper alloy annulars (AI,AJ) | copper alloy necklet |
| 100 | b | | | not ident. | tablet weave type 1a | ? | 10 warp coords and 8 weft | Pinned by annular brooch (AI) | | | |
| 102 | a | 002BA00159 | adult female | flax | ?2/2 | ZZ | ? | Probably pinned by annular brooch (AY) at left neck | Garment, probably tubular gown, of linen ?twill. Veil of fine linen tabby. | copper alloy annular (AY), copper alloy annular (BC) | iron object, copper alloy bead, copper alloy buckle, copper alloy strap ends |
| 102 | b | | | flax | tabby | ZZ | 16 x 14-16 | On front of annular brooch (AY) and on front and back of annular(BC) at right shoulder | | | |
| 103 | | 002BA00489 | adult gender unknown | flax | 2/2 | ZZ | 12 x 9 | Behind buckle-plate (AB),i.e. towards body | Garment of medium-weight linen twill, fastened with belt | iron & copper alloy buckle (AB) | iron knife |
| 107 | a | 002BA00939 | adult female | flax | 2/2 diam or chev | ZZ | 16-20 x 14 | Over small annular brooch(AO) under chin, over and around purse-group, behind knees | Tubular gown of medium-weight wool twill, pinned by annular brooches. Over this a fine chevron or diamond-patterned linen, probably a shawl, reaching to below knees. Fine tabby weave may be inner gown or veil tucked into shawl. A string of beads worn as a festoon between brooches | small copper alloy annular (AO), copper alloy annular (AP), purse-group AK, AR-AW | beads, copper alloy binding, worked bone & iron fragments, iron knife, key |
| 107 | b | | | wool | 2/2 | ZS | 10 x 9-10 | Almost certainly pinned by both annular brooches (AO,AP) at neck | | | |
| 107 | c | | | not ident. | tabby | ZZ | ? | Relatively fine. On small annular brooch (AO) behind chevron diamond twill below chin | | | |
| 107 | d | | | not ident. | cord | Z4S | - | Around pin of annular brooch(AP) at left of neck | | | |
| 108 | | 002BA00825 | juvenile (female) | wool | ?twill | ZZ | 8 x 8 | Pinned by annular brooch (AH) and on outer face of buckle (AD). | Garment of coarse wool twill pinned by annular brooch; worn over another, belted garment | copper alloy annular (AH), iron buckle (AD) | copper alloy binding, copper alloy bead |
| 109 | | 002BA00897 | young adult male | not ident. | tabby | ZZ | 18 x 16 | On back of buckle and buckle-plate (AB-D) at waist | Garment of fine tabby-weave fabric fastened with belt. | copper alloy buckle (AB-D) | none |
| 110 | a | 002BA00575 | adult (female) | wool | 2/2 | ZS | 10 x9 | On front and back of annular brooches at shoulders, possibly pinned by them | Garment of medium-weight wool twill, possibly tubular gown, pinned by annular brooches. | copper alloy fragments of annular brooches (AE, AT, BD, RM) iron ring | beads, iron chain links, brooch frags |
| 110 | b | | | not ident. | threads | Z | - | Appear to have been wrapped around around iron ring (AR) | | | |
| 111 | a | 002BA00420 | adult male or large female | not ident. | ?twill | ZS | ? | Coarse, loose weave in association with iron pins (BE-BI) and at hinge of pin with spangles (AF) on upper body | None | iron pin (AC), iron pins (BE, BF, BG, BH, BI), iron pin with copper alloy spangle (AF) | silvered disc, copper alloy object |
| 111 | b | | | not ident. | cord | S-ply | - | 10-15 mm diam cord around iron pin (AC). | | | |

*Table 9:(continued) catalogue of textile and costume evidence*

| Grave | Sample | Skeleton | Sex / (Gender) | Fibre | Weave | Spin | Count | Position of textile in grave | Costume interpretation | Objects with textile | Objects without textile |
|---|---|---|---|---|---|---|---|---|---|---|---|
| 113 | a | 002BA00441 | young adult female | flax/hemp | tablet braid type 2b | ZZ | 24-28 x 14 | Fine warp-faced braid pinned by annular brooch (AA) at right shoulder. In association with flax hemp textile | A full inner garment of medium-coarse tabby, much folded or pleated. Over this a tubular gown of spin-patterned linen twill, edged with braids and fastened with annular brooches. A veil of fine linen hangs down over the annular brooches in heavy folds. A cloak or blanket of matted wool twill covers many of the objects in the grave. Some copper alloy cylinders are stuffed with fine linen tabby and threaded on linen cords | copper alloy annular (AA, AL), copper alloy tubular ojects (AK), iron girdle-hangers (BG, BH, BI) | copper alloy rings, amber & silver beads, silver ring, amulet, iron ring |
| 113 | b | | | flax/hemp | ? | Z x ? | ? | Pinned by annular brooch AA.) Braid (above) is probably border or edging to this weave | | | |
| 113 | c | | | not ident. | ? 2/2 | S,Z x S,Z | ? | Spin-patterned twill pinned by annular brooch (AL) at left shoulder. ?Same as last entry. Braid plait (below) probably edges this fabric | | | |
| 113 | d | | | plant fibre | tablet braid or guilloche plait | Z2S x ? | 2 warp cords over 3mm, 4-5 ?weft over 10mm | Pinned by annular brooch (AL). Probably edging to spin-patterned twill and braid | | | |
| 113 | e | | | not ident. | tabby | ZZ | 9-10 x 8 | Folds or pleats on back of annular brooch (AL). inside spin-patterned twill and border | | | |
| 113 | f | | | flax | tabby | ZZ | 16-20 x 16-18 | Several layers on front and back annular brooch (AL) | | | |
| 113 | g | | | Wool | twill | ZS | 12 x 10 | Matted in places. On tip of mpin of annular brooch (AA), on iron girdle-hangers (BG-BI) and walnut & mount (BQ) at thighs | | | |
| 113 | h | | | flax | tabby | ZZ | 18-20 x 18-20 | Folded inside small tubular object (AK) in association with cord (below) | | | |
| 113 | l | | | flax/hemp | cords | Z2S | - | Inside tubular object (AK), through fine linen tabby (above). Two similar cords run through a second tube | | | |
| 114 | | 002BA00466 | adult female | not ident. | 2/2 | ZS | ? | Relatively fine textile in association with iron object (AX) at knees and over pin of annular brooch (BI) at throat | From comparison with other burials, a fine ZS twill over a shoulder brooch and reaching the knees may be a shawl | iron object (AX), copper alloy annular (BI) | amber beads, iron annular |
| 117 | a | 002BA00503 | juvenile gender unknown | plant stem fibre | fibres only | - | - | Inside copper alloy tube (AF) | Stuffing for cylinders, as in Grave 113, samples h and I. | copper alloy tubes (AF, AH) | none |
| 117 | b | | | not ident. | Fibres only | - | - | Different from above. Inside copper alloy tube (AH) | | | |
| 119 | a | 002EA00684 | adult (female) | wool | tabby | ZZ | 14 x 14 | Mainly on back of wrist-clasps (AI, AJ), where folded and stitched. Some traces also on front of clasps | Sleeved underdress of medium-fine wool tabby, cuffs of another wool fabric. A coarse wool textile and a linen of uncertain function also resent: one may represent a bag or purse. Outer gown of diamond or chevron-patterned twill, fastened with annular brooches and possibly edged with braid. | copper alloy wrist-clasps (AI, AJ), iron latch-lifters (AF AH), iron spike (AB), copper alloy annular brooches (AC, AD), large iron rng (AG) | iron knife, beads |
| 119 | b | | | wool | ? | ? | ? | Remains of another wool textile sandwiched between tabby (above) and wrist-clasps; all three stitched together with coarse Z-spun thread | | | |
| 119 | c | | | ?wool | 2/2 diam or chev twill | ZS | 12-14 x 11-12 | Pinned by annular brooch (AC) at right shoulder and with annular brooch(AD) at throat. Possibly edged by braid | | | |
| 119 | d | | | not ident. | ?tablet braid | Z x ? | ? | Braid or fringe on pin of annular brooch (AD) | | | |
| 119 | e | | | wool | tabby | ZZ | 7 x 7 | Adhering to latchlifters (AF AH) at waist | | | |
| 119 | f | | | flax/hemp | ? | Z x ? | ? | Loose in association with large iron rng(AG) at waist | | | |

*Table 9: (continued) catalogue of textile and costume evidence*

| Grave | Sample | Skeleton | Sex / (Gender) | Fibre | Weave | Spin | Count | Position of textile in grave | Costume interpretation | Objects with textile | Objects without textile |
|---|---|---|---|---|---|---|---|---|---|---|---|
| 120 | a | 002BA00587 | adult (?female) | not ident. | tabby | ZZ | 14 x 14 | On front of annular brooch (AD) | A garment, perhaps a veil, of medium-fine tabby. | copper alloy annular (AD), iron knife (AK) | copper alloy object |
| 120 | b | | | not ident. | fibres | - | - | Fibres on one face of knife blade (AK) | The knife may have had a fleece-lined sheath | | |
| 120 | c | Cremated | | not ident. | fibres | - | - | Matted fibres, on one side of knife blade (AG) | Possibly remains of a knife sheath made from skin pelt | fragment of iron knife (AG) | none |
| 121 | | 002BA00601 | juvenile gender unknown | not ident. | tabby | ZZ | 14 x 13 | In two layers, in association with copper alloy object and beads (AD) at throat | None | copper alloy object w. beads (AD) | iron buckle, glass & amber beads, wooden vessel |
| 122 | a | 002BA00594 | juvenile gender unknown | ?hemp | tabby | ZZ | 10 x 10 | On front and back of small-long brooch (AA) at left of shoulder, possibly pinned | None | copper alloy small-long (AA), iron knife (AE) | copper alloy binding w. wood, iron frags |
| 122 | b | | | not ident. | fibres | - | - | Fibres on one face of knife blade (AE). | | | |
| 123 | a | 002BA00606 | adult female | wool | 2/2 diam | ZS | 12-14 x 10 | Diamond pattern repeats every 12Z and 10S threads. On outside of iron buckle (AI) at waist. Probably pinned by brooches (BD,BE) at shoulders. In contact with back square-headed (BC) at right head, but not pinned by it. Also in contact with skull. | An inner garment of unknown material fastened with belt (buckle AI). An outer garment, probably tubular gown, of diamond-pattern twill fastened at shoulders with cognate brooches. A headdress of fine red gauzy fabric, edged with a patterned braid across the forehead and temples | skull, iron buckle (AI), iron ring (AY), iron knife (AZ), copper alloy cognate brooches (BD, BE), beads, copper alloy square-headed brooch (BC) | none |
| 123 | b | | | not ident. | tabby | ZZ | 24 x 24 | Very fine, gauzy fabric. Dyed red with bedstraw or wild madder. A fold of this textile runs above right ear, towards forehead (raw edge towards crown of head). The fold has the tablet braid (below) edging it | | | |
| 123 | c | | | wool | tablet braid type 2a | S-ply x ?l | - | Tablet-woven braid, 9mm wide, stitched to fold of fine tabby (above). | | | |
| 123 | d | | | not ident. | thread | ?plied | - | Knotted thread inside glass bead. | | | |
| 124 | a | 002BA00716 | elderly female | wool | 2/2 | ZS | 12-14 x 10-14 | Outside both annular brooches (AT, AU) at shoulders and on iron ring (AD) at left hip: probably with a fringe at hip | Inner garment of ?wool ZZ twill. Outer gown of ?wool ZZ ?tabby, probably fastened at shoulders by annular brooches. Cloak of wool ZS twill, with fringe, over shoulder brooches and objects at hip. Wool ZS tabby perhaps a bag or bag-lining | copper alloy annular brooches (AT, AU), iron ring (AD), iron knife (AE) | copper alloy pin |
| 124 | b | | | ?wool | 2/2 | ZZ | 16 x 10 | On back of iron ring (AD) at left hip | | | |
| 124 | c | | | wool | tabby | ZS | 12 x 10 | On one face of blade of iron knife (AE) at left hip | | | |
| 124 | d | | | ?wool | ?tabby | ZZ | 12 x 10 | On left collar-bone, in association with annular brooch (AT) | | | |
| 126 | | 002BA00673 | adult male | not ident. | tabby | ZZ | 12-14 x 12 | Along iron rod (AA) at side of body and with iron object and copper-alloy buckle (AC) | None | iron rod (AA), iron object & copper alloy buckle (AC) | iron object, iron knife |
| 127 | a | 002BA00737 | adult (female) | not ident. | tabby | ZZ | 16-18 x 14-16 | Folds pierced by pin of annular brooch (AS), at left shoulder. At hinge of annular brooch at right shoulder | Tubular gown of fine tabby pinned at shoulders by annular brooches. Over this an outer garment, perhaps a cloak, of chevron or diamond twill. A third garment or bag of medium-weight wool twill was found with the purse group at the knees | copper alloy annulars (AS,BM), iron buckle (BS) | copper alloy belt fitting, copper alloy finger ring, copper alloy wrist-clasp frags, iron knife, iron ring, amber & glass necklace |
| 127 | b | | | not ident. | 2/2 chev or diam | ZZ | 10 x 9 | On front of annular brooch (AS) above hinge; and on front of pin of annular brooch (BM) | | | |
| 127 | c | | | not ident. | 2/2 | ZZ | 12 x 10 | On both sides of buckle (BS) with purse group ?by knees | | | |

*Table 9: (continued) catalogue of textile and costume evidence*

| Grave | Sample | Skeleton | Sex (Gender) | Fibre | Weave | Spin | Count | Position of textile in grave | Costume interpretation | Objects with textile | Objects without textile |
|---|---|---|---|---|---|---|---|---|---|---|---|
| 130 | a | 002BA00754 | adult (male) | wool | 2/2 | ZZ | 10-11 x 9-10 | On back and sides of buckle (AA) and on both faces of tweezers (AD) at left waist | Garment of medium-weight wool twill fastened by belt. | iron buckle (AA), iron knives (AA,AC), iron tweezers (AD) | iron spearhead |
| 130 | b | | | animal fibres | fibres | - | - | Animal fibres, possibly too straight for wool, on one face of blade of knife (AA) | Fibres on knife may be sheath or cover | | |
| 132 | a | 002BA00770 | female | ?wool | 2/2 | ZZ | 9 x 6 | Loose and open weave close to copper alloy brooch in purse-group | Remains too jumbled and poorly preserved for interpretation. | iron circular object (AT), ?staple (AU), | copper alloy bracelet |
| 132 | b | | | not ident. | ?tabby | Z x ? | ? | Fine textile on amulet in purse-group and probably also on circular iron object (AT) | | copper alloy annular brooches (BK,BL), copper alloy pendant (BP), iron brooch buckle, iron | |
| 132 | c | | | not ident. | ? | ZS | ? | In purse-group, on one latch-lifter and on iron object (AU) | | object, copper alloy brooch, purse- | |
| 132 | d | | | not ident. | ?braid | ZZ | ? | ?Tubular braid intermittently through purse-group | | group: iron latch-lifters & copper alloy girdle-hanger | |
| 132 | e | | | not ident. | braid | Z3S | - | 3-strand plait worked from 3-ply yarn, at hoop-connector of latch-lifters | | | |
| 132 | f | | | not ident. | knot | Z's | - | Knotted bundle of Z-spun yarn, probably the end of the 3-strand plait (above), at hoop-connector of latch-lifters | | | |
| 132 | g | | | not ident. | cord | Z2S | - | Plied cord in association with circular iron object (AT). Other remains pinned by annular brooches (BK,BL) but weave and spin not identifiable | | | |
| 136 | a | 002BA00796 | adult (male) | not ident. | ? 2/2 | ZZ | 12 x 10 | On front and back of buckle (AA) at waist | Loose garment of medium-weight twill fastened by belt. | iron buckle (AA), iron knife (AC) | 2 iron spearheads, iron ?buckle |
| 136 | b | | | not ident. | fibres | - | - | Near tip of iron knife (AC). | Knife may have had a sheath of fleece or fur | | |
| 137 | | 002BA00799 | juvenile gender unknown | wool | ?tabby | ZS | 6 x 6 | In association with iron buckle (AA) at waist | None | iron buckle (AA) | none |
| 139 | a | 002BA00805 | adult female | wool | 2/2 | ZZ | 9-10 x 8-9 | Pinned by both annular brooches above waist and with latch-lifters below hip | Gown of medium-weight wool twill, pinned by annular brooches above waist. Other textiles only found with purse-group and therefore difficult to interpret. | copper alloy annular brooches (BO,BP), purse-group (BA-BN) - latch-lifters, purse ring | silver decorated disc, copper alloy frag |
| 139 | b | | | wool | 2/2 | ZZ | 13 x 12 | In association with latch-lifters | | | |
| 139 | c | | | wool | diamond twill | ZS | 12 x 10 | On copper-alloy strip with purse-ring. | | | |
| 139 | d | | | wool | braided fringe | Z2S x Z2S | - | Decorative fringe. Loose in association with purse-group | | | |
| 140 | a | 002BA00808 | adult gender unknown | ?hemp | ? | Z x S-ply | ? x 10 | On back of openwork brooch (AA) at throat and at pin-tip, possibly pinned by it | None | copper alloy openwork brooch (AA), large copper alloy ring (AL,AM) | none |
| 140 | b | | | wool | ?twill | ZS | 10 x 7 | In association with large copper-alloy ring at waist | | | |
| 141 | a | 002BA00940 | adult (female) | wool | 2/2 | ZZ | 10 x 10 | In association with annular brooch (AD) at shoulder | Coarse linen inner garment pinned by penannular brooch. Over this a tubular gown of medium weight wool diamond twill, pinned by at least one annular brooch at the shoulder; knife lies on this. Another wool twill at the shoulder may be a cloak. Beads run between undergown and ?cloak | copper alloy annular w. iron strip & amber bead (AD), copper alloy annular (AS), iron knife & iron flake (AR), small copper alloy penannular (BA) | copper alloy vessel, beads, copper alloy ring |
| 141 | b | | | flax | tabby | ZZ | 9-10 x 8 | In folds on back of penannular brooch (BA) and on annular brooch (AD) inside wool ZZ twill | | | |
| 141 | c | | | wool | 2/2 chev or diam | ZS | 10-11 x 12 | Pinned by annular brooch (AS) and on front penannular; also on knife (AR), in association with ?leather | | | |
| 141 | d | | | not ident. | Cord | Z3S | - | Cord, 2mm in diam, between ZZ twill and annular brooch (AD) | | | |

*Table 9:(continued) catalogue of textile and costume evidence*

| Grave | Sample | Skeleton | Sex / (Gender) | Fibre | Weave | Spin | Count | Position of textile in grave | Costume interpretation | Objects with textile | Objects without textile |
|---|---|---|---|---|---|---|---|---|---|---|---|
| 143 | a | 002BA00924 | adult (female) | wool | 2/2 | ZZ | 8 x 8 | On outer face of iron buckle plate outside medium twill. Also on latch-lifters at waist | Difficult to interpret: at least three garments of wool twill, but not clear which was clasped by brooches and which fastened by belt. The loose, open tabby is probably the remains of a veil | iron latch-lifters keys (AP), large iron buckle (AO), copper alloy annular (AF), copper alloy cruciform brooch (AG), copper alloy disc brooch (AH), copper alloy wrist-clasps (AL,AM) | beads, copper alloy ring |
| 143 | b | | | wool | 2/2 | ZZ | 10-12 x 10 | On outer face of iron buckle plate, behind coarser twill (above). On back of annular brooch (AF), cruciform brooch (AG) and disc brooch (AH) | | | |
| 143 | c | | | wool | 2/2 | ZZ | 14 x 14 | On front of wrist-clasps (AL,AM) | | | |
| 143 | d | | | wool | tabby | ZZ | 9 x 8 | Loose open weave on front of cruciform brooch | | | |
| 144 | | 002BA00820 | adult male | not ident. | ?tabby | ZZ | ? | On front of belt fitting (AC) at left waist | None | iron belt fitting (AC) | iron knife, spearhead |
| 146 | | 002BA00834 | gender unknown | not ident. | 2/2 | SS | 10 x 10 | On iron object (AA) | None | iron object (AA) | none |
| 147 | a | 002BA00904 | adult (female) | flax | tabby | ZZ | 14 x 14 | Behind square-headed brooch (AI) below throat but not pinned by it; behind ZS twill. Possibly also in association with annular brooch (AA) by left thigh | Inner garment of medium-fine linen tabby reaching from neck to at least thighs: this is probably the sleeved underdress, which has tablet-woven cuffs fastened by wrist-clasps. A cloak of matted wool twill, pinned by square-headed brooch, perhaps bordered with linen braid. A tubular gown with tablet-woven edgings pinned by copper alloy annular and iron penannular brooches. | copper alloy annular (AA,AJ), copper alloy wrist-clasps (AD,AE), copper alloy square-headed brooch (AI), iron penannular (AK) | none |
| 147 | b | | | wool | 2/2 | ZS | ? | Matted fabric, pinned by square-headed brooch (AI), over linen tabby. Possibly also in association with penannular (AK) on breast | | | |
| 147 | c | | | ?wool | tablet type 1a | Z x Z2S | 10 warp cords x ? | On back of both pairs of wrist-clasps (AD,AE). Secured to them with S-ply threads on AD and Z-spun on AE | | | |
| 147 | d | | | wool | tablet type 1a | Z2S x ? | 12 warp cords x ? | Two pieces both pinned by annular brooch (AJ) below shoulder; two more looped around pin of penannular (AK) | | | |
| 147 | e | | | plant stem fibre | ?tablet | S-ply x ? | ? | Possibly another tablet braid, pinned by square-headed brooch (AI) | | | |
| 152 | a | 002BA00909 | adult (female) | wool | 2/2 | ZZ | 14-16 x 14 | Below purse-group by legs; bordered by tablet braid type 1b | Most of the evidence comes from the jumbled area of the purse-group and is therefore difficult to interpret. Tentatively, an inner garment of medium-weight ZZ twill (perhaps the sleeved underdress). A second garment, (possibly the tubular gown) of medium-fine wool ZZ twill, with tablet-woven border (the annular brooches pin the tablet-woven braids but it is not clear which fabrics these braids are bordering. A veil of fine linen tabby hanging down in thick folds over the annular brooches. An outermost fabric - a cloak or cover to the burial - of matted ZS twill. The ribbed wool tabby may be the lining for the leather purse with ivory ring. It lies below the ZS twill (the cloak or cover) inside folds of the wool twill thought to be the tubular gown. | copper alloy annulars (AR,BA), copper alloy wrist-clasp (AG), girdle-hangers, knife, ivory ring, latch-lifters (AH-AI), strap ends | copper alloy wrist-clasp |
| 152 | b | | | not ident. | tablet type 1b | Z2S x ? | 10 warp cords by ? | Selvedge to finer ZZ twill (above) | | | |
| 152 | c | | | not ident. | 2/2 | ZZ | 12-14 x 10-12 | In layers behind finer ZZ twill (above) and purse-group; also above objects at edges of purse-group. Also on wrist-clasp (AG) at left waist | | | |
| 152 | d | | | wool | 2/2 (poss diam or chev) | ZS | ? | Matted fabric above purse-group | | | |
| 152 | e | | | not ident. | tablet type 2b | Z x ? | 16 warp cords x 10 weft | Under purse-group | | | |
| 152 | f | | | wool | tabby | ? x Z2S | 7 x 18 | Ribbed fabric in folds below purse group | | | |
| 152 | g | | | flax | tabby | ZZ | 18 x 16 | In thick layers of folds on front of annular brooch (AR) and probably also (BA), both at shoulders | | | |
| 152 | h | | | wool | tablet type 2b | Z2S x Z2S | ? | Pinned by annular brooch (BA & prob. also AR) | | | |
| 152 | i | | | wool | cords | Z2S | - | 9-10 parallel cords, one with knot, over girdle-hanger (AI) and latch-lifter (AK) | | | |

*Table 9:(continued) catalogue of textile and costume evidence*

| Grave | Sample | Skeleton | Sex / (Gender) | Fibre | Weave | Spin | Count | Position of textile in grave | Costume interpretation | Objects with textile | Objects without textile |
|---|---|---|---|---|---|---|---|---|---|---|---|
| 154 | a | 002BA00917 | juvenile gender unknown | not ident. | 2/2 | ZZ | 8 x 7 | On back at edge of one copper alloy brooch at shoulder | Linen tubular gown pinned at shoulders. | two small copper alloy brooches (AP, AQ) | none |
| 154 | b | | | flax | ? | ZZ | ? | Probably pinned by second copper alloy brooch at other shoulder | Beads strung between shoulder brooches | | |
| 154 | c | | | not ident. | cord | Z2S | - | Plied cord wrapped 3 times around pin of first brooch | | | |
| 157 | | 002BA00933 | sub-adult (?male) | not ident. | ? 2/2 | ZZ | ? | On blade and handle of knife at right waist | None | iron knife (AO) | none |
| 160 | a | 002BA00967 | adult gender unknown | wool | 2/2 | ZZ | 16 x 16 | In two layers on back of buckle & buckle plate (AD). Leather in association | Garment of fine wool twill fastened at waist by leather belt. | iron knife (AC), iron buckle (AD) | none |
| 160 | b | | | not ident. | ? 2/2 | ZZ | - | Coarser ?twill between knife and leather sheath | Knife appears to have a wrapping inside sheath | | |
| 161 | | 002BA00970 | adult gender unknown | not ident. | cord | Z's | - | Bundle of Z-spun threads given slight twist in S-direction over ?handle of ?knife (AA). | Possibly part of binding of knife-handle. | horn-handled ?knife (AA) | none |
| 163 | a | 002BA00976 | adult (female) | ?wool | 2/2 | ZS | 14 x 12-14 | On back of both annular brooches (AW, AX) below chin: pinned by at least one (AX). Also on rivet (AH) at waist | Tubular gown of medium-fine ?wool twill pinned by annular brooches and possibly edged with plaits. Two fine linen fabrics were worn outside this gown – the tabby probably the veil and the diamond-patterned the shawl | iron rivets (AH), copper alloy annulars (AW,AX) | 2 silver bells, copper alloy buckle & iron knife |
| 163 | b | | | flax | 2/2 diam | ZZ | 14 x 12 | Outside other textiles on front of pin of annular brooch (AX) | | | |
| 163 | c | | | flax | tabby | ZZ | 14 x 8-12 | On front of both annular brooches (AW, AX), behind diamond twill | | | |
| 163 | d | | | not ident. | threads | S | - | Threads around ring (AV) | | | |
| 163 | e | | | not ident. | plait | ? | - | 1.5mm diam. over pin, under hinge of annular brooch (AW) | | | |
| 163 | f | | | not ident. | tubular braid | ? | - | 2mm diam. around pin of annular brooch (AX) | | | |
| 164 | a | 002BA00980 | adult male | animal fibres | fibres | - | - | On socket of spearhead (AA) by head | None | fe spearhead (AA), | iron buckle |
| 164 | b | | | not ident. | ? 2/2 | ZZ | 8 x 7 | On one face of knife blade (AB) at waist | Knife appears to have a wrapping inside sheath | iron knife (AB) | |
| 165 | | 002BA00999 | adult female | not ident. | ? 2/2 | ZZ | ? | On front, over pin of annular brooch (AN) | None | frag. of copper alloy annular brooch (AN) | none |
| 167 | a | 002BA01082 | adult female | not ident. | 2/2 | ZZ | 11-12 x 10-11 | Along latch-lifters at left hips | Tubular gown of coarse ZS textile bordered with tablet braid pinned at shoulders by annular brooches. | iron chatelaine (BJ-BM), 2 copper alloy annular brooches (CD,CE), pin with spangle (CF), | copper alloy tweezers, copper alloy disc, buckle |
| 167 | b | | | not ident. | Tabby | ZZ | 14 x 12-14 | Fine open weave, on front of both annulars and on shank of copper alloy pin and pin with spangle below chin: over other textiles | Another garment of medium-weight ZZ twill, the underdress or cloak, in association with latch-lifters. Fine open-weave veil over all | copper alloy pin, bucket pendants & beads (BG,BI,CG) | |
| 167 | c | | | not ident. | 2/2 | ZS | ? coarse | Over hinge of one annular brooch behind tabby | | | |
| 167 | d | | | not ident. | tablet braid type 1a | Z2S x Z2S | 8 cords x 12 weft | Braid in loop over pin of annular brooch. Probably edging to a coarse textile behind the braid (possibly the ZS twill) | | | |
| 167 | e | | | not ident. | cord | S-cabled | - | String for amber beads | | | |

*Table 9:(continued) catalogue of textile and costume evidence*

| Grave | Sample | Skeleton | Sex / (Gender) | Fibre | Weave | Spin | Count | Position of textile in grave | Costume interpretation | Objects with textile | Objects without textile |
|---|---|---|---|---|---|---|---|---|---|---|---|
| 173 | a | 002BA01187 | adult (female) | wool | 2/2 | ZS | 10 x 12 | Pinned by cruciform brooch (AH) at neck. Probably also on front of buckle (AO) at upper waist | Tubular gown of medium-weight wool twill pinned at shoulders with annular brooches and fastened by belt with iron buckle. Over this gown another medium-weight wool twill fastened by cruciform brooch - probably a cloak. A tabby weave ?wool garment was also worn, the underdress or veil | copper alloy cruciform (AH), copper alloy annulars (AJ,AL), iron knife & latch-lifters (AN), iron buckle (AO) | wrist-clasps, beads, wire ring |
| 173 | b | | | wool | 2/2 | ZZ | 12 x 12 | Pinned by annular brooches (AJ,AL) at shoulders. Also on one face of latch-lifter (AN) by left hip and on back of belt-plate of buckle (AO) at upper waist | | | |
| 173 | c | | | ?wool | tabby | ZZ | 12 x 11 | On tip of pin of annular brooch (AJ) | | | |
| 175 | a | 002F 00009 | adult (female) | flax | tabby | ZZ | 14-15 x 11-12 | On front of both annular brooches (AH,AM) at throat | Garment of medium weight twill, possibly underdress, fastened by belt. | copper alloy annulars (AH,AM), iron buckle (AP) | copper alloy pin with spangle, amber & glass necklace |
| 175 | b | | | not ident. | 2/2 | ZS | 8 x 10 | On pin of annular brooch (AM) at right throat. | Tubular gown of coarser twill, fastened by annular brooch. Veil of medium-fine linen tabby. | | |
| 175 | c | | | not ident. | 2/2 | ZZ | 12 x 10 | On buckle (AP) at waist | | | |
| 176 | a | 002F 00012 | (male) | not ident. | 2/2 | ZZ | 6 x 5 | Over socket of spearhead (AA) on upper body | Tunic of wool diamond twill, fastened at waist by belt. Very coarse twill on spearhead may be wrapping fabric or cloak or grave cover | bent iron spearhead (AA), iron buckle (AB) | iron knife |
| 176 | b | | | not ident. | ZS | ZS | 10 x 8 | On blade of spearhead (AA) and back of buckle (AB) at waist | | | |
| 177 | a | 002F 00013 | (female) | not ident. | 2/2 | ZZ | 8 x 8 | On back of cruciform brooch (AA), on upper chest, probably pinned by it | Sleeved underdress with braided cuffs. Tubular gown perhaps of medium-weight wool twill. Third garment of coarser twill, perhaps a cloak fastened by cruciform brooch. Coarse tabby veil. | copper alloy cruciform (AA), copper alloy annulars (AD,DA), copper alloy wrist-clasps (AE,DD), copper alloy beads (AF) | copper alloy wire loop, amber & glass necklace, iron fragments |
| 177 | b | | | not ident. | tabby | ZZ | 9 x 9 | On front of annular brooch (AD) on left shoulder | | | |
| 177 | c | | | not ident. | tablet weave type 1a | ZZ | 12 warp cords x 12 weft | On back of wrist-clasps (AE) and perhaps also wrist-clasps (DD) | | | |
| 177 | d | | | not ident. | 2/2 | ZZ | 12 x 9 | In association with copper alloy cylinders (AF) under cruciform brooch | | | |
| 177 | e | | | not ident. | cord | Z2S2Z | - | Fine cabled cord, 1mm diameter, in association with copper alloy cylinders (AF) | | | |
| 177 | f | | | plant fibre | cord | S2Z | - | Close to pin of annular brooch (DA) | | | |
| 179 | a | 008AA00089 | adult male | ?wool | tabby | ZS | 6-7 x 6 | On inside of shield-grip (AY). Similar on iron ferrule (AD), with a straw or fibre binding | A loose garment of medium-weight fabric, fastened at waist with leather belt. A coarser ?wool tabby bound the grip of the shield - and probably also the iron ferrule. Some slight evidence for a fleece or sheepskin laid over the burial | iron shield boss (AC), iron ferrule (AD), iron staple (AF), iron buckle (AN), iron shield-grip (AY) | iron knife, 3 staples |
| 179 | b | | | not ident. | ? | Z x ? | ? | Finer textile loosely around iron buckle (AN), at right side of waist | | | |
| 179 | c | | | not ident. | ?fleece | - | - | Over shield boss (AC). | | | |
| 180 | a | 008AA00088 | adult (female) | wool | 2/2 | ZZ | 12 x 12 | Pinned by small annular (CC). Bound to wrist-clasps (CD) by cords. In association with leatherwork. | Inner garment or garments of medium-weight wool twill, fastened by small annular brooch; wrist-clasps bound to this garment. An outer garment, a cloak or blanket of coarser wool twill. Bag or sleeve-cuffs of leather | iron annular (AA), iron knife (CB), copper alloy small annular & copper alloy tweezers (CC), copper alloy wrist-clasps (CD,CE), iron suspension ring & knife (CB) | amber & glass beads |
| 180 | b | | | wool | 2/2 | ZZ | 8-10 x 10 | Over wrist-clasps (CE), annular brooch & tweezers (CC); and probably also over iron suspension ring (CB) and leather knife sheath (CB) | | | |
| 180 | c | | | not ident. | cords | Z2S | - | Wrapped around one half of wrist-clasp (CD), binding the clasp to the finer of the two twills | | | |

*Table 9:(continued) catalogue of textile and costume evidence*

| Grave | Sample | Skeleton | Sex / (Gender) | Fibre | Weave | Spin | Count | Position of textile in grave | Costume interpretation | Objects with textile | Objects without textile |
|---|---|---|---|---|---|---|---|---|---|---|---|
| 181 | a | 008AA00095 | probably adult | not ident. | ? | Z x ? | ? | Overlying leather knife sheath (AC) at waist | None | iron knife (AC), iron buckle (AD) | none |
| 181 | b | | gender unknown | not ident. | ?fleece | - | - | In association with iron buckle (AD) at waist | | | |
| 183 | | 008AA00112 | adult (male) | ?wool | 2/2 | ZS | 8-10 x 7-9 | On one side of spearhead (AL) and the outer face of shield-grip (AS), both on upper body | Coarse, loosely woven ?wool twill, possibly a blanket or cover | iron spearhead (AL), iron shield-grip (AS) | iron knife, iron shield boss, iron ferrule, copper alloy pin |
| 184 | | 008AA00168 | adult female (?male) | not ident. | ? | ZS | ? | Poorly preserved textile found with spearhead (AD) and knife (AI). | None | iron spearhead (AD), iron staple (AE), iron buckle (AH), iron knife (AI) | iron shield boss & fittings, iron staple, iron buckle |
| 185 | a | 008AA00167 | (male) | not ident. | ?2/2 | ZZ | 10 x 10 | On back of small buckle (AC); belt of leather | A garment of medium-coarse twill fastened with a leather belt. A second | small iron buckle (AC), iron knife (AD) | iron ferrule, iron spearhead |
| 185 | b | | | not ident. | 2/2 | ZZ | 6 x 6 | A fold on one side of leather knife sheath (AD) | garment of coarser twill | | |

*Table 9: (continued) catalogue of textile and costume evidence*

# The human bones

## Analysis and interpretation of the skeletal material

by Margaret Cox

## Background to the human bone report

The human bone recovered during the excavations undertaken by John Dent, Site 1HE, and much of the material recovered from the trial trenches on Site 2, 2B, 2C and 2F, was examined and reported on by Jean Dawes. Subsequently the full assemblage, derived from all areas, was examined by Margaret Cox. Where the bone was examined by both specialists the reports tally closely and therefore only the full report by Margaret Cox is included here.

## Summary

Skeletal remains considered to represent between 121 and 193 inhumations and 13 cremations have been examined in order to retrieve demographic, anthropological and pathological information. Analysis of these remains has been impaired by the condition of the skeletons; over 50% survived only as fragments of bone or teeth. Of the inhumations, 55 cannot be classified as either adult or juvenile. One hundred and four adults and 34 juveniles could be identified. Of the adults, 23 are female and 1 possibly female; 15 are male and 4 possibly male.

No perinatal deaths and only one infant death are represented. The most likely explanation for this is burial practice. Juvenile mortality was greatest between the ages of 5 and 6 years and from 11 to16. If dental attrition provides meaningful ages at death, adults appear to have died most frequently between the age of 25 and 35.

Dental and oral health was better than at most Anglo-Saxon sites. Apart from childhood anaemia, there is no evidence to suggest nutritional deficiency. Fracture rates appear to have been very low although there is other evidence of physical trauma. It seems likely that many adolescents were employed in fairly arduous physical labour.

The most interesting pathology is a possible stroke causing hemiplegia. This affected a young woman aged about 25 at death (G114). That she survived this condition for long enough for her skeleton to respond is testimony to a society in which the disabled were accepted and supported.

## The inhumations
### Preservation
Given the importance of the Anglian site at West Heslerton, it is unfortunate that the burial environment of much of the cemetery has proved incompatible with good preservation of human bone.

In archaeological contexts bone survival is affected by factors such as decomposition by bacteria, moulds and invertebrates; dispersal by vertebrates; chemical action such as soil water and acids; disturbance by other grave cuts; recovery during exhumation and post-excavation processes such as washing and sorting (Waldron 1987).

At West Heslerton, where bone has survived the cortex has frequently eroded. This has almost certainly resulted in the loss of pathological information. Generally teeth survived in better condition than bone, although in many cases the roots had been destroyed. It was not unusual, among the juveniles in particular, for only dentition to survive.

The preservation of each skeleton is described in two ways: first in terms of overall completeness for each burial number as described in Table 10, and secondly in terms of the representation of skeletal elements as shown in Table 11. For skeletal completeness, each individual was allocated a grade ranging from 1 to 6. Grade 1 indicates that only a small number of bone or tooth fragments survived. Grades 2 to 5 indicate that less than 25%, 50%, 75% and 100% respectively survived and grade 6 that the skeleton was complete.

Material from a total of 195 contexts identified in the

field as probably human bone were examined. This number includes two contexts 1A030, 1A011, both cleaning spits of blown sand from which the material was animal bone and a third 2BA774 the burrowed fill of G133 which also comprised animal bone. In addition to these, animal bone was found with human bone in four contexts 1A055, 2BA992 both windblown deposits sealing earlier features, 2BA1156 (G170 which had been cut by a modern sheep burial) and 2BA684 (G119); the latter context also contained and a single animal tooth. In the case of many from the grade 1 category, bone fragments were often so small and nondescript that it was not always possible to deduce whether the fragments were human or animal. These cases were not excluded from analysis of preservation.

In three cases a single context contained material from more than one individual. A sub-adult and a middle-aged adult in one bag were renumbered as 2BA172A and 2BA172B (G81). Grave 133, 2BA775 contained an adult female accompanied with a fragment of a juvenile femur and 2BA159 (G102) contained fragments clearly derived from 2BA242 (G101) buried in the same grave.

Contexts 2B4 and 2B5 contained material from the same individual, which had been incorrectly numbered in the field 2B4 representing the cut of G77, rather than the fill. Each consisted only of several incompletely calcified permanent teeth at the same stage of development. When combined these formed an almost complete set of dentition.

Six contexts included fragments of inhumations and cremated bone, 1A55 and 2BA656 both representing cleaning deposits incorporating residual and disturbed material, in the case of 2BA655 this material was mostly contained within a modern plough mark. In the four remaining cases, 2BA159 (G102), 2BA583 (G120), 2BA606 (G123) and 2BA1156 (G170) the material is also thought to be residual. Due to the small size of the cremated fragments, it was possible in only one case (2BA606 (G123), a single foot phalanx) to be certain that it was human.

Five other contexts, all upper fills of ditches or plough derived features, 1A38, 2BA668, 2BA662, 2BA654, and 2BA630 contained fragments of cremated bone. These were heavily calcined and have been excluded from the analysis. None of these could be considered as a 'whole' cremation; it seems likely that they represent the remains of redeposited cremations and may not reflect individual burials.

Table 11 illustrates that over half of the inhumations survived only as small fragments of tooth and or bone. Despite this, the material could survive extremely well. The hyoid bone and ossified thyroid cartilage survived in 2BA980 (G164) and also in an Early Bronze Age burial 2BA241. An incomplete ear bone, an incus, was

| Grade | Number | % |
|---|---|---|
| 1 | 98 | 51.0 |
| 2 | 60 | 31.2 |
| 3 | 14 | 7.3 |
| 4 | 12 | 6.3 |
| 5 | 8 | 4.2 |
| 6 | 0 | 0.0 |
| Total | 192 | 100 |

*Table 10: completeness of the West Heslerton inhumations*

recovered in the case of 2BA716 (G124) an adult female.

Proximity to bronze or copper objects promoted good survival. In several cases, for example 2BA940 (G141), green-stained bone survived in better condition than normal bone and occasionally, for example 2BA539 (G120), only green-stained bone and green-stained dentition survived. The reason for this is that copper salts produced during the corrosion process form an effective bactericide.

Faunal action was evident in two cases; 2B007 (G67), an adult of unknown sex and 2BA575 (G110), an adult female. The shaft of a tibia and the left femur respectively have what appear to be teeth marks incised horizontally across the shaft of the bone. Such activity could reflect either delayed burial or shallow graves.

Table 11 illustrates the representation of skeletal elements. Each bone was recorded not only in terms of representation (N) but also graded from 1 to 6 using the same criteria as in Table 10. For such elements as ribs and phalanges, the number represented was scored and not the state of preservation.

Very occasionally the condition of a bone was such that it could not be 'sided' with confidence. In such cases the bone was attributed to the left side, and this has resulted in an artificial side bias in some elements.

Apart from environmental factors affecting preservation, the representation of skeletal elements can be affected by failure to retrieve certain bones by inexperienced archaeologists, particularly in complex burial matrices. Small bones such as distal phalanges and carpals are frequently under-represented in skeletal samples, often in cases when the rest of the skeleton is recovered. Similarly, bones occupying an anterior position in the body such as the patellae and the sternum can be significantly under-represented (Waldron 1987). The reason for this is not apparent.

It has been demonstrated ( J Keilly pers comm) that in some burial environments sieving in the areas of hand and foot bones, and in juvenile and infant burials can significantly increase recovery rates of small bones. The

| Bone */Grade | No. | 1 | 2 | 3 | 4 | 5 | 6 |
|---|---|---|---|---|---|---|---|
| Skull | 121 | 44 | 23 | 29 | 13 | 12 | |
| Mandible | 74 | 8 | 18 | 15 | 18 | 13 | 2 |
| L. clavicle | 33 | 6 | 7 | 6 | 7 | 6 | 1 |
| R. clavicle | 29 | 4 | 2 | 8 | 7 | 8 | |
| L. scapula | 38 | 15 | 9 | 11 | 3 | | |
| R. scapula | 26 | 7 | 7 | 10 | 2 | | |
| Manubrium | 7 | 1 | 1 | 1 | 1 | 2 | 1 |
| Sternum | 6 | | 2 | 2 | | 1 | 1 |
| L. humerus | 62 | 14 | 6 | 15 | 14 | 13 | |
| R. humerus | 53 | 14 | 12 | 9 | 12 | 5 | 2 |
| L. radius | 38 | 13 | 4 | 9 | 5 | 6 | 1 |
| R. radius | 35 | 14 | 5 | 8 | 2 | 5 | 1 |
| L. ulna | 35 | 11 | 7 | 6 | 6 | 4 | 1 |
| R. ulna | 33 | 14 | 4 | 5 | 5 | 4 | 1 |
| L. innominate | 59 | 30 | 12 | 7 | 6 | 4 | |
| R. innominate | 58 | 24 | 13 | 13 | 7 | 1 | |
| Sacrum | 26 | 10 | 9 | 4 | 2 | 1 | |
| L. femur | 90 | 21 | 14 | 14 | 24 | 16 | 1 |
| R. femur | 89 | 10 | 16 | 26 | 23 | 13 | 1 |
| L. patella | 28 | 2 | 8 | 3 | 3 | 10 | 2 |
| R. patella | 16 | 1 | 1 | 6 | 2 | 4 | 2 |
| L. tibia | 81 | 23 | 17 | 15 | 16 | 10 | |
| R. tibia | 67 | 16 | 10 | 17 | 13 | 11 | |
| L. fibula | 54 | 25 | 11 | 8 | 7 | 3 | |
| R. fibula | 43 | 16 | 6 | 10 | 9 | 2 | |
| L. calcaneus | 48 | 9 | 14 | 7 | 13 | 5 | |
| R. calcaneus | 39 | 5 | 9 | 8 | 10 | 7 | |
| L. talus | 46 | 7 | 5 | 6 | 13 | 15 | |
| R. talus | 46 | 5 | 7 | 4 | 14 | 16 | |

| Bone */Grade | No | 1 | 2 | 3 | 4 | 5 | 6 | 7 | 8 | 9 | 10 | 11 | 12 |
|---|---|---|---|---|---|---|---|---|---|---|---|---|---|
| Cervical vertebrae | 48 | 12 | 12 | 3 | 6 | 3 | 3 | 9 | | | | | |
| Thoracic vertebrae | 47 | 9 | 11 | 2 | 2 | 4 | | 5 | 2 | 2 | 1 | 1 | 8 |
| Lumbar vertebrae | 27 | 9 | 5 | 2 | 1 | 10 | | | | | | | |
| L. ribs | 21 | 4 | 1 | 2 | 2 | | 2 | 2 | | | 5 | 2 | 1 |
| R. ribs | 22 | 5 | 1 | 2 | 2 | | 2 | 1 | 2 | 1 | 2 | 2 | 2 |
| ?ribs | 30 | 21 | 6 | 2 | 1 | | | | | | | | |

| Bone */Grade | No | 1 | 2 | 3 | 4 | 5 | 6 | 7 | 8 | 9 | 10 | 11 | 12 | 13 | 14 | 15 | 16 | 17 | 18 |
|---|---|---|---|---|---|---|---|---|---|---|---|---|---|---|---|---|---|---|---|
| Carpals | 25 | 3 | 1 | 2 | | 2 | 6 | | 5 | | 1 | | | 3 | 2 | | | | |
| Metacarpals | 22 | 4 | 3 | 6 | 1 | 2 | 2 | 2 | | 1 | 1 | | | | | | | | |
| Phalanges | 26 | 5 | 3 | 5 | 2 | 2 | | 2 | 2 | 1 | 1 | | 1 | 1 | | | | 1 | |
| Distal Phalanges | 13 | 5 | 6 | 1 | | | | | | 1 | | | | | | | | | |
| Tarsals | 34 | 6 | 6 | 5 | 3 | 2 | | 2 | 1 | 3 | 4 | 1 | 1 | | | | | | |
| Metatarsals | 30 | 8 | 2 | 1 | 4 | 1 | | 5 | 4 | 4 | 1 | | | | | | | | |
| Phalanges | 16 | 5 | 4 | 2 | 3 | 2 | | | | | | | | | | | | | |
| Distal Phalanges | 4 | 3 | | | | | | | | | | | | | | | | | |
| Sesamoid | 8 | 5 | 3 | | | | | | | | | | | | | | | | |

*Table 11: representation of skeletal elements. * = the number of each element recovered.*

extremely fragile state of much of the West Heslerton material was such, however, that sieving was considered to be potentially destructive and finger sifting was employed as a less abrasive measure (D Powlesland pers comm).

Those elements which appear to be under-represented in this sample are small bones from the hands and feet in particular. These may have been missed in the burial matrix. The manubrium, sternum and patellae are also notably few in number. This possibly reflects their anterior position.

Estimation of the minimum number of individuals represented by a cemetery sample is traditionally based on the skeletal element recovered in greatest numbers combined with contextual information. At West Heslerton the skull, though usually in a fragmentary and incomplete state, is represented most frequently. The minimum number of individuals represented skeletally is 121. Based on the earlier discussion, the maximum number represented from inhumations with surviving bone is 192. The reality probably approximates nearer the latter figure.

# Demographic profile

## The sex of the adults

The sexing of the adults from West Heslerton was based primarily on secondary sex characteristics which are manifest only after puberty. As advocated by the Workshop of European Anthropologists (1980) the criteria used in this analysis are based on cranial and pelvic differences between males and females. These methods have recently been tested blind on a sample of known sex (Molleson and Cox forthcoming) and proved to be accurate in over 97%.

The condition of the West Heslerton material is such that very few adults could be sexed on the basis of secondary sex characteristics. Nineteen adults were considered to be female with one further possible female. Eleven adults (aged 18 and over) and one sub-adult (aged approximately 12 to 17) were sexed as male with four further adults being probable males. A total of 69 further inhumations were considered to be adult but could not be sexed due to poor preservation.

Statistical analysis (unpaired t-tests at 95% confidence limits) of the differences between the sexed samples in several measurements indicates that, despite the small sample sizes, the femoral head, humeri head and mandibular condyle diameters are significantly different. The results are described in Table 12.

Using these dimorphic measurements, a further 8 adults were sexed, the combined totals for each sex being 23 female adults plus 1 further probable female, 15 male adults, 1 male sub-adult (sexed on the basis of a very tight sciatic notch) and 4 further probable male adults, leaving 61 adults unsexed. This represents a total of 104 adults. Because of the small size of the sexed sample and the large percentage unsexed no comment will be made on the apparently disproportionate sex ratio, as it is unlikely to be representative.

Given the comparatively good preservation of the teeth it was decided to examine the possibility that certain dental measurements might prove to be sexually dimorphic in this sample. Despite the fact that tooth size is genetically determined to an uncertain extent and can be modified by environmental factors such as maternal nutrition (Hillson 1986), dental measurements have been shown to be sexually dimorphic in several samples. If dental measurements proved to be significantly different in the sexed sample, this method of sexing could add to the demographic data of the sample, and given the good preservation of permanent dentition among the juveniles it had the potential of assigning sex to this group.

The mesiodistal and buccolingual diameters of each permanent tooth crown were measured (after Goose 1963). Repeatability was evaluated and proved to be difficult in the upper and lower 8s and the upper 7s. As is traditional, the measurements were taken from the left side or the right side if the left was absent. Unpaired t-tests were applied to the male and female samples and the results of significantly different dimensions, those close to significantly different dimensions and those close to significance are shown in Table 13 (95% confidence limits).

It was decided that as repeatability was difficult with the 8s, its use in sexing would be unwise. Histograms plotting the distribution of the upper and lower buccolingual 6 and the lower buccolingual 3 illustrated that with such small sample sizes the only measurements that could be used with any degree of confidence were as follows: with the upper 6 only those below 10.4mm could be considered as female, with the lower 6 only those below 10mm could confidently be classed as female and with the lower 3 only those of 8mm plus could be classified as male. The degree of overlap elsewhere in the range was such as to question the validity of the use of the means.

Using the upper 6, 18 females were classified, 4 of which were juveniles using the lower 6, 18 individuals were classified as female (8 juveniles and 1 sub-adult), 6 of these having been classified as female using the upper 6. These two dimensions added a total of 30 females to those classified using methods described above. Using the lower 3, a further 12 individuals were classified as male (including one juvenile and one sub-adult). However, three of these are classified as females using the 6s! Given

| Tooth | Sex | N | Mean | SE mean | T | DF | P |
|---|---|---|---|---|---|---|---|
| Maxilla | | | | | | | |
| 6B/L | F | 18 | 10.70 | 0.132 | 2.378 | 25 | 0.0254 |
| 6B/L | M | 9 | 11.24 | 0.187 | | | |
| Mandible | | | | | | | |
| 8M/D | F | 11 | 9.86 | 0.249 | 2.860 | 17 | 0.0108 |
| 8M/D | M | 8 | 10.96 | 0.292 | | | |
| 8B/L | F | 11 | 9.39 | 0.221 | 2.685 | 16 | 0.0163 |
| 8B/L | M | 7 | 10.34 | 0.227 | | | |
| 6B/L | F | 11 | 10.23 | 0.192 | 1.937 | 17 | 0.0695 |
| 6B/L | M | 8 | 10.80 | 0.225 | | | |
| 3B/L | F | 12 | 7.12 | 0.183 | 2.008 | 19 | 0.0591 |
| 3B/L | M | 9 | 7.68 | 0.211 | | | |

*Table 13: permanent dentition dimorphism in the males and females from West Heslerton*

| Measurement | Sex | No. | Mean (cm) | SE mean | T | DF | P |
|---|---|---|---|---|---|---|---|
| Femoral head | M | 6 | 48.6 | 8.99315 | | | |
| | F | 11 | 43.2 | 6.64188 | 4.838 | 15 | 0.0002 |
| Humerus head | M | 2 | 48.2 | 6.56379 | | | |
| | F | 3 | 40.9 | 5.35931 | 8.674 | 3 | 0.0032 |
| Mandibular condyle | M | 3 | 23.0 | 1.26932 | | | |
| | F | 4 | 17.9 | 1.09926 | 3.052 | 5 | 0.0284 |

*Table 12: sexually dimorphic measurements in the West Heslerton sample*

the disparity in these results it was decided not to use this data for demographic purposes but to report it for its considerable methodological interest.

## Age at death

Determination of the age at death of human skeletal material is dependent upon two processes. In the case of infants, juveniles, sub-adults and young adults, age is assessed by rates of development and growth. The main criterion used in this study was dental calcification (Ubelaker 1989); this was determined by the good survival of the dentition. Only once was a long bone length (Maresh 1955) used in conjunction. It was fortunate that a dental age could also be assigned to this individual, as the two ages differed by two years. The dental age was greater than the long bone length; this is not an unusual finding and has been observed elsewhere (Cox 1989). Skeletal maturation was used in conjunction when assigning ages to both sub-adults and young adults.

The most striking thing about the demographic profile of the children is the lack of foetal, perinatal (from the 28th week of gestation to seven days after birth) or infant (from one week to two years) bones or teeth. Archaeologically, there is also a lack of infant-sized graves (D Powlesland pers comm). Only one example of a one-year-old was seen 2BA601 (G121) and the condition of this material was particularly poor, making the age attribution rather tentative.

It has been asserted that infant and juvenile burials do not survive in cemetery samples as a result of their incompletely calcified bones (Gordon and Buikstra 1981). This theory ignores the fact that the bones of the young have comparatively high collagen content and that this should compensate for the lack of calcification. An evaluation of age bias in the skeletons exhumed from Christ Church, Spitalfields (Molleson and Cox 1990), has shown that bone preservation is greater in infants and gradually decreases with age.

The preservation of infant bones from earlier contexts at West Heslerton (D Powlesland pers comm) suggests that the lack of infant bones from the Anglian contexts indicates that few if any were buried in the excavated areas of the cemetery.

It has been suggested that perhaps none of the infants from the settlement died during the perinatal period or during infancy. This hypothesis is implausible in view of the fact that high infant mortality is a feature of contemporary third world populations and is attested both historically and archaeologically in both urban and rural contexts (Hassan 1981).

A lack or low frequency of perinatal and infant burials seems to be a feature of many Anglo-Saxon cemeteries. For example, at the School Street site in Ipswich (S Mays pers comm) only 2 out of 95 burials were aged below

five years. At Empingham in Rutland (S Mays pers comm) no infants aged below one year were apparent among a sample of 151 skeletons. Infant deaths at Kingsworthy are 4 (16% of the juveniles and sub-adults) and at North Elmham Park 3 (7.7%: Wells 1982). All of these samples are small, but if the results are representative they reflect either changed burial practice or a marked change in infant mortality rates between the Roman and Anglo-Saxon periods.

All known Romano-British cemetery sites of consequence have produced skeletal evidence of perinatal and infant deaths; in fact, the evidence for perinatal mortality alone is usually higher than that for both perinatal and infant mortality in Anglo-Saxon sites. One Roman site with low perinatal mortality (6%) is Poundbury Camp in Dorset (Molleson forthcoming). Most Roman cemeteries have perinatal mortality rates of over 20% (Cirencester 25.4%, Wells 1982, and Ancaster 28.6%, Cox 1989). No startling changes in the aetiology of infectious disease or improvements in the standards of hygiene have been suggested between the fourth century AD and the fifth and sixth centuries. It therefore seems probable that the lack of perinatal and infant remains reflects burial practice, and that for some cultural reason the people using the cemetery disposed of dead infants in a different manner or in a different place from dead children and adults. Burial rites as dictated by Christianity and paganism might well be the explanation. Figure 74 illustrates the distribution of juvenile and sub-adult mortality at West Heslerton.

While it is considered that infant and juvenile ages at death can be estimated fairly accurately and with a degree

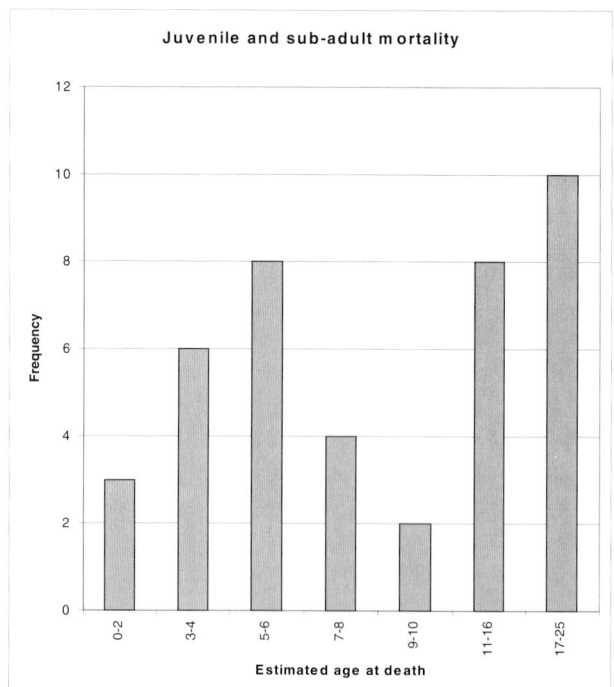

*Figure 74: juvenile and sub-adult mortality*

of confidence, the same is unfortunately not the case with adults. Age estimates of young adults are based on skeletal maturation and are considered to be reasonably accurate. However, once maturation is complete ageing is dependent on processes of degeneration and remodelling. Chronological ages are assigned on the basis of biological changes which can occur over a period of many years and whose rates reflect both environmental and genetic factors (see Molleson and Cox forthcoming).

The poor preservation of the human bone from West Heslerton has meant that age estimates have been based almost solely upon dental attrition. Attrition is the wearing away of occlusal surfaces during mastication by the rubbing of one tooth surface against another. The extent of the wear is determined by the abrasive effect of any hard material present in the diet and by the amount and strength of mastication (Brothwell 1981).

Brothwell's (1981) classification of age at death based upon molar wear has been used for this purpose. It must be considered, however, that the degree of wear may be different in males and in females, that it will be determined by the thickness and strength of the enamel surface (subject to environmental and genetic factors), it need not be at predictable rates depending on crown height and it will be different in individuals with different 'bites'. The small number of juveniles from West Heslerton prevents the calibration of attrition rates based upon molar wear as advocated by Miles (1963).

Table 14 describes the demographic profile of the West Heslerton adults based on dental attrition. In a small number of cases, this data has between supplemented by reference to other ageing indicators such as skeletal maturation in young adults, cranial suture closure (Perizonius 1984) and pubic symphysis morphology (Gilbert and McKern 1973; McKern and Stewart 1957), degenerative joint disease and osteoporosis. Only 51 adults could be assigned an age category.

Because of the small number of these which could be sexed, no attempt has been made to analyse the sexes separately. A further 53 inhumation numbers are believed to be adults but the condition of the material is such that more precise ageing is impossible. A total of 55 further inhumation numbers could not be classified as either adult or juvenile.

| Age group | No. | % |
|---|---|---|
| 17-25 | 12 | 23.53 |
| 25-35 | 31 | 60.78 |
| 33-45 | 5 | 9.80 |
| 45+ | 3 | 5.88 |
| Total | 51 | 99.99 |

*Table 14: demographic profile of the adults*

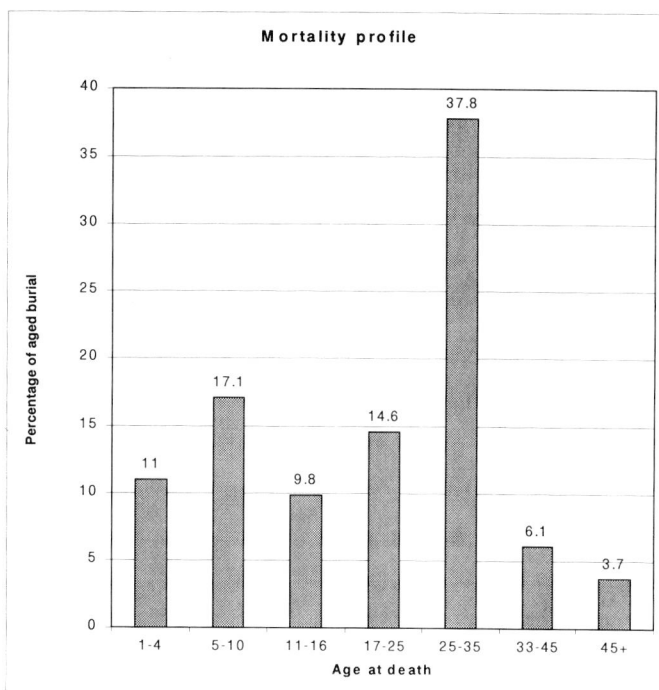

*Figure 75: West Heslerton mortality profile*

The age brackets used by Brothwell perpetuate the widely held belief that in the past the mean age at death of adults was low. With a top age range of 45+ any skeletal sample aged by this method would have a mean age at death of below that figure.

There is no historical evidence from the 'Dark Ages' in Britain which deals with life expectancy but there is epigraphic evidence from Roman Britain which attests to longevity. Examples are the tombstone of Claudia Crysis who lived for 90 years (RIB 263, Collingwood and Wright 1965) and Julius Valens who died aged 100 (RIB 363, ibid). If attritional age brackets were adjusted to allow for more precise longevity than 45+, this method might produce more meaningful demographic profiles. Figure 75 illustrates the mortality profile of the juveniles and adults, as represented in the cemetery sample.

Despite the lack of perinatal and infant deaths, 37.9% of the inhumations which could be assigned to an age category, were juveniles or sub-adults. A further three juveniles and 53 adults could not be assigned to age categories. Including these individuals, 24.6% (34) of the inhumations (N = 138) are juveniles and sub-adults with the remaining 75.4% (104) adults. Fifty-five further inhumation numbers were fragments which could not be identified as either juvenile or adult.

No comment will be made on the mean age at death of the cemetery sample. Mean ages rest very much on the confident estimation of tight and reliable age brackets for adults and there is no evidence to suggest that the ages assigned by dental attrition provide such data (the method was devised on an archaeological sample of unknown age at death). Furthermore, such estimates are spurious if the closed or open nature of the population is unknown (Johansson and Horowitz 1986). For similar reasons, no attempt has been made to generate birth rates from the mortality profile (Horowitz et al 1988).

| Sex | Mean | STDev | N | Range |
|---|---|---|---|---|
| Females | 160.0 | 7.46 | 6 | 149.7–168.2 |
| Modern F | 157.5 | | | |
| Males | 173.7 | 7.48 | 5 | 163.3–182.2 |
| Modern M | 167.6 | | | |

*Table 15: stature estimates for the West Heslerton adults*

# Physique

## Stature

Stature has been estimated from long bone lengths using the formulae of Trotter (1970). Because of the fragmentary and incomplete nature of the material very few statures have been estimated. Table 15 describes the mean stature (centimetres) of the males and females separately.

Despite the small sample sizes, the males appear to be significantly taller than the females. Within both groups there is great variation; 2BA890 (G145) is a short though robust male of only 163.3cm while 2BA939 was a tall and robust male of 177.8cm. Inhumation 2BA467 (G92)

was a very tall female but the condition of her long bones was such that her stature could not be estimated.

Both the males and females appear to have been taller than modern British adults (data from Wenham 1968) and are generally taller than adults from many Romano-British sites.

## Cranial and post-cranial measurements

Because of the condition of the material, only a limited range of cranial and post-cranial measurements were attempted. For comparative purposes these are described

| Measurements | Females N | Mean | STDev | Males N | Mean | STDev | Sex Unknown N | Mean | STDev |
|---|---|---|---|---|---|---|---|---|---|
| Max cranial L | | | | | | | 1 | 173.0 | |
| Max cranial B | 4 | 132.2 | 1.26 | | | | | | |
| Basi-bregmatic H | 2 | 132.5 | 9.19 | | | | | | |
| Basi-nasal L | 2 | 108.0 | 9.89 | | | | | | |
| Upper facial H | 1 | 68.0 | | | | | 1 | 70.0 | |
| Bimaxillary B | 1 | 99.0 | | | | | | | |
| Bizygomatic B | 1 | 130.0 | | | | | | | |
| Nasal H | 1 | 49.0 | | | | | 1 | 51.0 | |
| Nasal B | 1 | 25.0 | | 1 | 23.0 | | 1 | 22.0 | |
| Orbital B | 3 | 39.7 | 0.57 | | | | 1 | 42.0 | |
| Orbital H | 2 | 34.5 | 2.12 | | | | 1 | 36.0 | |
| Palatal L | 2 | 48.0 | 1.41 | 1 | 38.0 | | 1 | 49.0 | |
| Palatal B | 1 | 42.0 | | 2 | 42.5 | 4.95 | | | |

(L=length, B=breadth, H=height)

**Table 16:** *cranial measurements*

| Measurements | Females N | Mean | STDev | Males N | Mean | STDev | Sex Unknown N | Mean | STDev |
|---|---|---|---|---|---|---|---|---|---|
| Femur max.L | 4 | 42.4 | 3.66 | 3 | 46.3 | 3.10 | | | |
| Femur oblique L | 4 | 42.0 | 3.47 | 3 | 45.7 | 2.93 | | | |
| Femur min. a/p D | 11 | 23.4 | 2.41 | 7 | 26.7 | 2.04 | 7 | 24.6 | 5.00 |
| Femur trans D | 11 | 32.0 | 1.87 | 7 | 32.0 | 4.27 | 7 | 31.8 | 3.95 |
| Femur head D | 11 | 43.2 | 2.41 | 8 | 49.2 | 1.70 | | | |
| Tibia total L | 5 | 35.1 | 2.07 | 5 | 38.5 | 3.51 | 1 | 37.8 | |
| Tibia max. a/p D | 11 | 29.6 | 4.06 | 8 | 35.0 | 2.02 | 3 | 34.6 | 2.76 |
| Tibia projective trans D | 11 | 21.1 | 2.05 | 8 | 24.4 | 3.13 | 4 | 24.0 | 9.39 |
| Humerus max.L | 3 | 31.4 | 3.22 | 2 | 34.4 | 3.46 | | | |
| Humerus head D | 3 | 40.9 | 11.46 | 3 | 47.6 | 11.85 | | | |
| Radius max.L | 3 | 23.3 | 13.20 | 1 | 27.9 | | | | |
| Ulna max.L | 1 | 24.1 | | 1 | 30.5 | | | | |

(L=length, B=breadth, H=height, D=diameter, a/p=antero-posterior, trans=transverse)

**Table 17:** *post-cranial measurements*

in Tables 16 and 17, the measurements are as defined in Brothwell (1981).

## Meric index

The meric indices of the males and females from West Heslerton, assessed in accordance with the definition of Brothwell (1981), are described in Table 18. The significance of this index is uncertain. As a measure of the anterio-posterior flattening of the subtrochanteric part of the femoral diaphysis, it is considered to indicate either the amount of mineral available for bone formation or remodelling in response to mechanical stress.

| Sex | N | Mean | STDev | Range |
| --- | --- | --- | --- | --- |
| Females | 11 | 73.16 | 4.97 | 65.6-78.1 |
| Males | 5 | 77.06 | 6.21 | 69.3-83.2 |
| Unknown | 6 | 75.55 | 16.46 | 65.7-107.7 |

*Table 18: the meric index*

Both males and females fall into the platymeric range both in terms of the mean and the range. One unusual individual in the unknown sex category falls above the eurymeric range, the remainder being platymeric.

## Cnemic index

The cnemic index (as defined in Brothwell 1981) is taken at the level of the nutrient foramen of the tibia. Several explanations for platycnemia have been suggested, ranging from pathological to muscular factors, but the real significance remains in doubt. The cnemic indices of the West Heslerton adults are presented in Table 19.

| Sex | N | Mean | STDev | Range |
| --- | --- | --- | --- | --- |
| Females | 11 | 72.38 | 10.32 | 61.2-99.0 |
| Males | 8 | 69.74 | 7.34 | 54.3-77.6 |
| Unknown | 4 | 67.25 | 4.01 | 62.5-72.2 |

*Table 19: the cnemic index*

The male and unknown means fall within the mesocnemic range, the female mean being eurycnemic. The range for the females and unknowns extends from platycnemic to eurycnemic, the males extending from hyperplatycnemic to eurycnemic.

## Cranial shape; the cephalic index

The only cranial index which could be assessed for this sample was the cephalic index, and only for females. This index is designed to illustrate the degree of round or long-headedness; the formula used is as described by Brothwell (1981). Table 20 describes the cephalic index of the West Heslerton females.

| Sex | N | Mean | STDev | Range |
| --- | --- | --- | --- | --- |
| Females | 4 | 71.71 | 1.72 | 69.7-73.3 |

*Table 20: the cephalic index*

The head shape of the females, in terms of mean and range, falls within the dolichocephalic (narrow headed) range. This trend was also apparent in the skull shape of those who could not be measured with only one exception. Although his skull could not be measured, inhumation number 2BA1079 (G166), an adult male, is clearly brachycephalic, his skull shape being broad or round-headed. Recent work in Eastern Europe suggests that brachycephalisation is strongly associated with low social and economic status (papers presented at the 3rd Anthropological Congress of Ales Hrdlicka, Prague, Humpolec 1989).

## Discontinuous morphological traits

Non-metric traits are minor skeletal variations such as the retention of the metopic suture or squatting facets. The presence or absence of such traits is considered by some to be determined genetically although the frequency of some may be modified by the environment (Trinkhaus 1978; Sjovold 1984). The distribution of non-metric traits has been applied to a variety of questions such as biological distance between samples, matrilocal and patrilocal residence, differentiating between diffusion and migration (Ubelaker 1989) and genetic grouping within cemetery sites. Such analysis is dependent upon large samples, surviving in good condition; the West Heslerton sample is neither. The frequencies of a range of cranial and post-cranial non-metric traits are presented in Tables 21 and 22. Traits are as described by Brothwell (1981).

An interesting sample of non-metric cranial variation in this sample was observed in inhumation 2BA980 (G145). This adult female has unusual sutural variation. She has an inca bone, as illustrated in Brothwell (1981, 47 E), with three large ossicles at lambda.

# Dentition

## Oral and dental health: caries, abscesses and ante-mortem tooth loss

Dental and oral health can reflect both dietary considerations and oral hygiene. Dental caries is a localised, progressively destructive disease caused by organic acids produced in the immediate proximity of the teeth by the enzymatic action of masses of micro-organisms on carbohydrates. Caries are found most frequently on molars for two reasons. Firstly, molars are less effectively cleansed by the tongue than incisors. Secondly, they have more pits and fissures in which food debris can be retained. The caries rate in this sample is presented in Table 23. Males and females have not been described separately as the sexed sample with surviving dentition is very small, the majority remaining unsexed.

| Trait | N | Present | Unilateral | Bilateral | Only one side present |
|---|---|---|---|---|---|
| Metopism | 32 | 3 | | | |
| Mental foramen | 19 | | | 19 | |
| Coronal wormians | 12 | | 2 | 1 | 2 |
| Sagittal wormians | 14 | 9 | | | |
| Lambdoid wormians | 10 | | 3 | 4 | |
| Epipteric bone | 7 | | | | |
| Parietal notch | 7 | | 1 | | 1 |
| Mandibular torus | 24 | | | | |
| Maxillary torus | 20 | | | 1 | |
| Bregmatic ossicle | 17 | | | | |
| Coronal ossicle | 12 | | | | |
| Saggital ossicle | 11 | | | 1 | 1 |
| Ossicle at lambda | 12 | | | | 3 |
| Lambdoid ossicles | 13 | | | 1 | 6 |
| Parietal foramen | 14 | | 2 | | 5 |
| Asterion ossicle | 9 | | 2 | | |
| Supraorbital foramen | 21 | | 2 | 4 | |
| Double occipital facets | 6 | | | | |

**Table 21:** *the frequency of cranial non-metric traits*

| Trait | N | Unilateral | Bilateral | Only one side assessed |
|---|---|---|---|---|
| Allen's fossa | 13 | 1 | | |
| Porier's facet | 12 | | | |
| Plaque | 12 | | | 3 |
| 3rd trochanter | 17 | 1 | | |
| Exostosis introchanter | 6 | | 1 | 1 |
| Squatting facets medial left | 4 | 1 | 1 | |
| Squatting facets medial right | 4 | | 1 | |
| Squatting facets lateral left | 4 | 1 | | 1 |
| Squatting facets lateral right | 4 | 1 | | |
| Os trigonum | 16 | 2 | 7 | 2 |
| Talar extension | 16 | | 1 | |
| Talar facet medial | 16 | | | |
| Anterior calcaneal facet double | 19 | 3 | 7 | 2 |
| Vastus notch | 9 | 1 | | |
| Septal aperture | 12 | 1 | | 4 |
| Supracondyloid process | 13 | | | |
| Suprascapular foramen | 2 | 1 | | |
| Circumflex sulcus | 2 | | | 1 |
| Acromial articular facet | 3 | | | |
| Os acrimoniale | 4 | | 1 | |
| Sternal aperture | 5 | | 1 | 1 |
| Accessory sacral facet | 4 | | 2 | |
| Preauricular sulcus | 15 | | 6 | 3 |
| Pubic pitting | 3 | | | 1 |
| Acetabular crease | 12 | | 1 | 1 |
| Spina bifida occulta | 2 | | | |
| Atlas facet double | 6 | | | 1 |
| Posterior bridge | 6 | | 2 | 1 |
| Transverse foramen bipartite | 3 | | 2 | |

**Table 22:** *the frequency of post-cranial non-metric traits*

| | N | % carious |
|---|---|---|
| Adults | 123 | 15.45 |
| Sub-adults | 6 | 0 |
| Juveniles | 20 | 0 |

*Table 23: the frequency of individuals with dental caries*

The frequency of caries in surviving, erupted permanent teeth (including four juveniles) is 2.44% (41 of 1723).

Ante-mortem tooth loss per tooth position is presented below in Table 24 (frequency 1.2%, 21 of 1744). This can be caused by severe caries or by periodontal disease, it is impossible to tell which in skeletal material. If those teeth lost ante-mortem (21) are included in the caries frequency, both as carious and in terms of representing a tooth position, then the caries rate increases to 3.55% (62 of 1744). This frequency is lower than is usual for early Anglo-Saxon material, the average being 8.1% (Hardwick 1960).

The frequency of caries per tooth position is presented in Table 24. Two inhumations 2BA909 (G152) and 2BA921 (G86) were undergoing conservation and could therefore not be included in this analysis.

Dental abscesses are caused by a collection of pus surrounded by denser tissue. They can be caused in response to caries, periodontal infection or severe attrition exposing the pulp cavity. In skeletal material they are usually seen in the buccal surface of the alveolar bone as rounded cavities at the root apex.

The prevalence of dental abscesses in this sample is presented in Table 24. The frequency of adults with dental abscesses is 2.3% (2 of 86).

Not included in this figure is what appears to be a cyst associated with the upper right medial incisor of an adult male 2BA673 (G126). A smooth-walled cavity with a maximum diameter of 12.3mm, the cyst has drained lingually. The associated tooth (crown only survives) appears healthy. A possible cause could have been an embedded retained tooth. In such cases the epithelial covering proliferates causing a cystic reaction. Whether this was the cause is unknown as no embedded tooth survives.

The majority of individuals interred at West Heslerton had edge to edge bite, one exception being an adult female 2BA100 (G78) who had marked overbite. As a consequence of edge to edge bite, attrition was frequently severe on incisors and canines.

## Periodontal disease

Alveolar and palatal resorption and pitting is usually indicative of periodontal disease. Periodontal disease can, if resorption is severe, result in tooth loss. The major cause is poor oral hygiene (Costa 1982). Table 25 presents the distribution of periodontal disease among the adults (N = 49), it is scored as slight, moderate or severe. No juveniles (N = 4) were affected.

Three individuals appear to have experienced severe periodontal disease. Inhumation 2BA383, an adult female, had extreme resorption and pitting of the buccal alveolar around the upper left 5 and 6. This was almost certainly associated with the fact that approximately one-third of the crown of the 6 had been destroyed by caries and that the 5 was lost ante-mortem. Another female 2BA716 (G124) had severe resorption and pitting of the alveolar of both the maxilla and mandible. Severe attrition had contributed to ante-mortem tooth loss and severe interproximal caries were also responsible for poor oral health. Another female, 2B083 (G144), had severe periodontal disease affecting the maxilla and palate; this is associated with severe attrition.

## Calculus

A concretion mainly consisting of calcium salts, but containing some food debris, calculus develops from plaque forming mainly at the margin of the gums. The frequency of calculus (N = 77) is presented in Table 26; it has been scored as advocated by Brothwell (1981). None of the juveniles (N = 16) were affected.

Maxilla (L to R)

| Position | 8 | 7 | 6 | 5 | 4 | 3 | 2 | 1 | 1 | 2 | 3 | 4 | 5 | 6 | 7 | 8 |
|---|---|---|---|---|---|---|---|---|---|---|---|---|---|---|---|---|
| Teeth | 52 | 65 | 78 | 62 | 62 | 58 | 54 | 45 | 53 | 45 | 49 | 58 | 54 | 52 | 58 | 43 |
| Carious | 1 | 5 | 6 | 1 | 2 | 1 | 0 | 0 | 0 | 0 | 0 | 1 | 1 | 3 | 3 | 1 |
| A/M loss | 0 | 1 | 1 | 2 | 1 | 0 | 0 | 0 | 0 | 0 | 0 | 0 | 0 | 1 | 2 | 1 |
| Abscesses | 0 | 0 | 1 | 0 | 0 | 0 | 0 | 0 | 0 | 0 | 0 | 0 | 0 | 1 | 0 | 0 |

Mandible

| Position | 8 | 7 | 6 | 5 | 4 | 3 | 2 | 1 | 1 | 2 | 3 | 4 | 5 | 6 | 7 | 8 |
|---|---|---|---|---|---|---|---|---|---|---|---|---|---|---|---|---|
| Teeth | 51 | 61 | 64 | 58 | 59 | 48 | 51 | 48 | 43 | 49 | 38 | 57 | 55 | 60 | 61 | 52 |
| Carious | 0 | 1 | 5 | 0 | 1 | 0 | 0 | 0 | 0 | 0 | 1 | 0 | 0 | 0 | 4 | 3 | 1 |
| A/M loss | 0 | 1 | 2 | 0 | 0 | 0 | 0 | 0 | 0 | 1 | 0 | 1 | 0 | 1 | 2 | 2 | 1 |
| Abscesses | 0 | 0 | 1 | 0 | 0 | 0 | 0 | 0 | 0 | 0 | 0 | 0 | 0 | 0 | 1 | 0 | 0 |

*Table 24: distribution of carious permanent teeth, abscesses and ante-mortem loss per observed tooth position*

| | No. | % |
|---|---|---|
| Absent | 29 | 59.2 |
| Slight | 13 | 26.5 |
| Moderate | 7 | 14.3 |
| Severe | 0 | 0.0 |

*Table 25: periodontal disease*

## Variation in tooth number

Lack of the third molar is the most common example of congenital absence of teeth seen in archaeological and modern material. Thirteen (24.1% N = 54) individuals had what appear to be absent 8s. All four could be absent, three, two or only one, precise details are presented in Table 27. Inhumation 2B70/2B85 (G74) has an impacted lower left 8.

Several teeth which usually have a single root had split roots: 2BA939 (G107) in both 4s and the upper right 5; 2BA095 (G77) in the upper left 4 and 2BA141 (G94) in the lower left 3. The frequency of such variation is undoubtedly much higher but was only observed in teeth out of their sockets.

Two individuals had Carabelli's cusps 2BA154 (G98) and 2B071 (G70); 2BA1079 (G166) had an extra cusp on the upper right 7 and 2BA441 (G113) had an 8 with an extra cusp.

Peg-like lateral incisors (upper) were observed in 2BA594 (G122); a similar, but residual, tooth was present in context 2BA76. These teeth had comparatively short roots and slim conical crowns. An unusually small upper right 8 was present in 2BA1160 (G170). Its morphology and size were similar to a lower 5. What appears to be a re-

tained deciduous canine, probably from the maxilla, survived in 2BA587 (G120). Its total length is 8.6mm. Half of this is the crown, which is conical with a pointed apex.

## Metabolic disease; dental enamel hypoplasia

The result of faulty development during early childhood, enamel hypoplasia usually presents as irregular distribution and partial absence of enamel in the form of horizontal linear bands. Dental enamel hypoplasia is considered to reflect metabolic disease which has interrupted the progressive calcification of the developing teeth. The position of the hypoplastic bands on anterior dentition is thought to indicate the age at which the interruption, which seems to be caused by either infectious disease or nutritional stress, occurred.

Fourteen individuals interred at West Heslerton, exhibited enamel hypoplasia. Most cases were very slight and occurred between the ages of one and five years. The only severe case was inhumation 2BA154 (G98), a juvenile who died aged approximately four to five years. Calcification of the developing permanent dentition was interrupted when this child was aged approximately three to four years.

# Skeletal pathology

The majority of diseases and much of the trauma affecting man do not affect the skeleton. Of those that do, many cause discomfort and inconvenience, but very few are likely to have been fatal.

## Congenital and developmental pathologies

No cases of pathologies of certain developmental aetiology are evident in this material.

| | No. | % |
|---|---|---|
| Absent | 45 | 58.4 |
| Slight | 22 | 28.6 |
| Moderate | 10 | 13.0 |
| Severe | 0 | 0.0 |

*Table 26: calculus in the West Heslerton adults*

| Skeleton No. | Lower left 8 | Lower right 8 | Upper left 8 | Upper right 8 | |
|---|---|---|---|---|---|
| 2BA150 (G96) | P | A | A | A | also UL2 and UR2 |
| 2BA890 (G145) | P | A | A | A | also UR7 and UL2 |
| 2BA980 (G164) | A | A | A | P | |
| 2F005 (G174) | P | A | P | P | |
| 2BA805 (G139) | P | A | P | A | |
| 2BA159 (G102) | A | P | P | P | |
| 2BA466 (G82) | P | A | A | P | |
| 2BA420 (G111) | P | A | A | P | |
| 2B091 (G76) | P | A | M | M | |
| 2BA897 (G109) | A | P | P | P | |
| 2B085 (G74) | A | A | A | A | |
| 2BA775 (G133) | A | A | P | P | |

A=absent, P=present, M=site missing

*Table 27: agenesis*

## Metabolic disease

### Cribra orbitalia

The presence of cribra orbitalia is considered to represent a childhood episode of iron deficiency anaemia. This can reflect either nutritional deficiency or chronic intestinal blood loss through parasites (Stuart-Macadam 1985). Another possible explanation is that anaemia can be an adaptive response to increase immunity to pathogens (Stuart-Macadam 1988).

|  | Adults | | Juveniles | |
| --- | --- | --- | --- | --- |
| Grade | No. | % | No. | % |
| 0 | 13 | 72.2 | 1 | 33.3 |
| 1 | 2 | 11.1 | 0 | 0.0 |
| 2 | 3 | 16.7 | 2 | 66.6 |
| 3 | 0 | 0.0 | 0 | 0.0 |
| Total | 18 | 100.0 | 3 | 100.0 |

*Table 28: cribra orbitalia*

Presenting macroscopically as pitting of the roofs of the orbits, cribra orbitalia has been scored as described by Stuart-Macadam (1985), ranging from 0, which implies an absence of the condition, to 3, which reflects outgrowth in the trabecular from the normal contour of the cortical bone. The results are presented in Table 28.

Although the samples sizes are extremely small, the high frequency of more severe cribra orbitalia in juveniles is typical of many archaeological samples. It may reflect the fact that these lesions heal in some cases or that the cause of cribra in juveniles may be associated with their cause of death.

### Porotic hyperostosis

Of similar aetiology to cribra orbitalia, porotic cortical hyperostosis presents as areas of dense pitting on the cranium. Possibly reflecting the appalling condition of this material, only one case of porotic hyperostosis is apparent. Inhumation 2BA796 (G136), a young adult aged approximately 17 to 25 years, has widespread ectocranial porosity.

### Osteoporosis

Although it is usually associated with post-menopausal changes and senility, osteoporosis can occur as a result of endocrine disorders and renal disease. Only one elderly female 2BA606 (G123) is considered to have been affected by this condition. Had all of the adults been radiographed, it is likely that the prevalence would have been higher.

## Conditions of obscure origins or multiple aetiology

Neural arch separation, spondylolysis, can result from congenital defects, fractures or degenerative processes (Zimmermann and Kelly 1982). Spondylolysis usually occurs between the ages of 4 and 20, and despite the fact that males are considered more susceptible than females, one female and one probable female 2BA100 (G78) and 2BA078 (G89) from West Heslerton have bilateral spondylolysis. This usually occurs in the fourth and fifth lumbar vertebrae and is asymptomatic. Lumbar vertebrae three and four, the arch of which survives, are affected in inhumation 2BA100 (G78). Lumbar vertebra four is affected in 2BA078 (G89), both fall into the 25 to 35 year age group.

## Joint disease

### Osteoarthritis

Osteoarthritis or degenerative joint disease is probably the most common identifiable disease seen in archaeological material. The condition is characterised by deformation of joint surfaces, eburnation of the joint surface in severe cases and by periarticular and articular bone formation (Rogers *et al* 1987). It is a non-inflammatory disorder affecting diarthrodial, synovial and laminal intervertebral joints.

The causes can be diverse. It is more common in the elderly and appears to be part of the ageing process. The involvement of extra spinal joints can reflect the minor strains and stresses associated with everyday life and increasing age. Monarticular osteoarthritis can reflect trauma or infection. Osteoarthritis can reflect such factors as age, sex, hormonal influences, mechanical stress and genetic predisposition (Zimmermann and Kelly 1982).

It is considered by some (Wells 1982; White 1988) that the distribution of affected joints can serve to indicate lifestyle and occupations; this is a continuing and contentious area of debate. It is difficult to judge to what extent, if any, osteoarthritis affected the lifestyle and quality of life of past populations. Very severe cases would inevitably restrict mobility and cause some pain, but the correlation between the apparent severity of this condition and clinical symptoms is low in modern populations (Lawrence 1966).

The distribution of arthritic changes to the spinal and extra spinal skeleton are presented in Tables 29 and 30. Graded from 0 to 3 in terms of severity according to Sager (1969 in Brothwell 1981), no attempt has been made to deal with males and females separately as most individuals could not be sexed.

| Vertebra | N | 0 | 1 | 2 | 3 |
|---|---|---|---|---|---|
| OC | 11 | 10 | 1 | | |
| C1 | 26 | 23 | 3 | | |
| C2 | 22 | 17 | 3 | 2 | |
| C3 | 21 | 16 | 1 | 4 | |
| C4 | 17 | 13 | | 4 | |
| C5 | 12 | 9 | 2 | 1 | |
| C6 | 11 | 16 | 2 | 3 | |
| C7 | 12 | 10 | | 2 | |
| T1 | 13 | 10 | 3 | | |
| T2 | 13 | 10 | 3 | | |
| T3 | 17 | 14 | 3 | | |
| T4 | 19 | 13 | 6 | | |
| T5 | 19 | 11 | 7 | 1 | |
| T6 | 17 | 10 | 7 | | |
| T7 | 15 | 11 | 2 | 2 | |
| T8 | 13 | 10 | 1 | 2 | |
| T9 | 12 | 8 | 2 | 2 | |
| T10 | 11 | 8 | 1 | 2 | |
| T11 | 11 | 8 | 1 | 2 | |
| T12 | 10 | 8 | 1 | 1 | |
| L1 | 9 | 8 | 2 | 1 | |
| L2 | 10 | 7 | 2 | 1 | |
| L3 | 11 | 6 | 3 | 2 | |
| L4 | 12 | 5 | 5 | 2 | |
| L5 | 11 | 5 | 4 | 2 | |
| S1 | 11 | 4 | 4 | 3 | |
| LSIJ | 5 | 4 | 1 | | |
| RSIJ | 6 | 5 | 1 | | |

OC=occipital condyles, C=cervical,
T=thoracic, L=lumbar, S=sacral, L=left,
R=right, SIJ=sacroiliac joint

*Table 29: Spinal osteoarthritis*

Notable causes of spinal involvement are as follows. The articular facets of cervical vertebrae 6 and 7, are affected by severe osteoarthritis in a female, 2BA980 (G164). The vertebrae of 2BA938 (G158) are affected by moderate osteoarthritis from the lower thoracic region down. The surviving cervical vertebrae of 2BA606 (G123), an elderly female, are affected by moderate to severe osteoarthritis.

Particular cases of extra-spinal involvement include 2BA716 (G124), an elderly female with a severely affected right knee, the joint surfaces of which are eburnated. The left mandibular head of a probable female 2BA078 (G89) is sclerotic; it measures 16.7mm in diameter while the right, the joint surface of which appears normal, measures 20.4mm. A large robust adult male, 2BA938 (G123), has degenerative changes to both knees and to his right elbow. These joints exhibit moderate arthritic changes with periarticular bone proliferation.

No cases of erosive or infective arthropathy are evident in this material.

| Skeletal element | No. | 0 | 1 | 2 | 3 |
|---|---|---|---|---|---|
| L.mandibular condyle | 15 | 15 | | | |
| R.mandibular condyle | 14 | 13 | | 1 | |
| L.ribs | 10 | 6 | 3 | 1 | |
| R.ribs | 11 | 8 | 2 | 1 | |
| L.medial clavicle | 4 | 2 | 1 | 1 | |
| R.medial clavicle | 4 | 2 | 2 | | |
| L.lateral clavicle | 2 | | 2 | | |
| R.lateral clavicle | 2 | 1 | | 1 | |
| L.glenoid cavity | 9 | 9 | | | |
| R.glenoid cavity | 11 | 11 | | | |
| L.acromion | 4 | 4 | | | |
| R.acromion | 2 | | 1 | | 1 |
| L.proximal humerus | 8 | 8 | | | |
| R.proximal humerus | 5 | 4 | | 1 | |
| L.distal humerus | 14 | 13 | | 1 | |
| R.distal humerus | 8 | 8 | | | |
| L.proximal radius | 9 | 9 | | | |
| R.proximal radius | 5 | 5 | | | |
| L distal radius | 12 | 10 | 1 | 1 | |
| R.distal radius | 8 | 7 | | 1 | |
| L.proximal ulna | 14 | 14 | | | |
| R.proximal ulna | 6 | 1 | | | |
| L.distal ulna | 8 | 6 | 1 | | |
| R.distal ulna | 3 | 3 | 1 | | |
| L.carpals | 14 | 13 | | | |
| R.carpals | 13 | 12 | | 1 | |
| L.metacarpals | 12 | 11 | 1 | | |
| R.metacarpals | 12 | 11 | 1 | | |
| L.hand phalanges | 10 | 10 | | | |
| R.hand phalanges | 11 | 11 | | | |
| L.sacroiliac | 13 | 9 | 4 | | |
| R.sacroiliac | 11 | 8 | 3 | | |
| L.acetabulum | 22 | 21 | | 1 | |
| R.acetabulum | 22 | 21 | | 1 | |
| L.proximal femur | 21 | 20 | 1 | | |
| R.proximal femur | 20 | 17 | 1 | 2 | |
| L.distal femur | 19 | 18 | | | |
| R.distal femur | 20 | 17 | 2 | | 1 |
| L.patella | 15 | 13 | 2 | | |
| R.patella | 10 | 7 | 2 | | 1 |
| L.proximal tibia | 15 | 15 | | | |
| R.proximal tibia | 15 | 14 | | | 1 |
| L.distal tibia | 22 | 20 | 1 | | 1 |
| R.distal tibia | 18 | 18 | | | |
| L.proximal fibula | 5 | 5 | | | |
| R.proximal fibula | 4 | 4 | | | |
| L.distal fibula | 9 | 9 | | | |
| R.distal fibula | 11 | 11 | | | |
| L.talus/calcaneus/tarsals | 36 | | | | |
| R.talus/calcaneus/tarsals | 30 | | | | |
| L.metatarsals | 16 | 16 | | | |
| R.metatarsals | 15 | 15 | | | |
| L.foot phalanges | 7 | 7 | | | |
| R.foot phalanges | 6 | 6 | | | |

*Table 30: Extra-spinal osteoarthritis*

## Degenerative disc disease

Degenerative disc disease usually exists without symptoms unless the disc space narrows to such an extent that the nerve roots are entrapped within their foramina. The superior and inferior surfaces of the vertebral bodies become pitted and there is frequently associated osteophytosis. As with osteoarthritis this condition appears to be associated with increasing age.

Only one case were observed A female, 2BA980 (G164), has slight discitis affecting cervical vertebrae 6 and 7, lumbar vertebra 5 and sacral vertebra 1.

## Ankylosis

Fusion of two or more bones is apparent only in one individual. An elderly female, 2B83 (G144), who survives incompletely and whose bones are fragmented exhibits anklyosis of several joints. Both distal humeri are fused to the proximal ulnae with associated periarticular proliferation. It is possible that this represents the consequence of pyogenic arthritis of the elbow joints. The facets of two series of two unidentifiable thoracic vertebrae are fused; the bodies do not survive. Unfortunately the sacroiliac joints have not survived and neither have the hands or the feet. Identifying the probable cause of anklyosis rests very much on its distribution throughout the skeleton, and in this case the lack of joints makes attribution impossible.

# Trauma

## Fractures

Healed fractures usually survive very well in archaeological material. The reason for this is the post-trauma development of a raised cuff of bone, a callus, around the fracture site. New bone develops between the fracture ends and is accompanied by circumferential deposition beneath the periosteum. The callus is an area of dense cortical bone; it is very robust and usually survives most kinds of post-mortem degradation. In view of this fact, it is interesting that only one fracture is evident in the human bone from Anglo-Saxon burials at West Heslerton. This could indicate that despite the poor survival rate, the fracture rate was low in this sample.

Inhumation 2BA78 (G89), a probable female who died aged below 30, has a partially un-united Colles' fracture of the left distal radius. A Colles' fracture usually results from a fall onto an outstretched hand. Superior to the epiphyseal line there is remodelling proliferating anteriorly and across approximately half of the fractured surface. The rest of the fractured surface appears to have been broken off, probably post-mortem. The distal portion of this bone has not survived. The left radius is approximately 20.4mm shorter than the right.

## Cut marks

The cranium of 2BA775 (G133) bears the marks of four circumferential cuts running from the front to the rear. An adult female who died aged approximately 35 years, her skeleton survives in a fragmentary and incomplete state. The condition of the bone strongly suggests that the cuts were either ante-mortem or that they occurred at the time of death. Endrocranially the skull is pitted and the cortex is almost completely eroded; this is the result of post-mortem degradation and not of infection or of disease. On the left parietal, three distinct circumferential and straight cut marks run from the front to the rear. The most central incision measures approximately 66mm in length, the next moving laterally is 47mm and the outer extends for 34mm. A fourth cut of approximately 49mm is situated towards the squamous suture. These straight cuts have penetrated through the cortical bone deep into the diploe, but none have pierced the inner table. The loss of the outer table renders evaluation of healing and possible infection impossible and consequently it is not possible to estimate at what time before death these cuts were perpetrated. The underlying reason for this pathology is perplexing. Because of their length, the cuts are unlikely to have been the result of an accident. Similarly they bear no resemblance to cuts incurred as a result of scalping, either in terms of their position, morphology or angle, or cuts incurred during trephination.

## Exostosis

The skeletal evidence for trauma will only reflect either injury directly involving the bone, where soft tissue infection involves the bone, or where soft tissue injury results in calcification of the damaged tissue.

One case of exostosis, the calcification of soft tissue, is evident in this sample. In this case, an adult 1A77 (G16), the ossification is slight and is situated at the site of the interosseous ligaments of both the left and right distal tibia at the site of the fibulae notch. On the left tibia this is mainly on the posterior border of the attachment site and on the right at the apex. The exostoses are spicular in nature, measuring approximately 5mm from the normal bone contour.

A soft tissue injury which may have led to infection of the bone is one possible explanation for the infective osteitis affecting the right femur of inhumation 2BA172A (G81), a tall and gracile individual aged between 15 and 20 years. Despite the degraded condition of the bone, the cortex of the proximal third of the right femur is thickened and granular in appearance. The aetiology of this condition is uncertain.

Another instance of osteitis which may have resulted from soft tissue injury or infection is on the right parietal of an adult 2B85 (G74). A triangular area is pitted and irregular in appearance, one corner is situated on the coronal suture approximately 48mm from bregma, the lesion measuring *c* 54 x 27mm. Endocranially the bone is normal.

## Circulatory and haematological disorders

### Osteochondritis dissecans

Osteochondritis dissecans is a form of ischaemic necrosis probably reflecting trauma although there does seem to be a genetic predisposition (Jaffe 1972). This condition occurs when a fragment of subchondral bone becomes detached from the surrounding bone, cutting off the vascular supply to the detached fragment (Zimmermann and Kelly 1982). Macroscopically, osteochondritis dissecans presents as a crater-like defect in the subchondral bone. It can affect any diarthrodial joint. The condition usually occurs between the ages of 15 and 25 and it affects males up to 50% more frequently than females (Huskisson and Hart 1978). Although this condition arises from trauma, it is usually asymptomatic thereafter.

Only one individual at West Heslerton was affected by this condition. Inhumation 2BA802 (G138), a sub-adult probably aged about 15 years, has one crater-like defect on each of the medial condyles of the unfused epiphyses of the distal femorae. The left measures approximately 13.8mm in diameter and is clearly defined. The right measures 7.9mm and appears less clearly defined largely because the epiphysis is badly eroded.

### Scheuermann's disease

Scheuermann's disease is an epiphyseal ischaemic necrosis affecting the anterior and lateral zones of the superior intervertebral surface of vertebral bodies. It can reflect repeated trauma, congenital and hereditary factors, embolism or infection (Zimmermann and Kelly 1982). There is only one case apparent in this sample, 2BA927 (G155), an adult male. Three fragmentary and eroded lumbar vertebrae are affected by this condition; these are unusual sites, the thoracic vertebrae usually being affected. Two of these vertebrae also have irregularly shaped destructive lesions in the centres of the discal surfaces. These are in the same site as, but are not, Schmorl's nodes.

### Schmorl's nodes

If, during adolescence, the intervertebral disc is subject to stress. particularly compression forces such as those incurred during lifting, or frequent micro-trauma, a cavity, the Schmorl's node, is formed in the body of the vertebra by herniation of the nucleus pulposus in an axial direction. There can be a congenital propensity to this condition (Schmorl and Junghanns 1971).

Table 31 presents the frequency of Schmorl's nodes in both the superior and inferior discal surfaces.

Despite the very small sample sizes the frequency of Schmorl's nodes is high, particularly in the region of the lower thoracic and the upper lumbar vertebrae. This could indicate that many of this sample experienced considerable physical stress during adolescence and early adulthood. Schmorl's nodes can progress to spondylosis deformans (Kelly 1982), crescent-shaped lesions on the anterior portion of the discal bodies, the epiphyseal rings of the centrum being completely destroyed. Thoracic vertebrae 9 and 12 were affected in an adult female.

As with Schmorl's nodes, the infrequent mention of intervertebral osteochondrosis and spondylosis deformans in the medical literature reflects the lack of associated symptoms as well as their difficult radiographic detection (Kelly 1982).

## Benign neoplasms

### Osteochondroma

The right proximal humerus of inhumation 2BA927 (G155), an adult male who died aged approximately 35, is pathological. Approximately 25mm below the margin of the humerus head on the medial edge of the surgical neck is an irregularly shaped benign neoplasm arising from the epiphyseal cartilage. Osteochondroma is the most common of the benign tumours, the commonest sites being the metaphyses of the femur, tibia and humerus (Zimmerman and Kelly 1982). The cortex between the head and the osteochondroma has undergone some remodelling and the affected area (within the margin of the capsule attachment) is sclerotic. The proximal shaft of the bone is flattened as is often observed in such cases.

### Osteoid-osteoma

Benign neoplasms consisting of a core of osseous tissue surrounded by sclerotic bone, osteoid-osteoma usually occurs within the first three decades of life (Zimmermann and Kelly 1982). An elderly adult female, 2BA716 (G124), has an osteoid osteoma just below midshaft on the left femur. A longitudinal tumour measuring approximately 26 x 6mm and raised c 4mm from the normal bone contour, it issituated on the lateral side of the posterior aspect at the site of vastus intermedius.

### Miscellaneous

An adult 2BA633 (G125), probably a male, has unusual skeletal morphology in the region of the talar sulci. Extra bone is present; there is no indication of infection and the calcaneal sulci appear normal. The reason for this is obscure and there is no reason to suppose that it caused any discomfort or was
restrictive.

## A possible cerebral vascular accident

The most interesting pathological condition from the West Heslerton cemetery is evident in 2BA466 (G114), an adult female whose attritional age at death is at the top end of the 17 to 25 year age range. Cranial characteristics indicate a female as does the diameter of the right femoral

| Vertebrae | No. | Present |
|-----------|-----|---------|
| T3S | 6 | 0 |
| T3I | 7 | 0 |
| T4S | 9 | 2 |
| T4I | 11 | 0 |
| T5S | 11 | 1 |
| T5I | 11 | 2 |
| T6S | 10 | 4 |
| T6I | 11 | 3 |
| T7S | 10 | 4 |
| T7I | 12 | 5 |
| T8S | 9 | 4 |
| T8I | 10 | 5 |
| T9S | 10 | 4 |
| T9I | 10 | 4 |
| T10S | 10 | 4 |
| T10I | 8 | 4 |
| T11S | 8 | 4 |
| T11I | 8 | 5 |
| T12S | 8 | 5 |
| T12I | 8 | 4 |
| L1S | 9 | 4 |
| L1I | 8 | 4 |
| L2S | 8 | 4 |
| L2I | 9 | 2 |
| L3S | 10 | 2 |
| L3I | 11 | 1 |
| L4S | 9 | 3 |
| L4I | 9 | 3 |
| L5S | 9 | 0 |
| L5I | 1 | 2 |
| S1S | 8 | 0 |

*Table 31: Schmorl's nodes*

head at 38mm. Unfortunately this skeleton is incomplete and fragmentary.

The most striking feature of the surviving bones is the marked asymmetry of diaphyses in the post-cranial skeleton. The left clavicle is more gracile than the right, the left midshaft diameter measuring 7.5mm, the right 12.6mm. It is impossible to compare the length of these two bones. The left humerus, which despite being fragmented appears to be the same length as the right, has a diameter of 11.1m (medio-laterally) of the diaphysis at the level of the nutrient foramen is 16mm while the right is 23.1mm. Where they survive, the articular surfaces of the affected limbs appear normal. The cranium, which survives in unusually good condition, is normal both endo- and ectocranially, and the facial bones appear normal.

Possible explanations for this condition are those causing asymmetrical paralysis or hemiplegia, with subsequent muscle and bone wasting. Only conditions that might occur after growth was complete can be considered, since bone length appears unaffected. Poliomyelitis seems an unlikely cause because it usually affects in-

fants (hence its colloquial name, infantile paralysis). A viral infection of the central nervous system it usually causes paralysis of one or more muscle groups. In immature individuals, apart from diaphyseal wasting, it may affect growth of the affected limbs causing shortening (Manchester 1983). An example of this conditioning from the Anglo-Saxon site at Raunds is illustrated in Manchester (1983). It would be very unusual for poliomyelitis to cause total hemiplegia.

The possibility that trauma or disease caused spinal cord damage (unfortunately only fragments of the vertebrae and scapulae survive) has to be considered although it is highly unlikely that any lesion would only affect part of the cord. If such a case were possible, the damage would have been at the level of cervical vertebrae 5 to 6 or above (the level of the nerve to subclavius). It is extremely unusual for middle to upper cervical injuries, or to lesions resulting from disease, to cause hemiplegia; tetraplegia is usually inevitable. Furthermore, if the lesion had been at the level of cervical vertebrae 3, 4 or 5 it would have affected the phrenic nerve which controls the diaphragm and death would have inevitably resulted.

The most likely explanation for this hemiplegia is an upper motor neurone disorder affecting the right side of the brain. This may have been a stroke, a cerebral vascular accident. The young age of this female would suggest that the aetiology of the stroke, if that was the cause, may not have been the same as is usual in elderly individuals. Strokes can be caused by either thrombosis, embolism or haemorrhage.

The unilateral wasting of the diaphyses must reflect muscle inactivity. This implies that this young woman would have been severely disabled for some time before her death. Apart from mobility problems she may well have experienced partial or total loss of bladder and rectal control. In terms of contributing to the communal life of the village and her immediate family, her capabilities would have been severely restricted when compared to healthy and active women of her age. It is possible that she would have required special care. Her survival after her disability reflects the versatility and values of the society in which she lived.

# The cremations

Thirteen cremations (apart from those excluded as described in the introduction to this section) were examined. The procedure followed was that the contents, as received from the excavators, were first passed through a 5mm sieve to remove the larger bone fragments, the residue being passed through a 1mm sieve to retrieve smaller fragments and dentition. The weight of each cremation; the residue, fine sieved weight (1–5mm) and sieved weight (5mm+) and the colour of the cremated bone is described in Table 32.

The majority of the bone in most of the cremations is heavily calcined and white in colour, the remainder being various shades of bluish grey. This suggests that the firing temperature was over 800° Centigrade. The white fragments having been exposed to a high temperature for longer than the bluish grey (Ubelaker 1989). It has not been possible to identify any of the blue grey fragments to establish if they represent the more peripheral parts of the skeleton.

Fracture patterns are similar throughout. Some of the larger fragments are clearly warped with curved transverse fractures. A few fragments are 'checked' on the surface and there is some longitudinal fracturing. On balance, the majority of the fracture patterns suggest that the bones were not defleshed before cremation.

Impairing analysis of fracture patterns were breaks which probably resulted from pounding which took place after the cremation, presumably to enable the remains to be packed within a small container. The pounding was so thorough that very few recognisable fragments of bone survived from any context number. In some cases it was not possible to ascertain if the remains were human. A brief description of each cremation is presented in Table 33.

Of these 13 cremations, 9 are probably human and 1 possibly human. One cremation contains both animal and human remains. The efficient post-cremation pounding has ensured that very little pathological information is apparent and only very little demographic data can be deduced. One cremation may represent a juvenile and four are clearly adult. Of these four, one may be elderly; the others can be classified only as mature.

Small chalk and flint fragments were the most common inclusions.

## Acknowledgements
Sincere thanks go to Keith Manchester and Charlotte Roberts of the Calvin Wells Laboratory, the University of Bradford, for their invaluable expertise in palaeopathology, and their willingness to share their knowledge. Thanks are also due to those of Charlotte's students who radiographed the more interesting pathological specimens. Sincere thanks go to Sue MacLaughlin of the Department of Anatomy, UMDS. (Guy's Campus) for sharing her anatomical knowledge. Theya Molleson (The Natural History Museum) is thanked for commenting upon this report and for data from the Poundbury Cemetery report.

| ID No. | Residue weight (g) | Fine weight (g) | 5mm+ weight (g) | % White | % blue-grey |
|---|---|---|---|---|---|
| 2C4 (G196) | 283 | 112 | 1258 | 66.6 | 33.3 |
| 2BA55 (G193) | 1682 | 218 | 328 | 50.0 | 50.0 |
| 2BA58 (G190) | 788 | 60 | 162 | 80.0 | 20.0 |
| 2BA10 (G191) | 92 | 42 | 485 | 96.0 | 4.0 |
| 2BA1006 (G200) | 42 | 142 | 408 | 90.0 | 10.0 |
| 2BA18 (G187) | 276 | 179 | 82 | 100.0 | |
| 2BA1177 (G195) | 18 | 33 | 49 | 99.0 | 1.0 |
| 2BA1076 (G194) | 6 | 8 | 32 | 50.0 | 50.0 |
| 2BA56 (G189) | 12 | 10 | | 100.0 | |

*Table 32: the cremations: weight and colour*

| No. | Human | Adult | Juv. | Animal | Unknown | Complete | Chalk | Flint | Pot | Glass |
|---|---|---|---|---|---|---|---|---|---|---|
| 2C004 (G196) | | | | Y | Y | Y | Y | Y | | |
| 2BA055 (G193) | YF | Y | | | | Y | | Y | Y | Y |
| 2BA058 (G190) | Y | | Y? | | | N | Y | Y | Y | |
| 2BA010 (G191) | Y | Y | | | | Y | | Y | | |
| 2BA1006 (G200) | Y | Y | | | | Y | Y | Y | | |
| 2BA018 (G187) | Y | | | | | N | | Y | Y | |
| 2BA1177 (G195) | Y | | | | | N | | | | |
| 2BA1076 (G194) | | | | Y | Y | N | | | | |
| 2BA056 (G189) | Y? | | | | | N | | | | |

*Table 33: the cremations: demography and inclusions*

# Bibliography

**Aberg, N 1926** *The Anglo-Saxons in England during the early centuries after the invasion,* Cambridge

**Akerman, JY 1855** *Remains of pagan Saxondom,* London

**Alcock, L 1972** *Arthur's Britain,* Harmondsworth

**Alcock, L 1981** Quantity or quality: the Anglian graves of Bernicia. In Evison (ed), *Angles Saxons and Jutes: Essays presented to JNL Myres,* 168–86, OUP, Oxford

**Alcock, L 1987** *Economy, society and warfare among the Britons and Saxons,* Cardiff

**Aldhelm 1919** *De Virginitate (Monumenta Germaniae Historica, Auctores Antiquissimi xv: Aldhemi opera).*

**Alexander, M (trans) 1973** *Beowulf,* Harmondsworth

**Alexander, M (trans) 1977** *The Earliest English Poems,* Harmondsworth

**Anderson, A 1984** *Interpreting Pottery,* London

**Angilbert, A 1880** *Carmen de Carolo Magno (Monumenta Germaniae Historica, Poetae Latini Medii Aevi 1)*

**Annable, FK and Simpson, DDA 1964** *A guide catalogue of the Neolithic and Bronze Age collections in Devizes Museum,* Devizes

**Anon Rouen Museum catalogue 1985** *La Neustrie: catalogue de l'exposition,* Rouen

**Arnold, CJ 1982** *The Anglo-Saxon cemeteries of the Isle of Wight,* London

**Arnold, CJ, Janaway, RC, Jarvis, KS and Keepax, CA 1983** Catalogue and discussion of the graves and grave goods, in KS Jarvis (ed) *Excavations in Christchurch 1969–1980, Dorset Nat Hist Archaeol Soc* Monograph 5, 113–127

**Aston, M 1985** *Interpreting the Landscape,* London

**Atkinson, RJC 1951** The excavations at Dorchester, Oxfordshire, 1946-1951 *Archaeol Newsletter 4* (4) 56-9

**Atkinson, RJC, Piggott, CM and Sandars, NK 1951** Excavations at Dorchester, Oxon, Vol I Ashmolean Museum Oxford

**Bates, B 1983** *The way of Wyrd,* London

**de Baye, J 1893 (trans T Hardcastle 1990)** *The industrial arts of the Anglo-Saxons,* Lampeter

**Bayley, J 1991** Alloy Nomenclature, in G Egan and F Pritchard (eds) *Dress Accessories: Medieval finds from excavations in London,* HMSO London

**Bender Jørgensen, L 1986** *Forhistoriske textiler i Skandinavien: Prehistoric Scandinavian Textiles,* Nordiske Fortidsminder, Ser B, Vol 9, Copenhagen

**Bender Jørgensen, L 1989** European textiles in later prehistory and early history, *Journal of Danish Archaeology,* 8, 144–58

**Bender Jørgensen, L 1991** The textiles of the Saxons, Anglo-Saxons and Franks, *Studien zur Sachsenforschung* 7, 11–23

**Bender Jørgensen, L 1992** *North European Textiles Until AD1000,* Nordiske Fortidsminder, Copenhagen

**Bender Jørgensen, L and Wild, JP 1988** Clothes from the Roman Empire: Barbarians and Romans, in L Bender Jørgensen, B Magnus and E Munksgard (eds) NESAT II: Archaeological Textiles, Copenhagen, 65–98

**Bidder, HF and Morris, J 1959** The Anglo-Saxon Cemetery at Mitcham, *Surrey Archaeol Collect.* 56, 51–131

**Biek, L and Bayley, J 1979** Glass and other vitreous materials, *World Archaeology* 11,1, 1–125

**Blackburn, MAS (ed) 1986** *Anglo-Saxon monetary history: essays in memory of Michael Dolley,* Leicester

**Bonser, W 1968** *The medical background of Anglo-Saxon England,* London

**Boon, GC 1977** Gold-in-glass beads from the ancient world, *Britannia* 8, 193–207

**Brewer, CW 1976** Metallographic examination of six ancient steel weapons, *Hist Metallurgy Soc* 10(1), 1–9

**Brewer, EC 1981** *A dictionary of phrase and fable,* 2nd revised edition, London

**Brewster, TCM 1963** *The excavation of Staple Howe,* Scarborough

**Brewster, T C M 1980** *The excavation of Garton and Wetwang Slacks [Humberside N],* E Riding Archaeol Res Comm Prehist Excav Rep, NMR Microfiche, London

**Brothwell, DR 1981** *Digging up bones,* 3rd edn, Oxford

**Brown, D 1978** *Anglo-Saxon England,* London

**Burgess, C 1980** *The age of Stonehenge, London*

**Burgess, C 1986** 'Urnes of no small variety': collared urns reviewed, *Proc Prehist Soc 52,* 339-51

**Butzer, K 1982** *Archaeology as human ecology,* Cambridge

**Case, Humphrey 1977** An early accession to the Ashmolean Museum [The Ballyshannon 'sun-disc' and its comparanda] in Markotic, V (ed), Warminster, 18-34

**Chadwick, SE 1958** The Anglo-Saxon cemetery at Finglesham, Kent, *Med Arch 2,* 1–71

**Clarke, D 1970** *The Beaker pottery of Great Britain,* Cambridge

**Coghlan, HH and Tylecote, RF 1978** Medieval Iron Artefacts from the Newbury area of Berkshire: Metallurgical examinations, *Hist Metallurgy Soc* 12(1), 12–17

**Collingwood, P 1982** *The techniques of tablet weaving,* London

**Collingwood, RG and Myres, JNL 1937** *Roman Britain and the English settlements,* 2nd edn, Oxford

**Collingwood, RG and Wright, RP 1965** *The Roman inscriptions of Britain,* Oxford

**Cook, A 1981** *The Anglo-Saxon cemetery at Fonaby, Lincolnshire. Occ Papers in Lincolnshire History and Archaeology* 6, Sleaford

**Cook, AM 1974** The evidence for the reconstruction of female costume in the Early Anglo-Saxon period in the south of England, *unpublished MA thesis,* University of Birmingham

**Cook, AM and Dacre, MW 1985** Excavations at Portway, Andover 1973-75, *Oxford Univ Comm Arch Monograph No 4,* Oxford

**Cooke, B 1990** Fibre damage in archaeological textiles, in S O'Connor and M Brooks, Archaeological Textiles, *UKIK Occ Paper* 10, 5–13

**Costa, RL 1982** Periodontal disease in the Prehistoric Ipiutak and Tigara skeletal remains from Point Hope, Alaska, *American J of Physical Anthropol* 59, 97–100

**Cowgill, J, de Neergard, M and Griffiths, N 1987** *Medieval Finds from Excavations in London: 1 - Knives and Scabbards,* HMSO London

**Cowie, T 1978** *Bronze Age Food Vessel Urns,* BAR British Series 55, Oxford

**Cox, MJ Unpublished** The Human Bones from Ancaster, *AML Report* 93/89.

**Crowfoot, E 1958** The textiles, *in SE Chadwick,* The Anglo-Saxon cemetery at Finglesham, Kent, *Med Arch* 2, 36–7

**Crowfoot, E 1966** Appendix III: The textiles, *in PHutchinson,* The Anglo-Saxon cemetery at Little Eriswell, Suffolk *Proc Camb Antiq Soc* 59, 30

**Crowfoot, E 1967** The textiles, *in H Ellis Davidson and L Webster,* The Anglo-Saxon burial at Coombe, Kent, *Med Arch* 11, 20–1; 37–9

**Crowfoot, E 1976** The textiles and leather, in JF Barfoot and D Price Williams, The Saxon barrow at Galley Hills, Banstead Down, Surrey, *Surrey Archaeol Soc Res Vol 3,* 68–71

**Crowfoot, E 1978** The textile remains, in C Hills and P Wade-Martins, *The Anglo-Saxon cemetery at The Paddocks, Swaffham.* EAA Report 2, Gressenhall, 1–44

**Crowfoot, E 1978** The textiles, in B Green and A Rogerson, *The Anglo-Saxon cemetery at Bergh Apton, Norfolk: Catalogue,* EAA Report 7, Gressenhall, 98–106

**Crowfoot, E 1981** The textiles, in AM Cook, *The Anglo-Saxon cemetery at Fonaby, Lincolnshire, Lincs Hist Archaeol Occ Paper 6,* 89–101

**Crowfoot, E 1983** The textiles, in R Bruce-Mitford, *The Sutton Hoo ship burial* 3/1, London, 409–79

**Crowfoot, E 1985a** The textiles, in SM Hirst, *An Anglo-Saxon inhumation cemetery at Sewerby, East Yorkshire,* York, 48–55

**Crowfoot, E 1985b** Textiles, in JD Hedges and DG Buckley, Anglo-Saxon burials and later features excavated at Orsett, Essex 1975, *Med Arch 29, 15–16*

**Crowfoot, E 1987** Textiles, in B Green, A Rogerson and SG White, *The Anglo-Saxon cemetery at Morningthorpe, Norfolk, Vol 1: Catalogue* EAA Report 36/1, 171–88

**Crowfoot, E 1988** Textiles, in SE West *The Anglo-Saxon cemetery at Westgarth Gardens, Bury St. Edmunds, Suffolk,* EAA Report 38, 14–19

**Crowfoot, E 1990** Textile fragments from 'relic-boxes' in Anglo-Saxon graves, in P Walton and JP Wild (eds) *NESAT III: Textiles in Northern Archaeology,* London, 47–56

**Crowfoot, E and Jones, J 1984** The textiles, in C Hills, K Penn and R Rickett, *The Anglo-Saxon cemetery at Spong Hill, North Elmham, Part 3: Catalogue of Inhumations,* EAA Report 21, Gressenhall, 17–28

**Crowfoot, GM 1951** Textiles of the Saxon period in the Museum of Archaeology and Ethnology, *Proc Camb Antiq Soc 44, 26–32*

**Crowfoot, GM 1952** Anglo-Saxon tablet weaving, *in Antiq J, 32,* 181–91

**Crowfoot, GM 1956a** The braids, in CF Battiscombe (ed) *The Relics of St Cuthbert at Durham,* Oxford, 433–69

**Crowfoot, GM 1956b** The textile and impressions, in FH Thomson, Anglo-Saxon sites in Lincolnshire: unpublished material and recent discoveries *Antiq J 36,* 188–89

**Davidson, HRE 1962** *The sword in Anglo-Saxon England: its archaeology and literature,* Oxford

**Dedekam, H 1924–5** *To tekstilfund fra folkvandringstiden, Evebo og Snartemo, Bergen Museums Aarbok.*

**Dickinson, T 1980** The present state of Anglo-Saxon cemetery studies, in Rahtz, Dickinson and Watts, *Anglo-Saxon Cemeteries 1979,* BAR British Series 82, Oxford

**Dickinson, T and Härke, H 1992** Early Anglo-Saxon shields, *Archaeologia, 110, 1–94, Soc Antiq* London

**Dimbleby, G 1978** *Plants and archaeology,* London

**Drinkall & Foreman 1998** *The Anglo-Saxon cemetery at Castledyke South, Barton-on-Humber, Sheffield Excavation Reports 6,* Sheffield

**Eagles, BN 1979** *The Anglo-Saxon settlement of Humberside,* BAR British Series 68, Oxford

**Elsdon, SM 1989** *Later Prehistoric pottery in England and Wales,* Shire Archaeology 58, Aylesbury

**Evison, VI (ed) 1981** *Angles Saxons and Jutes: Essays presented to JNL Myres,* 168–86, OUP, Oxford

**Evison, VI 1987** *Dover: Buckland Anglo-Saxon cemetery,* HBMC Arch Rep 3, London

**Faull, Margaret L 1974** Roman and Anglian settlement patterns in Yorkshire, *Northern Hist 9,* 1-25

**Fell, C 1986** *Women in Anglo-Saxon England,* Oxford

**Geijer, A 1938** *Birka III: Die Textilfunde aus den Grabern. Uppsala*

**Genrich, A 1954** *Formenkreise und Stammesgruppen in Schleswig-Holstein nach geschlossen Funden des 3. bis 6. Jahrhunderts,* Neumunster

**Gerard, J 1633** *The Herball or Generall Historie of Plantes,* Facsimile Edition, New York

**Gibson, AM 1978** *Bronze Age pottery in the North-East of England,* BAR British Series 56, Oxford

**Goodyear, FH 1971** *Archaeological site science,* London

**Goose, DH 1963** Dental measurements: an assessment of its value in anthropological studies, in DR Brothwell (ed) *Dental Anthropology,* 125–48, London

**Gordon, CG 1981** Soil pH, bone preservation and sampling bias at mortuary sites, *American Antiquity 46,* 566–71

**Green, H Stephen 1980** *The flint arrowheads of the British Isles: a detailed study of material from England and Wales with comparanda from Scotland and Ireland* BAR British Series 75(i–ii), Oxford

**Graham-Campbell, J and Kidd, D 1980** *The Vikings,* British Museum, London

**Green, B and Rogerson, A 1978** *The Anglo-Saxon cemetery at Bergh Apton, Norfolk.* EAA Report 7, Gressenhall

**Green, B, Rogerson, A and White, S 1987** *The Anglo-Saxon cemetery at Morningthorpe, Norfolk,* EAA Report 36, I and II, Gressenhall

**Greenwell, W and Rolleston, G 1877** *British barrows,* Oxford

**Grieve, M (ed Leyel, CF) 1985** *A modern herbal,* London

**Guðjónsson, EE 1962** *Forn Roggvarvefnadur, Arbok hins Islenska Fornleifafelags,* Reykjavik, 12–71

**Guido, M 1978** *The glass beads of the Prehistoric and Roman periods in Britain and Ireland,* Rep Res Comm Soc Antiq London 35, London

**Hagg, I 1974** *Kvinnodrakten i Birka,* Uppsala

**Hansen, E 1990** *Tablet weaving,* Skive

**Hald, M 1950** *Olddanske Tekstiler.* Copenhagen

**Hald, M 1980** *Ancient Danish textiles from bogs and burials,* Copenhagen

**Harding, A F & Lee, G E 1987** *Henge monuments and related sites of Great Britain: air photographic evidence and catalogue,* BAR British Series175 ii, Oxford

**Hardwick, JL 1960** The incidence and distribution of caries throughout the ages in relation to the Englishman's diet, *British Dental Journal* 108, 9–17

**Harman, M, Molleson, T I & Price, J L 1981** Burials, bodies, and beheadings in Romano-British and Anglo-Saxon cemeteries *Bull Brit Mus Natur Hist (Geol)* 35, 1981 145-88

**Harke, H 1981** Anglo-Saxon laminated shields at Petersfinger, a myth, *Med Arch* 24, 141–44

**Harke, H and Salter, C 1984** A technical and metallurgical study of three Anglo-Saxon shield bosses, *Anglo-Saxon Stud Archaeol Hist* 3, 55–6, Oxford

**Haseloff, G 1974** Salin's Style I, *Med Arch* 18, 1–15

**Hassan, FA 1981** *Demographic archaeology,* London

**Hattatt, R 1982** *Ancient and Romano-British brooches,* Dorset

**Hattatt, R 1985** *Iron Age and Roman brooches,* Oxford

**Hedges, JW 1980** *Textiles and textile production in Dark Age Britain,* unpublished MPhil thesis, University of Southampton

**Hedges, J 1982** Textiles, in A MacGregor, *Anglo-Scandinavian finds from Lloyds Bank, Pavement and other sites,* The Archaeology of York 17/5, York, 102–7

**Henshall, AS 1959** Appendix II: Textiles on the back of a brooch from Blewburton Hill, Berks, *Berks Archaeol J* 62, 67–72

**Higham, NJ 1992** *Rome, Britain and the Anglo-Saxons,* London

**Higham, NJ 1993** *The Kingdom of Northumbria AD 35–1100,* Stroud

**Hills, C and Wade-Martins, P 1976** *The Anglo-Saxon cemetery at the Paddocks, Swaffham,* EAA Report 2, Norfolk, Gressenhall, 1–44

**Hills, C, Penn, K and Rickett, R 1984** *The Anglo-Saxon cemetery at Spong Hill, North Elmham Part III: catalogue of inhumations,* EAA Report 21, Gressenhall

**Hillson, S 1986** *Teeth,* Cambridge

**Hines, J 1984** *The scandinavian character of Anglian England in the pre-Viking period,* BAR British Series 124, Oxford

**Hines, J 1993** *Clasps Hectespenner Agraffen, Anglo-Scandinavian clasps of classes A-C of the 3rd to 6th centuries A.D. Typology, diffusion and function* Kungl. Vitterhets Historie och Antikvitets Academien, Stockholm

**Hines, J 1997** *A new corpus of Anglo-Saxon great sqyare headed brooches,* Rep Res Comm Soc Antiq London 51, London

**Hirst, SM 1985** *An Anglo-Saxon inhumation cemetery at Sewerby, East Yorkshire,* York Univ Arch Pub 4 York

**Hodges, H 1989** *Artifacts - an introduction to early materials and technology,* London

**Hoffmann, M 1974** *The warp-weighted loom,* Oslo

**Hope-Taylor, B 1977** *Yeavering: An Anglo-British centre of early Northumbria,* DOE Archaeological Report 7, London

**Horowitz, S, Armelagos, G and Wachter, K 1988** On generating birth rates from skeletal populations, *American Journal of Physical Anthropology* 76, 189–96

**Hoskins, WG 1977** *The making of the English landscape,* 2nd edn, London

**Hughes, R and Rowe, M 1982** *The colouring, bronzing and patination of metals,* Crafts Council, London

**Huskisson, EC and Hart, FP 1978** *Joint disease: All the arthropathies,* Chicago

**Hutchinson, P 1966** The Anglo-Saxon cemetery at Little Eriswell, Suffolk, *Proc Cambridge Antiq Soc.* 59, 1–32

**Jaffe, HL** 1972 *Metabolic, degenerative and inflammatory diseases of bones and joints*, Philadelphia

**Jakes, K and Sibley, L** 1983 Survival of cellulosic fibres in the archaeological context, *Science and Archaeology* 25, 31–8

**Jakes, K and Sibley, L** 1984a Survival of protein fibres in archaeological contexts, *Science and Archaeology* 26, 17–27

**Jakes, K and Sibley, L** 1984b An examination of the phenomenon of textile fabric pseodomorphism, *in JB Lambert (ed) Archaeological chemistry III*, Advances in Chemistry Series 205, Washington, 403–23

**Janaway, RC** 1985 Dust to dust: the preservation of textile materials in metal artefact corrosion products with reference to inhumation graves, *Science and Archaeology* 27, 29–34

**Janaway, RC** 1989 Corrosion preserved textile evidence: mechanism, bias and interpretation, in R Janaway and B Scott, *Evidence Preserved in Corrosion Products: New Fields in Artifact Studies*, UKIK Occ Paper 8, 21–9

**Johansson, SR and Horowitz, S** 1986 Skeletal mortality and growth rate, *American Journal of Physical Anthropology* 71, 251–57

**Jones, MU** 1975 A clay piece-mould of the migration period from Mucking, Essex, *Antiq J* 55 (2), 407–8

**Keepax, C** 1975 Scanning electron microscopy of wood replaced by iron corrosion products, *Journal of Archaeological Science* 2, 145–50

**Kelly, MA** 1982 Intervertebral osteochondrosis in ancient and modern populations, *American Journal of Physical Anthropology* 59, 271–79

**Kennett, DH** 1974 Some decorative aspects of the Anglo-Saxon shield, *BedsArch J* 9, 55–70

**Kennett, DH** 1989 *Anglo-Saxon pottery*, 2nd edn, Shire Archaeology 5, Aylesbury

**Kinnes, IA and Longworth, IH** 1985 *Catalogue of the excavated prehistoric and Romano-British material in the Greenwell collection*, British Museum, London

**Korber-Grohne, U** 1967 *Charakteristik rezenter Bastfasern von Lien*, Nessel und Hanf, Geobotanische Untersuchungen auf der Feddersen Wierde, 161ff

**Lamm, K** 1973 The manufacture of jewellery during the migration period at Helgo in Sweden, *Bulletin of the Historical Metallurgy Group* 7 (2), 1–7

**Lamm, K** 1980 Early medieval metalworking on Helgo in central Sweden, in WA Oddy (ed) Aspects of Early Metallurgy, 97–116, BM Occ Paper, London

**Langmaid, N** 1978 *Prehistoric Pottery*, Shire Archaeology 7, Aylesbury

**Lanting, JN and van der Waals, JD** 1972 British Beakers as seen from the continent, *Helinium* 12, 20–46

**Laporte, J-P** 1982 *La chasuble de Chelles, in* Bulletin du Groupement Archaeologique de Seine-et-Marne 23, 1–29

**Lawrence, JM, Bremner, JM and Bier, F** 1966 Osteoarthrosis: prevalence in the population and relationship between symptoms and X-ray changes *Annals of Rheumatic Diseases* 25, 1–24

**Leeds ET** 1936 *Early Anglo-Saxon art and archaeology*, Oxford

**Leeds, ET** 1945 The distribution of the Angles and Saxons archaeologically considered, *Archaeologia* 91, 1–106, Soc Antiq London

**Leeds, ET** 1949 *A corpus of great square-headed Brooches*, London

**Leeds, ET and Pocock, M** 1971 A survey of the Anglo-Saxon cruciform brooches of florid type, *Med Arch* 15, 13–36

**Leigh, D** 1990 Aspects of early brooch design and production, in E Southworth (ed) *Anglo-Saxon Cemeteries: a reappraisal*, Stroud

**Lepääho, J** 1964 **Spateisenzeitliche Waffen aus Finnland**, *Finska Fornminnesforeningens Tidskrift* 61

**Lethbridge, TC** 1936 *A cemetery at Shudy Camps, Cambridgeshire: report of the excavation of a cemetery of the christian Anglo-Saxon period in 1933, Cambridge Antiq Soc Quarto Pubs*, 5, Cambridge

**Luff, R-M** 1984 *Animal remains in Archaeology*, Shire Archaeology 33, Aylesbury

**MacGregor, A** 1985 *Bone, horn, antler and ivory: The technology of skeletal materials since the Roman period*, London

**Markotic, Vladimir (ed)** 1977 *Ancient Europe and the Mediterranean: studies presented in honour of Hugh Hencken*, Warminster (Wilts)

**McDonnell, JG** 1986 *The classification of early ironworking slags*, unpublished PhD thesis, University of Aston

**McDonnell, JG 1988** Ore to artefact, a study of ironworking technology, in E Slater, and JO Tate (eds) *Science and Archaeology,* Glasgow 1987, BAR 196

**McDonnell, JG 1989** Iron and its alloys in the Fifth to Eleventh Centuries in Britain, *World Archaeology* 20 (3), 373–82

**McWhirr, A 1982** *Roman crafts and industries,* Shire Archaeology 24, Aylesbury

**Manby, T G 1957** Food Vessels of the Peak District, *Derby Arch J* 77 1-29

**Manby, T G 1969** Bronze Age pottery from Pule Hill, Marsden, W R Yorkshire and footed vessels of the Early Bronze Age from England, *Yorkshire Archaeol J* 42(167) 273-82

**Manby, TG 1974** *Grooved Ware Sites in the North of England,* BAR British Series 9, Oxford

**Manby, T G 1980** Excavation of barrows at Grindale and Boynton, East Yorkshire [Humberside N], 1972, *Yorkshire Archaeol J* 52, 19-47

**Manby, TG 1988** *Archaeology in Eastern Yorkshire: Essays in honour of T.C.M. Brewster,* Sheffield

**Manchester, K 1983** *The archaeology of disease,* Bradford

**Maresh, M 1955** Linear growth of long bone extremities from infancy through adolescence, *American Journal of Diseases of Children* 89, 725–42

**May, Jeffrey 1976** *Prehistoric Lincolnshire,* History of Lincs Committee, Lincoln

**Meaney, A 1964** *A Gazetteer of Early Anglo-Saxon burial sites,* London

**Meaney, A 1981** *Anglo-Saxon amulets and curing stones,* BAR British Series 96, Oxford

**Meaney, A and Hawkes, SC 1970** *Two Anglo-Saxon cemeteries at Winnall, Winchester, Hampshire,* The Society for Medieval Archaeology Monograph Series No 4, London

**Megaw, JVS and Simpson, DDA 1979** *Introduction to British Prehistory,* Leicester

**Miles, AEW 1963** The dentition in the assessment of individual age in skeletal material, in DR Brothwell, *Dental Anthropology,* London, 191–209

**Molleson, TI and Cox, MJ (forthcoming)** *Spitalfields: the middling sort,* CBA, London

**Moore, J W 1965** An Anglo-Saxon settlement at Wykeham, North Yorkshire, *Yorkshire Archaeol J* 41(163), 403-44

**Morris, c 1982** Aspects of Anglo-Saxon and Anglo-Scandinavian lathe turning, *in S McGrail (ed) Woodworking Techniques Before AD 1500,* BAR Int Ser 129, 245–61

**Mortimer, JR 1905** *Forty years' researches in British and Saxon burial mounds of East Yorkshire,* London

**Myres, JNL and Green, B 1973** *The Anglo-Saxon cemeteries at Caistor-by-Norwich and Markshall, Norfolk,* Rep Res Comm Soc Antiq London, London

**Myres, JNL 1977** *A corpus of Anglo-Saxon pottery of the pagan period,* Cambridge

**Nockert, M 1991** *The Hogom find and other migration period textiles and costumes in Scandinavia,* Archaeology and Environment 9, Umea, Sweden

**Oddy, WA 1980** Gilding and tinning in Anglo-Saxon England, *in WA Oddy (ed) Aspects of Early Metallurgy,* BM Occ Paper, London

**Owen, G 1976** *Anglo-Saxon costume: A study of secular civilian clothing and jewellery fashions,* 3 Volumes, unpublished PhD thesis, University of Newcastle-upon-Tyne

**Owen-Crocker, GR 1986** *Dress in Anglo-Saxon England,* Manchester

**Pader, Ellen-Jane 1982** *Symbolism, social relations, and the interpretation of mortuary remains,* BAR Int Ser 130, Oxford

**Page, RI 1987** *Runes,* British Museum, London

**Perizonius, WRK 1984** Closing and non-closing sutures in 256 crania of known age and sex from Amsterdam (AD 1883–1909) *Journal of Human Evolution* 13, 201–16

**Pierpoint, S 1980** *Social patterns in Yorkshire Prehistory,* BAR British Series 74, Oxford

**Platt, HM 1980** Preserved worms on an Anglo-Saxon brooch, *Journal of Archaeological Science* 7, 287–88

**Potterton, D (ed) 1983** *Culpeper's colour herbal,* London

**Powlesland, DJ 1981** *West Heslerton,* Current Archaeology 76, 142–44

**Powlesland, DJ, Haughton, CA and Hanson, JH 1986** Excavations at Heslerton, North Yorkshire 1978–82, *Arch J* 143, 53–173

**Powlesland, DJ 1989** *West Heslerton 1989, The Anglian settlement, an interim report,* unpublished mss

**Powlesland, DJ and Haughton, CA, (forthcoming)** *West Heslerton - The Anglian Settlement,* Landscape Research Centre Monograph

**Pye, G.R. 1976** Excavations at Crossgates near Scarborough 1957-65, *Trans Scarb Arch Hist Soc* Vol. 3, No. 19, 1-22

**Pye, G.R. 1983** Further excavations at Crossgates near Scarborough 1966-1981, *Trans Scarb Arch Hist Soc*, No. 25

**Rahtz, P 1978** Grave orientation, *Arch. J.,* 135,1-14.

**Rahtz, P, Dickinson, T and Watts, L 1980** *Anglo-Saxon cemeteries, 1979,* BAR British Series 82, Oxford

**Ramm, H 1978** *The Parisi,* London

**Reichstein, J 1975** *Die Kreuzformige Fibel,* Neumunster

**Rogers, J, Waldron, T, Dieppe, P and Watt, I 1987** Arthropathies in palaeopathology: The basis of classification according to most probable cause, *Journal of Archaeological Science* 14, 179–93

**Ryder, ML 1978** *Sheep and wool for handicraft workers,* Edinburgh

**Samuels, LE 1980** *Optical microscopy of carbon steels,* Ohio

**Savory, H N 1957** A Corpus of Welsh Bronze Age pottery—Part II. Food Vessels and Enlarged Food Vessels. Middle Bronze Age (c 1500-1200 BC), *BCS* 17(3) 196-233

**Sawyer, PH 1978** *From Roman Britain to Norman England,* London

**Schaefer, G 1945** Flax and hemp, *CIBA Review 49,* 1762–95

**Schlabow, K 1965** *Der Thorsberger Prachtmantel,* Neumunster

**Schmorl, G and Junghanns, H 1971** *The human spine in health and disease,* (trans EF Beseman), New York

**Scott, A 1979** *The Saxon age,* London

**Seymour, J 1984** *The forgotten arts: A practical guide to traditional skills,* London

**Sherlock, SJ and Welch, MG 1992** *An Anglo-Saxon cemetery at Norton, Cleveland,* CBA Res Rep 82, London

**Sjovold, T 1984** A Report on the heritability of some cranial measurements and non-metric traits, in GN van Vark and WW Howells (eds) *Multivariate Statistical Methods in Physical Anthropology,* 223–46

**Speake, G 1980** *Anglo-Saxon animal art and its germanic background,* Oxford

**Starley, DE 1988** *A study of the morphology and composition of slag inclusions in archaeological ironwork from hamwih and coppergate,* unpublished graduate dissertation, University of Bradford

**Stenton, F 1971** *Anglo-Saxon England,* Oxford

**Strong, D and Brown, D (eds) 1976** *Roman Crafts,* London

**Stuart-Macadam, P 1986** Porotic Hyperostosis: Representative of a Childhood Condition, *American Journal of Physical Anthropology* 66, 391–98

**Stuart-Macadam, P 1988** Nutrition and anaemia in past human populations, in BV Kennedy and GM LeMoine (eds) *Diet and Subsistence: current archaeological perspectives,* Alberta, 284–87

**Swan, V 1980** *Pottery in Roman Britain,* 3rd edn Shire Archaeology 3, Aylesbury

**Swanton, MJ 1973** *The spearheads of the Anglo-Saxon settlements,* London

**Swanton, MJ 1974** *A corpus of pagan Anglo-Saxon spear types,* BAR British Series 7, Oxford

**Southworth, E (ed) 1990** *Anglo-Saxon Cemeteries: a reappraisal,* Stroud

**Tacitus (trans H Mattingly, rev S Handford) 1970** *The Agricola and the Germania,* Harmondsworth

**Taylor, GW 1990** Ancient textile dyes, *Chemistry in Britain,* Dec 1990, 1155–58

**Thompson, FH 1956** Anglo-Saxon sites in Lincolnshire: unpublished material and recent discoveries, *Antiq J* 36, 181–99

**Trinkaus, E 1978** Bilateral asymmetry of human skeletal non-metric traits, *American Journal of Physical Anthropology* 16, 79–123

**Trotter, M 1970** Estimation of stature from intact limb bones, in TD Stewart (ed) *Personal Identification in Mass Disasters*, Washington, 79–123

**Tylecote, RF 1976** *A History of Metallurgy*, London

**Tylecote, RF 1982** *Metallurgical examination of iron from Sewerby (East Yorks) pagan Saxon cemetery*, AML Report 3688

**Tylecote, RF 1986** *The prehistory of metallurgy in the British isles*, London

**Tylecote, RF and Thomsen, R 1973** The segregation and surface-enrichment of arsenic and phosphorus in early iron artefacts, *Archaeometry* 15 193–8

**Tylecote, RF and Gilmour, BJJ 1986** *The metallography of early ferrous edge tools and edged weapons*, BAR British Series 155, Oxford

**Ubelaker, DH 1989** *Human skeletal remains: Excavation, analysis, interpretation*, 2nd edn, Washington

**Vierck, H 1978** *Trachtenkunde und Trachtgeschichte in der Sachsen-Forschung, ihre Quellen, Ziele und Methoden, in C Ahrens (ed)* Sachsen und Angelsachsen, Hamburg, 231–93

**Waldron, T 1987** The relative survival of the human skeleton: Implications for palaeopathology, In AN Boddington, AN Garland and RC Janaway (eds) *Death, Decay and Reconstruction*, Manchester, 55–64

**Walker, PL, Johnson, JR and Lambert, PM 1988** Age and sex biases in the preservation of human skeletal remains, *American Journal of Physical Anthropology* 76, 183–8

**Walton, P 1986** Dyes in early Scandinavian textiles, *Dyes on Historical and Archaeological Textiles* 5, 38–41

**Walton, P 1988a** Dyes of the Viking Age: a summary of recent work, *Dyes in History and Archaeology (formerly Dyes on Historical and Archaeological Textiles)* 7, 14–20

**Walton, P 1988b** Dyes and wools in Iron Age textiles from Norway and Denmark, *Journal of Danish Archaeology* 7, 144–58

**Walton, P 1989** *Textiles, cordage and raw fibre from 16–22 Coppergate*, The Archaeology of York 17/5, York

**Walton, P 1990** Textile production at Coppergate, York: Anglo-Saxon or Viking? *in P Walton and JP Wild (eds) Textiles in Northern Archaeology: NESAT III*, London, 61–72

**Walton, P 1991** Dyes and wools in textiles from Mammen, Denmark, in M Iversen (ed) Mammen : *Grav, Kunst og samfund i vikingetid*, Aarhus, 139–43

**Walton, P 1992** Textile remains *in SJ Sherlock and MG Welch, An Anglo-Saxon cemetery at Norton, Cleveland*, CBA Res Rep 82

**Walton Rogers, P 1998** Textile and clothing, in G.Drinkall and M.Foreman, *The Anglo–Saxon cemetery at Castledyke South, Barton-on-Humber* Sheffield Excavation Reports 6, Sheffield, 274-79

**Walton Rogers, P forthcoming** *Textile and clothing in the Anglo-Saxon cemetery at Market Lavington, Wiltshire*

**Walton, P and Taylor, G 1991** The characterisation of dyes in textiles from archaeological excavations, *Chromatography and Analysis* 17, 5–7

**Waterman, DM 1951** Quernhow: food-vessel barrow in Yorkshire, *Arch J* 31, 1-24

**Watson, J 1988** The identification of organic materials preserved by metal corrosion products, in S Olson (ed) *The Use of the Scanning Electron Microscope in Archaeology*, BAR Int Ser 452, 65–76

**Watson, J and Edwards, G 1990** Conservation of material from Anglo-Saxon cemeteries, *in E Southworth (ed) Anglo-Saxon Cemeteries: a reappraisal*, Stroud, 97–106

**Welch, MG 1985** Rural settlement patterns in the Early and Middle Anglo-Saxon periods *Landscape Hist* 7, 1985 13-25

**Welch MG 1992** *Anglo-Saxon England*, Batsford, London

**Wells, C 1982** The human burials, in A McWhirr, L Viner and C Wells (eds) *Romano-British Cemeteries at Cirencester*, Cirencester, 135–202

**Wenham, LP 1968** *The Romano-British cemetery at Trentholme Drive, York*, HMSO, London

**Werner, J 1964** Frankish royal tombs in the cathedrals of Cologne and Saint-Denis, *Antiquity* 38, 201–16

**West, SE 1985** *West Stow, the Anglo-Saxon village*, EAA, 24, 1 and 2, Ipswich

**West, SE 1988** *The Anglo-Saxon cemetery at Westgarth Gardens, Bury St. Edmunds, Suffolk: Catalogue*, EAA Report 38, Bury St Edmunds

**White, R 1990** Scrap or substitute, Roman material in Anglo-Saxon graves, *in E Southworth (ed) Anglo-Saxon Cemeteries: a reappraisal*, Stroud

**White, W 1988** *The Cemetery at St. Nicholas Shambles,* London

**Whiting, M 1983** Dye analysis, in R Bruce-Mitford, *The Sutton Hoo Ship Burial* 3/1, London

**Whittle, A.W.R., R.J.C. Atkinson, R. Chambers and N. Thomas. 1992.** Excavations on the Neolithic and Bronze Age Complex at Dorchester-on-Thames, Oxfordshire, 1947-1952 and 1981, *Proc Preh Soc* 58, 143-201.

**Whitten, DGA and Brooks, JRV 1972** *The Penguin dictionary of geology,* Harmondsworth

**Wild, JP 1968** Clothing in the North-West provinces of the Roman Empire, *Bonner Jahrb.* 168, 166–240

**Wild, JP 1970** *Textile manufacture in the northern Roman provinces,* Cambridge

**Wild, JP 1985** The clothing of Britannia, Gallia belgica and Germania inferior, *in H Temporini and W Hasse, Aufsteig und Niedergang der Romischen Welt 2,* Berlin, 363–422

**Wild, JP 1988** *Textiles in archaeology,* Shire Archaeology 56, Aylesbury

**Williams, PW 1983** *An Anglo-Saxon cemetery at Thurmaston, Leicestershire,* Leicester Museums Publications 46, Leicester

**Wilson, DM 1971** *The Anglo-Saxons,* Harmondsworth

**Wilson, DM (ed) 1976** *The Archaeology of Anglo-Saxon England,* Cambridge

**Workshop of European Anthropologists 1980** Recommendations for Age and Sex Diagnoses of Skeletons, *Journal of Human Evolution* 9, 517–49

**Ypey, J 1982** *Europaische Waffen mit Damaszierung, Archaeologisches Korrespondentzblatt* 12, 381–88

**Zimmerman, MR and Kelley, MA 1982** *Atlas of Human Palaeopathology,* New York